Church Planting in Post-Christian Soil

Church Planting in Post-Christian Soil

Theology and Practice

CHRISTOPHER B. JAMES

OXFORD
UNIVERSITY PRESS

OXFORD
UNIVERSITY PRESS

Oxford University Press is a department of the University of Oxford. It furthers
the University's objective of excellence in research, scholarship, and education
by publishing worldwide. Oxford is a registered trade mark of Oxford University
Press in the UK and certain other countries.

Published in the United States of America by Oxford University Press
198 Madison Avenue, New York, NY 10016, United States of America.

CIP data is on file at the Library of Congress
ISBN 978–0–19–067364–2

5 7 9 8 6
Printed by Sheridan Books, Inc., United States of America

Contents

Acknowledgments

I AM GRATEFUL to the many people whose guidance and cooperation contributed in vital ways to this book. This work would not have been possible without the cooperation of Seattle's new churches and their pastors. I am indebted to the fifty-seven pastors who submitted the New Seattle Churches Survey, the sixteen pastors who welcomed interviews, the dozens of participants in focus groups, and the numerous denominational and network leaders who offered their local knowledge. I am especially grateful for the hospitality of the pastors and members of the three churches with which I spent extended time: Verlon Fosner and Community Dinners, Andrew Arthur and The Hallows Church, and Phil Nellis and Wits' End Church. These churches and leaders have shaped in profound ways my imagination for what church is and can be.

I offer my sincere thanks to the host of scholars who offered their expertise and support at critical junctures along the way. Bryan Stone not only introduced me to practical ecclesiology but also played a significant role in shaping both this project and my formation as a practical theologian. I am also deeply grateful to Nancy Ammerman for the benefit her expertise as a sociologist provided to me and to this project, and for teaching me that while all scholars are smart, kindness is a rarer trait, and one worth pursuing. These two provided multiple rounds of critical feedback on early drafts and offered exactly the kind of multidisciplinary sounding board that this project required. For this I am profoundly grateful. Christian Scharen and Ryan Bolger provided words of wisdom and affirmation at key moments. I appreciate the invitations I received to present this research at various stages from the American Society of Missiology, the Fuller Institute for Theology and Northwest Culture, and the Wabash Pastoral Leadership Program. My sincere thanks also go to Claire Wolfteich, Shelly Rambo, and Rady Roldán-Figueroa, whose engagement with the work and encouragement propelled me toward publication. The support of Cynthia Read and Cameron Donahue at Oxford University Press has also been a gift.

Scholarly projects require not only scholarly knowledge of what to do but also the motivation and means by which to get it done. I am deeply grateful to those who provided the encouragement, flexibility, and funding that enabled me to conduct this research and write this book. First, thanks to my parents, David and Ruth, whose generosity made doctoral studies feasible for my family. The support I received from the Reverend Dr. Allen J. Moore School of the Prophets Scholarship and the Center for Practical Theology at Boston University School of Theology, as well as the flexibility of Bradley Longfield at the University of Dubuque Theological Seminary, afforded me critical writing time. Thanks also go to Ellen Childs, Tim Snyder, Kristen Redford Hydinger, Gail Ray, and Allen Rascoe for their various contributions.

Finally, I want memorialize my gratitude to Lindsay, whose companionship, sacrifices, exhortations, and faith have done more to bring this book to print than all those previously mentioned put together.

Abbreviations

GCT   Great Commission Team
HS   Household of the Spirit
NC   New Community
NI   Neighborhood Incarnation

Introduction

LOOKING FOR THE FUTURE OF
CHURCH IN THE NONE ZONE

THIS BOOK IS about the future of church. In contrast to headlines trumpeting the demise of Christianity, it attends to the signs of new life that are already bursting forth in what would seem to be the most unlikely of places—Seattle, Washington. In 2004, researchers branded the Pacific Northwest "the None Zone" because of its distinctively high percentages of the religiously unaffiliated.[1] As the leading city in the region, Seattle is a hotspot for "Nones."[2] The latest research indicates that 37% of those in the Seattle metro area claim no religious affiliation.[3] Why look to Seattle, where less than 25% of people go to church on weekly basis, for the future of church? Wouldn't it make more sense to study the apparent success of Houston, Texas, where 67% do so?[4] Simply, no. National trends indicate that Seattle provides a better glimpse of our collective destiny. Not only is Seattle is one of the most post-Christian cities in an increasingly post-Christian nation, it is also one of the fastest-growing, most technological, and most progressive cities in a nation whose population is becoming increasingly urban, technological, and progressive. Seattle's perch on the leading edges of trends that are dramatically transforming the nation suggest that the new churches taking root in its future-trending soil are ecclesial pioneers of the new American frontier. The following chapters explore the four dynamic models of church I discovered among these ecclesial pioneers—the Great Commission Team, the Household of the Spirit, the New Community, and the Neighborhood Incarnation. Based on what I discovered, I am convinced that these first decades of the twenty-first century ought to be seen not only as a period of church decline but also, and more importantly, as a vibrant season of ecclesial renewal and rebirth. This book is about the future of church in the United States, a future that is already present in Seattle.

Toward Faithful Witness

Thousands of new churches and new forms of church are springing up each year across the country.[5] The sheer volume of church planting and innovation efforts under way across the Western world call for careful study and theological reflection as churches pursue Christian witness in increasingly post-Christian settings. As a practical theologian, I write this book as part of my commitment to equip church leaders with interpretive insight and theologically grounded counsel regarding faithful practice as they strive to faithfully lead their churches into spiritual and missional vitality in the midst of a changing context. The aim of this project is to share the practical wisdom of new Seattle churches with the broader church.

In some ways, this project is an extension of my biography. I grew up in Seattle in the 1980s and '90s within Seattle's conservative evangelical and charismatic subcultures. My family attended mostly Foursquare churches, and I went to a private Christian school through high school. As a kid, I wanted to become an FBI agent. Not just because I—like many of my youthful peers—was energized by visions of fighting bad guys, but also because I was convinced that the dark time was coming soon when the government would turn hostile toward Christians. It was clear enough to me and my church that the culture was already inhospitable to true Christianity. I wanted to be an FBI agent so I could see that day coming and be able to help my people, God's people, escape the worst of it somehow.

While I outgrew that professional ambition and that eschatological anxiety, my desire to serve the church remained. I went to Wheaton College and got involved in a summer evangelistic ministry to those traveling Europe's youth-hostel circuit. The challenge of sharing faith with mostly spiritual but not religious travelers was both disorienting and exhilarating. After college, I returned to the Seattle area, where I worked as a youth ministry intern at University Presbyterian Church, near the University of Washington campus, one of the nation's handful of evangelical PC(USA) megachurches. Feeling a sense of call to ministry, I headed to Fuller Theological Seminary, where I discovered the writings of Lesslie

Newbigin. Newbigin was a missionary in India who returned home to England in the 1960s only to discover and declare that the West was now as much a mission field as India had been. His impact on contemporary missiology, ecclesiology, and ecumenism is hard to overstate. As I delved into his writings, I found a deep resonance with my own experiences in Seattle and Europe, and with my aspirations for what the church could be if it lived into its identity as God's missionary people.

After seminary, my wife and I both took jobs at another evangelical PC(USA) megachurch, this time in the San Francisco Bay area. The church reflected the zest for innovation that is characteristic of its Silicon Valley locale, and it joined the burgeoning multisite church movement by launching three new video-venue campuses. As freshly minted seminary graduates sometimes do, I became somewhat disillusioned, frustrated in part by the church's size, priority on production value, and personality-centered culture. While we talked about evangelism a lot, I was disheartened when the leadership team of which I was a member tried to brainstorm names of recent converts who could share their testimony in worship, and none of us could think of any. I began looking for PhD programs in Practical Theology, largely because I wanted to find better and more beautiful ways to do and be church. Boston University School of Theology, a liberal United Methodist school with a multi-religious flavor, offered an escape from the evangelical orbit I had been in but did not diminish my evangelical drive to find and promote faithful forms of missionary engagement here in the United States. My dissertation gave me an opportunity to craft a project that would contribute to that end, and that work has ultimately resulted in this book.

These experiences and many others brought me to this project and have propelled me with a sense of its significance. This book was not written dispassionately; I have a stake in its subject. While the following chapters contain little personal commentary or explicit reflexivity, my biography and motivations are nonetheless a pervasive subtext.[6] I have lived in three of the "most Post-Christian" cities in the nation: Seattle, San Francisco, and Boston.[7] I have been part of Christian communities that share important features of each of the four models of church that are the focus of this book. I have already mentioned my sojourns in charismatic, evangelical, and mainline Protestant churches. I went to high school with a couple of men who have since become some of the most prominent pastors and church planters in the Seattle area. At Wheaton, I sang and toured with the multicultural Gospel Choir for three years, and I belonged to a charismatic Anglican church plant that gathered in an auditorium at a local community college. While in Boston, my family belonged to a Korean-American church plant that met in an elementary school and then later to a politically active church deeply rooted in its South Boston neighborhood. As a result of these and many other experiences, I felt a sense of familiarity in the diverse and ecumenical array of church plants that I studied in Seattle.

My story, my networks, and even my appearance have shaped this research by opening numerous doors while leaving others closed. My ties to evangelical institutions—Wheaton and Fuller—and genuine commitment to Christian mission earned me goodwill among many of the Evangelicals who dominate the field of new churches. On the other hand, my disillusionment and departure from an evangelical megachurch and my doctoral studies at Boston University School of Theology led liberal mainline Protestants to welcome me as one of their own. Local leaders who were critical of church planters moving in from other regions of the country responded warmly when I spoke of my Seattle roots. I am convinced that even my physical appearance as a young, white male with dark, thick-rimmed glasses and facial hair—a common look among both conservative and liberal innovators—facilitated kind receptions in several venues. The same characteristics made research among non-Anglo congregations more difficult. While I have made use of methodological precautions against bias and stand by the validity of my findings, I am also cognizant of some of the ways my own journey—my experiences and commitments—is reflected and implicated in this research.

A Case Study in Practical Ecclesiology

The central argument of this book is that *empirical and theological study of Seattle's newest cohort of churches yields practical wisdom for the U.S. church as it seeks to faithfully engage with its emerging context.* This thesis is simultaneously a practical and a methodological one. My argument leads ultimately to practical proposals for church leaders—specifically those engaged in church planting efforts. But inasmuch as these actionable proposals promote faithful practice, they serve to demonstrate the value of the method apparent in the following chapters to arrive at them.

I begin in chapter 1 by demonstrating parallels among four transformative national trends and four of Seattle's most distinctive characteristics. On the basis of this alignment, I argue that Seattle provides a serviceable proxy for a growing proportion of the U.S. context in the coming decades. In chapter 2, I provide an orientation to the field of new churches and report on the key findings of the New Seattle Churches Survey, including the discovery that Seattle's new churches take multiple, but not idiosyncratic, forms. Chapter 3 argues for my practical ecclesiological approach and synthesizes salient sociological and theological models of church. In dialogue with this body of research, chapter 4 develops the four dominant practical ecclesiological models in the field by drawing on original mixed-methods research. In chapter 5, I assess each practical ecclesiological model on the basis of missional theology and demonstrate that, while each has strengths and weaknesses, the Neighborhood Incarnation model is the missional exemplar. In chapter 6, I propose concrete practices for missional renewal among churches within each of the four dominant models. These proposals demonstrate the promise of a practical ecclesiological method that integrates robust empirical research with missional theological evaluation. Chapter 7 explores the five threads of practical wisdom I found woven into the fabric of new Seattle churches as a whole, and translates them into actionable guidance for leaders in church planting efforts, as well as trajectories for doctrinal ecclesiology.

This book makes contributions to a handful of scholarly and professional discourses. First, it provides a critical supplement to the professional literature on church planting, renewal, and innovation. Too many of these books rely upon idealized visions of the church rather than on disciplined study of real churches.[8] More troubling, most of what is written about church planting and renewal derives from productionistic concerns with what is "effective" at producing conversions and church growth that are validated by narrow claims regarding "what's biblical."[9] The results are crass strategies for boosting attendance, multiplying baptisms, and maximizing growth that lack appropriate sensitivity to the profound theological and contextual dimensions of making faithful witness. In contrast, this book is based on extensive research among real Christian communities, and it provides church leaders with theologically grounded practical wisdom for faithful and viable forms of ecclesial life.

Second, I offer two straightforward contributions to the field of congregational studies. The research adds to the limited social scientific knowledge regarding new churches by providing original data on the churches that have been founded between 2001 and 2014 in Seattle. Additionally, it offers a new interpretive typology for these faith communities. This typology, unlike others in the literature, reflects attention to the unique character and features of new churches.[10]

The third and most significant contribution lies at the intersection of sociology and theology. This study thoroughly integrates empirical and theological tools and perspectives in its analysis. Not surprisingly, theological and spiritual concerns have been downplayed in social scientific research in favor of attention to social and cultural features.[11] Recently, however, The Network for Ecclesiology and Ethnography has convened social scientists and theologians, and has called for projects that explore various ways of connecting theology and qualitative research in the study of churches.[12] These calls reflect two primary critiques. The first critique challenges the "methodological atheism" of classic congregational studies and appeals for more theologically informed congregational research.[13] The second critique is directed at classical approaches to ecclesiology and challenges the production of doctrines that are so incongruous with actual churches as to be implausible and unbelievable. These well-founded critiques have led me to give disciplined attention to concrete churches as a critical element of my ecclesiological method.[14] As a contribution to this discourse, this book provides both an argument for a mixed-methods (rather than purely qualitative) approach and an example of how it might take shape and bear fruit.[15]

Missional Practical Ecclesiological Reflection

As a work of practical theology, this book is interdisciplinary and invites readers who are at home in several discourses. Sociologists and congregational studies researchers can find data and interpretive models in chapters 2 and 4. Chapters 5 and 7 contain theological critique and doctrinal construction that will likely be of most interest to theologians. Church practitioners and missiologists may gravitate to the actionable proposals found in chapters 6 and 7.

While this book is written with each of these audiences in mind, taken as a whole it is addressed to practical theologians and, more precisely, to an emerging network of theologians and social scientists working in the area of practical ecclesiology. By "practical ecclesiology" I refer both to an ecclesiological method that utilizes study of concrete churches and to the written products of such work. Participants in this discourse will find in this book a mostly implied methodological argument in keeping with the conviction that understanding the church requires recognizing it as "simultaneously theological and social/cultural."[16] The methodological argument is, simply stated, that the method of practical ecclesiological reflection utilized for this project yields promising proposals for viable, faithful, ecclesial, missional engagement in the changing U.S. context. The basis for this methodological argument is most explicitly treated in chapter 3, but the method itself is outlined in the following pages and supported by the more detailed discussion found in appendix A.

Practical theology is a contested discipline, so allow me to clarify what I mean when I describe this book as a work of practical theological reflection. Practical theology proceeds by use of theological methods that include theological description, interpretation, evaluation, and proposals that arise from and are addressed to concrete contemporary situations and practices relevant to the church. The method underlying such work welcomes relevant human disciplines into the church's critical reflection in order to discern the presence, praxis, and call of God. This is done so that Christ's church in the world can respond faithfully in discipleship and witness to the glory of God and for the good of the world.

This is a practical theological project, but it is also a practical *ecclesiological* one, in that it takes the church's whole praxis as its object and intends its assessment and proposals to yield more faithful forms of ecclesiopraxis. "Ecclesiopraxis" is the whole constellation of theory-laden practices that animate a particular church or practical ecclesiological model. To add a final layer of precision, the methodology I employ is *missional* practical ecclesiological reflection. I seek specifically to assess and advance the church's contextual witness and thereby to foster the church's increasing faithfulness to its divine call to participate in the *missio Dei*.[17] In order to fulfill this missional aim, the chapters of this book progress through four basic movements that are common in practical theology: description, interpretation, evaluation, and proposals.

Description: The Context and Contours of New Seattle Churches

Richard Osmer suggests that the first question a practical theological project must entertain is, "What is going on?"[18] It is the kind of question one might ask when encountering the scene in figure I.1, a signboard for Community Dinners (a church) placed in the heart of the iconic Pike Place Market. This book begins by asking what is going on in three domains: the U.S. context, the Seattle context, and the field of new churches in Seattle.

FIGURE I.I Community Dinners signboard at Seattle's Pike Place Market.

In response to this question, I offer descriptions of (1) Seattle within the larger U.S. context and (2) the field of new Seattle churches.

In fulfilling this initial descriptive task, I demonstrate in chapter 1 that Seattle is a profoundly urban, progressive, technological, and post-Christian context in the midst of a nation whose population is becoming increasingly urban, progressive, technological, and post-Christian. As such, I argue that Seattle provides a serviceable proxy for the future U.S. context more broadly and, by extension, other places marked by these four characteristics, such as can be found in Western cities across Canada, Europe, and Australia.

My description of the field of new Seattle churches in chapter 2 draws on what I learned about the 105 churches that were founded within the Seattle's city limits since January 1, 2001, and that remained active into 2014.[19] This includes the information that was available through church websites, social media pages, and denominational sources, as well as, importantly, the surveys that were submitted by pastors from more than half of these new churches (see survey in appendix B).

The New Seattle Churches Survey also allowed me to confirm my hypothesis that the field could be characterized by a limited number of types. This hypothesis was based on the findings of two previous geographically delimited congregational studies.[20] The four paradigms that emerged from statistical analysis of the survey responses provided a framework to structure the interpretive analysis.

Interpretation: Moving from Statistical Paradigms to Practical Ecclesiological Models

The task of the interpretive move is to make sense of what has been described using the most relevant disciplines and theories. At the outset, I was convinced that the best way to adequately comprehend the variety among new Seattle churches would require drawing on both theological and social science perspectives, since both fields have significant histories of reflection on church. While the survey was critical in setting the stage for this interpretive work, it was not expected to make possible a sufficiently thick understanding of the ecclesial cultures and practices that make up the field. To gain this thick understanding I took a mixed-methods approach that included various levels of qualitative research in churches across the ecclesial spectrum.

The four paradigms that emerged from analysis of the survey served to guide my qualitative research among a number of churches that were prime examples of each paradigm. In this way, the survey-based paradigms provided skeletons of ecclesiopraxis that the qualitative research built upon in the development of the four practical ecclesiological models. From several *exemplar* churches in each paradigm, I collected and analyzed pastoral interviews, field notes, transcripts from worship gatherings, online recordings, media coverage, newsletters, brochures, web pages, and social media posts. In addition, as a subset of these twenty-five exemplar churches, three *focus* churches were selected for intensive study on the basis of their ecclesiological diversity and the feasibility of participant observation among all three on a single Sunday. Focus church research included extensive participant observation, multiple focus groups, and a congregational survey.

The qualitative materials from exemplar and focus churches were coded and analyzed for themes within each of the four paradigms. These themes compose the major part of the practical ecclesiological models I develop in chapter 4. The models are situated alongside prominent types in the existing literature—which are surveyed in chapter 3—in order to highlight key similarities and differences. The four practical ecclesiological models that resulted provide an interpretive typology for dominant forms of ecclesio-praxis among new churches. The models broadly correspond to recogniz-able categories as follows:

Great Commission Team: Evangelical, mission-centered churches
Household of the Spirit: Pentecostal and charismatic, worship-centered
    churches
New Community: Mainline and emerging, worship- and community-
    centered churches
Neighborhood Incarnation: Community- and mission-centered neigh-
    borhood churches

Evaluation: Missional Theological Assessment of the Models

The task of theological evaluation is to proceed from the interpretive understanding of "what is" toward "what should be." This task seeks to collaborate with the ongoing work of the evangelizing, converting Spirit of God, which is always inviting human agents to repent and realign their lives with the inbreaking Reign of God.

Chapter 5 is dedicated to an evaluation of the four models from the perspective of missional theology. Missional theology is a discourse largely about the theology and practice of mission in the post-Christian West. As such, it makes an invaluable partner in promoting faithful and vital forms of ecclesial mission in the United States. This assessment high-lights both the strengths and weaknesses of each model, but ultimately judges the Neighborhood Incarnation model to most thoroughly embody the commitments of missional theology. In addition, I find this model to be vibrantly contextual in its engagement with the four future-trending characteristics of Seattle.

Proposals: Toward Renewed Ecclesial Practice and Doctrine

This culminating move answers the "So what?" question, venturing prac-tical proposals and fresh ecclesiological formulations. Chapter 6 offers concrete practices to on-the-ground practitioners within each of the four models. The proposed practices are intended to simultaneously capital-ize on the strengths of their model and open the church to transformative encounters with the Spirit of God, yielding greater alignment with the insights of missional theology. These strategic proposals, on the surface quite modest, are calibrated to walk a fine line between authentic resonance within the model's cultural logic and progressive disruption of some of the more problematic characteristics of its theology and practice.

The proposals found in the concluding chapter arise from the five threads of practical wisdom I discovered among new Seattle churches as a whole. This practical wisdom includes: (1) embracing local identity and mission; (2) cultivating embodied, experiential, everyday spirituality; (3) engaging community life as means of witness and formation; (4) prioritizing hospitality as a cornerstone practice; and (5) discovering ecclesial vitality in a diverse ecclesial ecology. These threads represent themes among new Seattle churches that are promising for their potential to foster ecclesiological and missional vitality. On the basis of each of these threads, I offer strategic proposals to leaders among church planting efforts and also propose doctrinal trajectories for theologians to explore.

Writing the Church

This book is about the future of church—but is also about the study of church. It *is* ecclesiology and it is *about* ecclesiology. As an exercise in missional practical ecclesiological reflection, this book offers an interdisciplinary and multi-genre engagement with the field of new churches in Seattle. Writing about church, I am convinced, is at its best when it is pluriform. Church is a diverse, complex, and simultaneously sociocultural and theological reality. Expressing this reality faithfully can be done only by exceeding genre boundaries and integrating them as a spectrum of multidisciplinary perspectives.[21] It is this kind of work that can engender faithful ecclesiopraxis and thus fulfill the task of ecclesiology. Inasmuch as this book demonstrates the validity of this claim, it not only advances the central thesis about the practical wisdom to be gleaned from new Seattle churches but also embodies an argument for practical ecclesiological reflection. The book is an effort not only to write *about* church but also to write *as* church and *for* church. While I will make an argument for the practical ecclesiological method I use, the strongest case for this approach is to be found in the fruit it produces. That fruit is found in the proposals toward renewed ecclesiopraxis in the final chapters and their impact when put into practice in real congregations.

In the midst of dramatic cultural shifts and declining religious institutions, new churches are taking root. What are these churches like? How are they responding to their contexts? What do they have to teach churches about faithful witness in their emerging environment? These are the questions at the heart of this book. It is my hope that the answers I found in Seattle will prove themselves to be assets as churches seek to discern God's call to discipleship, join the Spirit's missional initiatives, and witness faithfully to Jesus Christ in the midst of our rapidly evolving U.S. context.

I

The Lay of the Land

SEATTLE AS A FUTURE-TRENDING CONTEXT

AT ITS CORE, this project is about helping Christian communities fulfill their vocations as witnesses to the good news of Jesus Christ in rapidly evolving Western contexts. Because Christian witness is always a deeply contextual practice, providing the U.S. church with wise counsel requires an understanding of key dynamics in the U.S. context that bear upon the practice of Christian witness. This chapter lifts up four such national trends: urbanization, technological culture, progressive social values, and post-Christian society. Furthermore, I show how each of these trends is a distinguishing feature of the Seattle context, which for this reason I identify as a future-trending city. On this basis, I make the central argument of this chapter: Seattle—by virtue of its epitomization of four major national trends—provides a serviceable proxy for the urban U.S. context in the coming years.

Vanguard Characteristics of the Emerald City

The decision to locate this practical ecclesiological study in Seattle was grounded in Seattle's unique characteristics as a city on the leading edges of wider contextual changes that the church cannot afford to ignore. Northwest resident and religion scholar Patricia Killen has said it plainly: "The rest of the nation is beginning to look more like us."¹ She aptly compares the Pacific Northwest to a "canary in the mine." In a similar vein, historian Jan Shipps has described Seattle as "a harbinger of urban religion in the future."² The basis for these grand declarations can be grounded in several distinctive characteristics of the Seattle context that map to wider trends—including urbanization, progressivism, the digital revolution, and post-Christian religious dynamics. These trends promise to significantly shape the United States as a context for Christian witness in the coming decades. In each of the following sections, I describe one national trend with major cultural significance and demonstrate how Seattle is on the leading edge of this national shift.

City Living: Urbanization, Neighborhoods, and Urban Isolation

Seattle is a prime example of the overwhelmingly and increasingly urban character of the nation as a whole. More than 82% of the U.S. population currently lives in urban areas, though these take up only about 2% of the nation's land area.[3] This figure is expected to approach 90% by 2050.[4] Urbanization—the flow of people into urban areas—is not just an American phenomenon; it is a global one that is changing the shape of human society in ways that have deep implications for ecclesial life and witness. A century ago, only 10% of the global population lived in cities. Humanity reached a tipping point in 2008, when urbanites became the population majority. We are now a predominantly urban species; it seems certain we will only become more so. United Nations projections through 2050 chart a steady climb in global urban populations, with dramatic transformations taking place in many underdeveloped nations.

Urban areas in developed nations like the United States predictably undergo a process of land use typified by multiple waves of urban sprawl into several suburban rings, urban decay followed by population growth in the inner rings, and consequent expansion of the urban core and gentrification of nearby neighborhoods.[5] This extension of the urban core entails significant replacement of traditional home-and-yard lots with apartment complexes, facilitating increasing population density and resulting in a demographic shift away from families and toward singles. The processes of urban growth can bring an array of challenges, including increases in pollution, crime, and cost of living that in turn feed suburban sprawl and displacement of the poor.

As one of the fastest-growing cities in the nation, Seattle is a case study in urbanization.[6] In recent years, Seattle has ranked among the fastest growing large U.S. cities. Between 2000 and 2012, the city grew 12.6%, and between July 2012 and July 2013 alone, Seattle's population increased

2.8%—the steepest rise in the country.[7] With 100,000 new residents added since 2010, Seattle's population now exceeds 700,000—making it the 18th most populous city in the United States. Conscious of the challenges of urbanization, Seattle officials have taken a proactive approach; in 2005, they embraced—and have since reaffirmed multiple times—a strategic plan to focus its population growth in urban villages that intentionally "match growth to the existing and intended character of the city's neighborhoods" in a mix of housing, employment, and services (see figure 1.1). Such urban planning efforts aim to capitalize on the economic, environmental, and human benefits of high-density, city-center development. These benefits are said to include increased productivity, innovation, walkability, and quality of life, as well as decreased demand for the costly facilities and services that accompany urban sprawl. Bolstered by these efforts, two-thirds of Seattle's recent urban growth has been concentrated in just thirteen of Seattle's fifty-three neighborhoods, with a heavy concentration in the downtown area.[8] This urban boom has led to several consecutive years in which population growth in the city has outpaced that in the surrounding suburbs of King County, reversing a 100-year trend.[9]

The influx of new residents has also substantially shifted city and neighborhood demographics. A remarkable 92% of the population growth in the Puget Sound area, which includes four counties, has been among minority segments, but Seattle itself is a different story.[10] Within Seattle city limits, Hispanic and "two or more races" demographics have grown and the Asian demographic has basically held steady since 2000, but African Americans have been substantially displaced.[11] These changes have been most dramatically on display in the Central District, where gentrification has transformed a neighborhood where blacks in 1990 made up 64% of the population into a majority-white neighborhood with only 28% black residents.[12] Citywide gentrification has pushed minorities and the less affluent to the southern edges of the city and beyond.

The Seattle metropolitan area is a magnet for the young, white, educated, and upwardly mobile, thanks in part to numerous tech company hubs including Amazon and Microsoft. The largest ten-year age category in the city itself is 25 to 34 years and the median age for residents is 36.[13] A study out of Portland State University found that the Seattle metro area ranked in the top third of fifty metro areas for attracting and retaining college graduates between 25 and 39 years.[14]

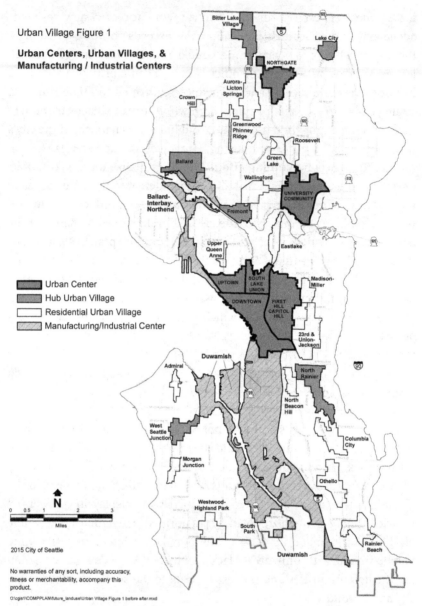

FIGURE 1.1 Seattle's urban villages.

(*Seattle's Comprehensive Plan: Toward a Sustainable Seattle*, 2015, www.seattle.gov/dpd/cs/ groups/pan/@pan/documents/web_informational/dpddo16610.pdf)

These population flows come with increasingly mobile urban dwellers. In fact, about 62% of Seattle residents were born outside of Washington State, ranking it among the top ten big cities in the nation for out-of-state transplants.[15] The mobility (and instability) of Seattleites is also evident in the nearly one in four (22.9%) city residents who have been in their current housing situation for less than a year.[16] Sociologist Rodney Stark, formerly at the University of Washington, purportedly quipped that "people in Seattle have lived in three places in the last 10 years."[17]

Urban transplants are often seeking to start afresh in a new place, with a new group of friends. Unfortunately, the same longings that drive many to Seattle may be inhibiting the realization of meaningful community. The concentration of relocated individuals in the Greater Seattle area yields significant social and cultural impacts. Killen expresses this well:

> Few people come to the Far West seeking what they left behind. Most hold dreams of a better life. Physical mobility and psychological mobility reinforce each other. When people move west they must choose to reconnect to social institutions, to be part of communities. Having left one community, they find it easier to leave another and harder to reconnect.[18]

The challenges that transplants face in finding community are so common that Seattle has earned itself a reputation as a hard place to make friends. It is not that Seattleites are rude; to the contrary, newcomers' first impressions often include celebration of the city's "niceness." Indeed, Marjabell Young Stewart, author of a dozen etiquette books, ranks Seattle as the third most polite city.[19] So, Seattleites may hold the door for you and make warm chit-chat, but these superficial actions should not be mistaken as heralding a real opening toward friendship, and so the nice soon turns to ice.

The phenomenon has been dubbed the "Seattle freeze," and the phrase resonates so strongly that since it was first put in print in 2005, a steady stream of articles have been written about it.[20] Among the 1,040,000 google search results for "Seattle freeze" are links to entries in Wikipedia and the Urban Dictionary, as well as a meetup.com group with more than 11,700 members calling itself "Seattle Anti-Freeze." Theories explaining the Seattle Freeze abound, and variously attribute the frostiness to ethnicity ("Can we blame the Norwegians?"),[21] residual frontierism ("This is my land, find your own!"), and weather ("Gray skies make me want to hunker down"). More recently, the Seattle Freeze has been linked to the ubiquity of technology, another important national trend that is on display in Seattle.

Seattle's unsociable behavior is not limited to giving newcomers a chilly reception. The Greater Seattle Civic Health Index in 2013 found that Seattle's "social cohesion" was among the lowest in the nation.[22] Out of fifty-one similar U.S. communities, Greater Seattle ranked forty-eighth in frequency of residents' talking to their neighbors and thirty-seventh in giving to and receiving favors from neighbors.

The residential practices of many Seattleites certainly are not helping to build bonds. Roughly half of the those who live in Seattle rent their housing, and more than half of Seattle apartments have a solitary occupant.[23] This percentage of solo renters is the second highest in the nation. Moreover, 31% of owner-occupied residences have only one resident. Altogether, then, roughly four out of every ten Seattle dwellings house someone who is living alone. While there are undeniable perks to the solitary housing situation, there are also personal (and civic) liabilities.

It is hardly surprising that this antisocial urban cocktail of mobility, unneighborliness, and solitary housing is accompanied by widespread feelings of isolation and despair. Indeed, one study named Seattle the fifth loneliest city in the nation.[24] The Greater Seattle area is also a hotspot for suicide attempts, earning it a lamentable second-place ranking out of thirty-three metropolitan areas.[25]

Urban living—with all its benefits and challenges—is the way of the future. The overwhelming majority of Americans already live in urban areas, and the percentage will keep rising. The significance of this for Christian witness in the United States is plain: if the church wants to provide viable and faithful witness to the overwhelming majority of the population, it must discern how to do so in urban settings shaped by dynamics such as urban villages, gentrification, and social isolation. As one of the fastest-urbanizing cities in the United States, Seattle offers church futurists a prime context in which to seek such discernment.

Progressive Values

Despite the unexpected election of Donald Trump in November 2016, the last decade has nonetheless seen significant national and urban shifts toward progressive social values, including Lesian-Gay-Bisexual-Transgender-Queer (LGBTQ) inclusion, minimum-wage increases, environmental sustainability, and legalization of marijuana, to name a few.[26]

Each of these progressive trends is exemplified in Seattle, a city with a reputation as one of the most progressive in the nation. In 2014 alone, Seattle approved an increase of the minimum wage to $15 an hour, saw its first recreational marijuana store open,[27] and was named the nation's "most LGBT-friendly" city.[28] On these and other progressive issues, Seattle is at the front edge of wider trends that have profound implications for ecclesial witness.

Major shifts toward LGBTQ-positive attitudes and policies have taken place across the nation since the early years of the millennium. In 2001, only 35% of Americans supported same-sex marriage, while 57% opposed it.[29] But by 2016, these figures had nearly flipped, with 55% in favor and only 37% opposed.[30] This trend is set to continue owing to generational replacement; nearly seven in ten millennials favor same-sex marriage compared to roughly half that among those 68 and older.[31] The last decade has also included landmark political and legislative moves. Starting in 2008, the United States saw a steady increase in the number of states with legalized same-sex marriage. In 2012, President Obama became the first president to come out in support of gay marriage, and in 2014 he made an executive order prohibiting federal contractors from discriminating on the basis of sexual orientation or gender identity.[32] In 2013, the Supreme Court struck down the Defense of Marriage Act in a landmark ruling that state-approved same-sex marriages must be federally recognized. In 2015, the court made same-sex marriage legal in all states. Even Donald Trump—by no means a progressive figure—broke ranks with the Republican Party, declaring at the 2016 Republican Convention, "As your President, I will do everything in my power to protect LGBTQ citizens."[33] After winning the election, he told Barbara Walters on *60 Minutes* that he regards same-sex marriage as having been "settled in the Supreme Court," saying "I'm fine with that."[34]

Seattle's recognition as one of the most LGBTQ-friendly cities in America has much warrant. Most notable is its high concentration of same-sex couples. A Census Bureau Report in 2012 noted that one out of eighteen couples living together in Seattle were of the same sex. Moreover, 2.6% of all Seattle dwellings were found to same-sex couples—the highest density in the nation.[35] Also in 2012, Washington passed legislation that recognized gay marriage, backed by 82% of Seattle voters.[36] When the first same-sex couple was married in Seattle in 2013, they were invited to hoist a giant marriage equality flag atop the iconic Space Needle (see figure 1.2). The Human Rights Campaign's Municipal Equality Index is another key indicator that combines nondiscrimination laws, relationship recognition,

FIGURE 1.2 Marriage Equality flag atop Space Needle in 2013.
("Space Needle Marriage Equality Flag," *AP Images*, June 30, 2013)

employment practices, city services, law enforcement, and city leadership; Seattle has earned consecutive perfect scores since its inception.

In a nation whose population is becoming increasingly urban, urban areas are swinging increasingly left. While Donald Trump, the Republican nominee, won the 2016 election by claiming a victory in the Electoral College, he lost the popular vote to Democrat Hillary Clinton by nearly 3 million votes.[37] Most counties with a population above 500,000 moved further left in 2016.[38] Clinton won nearly 90% of counties that include urban cores.[39] Large U.S. cities overwhelmingly have Democratic mayors, a marked difference from twenty years ago, when half of the largest dozen cities had Republican mayors.[40]

Seattle reflects these national and urban trends. In the 2012 presidential election, every Mitt Romney voter in Seattle was matched by six Barack Obama backers. In 2016, Clinton outperformed Trump in Seattle by nine to one.[41] The only non-Democratic member currently on the City Council is Kshama Sawant, a member of the Socialist Alternative Party, who campaigned on promises of a $15 an hour minimum wage. The city's support of this landmark wage hike in 2014 has gained national attention, spurring similar efforts across the country. In 2016, the movement won minimum-wage increases in twenty-five states, cities, and counties, including graduating increases to $15 an hour in Washington, D.C., parts of Oregon and New York State, and all of California.

Washington was one of the first two states, along with Colorado, to legalize recreational use of marijuana. Public opinion on the issue has been steadily trending positive since the early 1990s. The progressive shift accelerated in 2010, and by 2013 a majority of Americans (52%) favored legalization.[42] Marijuana was legalized for medical use in Washington State as early as 1998, and since about that time twenty-seven other states (and the District of Columbia) have followed. In 2016, California, Nevada, Maine, and Massachusetts also legalized the sale of recreational marijuana. The trend in popular opinion is likely to lead to recreational legalization in more states, especially in view of the financial upside. Seattle's first pot shop ran out of supply only three days after opening, but in that short time it had generated about $150,000 in excise taxes.[43] Colorado's cannabis market contributed $2 million in tax revenues in its first month of operation.[44]

Another progressive value—environmental sustainability—also has had the Emerald City in the vanguard. The trend toward energy-efficient buildings is illustrative. As of 2003, only 1,100 buildings nationwide had earned the Energy Star label, but by 2016 the certification had been awarded to 28,000.[45] Seattle was among the early adopter cities, and when the EPA began ranking cities in 2009 based on how many Energy Star buildings they included, Seattle ranked tenth despite being only the twenty-third largest city in the nation. Since then it has ceded a few spots in the ranking to larger cities, but this is more indicative of the national trend gathering momentum than any waning commitment in Seattle; during the same period, the Emerald City has nearly doubled its number of qualifying structures.[46]

When the United States declined to adopt the Kyoto Protocol with 141 other nations in 2005, Seattle Mayor Greg Nickels launched the U.S. Conference of Mayors Climate Protection Agreement, pledging to strive to meet the Protocol in their own cities.[47] Since that time, more than 1,000 mayors across the country have signed on. Seattleites themselves also show an active commitment to green living by fueling a key market for electric vehicles,[48] carpooling,[49] and passing major legislation, such as a 2008 levy that committed $146 million to Seattle Parks. The Pacific Northwest's proximity to the Pacific Ocean, its abundance of rain, and its steep landscapes not only offer residents daily prompts for environmental consciousness but also promise to make the region a refuge from the negative impacts of climate change.[50] In light of these facts it is not surprising that Seattle has earned numerous recognitions in recent years as a leading green city.[51]

Environmental sustainability, LGBTQ equality, legal marijuana, and minimum-wage increases are just a handful of the nationally trending progressive values that Seattle has championed, and for which it has earned recognition as one of the nation's most progressive cities.

Technological Culture

Technology is changing the nation. Seattle is a key site where these changes can be observed and is a catalyst for advancing them. Pew Research highlights three technology revolutions in the new millennium: broadband connectivity, mobile devices, and social media. Home broadband internet connectivity rose from a mere 1% in 2000 to 73% in 2016, supporting dramatic rises in internet use, video streaming, and time spent online.[52] Mobile connectivity via smartphones, e-readers, and tablets has also taken off, especially since 2010.[53] Between 2005 and 2016, the use of at least one social media site jumped from 5% to 69% of all U.S. adults.[54]

These nationwide tech trends have recently become a subject of some popular self-reflection and scholarly scrutiny surrounding concerns about their impacts. One study found that 60% of smartphone users did not go an hour without checking their phone.[55] More troubling, perhaps, are the 30% who check their phones during meals with others. Nielsen found that smartphone users were spending thirty hours a month using apps.[56] Parents of teens and tweens spend more than nine hours a day using screens.[57] Studies have confirmed the highly addictive nature of digital connectivity and the deleterious effects mobile tech can have on relationships.[58] A slew of (ironically) viral videos and independent films, including the award-winning *Her*, have emerged in recent years challenging the cultural obsession with staying digitally linked.[59]

Seattle is one of the nation's most digitally connected cities. As the New America Foundation notes, "the information technology industry employs 90,000 people in the Seattle region, and the Puget Sound area is home to 150 interactive media companies," including Microsoft, Google, RealNetworks, and Amazon, whose latest contribution to the city is some transparently futuristic architecture (see figure 1.3).[60] The City of Seattle's study of technology access in 2014 found that Seattle reflects the national trends of rapid adoption: home internet access had jumped from 57% to 85% in the preceding decade; smartphone use increased from 35% in 2009 to 58% in 2013; and two-thirds of Seattleites were using Facebook.[61] The city frequently ranks among *Forbes* magazine's Most Wired Cities, in

FIGURE 1.3 Amazon Biosphere rendering.
(NBBJ)

part due to its ubiquitous Wi-Fi hotspots.[62] Richard Florida ranked Seattle as the nation's "top tech city" in 2012.[63] In 2013, a couple of researchers found that Seattle was the source of more trending Twitter topics than any other city.[64] Seattle's connectivity has earned it distinctions and influence, but its residents are not immune to the psychological and social impacts. One study found Seattle to be the second most social media–addicted city in the nation.[65] Appropriately, Seattle metro became home to America's first internet addiction clinic in 2009.[66]

The three characteristics already discussed—urbanization, progressivism, and the technological culture—combine in various ways and with other elements in the formulas behind declarations that Seattle is a "next frontier,"[67] an "up and coming"[68] city, and among the nation's "smartest"[69] and most "creative"[70] urban areas.

Post-Christian: Dynamics of Religious Life in the None Zone

In the forefront of the minds of the region's church planters is Seattle's status as one of the most post-Christian cities in an increasingly post-Christian nation. "Post-Christian" can have a number of meanings, but here I refer chiefly to low levels of Christian church affiliation and participation.[71] Downward national trends for both are well documented. According to the General Social Survey, weekly church attendance has fallen steadily in the United States since 1972, dropping from 28.5% of the population to 17.5% in 2014. During the same period, the percentage of Americans reporting they never attend religious services jumped from less than one in ten to more than one in four.[72]

Even more dramatic than steady declines in participation is the uptick in the number of religiously unaffiliated Americans, as seen in figure 1.4.[73] The last four decades of the General Social Survey show the number of those with "no religious preference" more than tripling. A 2016 study by Public Religion Research Institute found that the unaffiliated—or "Nones," as they are frequently called—included 25% of all Americans.[74] Already, the unaffiliated are the largest religious grouping in thirteen states.[75] The Pew Research Center predicts that 52 million new individuals will be added to the number of unaffiliated Americans by 2050.[76] This dramatic "Rise of the Nones" mostly began in the early 1990s, and thus far the majority of it has come at the expense of Protestants, especially white Protestants, whose share has dropped dramatically since the same time to less than half of the U.S. population for the first time on record.[77]

The "Nones" are a composite group, mainly made up of those who religiously claim "nothing in particular," but also including a growing

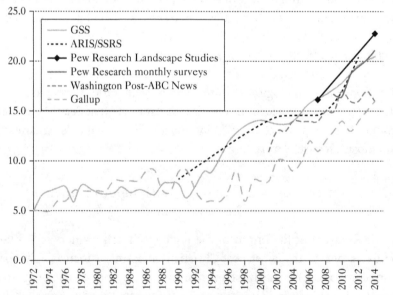

FIGURE 1.4 Size of the unaffiliated population: long-term trends.

(Appendix C: Putting Findings from the Religious Landscape Study into Context, Pew Research Center, May, 2015, www.pewforum.org/2015/05/12/appendix-c-putting-findings-from-the-religious-landscape-study-into-context/pr_15-05-12_rls_append-c-00/)

number of agnostics and atheists. They are disproportionately young, with each successive generation increasingly unlikely to affiliate, as figure 1.5 shows. While 88% of the unaffiliated are not searching for a religion that fits, it would be a mistake to assume that the majority are secular.[78] In fact, two-thirds of "Nones" believe in God.[79] According to Peter Berger, "Most "nones" have not opted out of religion as such, but have opted out of affiliation with organized religion."[80] The unaffiliated are also more likely to think of themselves as either "religious" or "spiritual" than nei-ther.[81] The "spiritual-but-not-religious" are a related group defined not by their religious affiliation but by their responses to two other survey ques-tions: Do you consider yourself to be spiritual? Do you consider yourself to be religious? As a group they account for only 18% of U.S. adults, but they account for 37% of the "Nones."

The spiritual-but-not-religious have been the subject of much discus-sion in recent years.[82] As sociologist Nancy Ammerman has clarified, those who occupy the spiritual-but-not-religious category are rarely the freewheeling, Eastern/eclectic practitioners that the spirituality vs. religion binary imagines. Their spirituality may be a patchwork, but the scraps of cloth at hand for many are well worn and patently Christian. Indeed, a significant number of the spiritual-but-not-religious are basically "white label" Christians who hold recognizably Christian beliefs (about God, the Bible, and Jesus), engage in central Christian practices (Christmas and Easter services, prayer, Bible reading), and may even identify with a local congregation, all while eschewing self-identification as a "religious

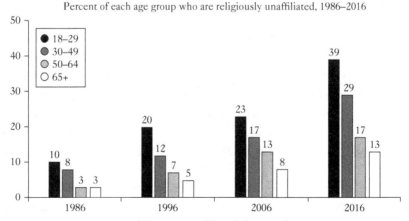

Percent of each age group who are religiously unaffiliated, 1986–2016

FIGURE 1.5 More young adults are unaffiliated than in the past. (PRRI)

person."[83] This is despite the fact that fully two-thirds of the spiritual-but-not-religious *are* religiously affiliated.[84] Often, identifying as "spiritual" but not "religious" is evidence of an individual's desire to distance him or herself from the perceived evils perpetrated by organized religion, rather than descriptive of the individual's beliefs and practices.[85] Ammerman highlights important overlaps in the imagined spiritual vs. religious binary:

> The "religion" being rejected [by the spiritual-but-not-religious] turns out to be quite unlike the religion being practiced and described by those affiliated with religious institutions. Likewise, the "spirituality" being endorsed as an alternative is at least as widely practiced by those same religious people as it is by the people drawing a moral boundary against them.[86]

When it comes to being spiritual and/or religious in practice, it is usually both or neither.[87] This is in part due to the role of religious communities in providing the "sustaining conversations" that make day-to-day spiritual perspectives viable.[88] "If [people] do not learn the language of spirituality in a religious community, it does not shape their way of being in the world." Ammerman quips, "'Spiritual but not religious?' Probably not."[89]

These national post-Christian trends are reflected and exaggerated in the Pacific Northwest. As Patricia Killen notes, the defining feature of religion in the region is its unchurched and unaffiliated majority.[90] This is why the team of scholars who produced *Religion and Public Life in the Pacific Northwest* first dubbed the region "The None Zone."[91] Moreover, it has pretty much always been this way.[92] While religion has been on the decline in the Northwest as elsewhere, this has not been a fall from cultural dominance as in other parts of the country; Christendom never really took hold in Cascadia. The historic weakness of religious institutions and absence of a dominant religious institutional reference group have shaped the religious ecology in several important ways. First, these dynamics have created an open religious environment that fosters innovation and has proved relatively hospitable to nontraditional religions and sectarians alike. This has benefited a diverse range of groups, including Wiccans, Mormons, Adventists, and Holiness-Pentecostals, all of which are regionally overrepresented.[93] Second, the Northwest's open ecology has led the religious institutions present in the region to "become concerned with boundaries of identity and exhibit . . . alternation between expansiveness and self-absorption" as some choose to embrace the region's pluralism and others to adamantly reject it.[94]

The region's openness has a parallel impact on individuals, for whom establishing religious identity can mean a lifelong project, often along one of two paths.[95] Killen describes the primary options:

> The ambiguity of this macro religious environment . . . [causes] many [to] pursue a spiritual quest of their own, drawing from multiple traditions and practices on a journey of religious experimentation. . . . But for others the ambiguity . . . propels them toward commitment that is clearly defined, emotionally significant, and often inflexible because it is hard won, and thus in need of protection. For these people, highlighting boundaries between one's religious community and others helps to reinforce identity and commitment. Hence, the same environment that provides space for wide-ranging religious experimentation feeds a sectarian impulse.[96]

The result of weak religious institutions, then, is counterintuitively both diversity and vitality of religious and spiritual identities. Though institutional affiliation is low, personal ownership of the religious beliefs and practices one has forged and cultivated is high. As Killen told the *Seattle Times*, these dynamics have also made the Northwest "the only region outside of the South and Old Southwest where Conservative Protestants are a group equal to Catholics in size and where they constitute a major share of the adherent pie."[97] It turns out the None Zone can be a rather fertile place for certain types of religion.

In many ways, Seattle—as Cascadia's largest city—epitomizes these longstanding features of the Pacific Northwest. The 2016 American Values Atlas found the Seattle metro to have the highest percentage of religiously unaffiliated inhabitants among major metropolitan areas (40%).[98] Barna's Cities survey, which includes questions ranging from Bible reading and prayer to church participation, also ranks the Seattle-Tacoma area among the nation's most post-Christian metros.[99] The Greater Seattle area is home to a higher percentage of atheists—10%—than any other large U.S. metro area.[100] By these measures, Seattle is an irreligious place indeed.

But Seattle's apparent irreligiosity can be surprisingly spiritual. Two-thirds of the Northwest's "Nones" believe in God and half of them agree that God helps them personally.[101] Seattle's open religious environment and majestic scenery combine in charging its magnetism among the spiritual-but-critical-of-institutional-religion demographic. Historian Jan Shipps has described spirituality as the "the hallmark of Seattle religiosity," noting that "[Northwest] spirituality is connected to nature, to the human body, to animals, even to free trade."[102] She continues: "Altars exist in gorgeous religious structures, but are as often found as stopping points on hiking trails or mountainside overhangs. What is revealed when the pie chart's confines are removed is that the apparent secularity is a veneer."[103] Sociologist Mark Shibley describes ubiquitous "nature religion" as the most central alternative spirituality to the cultural ethos of the region. There is cultural resonance, of course, between this spiritual sensibility and the progressive concern for the environment. As Shibley asserts, much environmentalism in the Northwest should be considered religious because "it facilitates religious experience, ritualizes daily life, contains a coherent worldview regarding the sacred [and profane] and provides a basis for community."[104]

Indeed, as a post-Christian context, Seattle puts to rest the daydreams of some secularization theorists who foretold the end of religion. The None Zone is not a religious "no man's land."[105] By designating Seattle as "post-Christian," I do not mean that it is devoid of religious presence, nor that it is characterized by a demoralized, retreating Christianity. To the contrary, while almost half of Seattle metro residents are not religious, more than a quarter are "highly" religious.[106] The persistence of devout religionists amid secularization is consistent with the national trend; while the percentage of Americans with no religious affilation has tripled since 1972, the percentage with "strong" religious affiliation has remained remarkably stable above 33%.[107] Rather than demoralizing the faithful, the minority status of confessional Christians seems to counterintuitively contribute to the vitality of their religious identity and mission. As sociologist Christian Smith has argued, Evangelicals can thrive on the sense of embattlement they feel in secularizing, pluralistic settings.[108] The None Zone's dominant secularism has proved to be a rather fertile environment for fervent Christianity.

The None Zone, then, is not so irreligious after all. Rather, it is characterized by distinctive religious dynamics. As Killen put it, the Northwest "is alternately indifferent or inviting to religion, an obstacle or opportunity, a refuge or revelation. Here, more than in other regions of the United States, weak religious institutions and the absence of a dominant institutional reference group allow for a highly elastic religious reality."[109] Institutional weakness has made the Northwest "differently religious" and "a uniquely attractive place for proselytizing churches and countercultural spirituality movements."[110] Thus it is that Seattle is simultaneously home to an unaffiliated, unchurched majority and to a fierce Evangelical Christian minority.[111]

A sense of the ecology of Christian congregations and adherents in Seattle provides a key context in which new churches are emerging.[112] A 2010 dataset reported the existence of 327 Christian congregations inside the city limits.[113] Nearly half of these churches were classified as Evangelical, though not all were affiliated with Evangelical denominations; nondenominational churches made up a fifth of the Evangelical set and about 8% of the whole. Mainline Protestant congregations accounted for the next largest group at 37% of the congregational ecology. Catholic and Orthodox parishes constituted about 10% of Seattle churches, and about 5% were in the historic black church tradition.

Of course, the number of congregations reveals relatively little about the proportions of adherents, since church size can vary dramatically. The best available data on adherents come from Pew Research's 2014 Religious Landscape Study, which reports that Evangelicals make up the largest group, accounting for 44% of adult Christians in the Seattle metro area. Catholics are the next largest group with 29%, followed by those identifying with mainline Protestant denominations at 19% of Seattle's Christians.[114] All other Christian groups each account for less than 1%. To summarize, Evangelicals are better represented in numbers of adherents and congregations in the Seattle area than are either Catholics or mainline Protestants.

Seattle: Western Pioneer

This is Seattle—a place of rapid urban population growth, progressive social values, technological culture, and post-Christian dynamics. As such, the Emerald City embodies wider national and urban trends, and warrants the attention of those invested in the future of the church in the American context. In the words of Mark Driscoll—the highly controversial pastor responsible for more of Seattle's newest churches than any other— "Christendom is Dead: Welcome to the United States of Seattle."[115]

Though the study of churches anywhere, of any vintage, can offer promising theological and practical insights, the future-trending character of the Seattle context marks it as particularly significant, and invites careful analysis of the new ecclesial life putting down roots in its Cascadian soil. What makes new Seattle churches important is not that they merely happen to be located in a trend-leading place, but that they have been— inevitably and often intentionally—shaped in and for such a context.[116] "New congregations . . . even if unconsciously, take on elements of their environments and can thus be expected to have a competitive advantage over older ones which were 'imprinted' by the bygone eras in which they were founded."[117] As a result, new churches in a future-trending context have the potential of revealing clues about what it takes to be viable as trends progress.

Attention to the contours of new Seattle churches reveal various con-nections with the trends already discussed. Many of Seattle's newest churches have been started (and funded) precisely because Seattle is such a post-Christian, unchurched place. The dynamics of rapid urbanization have shaped everything from where new churches are located to what they regard as top mission priorities and how they structure their corporate life. Most new churches embrace—and appeal to—the digital culture of the city. In contrast, Seattle's progressive values are highly controversial among church starts; they are demonized by resurgent Christian conservatives but embraced as gospel by theological liberals. These broad strokes can only begin to characterize the complex relationships between gospel, com-munity, and culture incarnated in these churches. Indeed, every church is unique in the way various contextual features influence its ecclesial spiri-tuality, identity, and mission. However, making sense of the inimitable particularity of any given church can be aided by an understanding of the larger contours and patterns in which that particular church participates and exists. Describing this rich ecclesial ecology is the task of chapter 2.

2

Surveying the Field

SEATTLE'S RELIGIOUS ECOLOGY is being reshaped by new churches and the ways their approaches to spirituality, mission, and identity foster engagement with Seattle's urban, progressive, technological, post-Christian context. This chapter provides a description of this new cohort of churches. In the first section, I offer a broad overview of the field in terms of denominational affiliation, founding dates, locations, web presence, and ethnic composition. In the rest of the chapter, I unpack the findings of the New Seattle Churches Survey. These findings shed light on how new Seattle churches approach spirituality, mission, and identity. In each of these ecclesial dimensions, I note key *currents* across the field, such as the prevalence of weekly Communion. In addition, I identify the significant *patterns* present within each dimension—for example, the mission pattern constituted by correlated priorities on service and hospitality. Finally, I show how these patterns cluster to form four ecclesial paradigms. These four paradigms represent, in skeletal form, the dominant varieties of ecclesial presence in the future-trending city of Seattle.

By the Numbers

The identification phase took place between spring 2013 and summer 2014, and involved extensive internet research, as well as phone and on-site research. More information regarding methodology are available in appendix A. The result of this research was the identification of 105 new churches started, rebirthed, and/or relocated between January 1, 2001 and June 1, 2014, which were gathering regularly for worship at a Seattle address.[1] All these churches were confirmed as fitting the parameters of the study, but roughly another dozen churches were identified that may have qualified for inclusion but could not be verified in terms of founding date, address, or current status.[2] Nine of the confirmed churches were in the middle or late stages of development; they were included only if they had started holding regular—but not necessarily weekly—gatherings. The great majority of the churches included in the study are brand new and self-governing, but the field also includes fourteen multisite campuses, five churches resulting from church splits, four mergers, seven churches that relocated from outside to inside the city limits, and one rebirth.[3]

Multiple surviving new churches were founded in Seattle every year between 2001 and 2014. Generally, the number of new starts hovered around six or seven, but 2010 saw a spike of sixteen. This tapered off to twelve and ten in 2011 and 2012, respectively. Multisites played a role in this bump, as six of the fourteen multisites in the city were launched between 2010 and 2012. On average, 7.5 new churches were started per year in Seattle between 2001 and 2014.

Churches have taken root in neighborhoods scattered across the city, but several hotspots are noteworthy, as shown in figure 2.1.[4] The heart of the city (Downtown, Belltown, South Lake Union, Capitol Hill) is home to more than one in six new Seattle churches (18/105).[5] North of Downtown, the Phinney Ridge and Ballard neighborhoods host ten church starts. The areas by Zip code that are most populated with new churches center on major thoroughfares. Aurora Avenue is the spine of 98103, which stretches between Fremont and Greenwood, and is home to fourteen new churches. The main street through 98118—once considered the "most diverse Zip code in the nation"—is Rainier Avenue.[6] Fourteen churches have sprouted in Rainier Valley, the ethnically diverse southeastern section of Seattle. This includes Columbia City, a rapidly gentrifying neighborhood that has added four new churches just since 2008.[7]

The Christian traditions of new Seattle churches shed light on the scene. Slightly less than one in five are in the mainline Protestant tradition (18%). The most active denominations in this tradition are the Evangelical Lutheran Church in America (6%), Presbyterian Church USA (5%), and United Methodist Church (4%). The new churches in the historic black church tradition are mostly (6/7) nondenominational and constitute 7% of the field. Orthodox and Catholic communities account for 4% and 3%, respectively.

Not surprisingly, Conservative Protestants with their missionary zeal make up the lion's share (68%) of new churches, as figure 2.2 shows. The Conservative Protestant category includes churches affiliated with

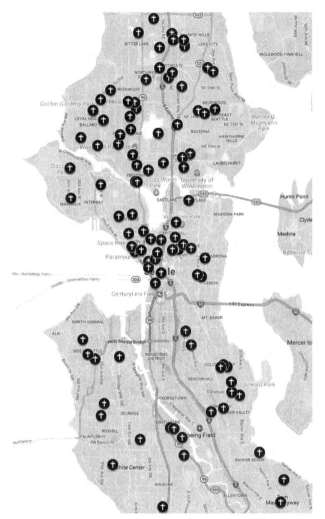

FIGURE 2.1 Map of new Seattle churches.
(Google Maps)

Evangelical, Pentecostal, and Charismatic denominations, as well as non-denominational churches.[8] Eighteen percent of Seattle church starts are affiliated with Charismatic or Pentecostal denominations, but nearly twice that (35%) have identifiably Pentecostal or Charismatic theology and/or worship. Conservative Protestants associated with Evangelical denominations that are neither Charismatic nor Pentecostal constitute a fourth of all new churches. The Conservative Protestant denominations responsible for the greatest percentage of all new churches are the Assemblies of God

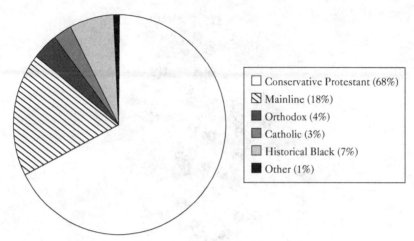

Conservative Protestant (68%)
Mainline (18%)
Orthodox (4%)
Catholic (3%)
Historical Black (7%)
Other (1%)

FIGURE 2.2 Christian traditions among new Seattle churches.

(9%), Southern Baptists (8%), Foursquare (7%), and Christian Reformed Church (4%). Nondenominational Conservative Protestant churches account for a fourth of new churches and are discussed later.

The strong majority—69.5%—of new Seattle churches are affiliated with a denomination, as table 2.1 illustrates. Still, 30.5% percent of new Seattle churches are nondenominational.[9] More than a third of these (38%) are multisite campuses of nondenominational churches.[10] That these churches have no denominational affiliation does not mean they are disconnected from the wider church. Nearly half (14/32) are affiliated with networks that exist to provide resources and relationships, especially for new church development and mission. The most prevalent network in Seattle is Acts 29, which, during the research window, linked not only five campuses of the now defunct Mars Hill Church but two other new Seattle churches as well. Other nondenominational churches have ties to specific sponsoring or supporting churches, either locally or out of state. As a result, less than a third of (10/32) new Seattle nondenominational churches appear to lack institutional connections. Several of these independent churches started off with denominational identity and support but later cut formal ties, and virtually all are relationally connected via relationships with other area pastors.

The most common ethnic composition found among Seattle church starts is predominantly Euro-American, English-language speakers (38%). However, more than a third (37%) are identifiable with a specific

Table 2.1 New Seattle Churches, by Tradition and Denomination

Tradition	Family	Denomination	# of churches		
Conservative Protestant					71
	Evangelical Denominations			26	
		Southern Baptist	8		
		Christian Reformed Church	4		
		Other	14		
	Pentecostal & Charismatic Denominations			19	
		Assembly of God	9		
		Foursquare	5		
		Other	5		
	Nondenominational (not black)			26	
Mainline Tradition					19
		Evangelical Lutheran	5.5[a]		
		Presbyterian (USA)	5		
		United Methodist	4		
		Other	4.5[a]		
Catholic and Orthodox Traditions					7
	Orthodox			4	
	Catholic			3	
Historically Black Church Tradition					7
		Nondenominational	6		
		Church of God in Christ	1		
Other Christian Groups					1
	Messianic Judaism		1		

[a] The .5 reflects a congregation that is formally affiliated with both the ELCA and Episcopal Church.

non-Euro-American or non-English-speaking minority cultural group. In light of the difficulty of identifying ethnic and immigrant communities, this figure almost certainly underrepresents these churches; I suspect they outnumber new Euro-American churches. Of the confirmed ethnic/cultural group churches, African Americans have the most new churches at seven (18% of new ethnic churches). Spanish-speaking churches are the second largest group (13%), and are mainly split between Episcopal and Pentecostal affiliations. Ethiopian and Eritrean churches combined account for 18% of new ethnic churches; most of these are either Orthodox or Pentecostal. Korean, Vietnamese, and Indonesian communities have started two churches each, and the remainder are one of a kind, though there are multiple churches with ties to Central Asia, Southeast Asia, and Africa.

As figure 2.3 shows, a quarter of new Seattle churches are multicultural, by the low-bar measure that no ethnic group is more than 80% of the congregation.[11] Most multicultural churches are majority white, with Asians making up the largest minority group. This reflects the ethnic composition of the city.[12] Multicultural churches were somewhat more likely to belong to the Conservative Protestant tradition than others.

The names of new Seattle churches also reflect some significant tendencies. While 69.5% of new churches are denominationally affiliated, only a fourth include a denominational affiliation in their church name—a sign of the declining cache of denominational identity.[13] Also showing a move away from traditional church identity are the nearly one in three (31%) new churches that have opted to leave "church" out of their moniker. Among these "church"-less names, "Community Dinner," "Communities," "Fellowship," and "Center" are the most popular alternatives, but more than half use none of these.[14] The importance of offering a place to belong among new churches is evidenced by the popularity of including some variation of the word *community* in their name; 15% of new church names include related terms.[15] The cultural shift toward localism and urban villages (something embraced by Seattle's urban planners) is, perhaps, reflected in the fourth (24%) of new churches— including all the multisites—whose names include that of their neighborhood location.

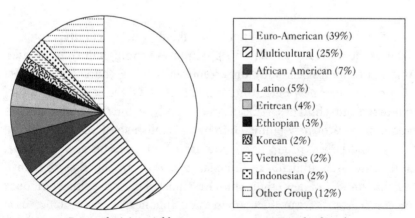

FIGURE 2.3 Race, ethnicity, and language among new Seattle churches.

Attuned to their digitally connected context, most Seattle church starts have a substantial web presence. Eighty-seven percent have their own dedicated websites. Often these websites highlight links to social media platforms, most notably Facebook, Twitter, Instagram, and YouTube or Vimeo. The popularity and functionality of Facebook for distributing announcements contributes to its being the most important site for many new churches. Facebook pages were nearly as common as church websites; only one church in six (17%) lacks a community presence on the social media site. Nearly half (47%) have Twitter accounts. Twitter is, apparently, for those most dedicated to online presence; those with Twitter accounts universally also have both a website and a Facebook page. The most likely tradition to be utilizing these three key web platforms are Conservative Protestants, and they are standard for multisite, multicultural, and nondenominational churches. Ethnic minority churches were the least likely to have a substantial web presence, though mainline Protestant and Orthodox churches were also somewhat less connected.

While new Seattle churches are, on the whole, keeping pace with the technological culture of Seattle, the same cannot be said with regard to Seattle's social progressivism, at least as far as this can be judged by their practices concerning gender and sexual identity. Only sixteen new churches (15%) have female staff identified as "pastors." Seven of these occupy the senior pastoral role, but this still lags significantly behind the best national estimates regarding female congregational leadership.[16] New mainline Protestant churches are the most likely to have a woman at the helm, but two nondenominational multisites also have female campus pastors. Just nine of the new churches are open and affirming with regard to LGBTQ inclusion; seven of these are connected to mainline Protestant denominations.[17]

Sunday mornings continue to be the favorite worship time, and more than half (54%) gather during that prime slot. Sunday afternoons are also common. More than a third gather then, and many of these are ethnic churches that do so in order to rent worship space from more established churches. Some of the larger multisite churches hold full services both Sunday morning and Sunday evening.

Church buildings are the most common places of worship, but 44% of new churches do not meet in these traditional sacred spaces; eschewing sanctuaries is a predominantly Conservative Protestant practice. Seven percent of those meeting in churches gather in basements or other rooms rather than sanctuaries. New churches that do not meet in church buildings are most likely to gather in community centers (18% of total) or various other public spaces including schools (3%), movie theaters (3%), or church-owned mixed-use community assets like coffee shops or co-working offices (2%). Nearly 10% of new Seattle churches reported holding their primary gatherings in homes.

The typical Seattle start is a white, Conservative Protestant, denominationally affiliated, self-governing church led by a male pastor. They worship on Sunday morning in a church building located near a major thoroughfare, and have both a website and Facebook page. But to stop at this rather traditional-sounding composite picture would be to fail to appreciate the rich diversity present among new Seattle churches. The preceding description by the numbers has provided some insight into this richness, but the more textured sense of the variety in the field I sought required closer study, and a means of hearing more directly from the practitioners themselves.

The New Seattle Churches Survey

This project is grounded in the belief that new Seattle churches have much to teach the U.S. church as it navigates significant contextual change. Who better to speak to what is involved in establishing viable forms of ecclesial witness in post-Christian contexts than church planters who have done it themselves? For this reason, I designed a survey for the pioneers, one that would reveal significant currents, patterns, and paradigms in ecclesial spirituality, mission, and identity. Pastors from 57 of the 105 (54%) new Seattle churches identified took the New Seattle Churches Survey.[18] The survey instrument is available in appendix B.

Survey Findings: Currents and Patterns

Analysis of responses to the New Seattle Churches Survey revealed noteworthy currents and patterns in spirituality, mission, and identity. It is unavoidably problematic to delineate between these interrelated aspects of ecclesial life, but for the sake of analysis survey questions were designated as related *primarily* to spirituality, mission, or identity. These three dynamics of ecclesial life can be envisioned as three dimensions, each of which addresses a fundamental ecclesiological question pertaining to the church's relationships. *How do we relate to God?* is the basic inquiry behind the classification of survey questions as most relevant to ecclesial spirituality. Thus, spirituality is explored through survey questions about worship practices, personal spiritual practices, theology, names for God, ideals of Christian maturity, and leadership practices.

The basic question of the mission dimension is *What are we supposed to do?* Often—but not always—this is expressed in terms of how the church believes it ought to relate to its context. Mission questions in the survey include an important series regarding "potential priorities" of the church and a follow-up question ranking the time and energy devoted to the most important priorities. Also important are responses regarding the church's primary approach to mission, Scriptural passages that imply the church's task, motivations for new church development, and outward-focused practices such as mission trips.

Identity variables offer various answers to the question *Who are we corporately?* Included are understandings of what makes a church community distinct from others, what affiliates share in common, and affiliations with other organizations and reference groups. As such, this classification is a collection of survey questions pertaining chiefly to demographics, denominational affiliation, the importance of the neighborhood location, and the organizational form of Christian community (congregational or otherwise).

These three ecclesial dimensions, while based in the primary relationships in which church exists—with God, among members, and toward the wider world—also relate to the three core tasks that congregational sociologists have identified—namely, *"religious reproduction* through worship and education, *building religious community* within the congregation, and *witness* to outsiders."[19] To make the parallels clear, the ecclesial dimension of spirituality points to religious reproduction, identity relates to building religious community, and mission corresponds with witness.

Currents and patterns in spirituality, mission, and identity are discussed in the following pages. To be clear, "currents" refers generally to the most and least common responses to specific questions across all survey responses, with significant differences among groups noted. "Patterns," on the other hand, are groups of mutually correlated responses to multiple questions within the same dimension. For example, the mission pattern of "discipleship" was created as a composite of priorities on teaching, formation, and equipping—all three of which are strongly correlated to one another in survey responses.[20] As a result, significant currents typically indicate how a significant number of churches responded, whereas a pattern may be significant even if a set of strikingly similar responses were found among only a handful of churches.

As will be apparent in what follows, analysis of the survey revealed significant differences between the various Christian traditions and ethnic compositions represented.[21] Foremost among these are how very *different* mainline and Conservative Protestant churches are, as well as precisely *how* they are different. In general, the new black churches run parallel with Conservative Protestants, though with some notable exceptions. The same is true of the lone Messianic Synagogue. The ethnic churches in the sample tend to reflect Pentecostal/Charismatic perspectives.[22] The multi-cultural Catholic parish, however, exists outside the Protestant polarity; it resembles the mainline in matters of worship and mission practices but is more like the Conservative Protestants views on matters of theology, personal piety, and authority. The Euro-American and multicultural churches have much in common, though diverse churches are bigger while homogeneous white churches have greater fondness for the liturgical calendar and small-group Bible studies. These and other differences, as well as overall currents, are explored in the following section.

Spirituality: How Do We Relate to God?
Currents in Spirituality

One way of conceiving of spirituality is in terms of ideals—views regarding the most important virtues and practices, of aspirations and markers of enlightenment or excellence. Among the list of indicators of Christian maturity shown in table 2.2, the most often selected as a point of emphasis was "relational closeness with God." The ethnic churches in the sample valorize "having Christ-like character" and "being obedient to God's will" as chief virtues. "Living missionally in relationships with friends and neighbors" was given added importance among multicultural and Conservative Protestant churches. "Serving those in need" was highly ranked among responding Pentecostals and multicultural churches. The least emphasized mark overall, by far, was "standing up against injustice," though the lone Catholic priest in the sample ranked it highly. White and multicultural mainline Protestant churches, unlike all other groups, highly ranked "embracing ambiguity and divine mystery" as indicative of Christian maturity.

The most emphasized name for God among survey respondents was Jesus, followed by Spirit. The least popular names in the listing were Sanctifier, Almighty, and Friend. Conservative Protestants tended to put strong emphasis on the whole list of names for God suggested, while

Table 2.2 Markers of Christian Maturity

Christian Maturity: Comparison of Means	Religious Group					Ethnic Composition			
Which potential indicators of Christian maturity are emphasized most strongly in your church? Please rank the top four.[a]	Conservative Protestant, Evangelical (n = 15)	Conservative Protestant, Nondenom (n = 17)	Conservative Protestant, Pentecostal/Charismatic (n = 10)	Mainline (n = 9)	Historically Black Tradition (n = 3)	Ethnic Minority (n = 8)	Multicultural (n = 19)	Euro-American (n = 29)	Total (n = 56)
Relational closeness with God	1.7	2.2	2.0	1.0	0.7	1.8	2.1	1.6	1.8
Living missionally in relationships with friends and neighbors	2.4	1.8	1.7	0.8	0.0	0.1	2.4	1.6	1.6
Having Christ-like character	1.6	0.9	2.2	2.0	3.0	2.6	1.1	1.1	1.3
Serving those in need	0.8	1.1	1.5	1.0	1.7	0.9	1.4	1.0	1.1
Walking the power of the Spirit	0.5	0.9	1.5	0.0	1.7	1.4	0.6	0.8	0.8
Being obedient to God's will	0.2	1.1	1.3	0.1	2.7	2.1	0.7	0.5	0.8
Humility, listening, and openness	0.8	0.7	0.6	1.2	0.3	0.4	0.6	1.0	0.8
Embracing ambiguity and divine mystery	0.6	0.2	0.0	2.1	0.0	0.0	0.4	0.8	0.6
Commitment to devotional/spiritual practices	0.6	0.4	0.2	0.8	0.0	0.8	0.5	0.4	0.5
Standing up against injustice	0.7	0.1	0.0	0.3	0.0	0.0	0.3	0.1	0.2

[a]Numbers indicate the average ranking on a scale from 0 to 4.

mainline respondents were more discriminating and put significantly less stress on several referents, including Lord, Father, and Savior. Nine respondents—half of whom are in mainline denominations—added their own emphasized names for God, several of which drew on themes of divine mercy, femininity, and life-giving.

The most commonly selected theological label was "Evangelical," though fewer than half of respondents (45%) claimed it and none in the mainline tradition did. The second most popular label indicated was "Other (please specify)"; 30% of the pastors were apparently unsatisfied with their options or eager to clarify the meaning of their other selections. "Progressive" theology was popular with white (83%) and multicultural (50%) mainline Protestant churches, but more than a fourth (27%) of multicultural Conservative Protestants also identified as "progressive" as well. None of the ethnic churches that completed the survey identified its theology as progressive, but 57% selected Pentecostal. Respondents very rarely identified with "Anabaptist" or "Conservative" theological labels.

While only 23% identify with "Sacramental" theology, this figure is in fact remarkably high, given that only 4% of respondents are in classically sacramental traditions.[23] Half of the Euro-American churches in Evangelical denominations resonate with Sacramental theology, as do a majority of the Anglo mainline churches. This Sacramental turn can also be seen in the notably prominent place new churches have for Communion. Forty-four percent said the sacred meal is part of their worship "very often or always" and another 35% practice it "often." As can be seen in table 2.3, the Lord's Table is celebrated slightly less frequently among the black and ethnic churches in the sample.[24] Baptism is an occasional practice in most new churches (54%) and varies little across subgroups. Other traditional liturgical practices, such as use of the liturgical calendar, the Lord's Prayer, and a time of confession, distinguish mainline and Catholic churches, in which they are commonplace, from Conservative Protestant and black churches, in which they are rare.[25]

Fifty-three percent of respondents consider "passionate worship" to be very or extremely important to their church culture. Hand-raising in worship is common for more than two-thirds (69%) of respondents, but is especially so among ethnic Conservative Protestants, while it is rare in worship among white and multicultural mainliners. Singing of "hymns" remains fairly popular and happens at least "often" in more than half of new churches (52%). Charismatic gifts such as prophesy, healing, and speaking in tongues rarely or never occur in worship in

Table 2.3 Worship Practices

Worship Practices: Comparison of Means

How often are these practices included in your worship?

1 = very rarely or never
2 = rarely
3 = occasionally
4 = often
5 = very often or always

	Religious Group[a]					Ethnic Composition			
	Conservative Protestant, Evangelical (n = 16)	Conservative Protestant, Nondenom (n = 15)	Conservative Protestant, Pentecostal / Charismatic (n = 9)	Mainline (n = 8)	Historically Black Tradition (n = 2)	Ethnic Minority (n = 8)	Multicultural (n = 19)	Euro-American (n = 27)	Total (n = 54)
Communion/Eucharist	4.4	4.1	4.0	4.4	3.5	3.3	4.1	4.4	4.2
Youth and children are present	4.3	3.4	4.1	3.5	4.0	3.7	4.4	3.6	3.9
Verse-by-verse biblical preaching	4.0	3.7	4.3	2.0	5.0	4.3	3.8	3.5	3.7
Passionate worship[b]	3.4	3.5	3.4	3.6	4.5	4.4	3.3	3.5	3.6
Hand-raising during signing	3.4	3.9	3.8	2.1	4.5	4.7	3.3	3.3	3.5
Singing hymns	3.1	3.3	3.7	4.1	3.5	3.4	3.4	3.5	3.4
Preaching on a topic or theme	3.4	3.5	3.1	2.9	4.5	3.9	3.6	3.2	3.4
Church members share personal thoughts or experiences of God	3.6	3.0	3.2	3.8	3.0	3.3	3.5	3.3	3.4
Opportunity to share prayer requests	3.2	2.7	3.7	3.8	4.0	3.9	3.4	3.0	3.3
Time of confession	3.3	2.4	2.6	3.1	3.5	2.6	3.0	2.9	2.9
Baptism	3.1	2.5	2.8	2.5	3.0	2.7	2.9	2.7	2.8
Reciting the Lord's Prayer	3.0	2.3	2.1	3.6	1.5	2.0	2.6	2.9	2.7
The liturgical Christian calendar[b]	2.8	2.1	2.3	3.3	1.5	2.4	2.2	2.8	2.5
Charismatic gifts: speaking in tongues, prophesy, healing, etc.	1.6	1.9	2.7	1.3	2.0	2.7	1.7	1.7	1.8
Sermon length (minutes)[c]	32.1	38.8	28.9	15.6	35.0	32.1	29.1	32.1	31.1

[a] Data from the Catholic and Other Christian group (Messianic Jewish) have not been included in this table, because each represents a single survey.

[b] In response to "How important are these practices to your church's culture?"

[c] In response to "How long is a typical sermon?"

81% of responding churches, though they are, of course, more frequent among the Pentecostal/Charismatic and ethnic churches surveyed. Three-fourths often or always have youth and children present, a practice especially prevalent in multicultural churches, though it is uncertain how respondents interpreted this question—whether kids in another room of the church were presumed to qualify. Half (52%) make space for members to share personal thoughts or experiences of God often or always. Slightly fewer (42%) include time for sharing prayer requests with the same frequency.

The average sermon length is just over 30 minutes, but the standard deviation is almost half that amount. Conservative Protestants favor long, exegetical sermons, while mainline Protestant and Catholic churches favor shorter, more topical homilies.[26] Mainline sermons averaged 16 minutes, while nondenominational preaching typically surpasses the 35-minute mark. More than a third of the sample exceeds 40 minutes; these are all Conservative Protestant churches. Verse-by-verse preaching is more common among survey respondents than preaching on a topic or theme, but almost half (47%) go the topical route at least "often."

Worship gatherings are not the only significant spiritual practice for new churches. Two-thirds (66%) of new church pastors consider small groups and Bible studies to be very or extremely important to the culture of the church. This is a central practice shared by conservative and mainline Protestant churches, but is more central to white churches and least important to the two nondenominational black churches that responded. Church retreats, while important to the multicultural mainline and Catholic churches in the sample, are regarded by a majority (59%) as of little or no importance.

The theology and practice of church leadership is also a spiritual matter, especially in new churches where leaders often serve as both spiritual exemplars and mediators while shaping how the church relates to God in everything from worship practices and events to practical discernment. More than two-thirds (68%) are led in decision making by a "core team which includes the pastor(s)." This model is dominant among Conservative Protestants (more than 75% chose it), but it is also the most popular arrangement (or conceptualization) for decision making among mainline churches.[27] However, a third of new white mainline churches said they are "led by the whole church" in times of decision. Only one in seven (14%) say they look to the pastor as the "key leader and decision maker."

Gender is also a significant factor in how new churches practice leadership. Virtually all the churches that responded allow women to volunteer in various capacities and lead in ministry to women and children, but when it comes to ordained positions, the results were different: 8% do not allow female deacons, one in five prohibits female board members/elders, and a fourth do not allow women to be associate pastors. Thirty-eight percent reserve senior pastoral leadership for men only. Among the sample, limitations on women's roles are as closely linked to ethnic composition as they are to religious tradition. More than two-thirds of the multicultural, mainline, and black churches surveyed do allow women as senior pastors, but half of the churches in the nondenominational and ethnic groups do not. Still, a strong majority (62%) of respondents have no objection to female lead pastors—at least in principle (only 6% actually have a woman as lead pastor).[28]

Some spiritual practices are less structured by the church and more a matter of personal initiative or organic collective action. Echoing the centrality of Communion as a ritualized sacred meal, four of five new churches indicated that "sharing meals together" is extremely (42%) or very (38%) important to their church culture.[29] Personal Bible reading and prayer are far less central, as they are very or extremely important in only 57% of new churches. Its significance is markedly less among white mainline churches. Spiritual practices of restraint have a negligible role in the culture of Seattle's newest churches; 64% said fasting was no more than a little important and 51% said as much about living simply.

Patterns in Spirituality

Correlation of spirituality variables revealed four strong spirituality patterns, and they are consistent with currents already described. A recognizably *Evangelical* spirituality included more mutually correlated variables than any other pattern, suggesting that this pattern is strongly institutionalized and more widely recognized as normative than others. Most central to the Evangelical spirituality pattern is the importance of personal bible reading and prayer, and the frequency with which worshipers raise their hands during singing. Also important is the prevalence of long, exegetical sermons, fasting, passionate worship, an emphasis on God as Lord, Father, and Savior, and the reservation of pastoral authority for men only.[30]

An overlapping but distinguishable pattern of *Spirit-filled* spirituality shares the practice of hand raising in worship, but distinctively centers on the frequency of charismatic gifts such as speaking in tongues, prophesy, and healing. Not surprisingly, this pattern includes identification with Pentecostal and/or Charismatic theology.[31]

Progressive Christian spirituality is centered on identification with Progressive theology and recognition of "embracing ambiguity and divine mystery" as a key mark of Christian maturity. Maturity, for these Progressives, is also indicated by "humility, listening, and openness." These two key virtues are paired with—and enacted in—distinctive practices of including shared leadership (in which the "whole church" participates in making decisions) and shared meals (sacramental and informal).

A fourth pattern in spirituality has at its center in Sacramental theology and liturgical worship practices, including use of the liturgical calendar, recitation of the Lord's Prayer, a time of confession, and frequent Communion/Eucharist. In addition, this *Sacramental-liturgical* pattern overlaps with Progressive spirituality in its esteem for those who embrace ambiguity and mystery. Finally, church retreats were a uniquely important practice for this pattern.

Not surprisingly, given what has already been noted, Evangelical and Spirit-filled spiritualties are positively correlated, as is Progressive spirituality with the Sacramental-liturgical pattern. The negative correlations between the four patterns are also illuminating. Most important, Evangelical and Progressive patterns are almost diametrically opposed. Progressive spirituality has strong negative correlations to every one of the elements composing the Evangelical pattern, and Evangelical spirituality has strong negative correlations to nearly all the variables that form the Progressive pattern. Progressive spirituality is also in tension with Spirit-filled distinctives, but to a lesser degree. Sacramental-liturgical spirituality, however, is not negatively correlated to the Spirit-filled pattern, though it is in tension with Evangelical spirituality.

To summarize, four discernible patterns of spirituality characterize new Seattle churches. Evangelical and Spirit-filled spiritualties are both typified by hand-raising in worship and by detachment from both "Progressive" theology and the notion that Christian maturity is best indicated by being at peace with ambiguity. Progressive and Sacramental-liturgical spirituality both welcome mystery and have a prime place for sacred meals while de-emphasizing key characteristics of Evangelical and Spirit-filled piety such as lifted hands and verse-by-verse sermons. As polarized as these streams are, it should also be noted that Evangelical and Progressive spiritualties exist in sharpest distinction from one another, while Spirit-filled and Sacramental-liturgical patterns are markedly less at odds. This difference is, in part, the result of the handful of surveyed churches that self-consciously integrate Evangelical, Spirit-filled, and Sacramental-liturgical spiritual practices and outlooks.

Mission: What Are We Supposed to Do?
Currents in Mission

The top priorities of new churches, displayed in detail in table 2.4, shed light on their sense of mission. The most highly rated priority from a list of seventeen was "proclaiming the gospel of Jesus." More than three-fourths (76%) of responding churches consider this to be "extremely" important, though it is likely that both "proclamation" and the "gospel of Jesus" are diversely interpreted across different groups.[32] There are certainly differences in the degree of importance it is given. While at least "very" important across the board, white mainline churches ascribe it notably less weight than all other groups. Proclamation of the gospel is followed by "offering a community in which to belong and be loved," which is the highest-rated priority among new mainline Protestant churches.[33] "Modeling God's intentions for humanity" is a priority shared by all groups. Also very important to the sample was "equipping people to go out as agents of God in the world," and "forming Christians into Christ-like character." The former is more highly rated among mainline churches and the latter is especially important among Evangelical and nondenominational churches. Both, however, are top-rated priorities in the black nondenominational churches surveyed. African American churches, along with other ethnic churches, also put somewhat more emphasis on "building a refuge from the world's dangers and temptations," while Catholic and white mainline starts expressed unique interest in "improving society through political action and community organizing." However, both refuge building and society improving are no more than "a little important" to the solid majority of new Seattle churches surveyed.[34]

In addition to *rating* these priorities, survey respondents were asked to *rank* the top four from those they had rated most highly in terms of how much time and energy were devoted to those tasks. Not surprisingly, the pastors see proclaiming the gospel of Jesus as the most demanding top-rated priority; 39% listed it as the single most time- and energy-consuming priority. However, this is another instance where mainline churches

Table 2.4 Church Priorities

Church Priorities: Comparison of Means	Religious Group				Ethnic Composition				
How important are these potential priorities for your church? 1 = not important 2 = a little important 3 = important 4 = very important 5 = extremely important	Conservative Protestant, Evangelical (n = 15)	Conservative Protestant, Nondenom (n = 16)	Conservative Protestant, Pentecostal/ Charismatic (n = 10)	Mainline (n = 8)	Historically Black Tradition (n = 3)	Ethnic Minority (n = 8)	Multicultural (n = 19)	Euro-American (n = 27)	Total (n = 54)
Proclaiming the gospel of Jesus	4.9	4.6	4.8	4.3	5.0	5.0	4.7	4.6	4.7
Offering a community in which to belong and be loved	4.3	4.4	4.5	5.0	4.7	4.5	4.5	4.6	4.5
Modeling God's intentions for humanity	4.3	4.6	4.1	4.5	4.7	4.4	4.3	4.6	4.4
Forming Christians into Christ-like character	4.7	4.4	4.1	4.1	4.7	4.8	4.3	4.4	4.4
Teaching and learning about God, the Bible, and our world	4.4	4.4	3.9	4.1	5.0	4.6	4.3	4.3	4.3
Equipping people to go out as agents of God in the world	4.3	4.4	4.2	4.5	5.0	4.8	4.3	4.4	4.3
Welcoming all—especially those excluded—as an inclusive community	4.3	4.3	4.0	4.5	3.7	3.5	4.4	4.4	4.3
Serving the needs of the community	4.3	3.9	4.5	4.4	4.3	4.0	4.3	4.3	4.2
Giving opportunities to worship God	4.0	4.1	4.1	4.0	4.3	4.5	4.0	4.1	4.1
Seeking God through prayer and contemplation	4.0	4.0	3.1	4.5	4.7	4.3	3.7	4.1	4.0

Engaging culture and being relevant	3.9	3.5	3.7	3.9	3.7	3.8	3.8	3.7	3.8
Innovating and experimenting for the sake of the broader church's future	3.5	3.4	3.2	3.9	3.7	3.6	3.6	3.4	3.5
Adding beauty to the world	3.9	3.3	3.0	3.9	3.3	2.9	3.2	3.9	3.5
Witnessing to and experiencing God's miracle-working power	3.5	3.4	3.5	2.9	4.7	4.6	3.2	3.4	3.5
Speaking out about evil and injustice	3.8	3.4	2.6	3.6	3.3	2.9	3.3	3.7	3.4
Improving society through political action and community organizing	2.2	2.2	2.8	2.8	2.7	2.5	2.4	2.5	2.5
Building a refuge from the world's dangers and temptations	1.7	2.1	2.5	2.0	3.7	3.3	2.1	1.8	2.1

and Conservative Protestants diverge strongly; 80% of white mainline churches did not rank proclamation of the gospel among the top four, but almost 70% of Conservative Protestants did.[35] Instead, mainline churches give the highest rank to "offering a community in which to belong and be loved," which was ranked the second most intensive priority among survey respondents as a whole.[36]

New churches are also making substantial investments in equipping (43% include this in their top four) and formation (38%) efforts, though the latter is especially central for white nondenominational churches (73% rank it in the top four). Teaching and learning about God, the Bible, and the world along with modeling God's intentions for humanity are also central foci, and were among the top ranked for 26% and 21%, respectively. "Welcoming all—especially those excluded—as an inclusive community," ranks among the top two for roughly half of the non-ethnic mainline, white nondenominational churches, and multicultural Pentecostal churches. Two-thirds of the black nondenominational churches surveyed ranked "witnessing to and experiencing God's miracle working power" as a top-tier commitment.

While the Bible is a center of spiritual reflection, it is also utilized as an authoritative source on the proper mission of the church. Often churches validate their sense of mission by scriptural appeals to Jesus's own ministry and teaching. Several texts were selected for their thematic relevance to the mission of the church and popular familiarity, and survey respondents were asked to rate them in terms of the frequency with which they are referenced or alluded to in the church. Jesus's declaration in John 13 that "By this everyone will know you are my disciples, if you love one another," was the highest rated overall—it is cited "often" or "very often" in three-fourths of new churches.[37] It is frequently utilized in churches of various theological persuasions, though perhaps with differing emphases. Also noncontroversial is Jesus's soothing invitation, "Come to me all you who are weary . . . and I will give you rest" (Matt. 11), which 62% of churches reference often or very often. The most polarizing text was the Great Commission of Matthew 28 ("Go and make disciples of all nations, baptizing them"). A third of surveyed churches have a central role for this passage and invoke it very often, but 15% rarely or never use the classic mission text.[38] Unsurprisingly, the groups that most elevate this text are ethnic, black, or Conservative Protestant churches, while white mainline churches scarcely reference it. The least referenced passage among the set, however, was Jesus's overturning of the money-changers tables (Matt.21

and Mark 11); nearly half (46%) rarely or never mention it. An emphasis on the role of the Spirit—a centerpiece of Pentecostal missiology—is shared by all the Conservative Protestants and black churches surveyed, but is less common among new mainline churches. Mainline Protestant starts were somewhat more likely to reference Jesus's manifesto in Luke 4: "The Spirit of the LORD is upon me for he has anointed me to proclaim good news to the poor"[39] than Jesus's pre-Pentecost announcement in Acts 1 that his disciples would "receive power when Holy Spirit has come upon you; and you will be my witnesses."

The reasons that motivate the development of new churches also reflect their sense of mission. Far and away the most important consideration is an intentionality around "reaching unchurched people," reflecting their cognizance of Seattle's post-Christian character. Sixty-four percent rated this impetus as extremely important, without significant differences between groups. In open-ended questions asking for whom the church was started, significant numbers also indicated a focus on the unchurched (21%), disillusioned (14%), and nonbelievers (16%). Though this desire is basic to church starts nationwide, it is likely heightened by the great numbers of people in Seattle who are unaffiliated and/or not participating in church. Another important reason churches across the board start is to "help new Christians mature"; 46% indicated this was extremely or very important.[40] Also extremely or very important to many churches is the pull toward "embodying our convictions about the church" (70%) and the need for "engaging with contemporary culture" (59%). These two reasons are, however, both less central in motivating ethnic church starts, who are—as one would expect—uniquely intent on "reaching specific cultures or networks." While "replacing closed churches" was of little consequence to 71% of new churches, about three in eight churches (37%) felt compelled to "offer an alternative to unfaithful or ineffective churches." The same percentage started intending to "create a different expression of church."

When it comes to mission, strategies are at least as important as intentions. The way many starts approach "mission, social action, and evangelism" resists the tired evangelism/social justice dichotomy. Altogether, only one in five pastors felt that "sharing the good news of Jesus through evangelism" (15%), on the one hand, or the pursuit of "social justice through political action" (6%), on the other, best described their church's approach.[41] Significantly more (36%) combine soul-saving with serving in one of three ways.[42] Twelve percent "offer ministries of compassion, in part, as a means for evangelism." More (17%) "integrate social services and evangelism" and another 12% do both, but separately. However, the single most popular mission approach overall—and among all groups except the ethnic churches—apparently involves neither explicit evangelism nor direct social action and is accomplished by simply being "present and modeling different values to the community" (42%).

The importance of three specific mission practices to church culture are instructive: mission trips, evangelism, and environmental stewardship. Mission trips are of little or no importance to 57% of surveyed churches. This likely reflects both the difficulty of church starts engaging in such resource-dependent mission efforts and a turn toward an emphasis on local mission. The cultural importance of personal evangelism is quite high among all groups except mainline Protestant churches, which seem to reflect progressive Northwest values by indicating greater emphasis on saving the environment than on saving souls, as shown in table 2.5.

One of the essential tasks of new churches is recruitment, at least until a degree of viability is achieved. One of the most touted strategies for numerical success in the church-planting literature is starting with a "launch" service, and 40% of responding churches had followed this advice. Many new churches set out signboards, like the one shown in figure 2.4, placed on a busy corner in Fremont by The Hallows Church. The most popular outreach strategies, however, are use of social media (60%) and sponsoring community events (51%). Overwhelming majori-ties eschew traditional, aggressive marketing strategies such as going door-to-door (84%), direct mail (71%), and advertisements (69%). More than a fourth of white churches said they use no strategy to reach others, and more than a third of respondents (35%) described some other form of outreach not listed; most of these pointed to relational, word-of-mouth approaches.

Table 2.5 Evangelism vs. Environmentalism

Comparison of Means *How important are these practices to* *your church's culture?* 1 = not important, 2 = a little important, 3 = important, 4 = very important, 5 = extremely important	Conservative Protestant	Mainline Protestant
Personal evangelism	3.39	2.25
Creation care/environmental stewardship	2.64	3.63

FIGURE 2.4 The Hallows Church signboard competes with massage center and fitness club.

Patterns in Mission

Analysis of mission-oriented survey questions revealed ten noteworthy, interrelated combinations of mission variables, each with significant correlations to spirituality patterns—and to other mission patterns.

Questions related to *Evangelism* were highly correlated, and included emphases on personal evangelism, church mission trips, and the Great

Commission and a corporate approach to mission best described as "sharing the good news of Jesus." Evangelistic mission syncs with Evangelical spirituality and, like Evangelical spirituality, is at odds with Progressive and Sacramental-liturgical ways of relating to God. *Proclamation*—a pattern that combines the rated importance of and the ranked time and energy commitment to "proclaiming the gospel of Jesus"—has a significant positive correlation to Evangelical spirituality and is negatively correlated to the Progressive stream.[43] The mission priority of *Discipleship* combines correlated emphases on teaching the Bible, forming Christians in Christ-like character, and equipping people as agents of God in the world. Like Proclamation, Discipleship is de-emphasized by pastors embracing a Progressive spirituality and embraced by Evangelicals.

Together these three mission priorities—Evangelism, Proclamation, and Discipleship—form what I have come to call the *Great Commission* approach, as that text from Matthew 28 has, for the last 200 years, served as the battle cry of Evangelicals committed to mission in primary forms of evangelism, proclamation, and discipleship. Each of the elements of the Great Commission mission, not surprisingly, correlate with Evangelical piety. Together these four patterns form the ecclesial paradigm that provided the skeleton for the Great Commission Team practical ecclesiology that is developed in chapter 4. While combined in the paradigm, these three mission approaches have been distinguished from one another here to highlight their relations with other patterns. Although Evangelism is highly correlated to both Proclamation and Discipleship, these two are not significantly correlated to one another. In addition, while Progressive spirituality is in tension with all three elements of the Great Commission approach, the Sacramental-liturgical pattern is negatively correlated only with an emphasis on Evangelism.

As noted earlier, "offering a community in which to belong and be loved," was second in both the ratings and ranking and especially important among mainline Protestant churches. A high valuation and commitment to offering *Community* was found to correlate with a corporate approach to mission enacted by being "present and modeling different values to the community."[44] This mission pattern resonates with both Progressive and Sacramental-liturgical spiritualities. On the flip side, Evangelical spirituality showed a strong negative correlation with Community as mission and almost an equally negative relationship with the mission priority of "Welcoming all—especially those excluded—as an inclusive community."

However, the *Inclusive Welcome* pattern did not show a significant relationship to Progressive spirituality.

An emphasis on welcoming all is often coincident with a priority of "serving the needs of the community," and together these priorities compose the mission approach of *Hospitality & Service*. This mission package is somewhat negatively correlated to Evangelical piety, but it is not positively related to other patterns in spirituality. Its importance lies largely in its correlation with identity patterns which will be discussed in the following sections.

Worship is a mission priority centered on "offering opportunities to worship God" that includes related emphases on "engaging culture and being relevant" and "seeking God through prayer and contemplation." This focus on creating relevant experiences of divine worship has a significant positive relationship with Sacramental-liturgical spirituality.

Contemplative Advocacy is a mission approach consisting of an intriguing combination of priorities, including "seeking God through prayer and contemplation" and "speaking out about evil and injustice," as well as the importance of "creation care/environmental stewardship" to church culture. Fueled by contemplative practice and sacramental theology, this mission package is common among Progressive and, especially, Sacramental-liturgical churches. It is expressed in personal practice and corporate declarations, but is not necessarily matched with activism. The *Activism* pattern consists of correlations between the uncommon "social action" approach to mission and commitments to advocacy, environmental stewardship, "improving society through political action and community organizing," and regarding "standing up against injustice" as a key marker of maturity. The two churches represented in the survey sample that serve as prime examples of Activist mission are also exemplars of Sacramental-liturgical spirituality and both are also connected to well-established institutions (Roman Catholicism and the United Methodist Church).

Innovation emerged as a high-rated priority and high-ranked commitment to "innovating and experimenting for the sake of the broader church." There is a significant relationship between the Innovation pattern and Hospitality & Service, though this is the result of its correlation with the service variable only. In addition, this commitment to pioneering is slightly correlated, somewhat surprisingly, to Sacramental-liturgical spirituality, as the product of the "ancient-future" trend in which new churches reappropriate traditions in pursuit of the church's future.

The final pattern in mission that arose from the survey combines relative emphases and commitments to "building a refuge from the world's dangers and temptations" and "witnessing to and experiencing God's miracle-working power." This mission of *Temple-building* seeks to establish a place of safety in which the church can encounter the power of God; it is, not surprisingly, highly correlated to Spirit-filled spirituality and to a lesser degree related to the Evangelical stream.[45]

Identity: Who Are We Corporately?
Currents in Identity

Several of the identity variables included in the survey were also discoverable for all new churches, rather than only those who completed the survey, and thus have already been noted.[46] Among those already discussed are denominational and/or network affiliation, gathering times and spaces, church names, and ethnic composition.

However, the survey does offer additional insights on several salient aspects of corporate identity. As displayed in table 2.6, two-thirds of respondents see their community as a "congregation," the most common ecclesial form for all groups. However, nearly as many (63%) identified their faith community as something other than a congregation, indicating either an alternative or an additional designation. The most commonly selected noncongregational designation was "missional community," and it was claimed by half the white churches in Evangelical, Pentecostal/ Charismatic, and mainline denominations. Almost one in five churches identifies as a multisite campus, including a few Pentecostal dinner church sites that do not fit the typical multisite mold. Fourteen percent consider themselves an "emerging church," and most of these are multicultural churches. Mainline starts were the most likely to understand themselves as new monastic or intentional communities (22%), while it was exclusively Conservative Protestants who wished to designate themselves as "Other," either instead of or in addition to the options provided.

Several survey questions touched upon a church's degree of identification with its geographical location, an identity feature that is important across religious groups but varies in significance across ethnic compositions. A third of respondents indicated that "identifying with our neighborhood" was extremely important, and another third considered it very important. However, only 19% ranked this priority among the top four in terms of time and energy committed. Thirty-nine percent said that

Table 2.6 Christian Faith Community Type

Faith Community Type: Comparison of Means	Religious Group					Ethnic Composition			
What kind of Christian faith community is it? (check all that apply) 1 = yes 0 = no	Conservative Protestant, Evangelical (n = 16)	Conservative Protestant, Nondenom (n = 17)	Conservative Protestant, Pentecostal/ Charismatic (n = 10)	Mainline (n = 9)	Historically Black Tradition (n = 3)	Ethnic Minority (n = 7)	Multicultural (n = 19)	Euro-American (n = 30)	Total (n = 56)
A congregation	0.63	0.65	0.56	0.67	1.00	0.86	0.68	0.60	0.66
A missional community	0.44	0.18	0.44	0.67	0.00	0.14	0.37	0.40	0.36
A multisite campus of a church	0.00	0.35	0.44	0.00	0.00	0.00	0.16	0.23	0.18
An emerging church	0.19	0.12	0.22	0.11	0.00	0.00	0.21	0.13	0.14
A new monastic or intentional community	0.06	0.00	0.00	0.22	0.00	0.00	0.11	0.03	0.05
A house/cell/ organic church	0.06	0.06	0.00	0.11	0.00	0.00	0.05	0.07	0.05
A para-church group	0.00	0.00	0.00	0.00	0.00	0.00	0.00	0.00	0.00
Other (please specify)[a]	0.25	0.18	0.33	0.00	0.00	0.00	0.16	0.23	0.18
Selected something other than congregation alone	0.56	0.71	0.80	0.78	0.00	0.13	0.63	0.77	0.63

[a] Two churches who selected "Other" described themselves as a "network of missional communities." Several others identified as a church with various qualifiers such as neighborhood, community, or sending.

"a neighborhood with needs a church could address" was an extremely important consideration motivating the development of the church. Unsurprisingly, all three indications of neighborhood identity were much stronger among white and multicultural churches and weaker among ethnic churches whose identity is typically tied to an ethnic group rather than particular place.

While the survey sample has relatively little representation from ethnic churches, those that did respond indicated that their ethnic character is an important part of their identity; they place greater priority on and invest more time in "providing an extended family for a cultural group" than other streams. Ethnic churches also asserted the importance of "embodying multicultural diversity," though unsurprisingly it is multicultural churches that invest most heavily in this aim.

Most new Seattle churches have relatively young affiliates. In open-ended descriptions of the demographics of their churches, 62% of respondents indicated that a majority of their participants are under the age of 40. Similarly, in response to an open-ended question about who the church was started *for*, several indicated intentionality around reaching college and young adult populations (13%) and/or young professionals (7%).

As table 2.7 shows, the median size of primary church gatherings among respondents was 75, with slightly more—100—who would consider the church their own. Multicultural churches have roughly twice as many attendees and affiliates as white churches. Similarly, the size of nondenominational congregations is about twice that of their mainline counterparts. The average new Seattle church in the sample has one weekly worship service and two staff members.

Patterns in Identity

Seven salient patterns among identity variables emerged. Two pertain to cultural/ethnic identity and three reflect denominational affiliation. A strong identity as an *Ethnic Family* formed around the importance of and investment in "providing an extended family for a cultural group," open-ended mention of a primary nonwhite or non-English-speaking group, and researcher confirmation of the ethnic composition of the church. Similarly, a *Multicultural* identity pattern was expressed as ratings and rankings for "embodying multicultural diversity," matched with open-ended descriptions and researcher confirmation of the multicultural mix. Both cultural identity patterns also included a supplementary variable

Table 2.7 Church Size

Church Size: Comparison of Means over Medians[a]

	Religious Group					Ethnic Composition			
	Conservative Protestant, Evangelical (n = 15)	Conservative Protestant, Nondenom (n = 15)	Conservative Protestant, Pentecostal/Charismatic (n = 9)	Mainline (n = 9)	Historically Black Tradition (n = 3)	Ethnic Minority (n = 7)	Multicultural (n = 18)	Euro-American (n = 28)	Total (n = 53)
Average attendance at largest, weekly gathering	84 / 45	184 / 150	110 / 110	60 / 35	92 / 75	61 / 50	161 / 120	101 / 53	116 / 75
Pastors' estimates of how many consider this "their" church	111 / 75	216 / 200	242[b] / 100	109 / 75	162 / 113	89 / 40	263[b] / 180	134 / 75	172 / 100
Worship services each weekend	1.1 / 1	1.5 / 1	2 / 1	1.1 / 1	1.3 / 1	1.13 / 1	1.74 / 1	1.17 / 1	1.35 / 1
Current staff (full and part time)	3.1 / 2	2.1 / 2	2.9 / 2	5.5[c] / 2.5	.5 / .5	.67 / 1	4.8[c] / 3	2.7 / 2	3.2 / 2

[a]Means are listed above medians.

[b]This mean is inflated by a multicultural Pentecostal dinner church that claims 1,000 affiliates (across five sites) where the maximum weekly attendance at any one site is 160.

[c]This mean is inflated by one mainline church with a chocolate/coffee shop and 28 employees.

from outside the survey; online images from church websites and social media were analyzed for ethnic composition. Spirit-filled spirituality is significantly correlated to both forms of ethnic/cultural identity, but it is the Ethnic Family pattern to which it is most strongly linked.

Unlike all other patterns, which are composed of multiple correlated variables, the three "patterns" in denominational identity are constituted by a single variable demarcating their specific affiliation with either a mainline denomination, a Pentecostal/Charismatic denomination, or no denomination.[47] *Nondenominational* identity had a negative relationship with Sacramental-liturgical spirituality, but nondenominational identity had no other significant correlations.

Not surprisingly, *Pentecostal/Charismatic* denominational identity is highly correlated to Spirit-filled spirituality, as well as to the Ethnic Family identity pattern. In addition, these three patterns have a significant co-occurrence with the Temple-building mission approach. These four interrelated patterns form the Household of the Spirit paradigm that is developed along with the other practical ecclesiological models in chapter 4.

Mainline denominational identity is highly correlated with both Progressive and Sacramental-liturgical spirituality, as well as to Community and Contemplative Advocacy mission approaches. These five patterns combine to form the New Community paradigm.

Neighborhood identity is a sense of being church in, of, and for a delimited place. This pattern emerged in the survey in links between an enacted priority on "identifying closely with our neighborhood" and responses indicating that "the church was started for a specific neighborhood" in view of "needs a church could address." This rootedness in place was not correlated to any of the four spirituality patterns, but it is strongly linked with the mission approach of Hospitality & Service. Neighborhood identity also has significant relationships with a few other identity patterns. This place-shaped identity exists in tension with the people-shaped pattern of the Ethnic Family. It also is uncommon among nondenominational churches, despite the fact that nondenominational multisites are universally named after their neighborhoods. A strong positive relationship exists, however, between Neighborhood rootedness and the final identity pattern, an extra-congregational form of Christian community.

Extra-congregational identity self-consciously breaks the dominant American mold for ecclesial life. The pattern primarily reflects respondents who shied away from identifying the church as a "congregation" and preferred to designate their fellowship as one or more of the following: a missional community, an emerging church, a new monastic or intentional community, a house/cell/organic church, or "other." Holding primary church gatherings in a nontraditional space—such as a community center or home—is another element of Extra-congregational identity. Also supplementing this pattern is the importance placed on "creating a different expression of church" as a motivation for starting the church. This pattern of novelty in ecclesial form is in some tension with Evangelical spirituality, Evangelistic, and Temple-building mission approaches, and with the Ethnic Family identity pattern. It is strongly correlated, however, with both Neighborhood rootedness and Hospitality & Service, and these three patterns constitute the Neighborhood Incarnation ecclesial paradigm outlined in this chapter and developed in chapter 4.

Summarizing the Currents

In many ways, new Conservative Protestant and mainline Protestant churches in Seattle are a study in contrasts. Striking differences exist in worship practices with long, exegetical sermons, and hand-raising characterizing the former, and the Lord's Prayer and liturgical calendar distinguishing the latter. Maturity among Conservative Protestants is lived out missionally in relationship with friends and neighbors, while among mainline Protestants it is recognized in the acceptance of ambiguity and divine mystery. When it comes to priorities, mainline churches stand out for their elevation of offering community over proclaiming the gospel, the centerpiece of Conservative Protestant mission. The two traditions are similarly divided over the relative importance of personal mission practices, including personal evangelism and environmental stewardship.

Churches in historically black church traditions, as well as other ethnic churches, bear a much stronger resemblance to Conservative Protestants than to mainline churches, though they are significantly less committed to small groups, less concerned about inclusivity, less identified with their neighborhoods, and more regularly invoke the Great Commission.[48] Multicultural churches place distinctive emphasis on the presence of children and are dramatically larger than ethnic and white churches.[49]

While these contrasts between groups are important, the broad consensus among new Seattle churches is also significant. This diverse cohort of new churches overwhelmingly places "offering a community in which to belong and be loved" among their top two most important priorities. They agree that the church ought to model God's intentions for the world, and most approach mission through a public display of unique values. They are engaged in the world—rather than building a refuge from it—but not involved in political action or community organizing. New Seattle churches start with hopes of reaching the unchurched masses, and many are largely composed of young adults. They have readily adapted to the digital revolution and have robust online presence, but they avoid use of other aggressive marketing strategies such as going door-to-door, direct mail, and advertisements. Jesus and the Spirit are more central to how new churches speak of and relate to God than is the Father. Shared meals—both ritualized and informal—are central and frequent practices. Denominational affiliation is predominant, but publicizing it is uncommon. Seattle's church starts mostly understand themselves as congregations, but also resonate with other ways of conceiving of and describing their ecclesial identity and form. Differences notwithstanding, these widely shared tendencies among new Seattle churches offer important content for theological reflection on ecclesial witness in post-Christian contexts.[50]

Making Sense of the Patterns

One of the key findings of this research is the identification of four paradigmatic ecclesial combinations of patterns across spirituality, mission, and identity dimensions. These paradigms and their constituent patterns are shown in table 2.8. The first cluster of patterns brings together Evangelical spirituality with three interrelated mission priorities often linked to the Great Commission (Matt. 28)—evangelism, proclamation, and discipleship. In light of the mission-centric nature of this type of Christian community, I have designated it as the Great Commission Team. The Household of the Spirit ecclesial paradigm brings together identity patterns grounded in Pentecostal/Charismatic denominations and non-majority ethnic composition, with Spirit-filled spirituality and a mission of Temple-building. Mainline identity correlates with Progressive and Sacramental-liturgical spirituality patterns, as well as Community and Contemplative Advocacy mission approaches to form the New Community paradigm. Finally, the Neighborhood Incarnation paradigm subsists in the interrelationship between Extra-congregational and Neighborhood-rooted

Table 2.8 Paradigms: Multidimensional Pattern Clusters

Paradigm Name	Spirituality Pattern(s)	Mission Pattern(s)	Identity Pattern(s)
Great Commission Team	Evangelical	Evangelism Discipleship Proclamation	
Household of the Spirit	Spirit-filled	Temple-building	Pentecostal/ Charismatic Ethnic Family
New Community	Progressive Sacramental- liturgical	Community Contemplative Advocacy	Mainline
Neighborhood Incarnation		Hospitality & Service	Neighborhood Extra- congregational

Note: Paradigms were formed as mutually correlated patterns across dimensions. The majority of the correlations between patterns in each paradigm are at the 0.01 level (two-tailed significance).

The empty cells in the table indicate that the several patterns that make up the indicated paradigm do not consistently have a significant correlation with other identified patterns in that dimension. This is not to suggest, however, that these patterns have no significant correlations with select variables in that dimension.

identity patterns and mission that take shape as Hospitality & Service. The names assigned to these paradigms have ecclesiological significance and will be discussed in chapter 4, where the central task is theological development of these prevalent forms of ecclesiopraxis.

3

Modeling Church

WHILE ECCLESIOLOGY HAS historically focused on the universal nature of the church, some scholars of the late twentieth century turned their attention to the multiple models of church or, as one team of sociologists called it, the *Varieties of Religious Presence*.[1] Indeed, when one considers the diversity of expressions of church that can be found in a single metropolitan area such as Seattle—from Evangelical multisites and a Pentecostal Skate Church to an Ethiopian Orthodox Parish and an activist Methodist community partnered with an arts collective—the need for developing coherent ways of mapping salient similarities and differences becomes apparent. As I discovered in Seattle, the fact of ecclesial diversity raises questions about the best ways of making sense of the dynamic field and the most useful means of comparison.

Theological and Sociological Interpretations of Church

Practical ecclesiological models, such as chapter 4 will develop, are informed by both sociological and theological approaches to interpreting the church. In order to set the stage for that constructive work, this chapter offers a survey some of the most significant models and typologies in the literature. It begins, however, with consideration of the nature and limitations of models for understanding ecclesial life.[2]

Sociological approaches view churches as human organizations. Sociologists are interested in the character of the church rather than its essential nature. Congregations are classically studied by sociologists through several "frames," including ecology, culture, resources, and process.[3] Some attention is given to theology in the congregation, but mostly as a necessary aid for making sense of congregational culture or in the interest of exploiting congregational theology as a potential resource for organizational vitality. Theology matters, for sociology, because what the congregation believes has organizational and social impacts; the correspondence of theological beliefs to spiritual reality (or not) is methodologically irrelevant because it cannot be scientifically verified.

Indeed, sociological frames can be revealing because churches, like all organizations, are situated in an ecology, shaped by a culture, dependent upon resources, and operate by various processes. However, from the standpoint of the faithful, disciplinary disregard for the theological nature of the church presents a serious limitation. Sociologists' methodological atheism (or even agnosticism) is in tension with the deep conviction of church members and theologians that there is more to the church than meets the eye—that is, more than a survey or series of focus groups can discover.[4] Confessional theologians, such as myself, do not believe that a study of the church can be considered adequate that does not include within its scope attention to the spiritual nature of the church. As Avery Dulles, author of the landmark *Models of Church*, has suggested, "the mysterious character of the Church has important implications for methodology."[5] Some of these implications are being explored currently in scholarly circles calling for and experimenting with what might be termed a methodological Trinitarianism: attempts to integrate qualitative methods with doctrinal construction and/or inclusion of various nontraditional research methods such as prayer and Scripture study, all undergirded by the belief that God is indeed present among the faithful.[6]

One result of the methodological atheism of sociology can be seen in congregational studies literature that evinces a mostly unstated but fundamental assumption that the *telos* of the church is society. That is, the sociological literature produced about churches largely assumes that the proper goal of the church—and the basis on which it ought to be evaluated and guided—is its contribution to the larger society (or even the nation-state). Thus, much work in the field has sought to demonstrate the validity of religion, and congregations in particular, by highlighting the positive contributions churches make to society via building social capital and delivering social services.[7] A good church contributes to society; churches are good because they contribute to society. Some sociologists have developed typologies explicitly to help churches survive, thrive, and contribute more substantially to the wider public. In this view, society—the neighborhood, the nation, the world—is understood as the locus of meaning for human history, such that the church's purpose is to help society realize its potential. This guiding conviction is appropriately understood as teleological (and thus theological) in nature. While much of liberal Protestant theology has endorsed this vision, Catholic and Anabaptist theologians generally have not.[8]

Theological models of the church, by contrast, begin with the conviction that the church is a manifestation of God's work and that its fellowship includes not only voluntary human participants but also the Godhead whose unique relationship to this social body constitutes it as church and endows it with a mysterious and super-human nature. According to Dulles, theological models for expressing the church's nature have typically been developed from biblical images.[9] In any given context, he suggests, the surplus of scriptural metaphors has been channeled into a fairly modest set of dominant models on the basis of the psychological conditions of the church and broader cultural and historical trends.[10]

Dulles borrows the concept of models from physical and social sciences, and he understands them as "realities having a sufficient functional correspondence to the object under study so that they provide conceptual tools and vocabulary; they hold together facts that would otherwise seem unrelated." Their chief functions are explanatory—"to synthesize what we already know"—and exploratory—"to lead to new theological insights." Unlike models in the sciences, Dulles insists, ecclesiological models are not subject to "deductive or crudely empirical tests" for validation because of the mysterious character of the church. Instead, he suggests that theological verification is accomplished by "a kind of corporate discernment of spirits" informed by the religious experience of the faithful (by the Spirit they accept what adds to their faith, hope and love) and proven by its practical outworkings, whether they build up the church and its witness or result in abuses. The five models that Dulles describes (summarized in this chapter) are, in his language, paradigms: dominant models that have proven capable of solving numerous problems and that have future potential. While these are useful, Dulles acknowledges that all models are unavoidably inadequate. While some will be better than others in a given context, no perfectly satisfactory "supermodel" can possibly be discovered or developed. Thus, Dulles quips, "no good ecclesiologist is exclusively committed to a single model of the Church."[11]

In *Church, World, and the Christian Life: A Practical-Prophetic Ecclesiology*, Nicholas Healy concurs with Dulles but goes further to offer a needed critique of modern approaches to ecclesiology. Healy contends that most modern ecclesiologies have, indeed, foolishly chased ecclesiological "supermodels" in hopes of providing "blueprints" for ecclesial reform. These ecclesiologies have taken shape as normative, doctrinal claims about the nature of the church meant to facilitate an equation such as "'the church is x, therefore the church should look like abc and reform y must be initiated.'"[12] The problems with this approach, Healy suggests, are multiple. First, no agreement on a single ecclesiological model as supreme has been or can ever hope to be reached, and this diminishes the force of such proposals substantially. Second, and more important, the implied logic of such ecclesiologies is a movement from the church's essential nature to its right practice, without "explicit and careful analysis of the church's present practices."[13] Theory-to-practice logic of this type has been the object of crippling criticism by practical theologians for decades. Healy summarizes: "Blueprint ecclesiologies thus foster a disjunction not only between normative theory and normative accounts of ecclesial practice, but between ideal ecclesiology and the realities of the concrete church, too."[14]

The result of these disjunctures, according to Healy, is that blueprint approaches are not adequate to the central purpose of ecclesiology; their preoccupation with finding the single best formulation and applying it without regard to context is more likely to harm than "aid the church in performing its task of truthful witness within a particular ecclesiological context."[15] What is needed, Healy suggests, is ecclesiology that incorporates "critical analyses of the concrete church and its context into the arguments for its proposals, so that these can be analyzed, challenged and improved."[16]

It is with Healy's vision in view that this project was conceived.[17] This research has been motivated by a practical desire to assist the church in its task of witness in Seattle and similar contexts. Moreover, it began with extended "analyses of the concrete church and its context" rather than with construction of a normative doctrinal ecclesiology for application in new church development, such as is common in church planting literature.[18] Like Dulles's *Models*, this project seeks to advance the church's witness by use of a comparative approach, synthesizing each of the dominant types of ecclesiology "in order to assess its relative merits and drawbacks by comparison to other models."[19] Theological and missiological assessment of these models is the task of chapter 5.

The task of developing the four models themselves is undertaken in chapter 4. In the remainder of this chapter, I consider the various examples of modeling church that are available, and make a case for the practical ecclesiological approach taken in the following chapter. My approach, it should be stressed, offers interpretive rather than prescriptive models of church. Instead of handing down authorized blueprints, the models I develop attempt to make sense of ecclesial footprints. They describe in practical and theological terms the paths new churches are following and forging as they go about their lives and witnesses in Seattle.[20] Thus, these models are footprint ecclesiologies rather than blueprint ecclesiologies. They have arisen from theologically motivated and theologically oriented mixed-methods research and multidisciplinary analysis among concrete churches in context, focusing on their distinctive characteristics and practices in spirituality, identity, and mission. These ecclesiologies are lived out in actual churches, therefore they should be acknowledged as practically coherent and organizationally viable embodiments of church. Because they exist as actual communities, their practical coherence is demonstrable. These practical ecclesiologies *work*, though as chapter 5 will manifest, their functionality (even effectiveness) does not place them above theological scrutiny. Nonetheless, I join the ecumenical consensus in presuming that these communities are indeed local gatherings of the People of God by virtue of their practice of Trinitarian baptism.[21] Inasmuch as these coherent communities are Christians united in Jesus's name, they have valuable insights to offer the wider church, though it is also assumed each model comes with a set of characteristic weaknesses. Moreover, these models have contributions to make not only to practitioners but also to doctrinal ecclesiology—a subject treated in the final chapter of this book.

To summarize, the models of church developed and explored in the following chapters are understood as practical ecclesiologies on the basis of several defining features. First, the models are constructed with the presumption of the presence and activity of God in and among the lives of the Christian communities under study. Second, I have developed these models with the intention of assisting the church in its task of contextual witness. Third, the models attend to the multidimensioned relational life of the church, including its theory-laden practices of spirituality, identity, and mission. Fourth, they are deeply enriched by both theological and sociological approaches such that they begin with analysis of concrete churches, make use of qualitative research methods, attend to both espoused and operant theologies, and reflect substantive conversation with doctrinal formulations of the nature of the church. Fifth, the models are understood as culturally coherent and theologically valid.[22] Sixth, and finally, the

models have potential to offer constructive insights to doctrinal ecclesiology. Together, these features warrant designation of the models developed
in chapter 4 as practical ecclesiologies.

To set the stage for describing the prevalent practical ecclesiological
models among new Seattle churches, it will be beneficial to provide a
review of key theological and sociological models of church. This review
will help to situate the four models with respect to these discourses, as well
as provide useful points of reference and comparison.

Theological Models of Church

The church has been a topic of its own faithful reflection from its inception. "Who are we?" was a key question answered implicitly and explicitly
by the new community that emerged during the life and ministry of Jesus,
and that reformed and crossed ethnic lines in the wake of the Resurrection
and Pentecost. It remains a vital question today for the church qua church,
as well as for local congregations. While the Reformations generated considerable reflection and debate regarding the nature of the true church, it
is the last century that has seen the greatest blossoming of a formal discipline of ecclesiology, entertaining focused reflection on questions of the
relationship of the church to the world, the Reign of God, and the Trinity.
This section offers a necessarily brief treatment of some of the key ecclesiological models developed by canonical and contemporary authors so
they can be utilized later in interpreting the ecclesiologies of new Seattle
churches.

New Testament Ecclesiological Models

Libraries are filled with ecclesiological analysis of New Testament texts and
attempting here to synthesize such volumes would be foolhardy. Indeed,
in 1960, Paul Minear catalogued ninety-six ecclesial metaphors in *Images
of the Church in the New Testament.*[23] Instead, here I offer simplified formulations of four of the most potent, distinctive, and enduring models of
church found in the writings of three of the most prolific New Testament
authors—Paul, Luke, and John, and their respective schools.

One of the central identity questions that faced the early Jesus community was the nature of its relationship to the Hebrew people. Aspects of
continuity and discontinuity between the Jews and the followers of Jesus
were central topics for Paul of Tarsus, the earliest New Testament author.

Its significance for Paul was deeply personal, as he sought to reconcile his own Jewish identity with his Christic epiphany and missionary call to the Gentiles. This complexity was amplified as he instructed newly established congregations of mixed ethnic and class compositions in areas around the Mediterranean. Paul's resolution of this complex question was to assert a fundamental continuity that can be encapsulated in his dominant image of church as the People of God. As the Hebrew Scriptures attest, Israel knew itself to be a people chosen by the creator God through which God would somehow right what had gone wrong in creation brought about by human sin.[24] For Paul, this Jewish paradigm of God's elect as a people set apart *from* the world *for* the world was retained, but significantly reshaped. This reshaping replaced the Torah as the vehicle of membership in God's people with belief in Jesus as Messiah and Lord as the means of incorporation. Thus, for Paul, the *church as the People of God are one people of all nations, a new humanity born of God's covenant faithfulness whose novel social existence witnesses to the "principalities and powers" (namely, the pagan Roman Empire) the wisdom of God.*[25]

While historians and theologians have given considerable attention to Paul's negotiation of the church's relation to Israel, everyday Christians and clergy are much more likely to cite his better known ecclesial image: the Body of Christ. The recurring language in Pauline literature has a recurring theme—namely, a dialectical tension between unity and diversity in the local church, grounded in a common Spirit that distributes a multiplicity of gifts toward a singular purpose, which is the upbuilding of the whole.[26] The purpose of this metaphor for Paul is to urge relationships of mutuality and respect in contrast to the arrogance, self-effacement, and animosity that were presumably occurring. The metaphor also serves to validate diverse forms of ministry within the community and extending out from it.[27] For Paul, what unifies the church is the one Spirit who gives gifts to every member for ministry. This appeal for unity is not, however, for Paul, inconsistent with ranking empowerments in terms of their relative importance and authority when it comes to practical tasks. The Deutero-Pauline references employ the Body of Christ metaphor not only to appeal for horizontal harmony among the members of the church but also to add a vertical dimension by identifying Christ as the head of the body—its authority and source. The Body of Christ model, then, represents the *church as a unified body of diversely Spirit-gifted persons called to mutual respect as they each contribute to the Spirit's common purpose under the Lordship of Christ.*[28]

Lukan literature, which verse for verse composes more of the New Testament even than those writings attributed to Paul and his school, also explores the church as the People of God, but in addition presents a distinctive ecclesiological paradigm. Kevin Giles's analysis of Luke's language for the Acts community highlights the significance of their repeated designation as "the disciples."[29] This language foregrounds the practically oriented commitment of the new community to emulate their founder, Jesus. This practical imitation finds characteristic expression in the Lukan presentation of the church as followers of "the Way" and references their later designation by outsiders as "Christians."

The Spirit is also essential to Lukan ecclesiology—so much so that Darrell Bock asserts "the essence of the church is that she is a Spirit-indwelt community."[30] Jesus's disciples had waited on the Spirit's power to witness across all cultural boundaries "in Jerusalem, in all Judea and Samaria, and to the ends of the earth" (Acts 1:8; NRSV). Accordingly, Graham Twelftree's treatment of Lukan ecclesiology designates the church as the "People of the Spirit," but he nonetheless insists that for Luke the church is primarily Christo-centric rather than Pnuema-centric. "The Church came into existence before the coming of the Spirit . . . in Jesus' simple choosing of the apostles."[31] The church's Christo-centrism was neither merely doctrinal nor simply a matter of imitating the rabbi, but was rooted in the belief that the same Spirit who empowered Jesus's ministry of seeking and saving the lost[32] was the animating force behind the mission of the church. Thus, as Twelftree claims,

> above all else, Luke would say that the Church is the present and ongoing embodiment of Jesus and his mission. It is not that the Church is simply Christ-like or is to mirror and maintain the ministry of Jesus through emulating his activities and message. Rather, through receiving the empowerment and direction of the Spirit [at Pentecost], the Church embodies and expresses the same powerful presence of God apparent in Jesus and his ministry. . . . For Luke, the Church is called into existence by Jesus and has as its *raison d'etre* in its ongoing embodiment of his life and mission.[33]

This distinctively Lukan ecclesiology, then, could be summarized as modeling the *church as followers of Jesus empowered by the Spirit to extend God's saving mission across ethnic and cultural lines to the ends of the earth.*

Johannine ecclesiology is unique in part because of the dearth of material that explicitly addresses ecclesial matters such as church structure and sacraments. While it is true that "one can at most infer a doctrine of church" from Johannine sources, here at least some inferences from silence can be both valid and productive.[34] For instance, the absence of references to church hierarchy, when combined with the Johannine emphasis on mutual love ("love one another") and the foot-washing scene, presents an image of the church as a community characterized by mutuality. As Raymond Brown notes, "in the Johannine tradition the position of the Paraclete as the authoritative teacher and the gift of the Paraclete to every believer would have relativized the teaching office of any church official."[35] In this way, the Johannine vision of church is marked by a striking equality.

Additionally, while John's gospel says little about the church directly, interpreters have offered compelling readings of the Beloved Disciple as a stand-in for the church. D. Moody Smith concludes his remarks on Johannine ecclesiology with these words: "[The Beloved Disciple] is the paradigmatic disciple, a model not so much for the disciples contemporary with Jesus as for future disciples. . . . Perhaps for this reason he remains unnamed, for any and all disciples of Jesus may become beloved disciples. Such disciples, whom Jesus loves, are the church.[36]

John's church is also distinctive for its sectarian character.[37] The Johannine community defined itself in contrast to other groups, including other Christian groups.[38] This sectarianism is also evident in the Gospel's portrayal of those who come to Jesus as those who are already righteous versus the synoptic view that highlights the sinfulness of those who come. This sentiment is most clearly expressed in John 3:21: "But those who do what is true come to the light, so that it may be clearly seen that their deeds have been done in God." This suggests that the early Johannine community regarded itself as a righteous community, embattled in a sinful world. While the epistle's refrain to "Love one another" has often been preached alongside Jesus's call to love of neighbor, Johannine love—in Gospel and Epistles alike—is strictly a family affair. In fact, calls to love those outside the community are not only absent but also cautioned against, for fear that heresy might infiltrate the community in this way (2 John:10–11). In sum, Johannine ecclesiology presents the *church as Christ's Beloved Embattled Community of righteous equals in the Spirit.*

In review, as the Pauline People of God, the church is a chosen people of all nations, testifying to God's covenant faithfulness. Paul's Body of Christ is a unified group of diversely Spirit-gifted persons called to mutual respect as they each contribute to the Spirit's common purpose under the Lordship of Christ. In the Lukan model, the church is the Spirit-empowered Followers of Jesus boldly advancing God's saving mission to the ends of the earth. Johannine ecclesiology presents the church as Christ's Beloved Embattled Community of righteous equals in the Spirit. In various ways the themes found in these biblical ecclesiologies are integrated, reappropriated, and reconfigured among new Seattle churches as we shall see.

Contemporary Ecclesiological Models

Two twentieth-century ecclesiological typologies have definitively shaped the field: H. Richard Niebuhr's *Christ and Culture* and Cardinal Avery Dulles's *Models of the Church*. In this brief section I summarize these classic texts so they may be utilized in describing the practical ecclesiologies prevalent among Seattle church starts.

The focus of Niebuhr's typology in *Christ and Culture* is the relationship between Christianity and the culture in which it exists.[39] Niebuhr presents five models, which he suggests represent legitimately Christian ways of resolving the "enduring problem" of an intrinsic tension between the radical call of Christ to a single-minded devotion to God and the inescapable reality that followers of Christ live within cultures that necessarily balance multiple and irreconcilable values in a "great pluralism."[40] For each, Niebuhr offers historical examples, biblical precedents, and—with the exception of his favored fifth type—theological critique.

The first model pits *Christ Against Culture*. Christians of this sort are "radicals" who, stressing the Lordship of Jesus Christ, call for uncompromising loyalty to the authority of Christ and rejection of the rival claims of culture. Niebuhr points to early Christians, Mennonites, and Benedictine Monasticism as historical examples of this posture, and cites 1 John and Revelation as supporting biblical sources. In stark contrast, the second model offers a *Christ of Culture*, an accommodating Christ whose truth and beauty are recognized though the values of culture. These "liberals" have historical antecedents in the Gnostics and their writings, as well as in Abelard, Kant, and Schleiermacher, each of whom, Niebuhr suggests, sought to bring together Christian ideals with those celebrated by the culture of their time. These first two types provide the black and white extremes for Niebuhr's spectrum, which he synthesizes into varying shades of gray to produce the three remaining types that more closely describe the great majority of Christians who live out their faith in what he calls "the church of the center."[41]

The first synthesizing answer places *Christ Above Culture*, as neither synonymous with nor in opposition to it. In this view, Christians are called to a dual, though unequal, allegiance, typified in Jesus's instruction to "Render to Caesar what is Caesar's and to God what is God's." These "synthesists," exemplified by Catholic and Orthodox churches, see culture as simultaneously human and divine in origin and thus accept that certain cultural claims and values are not only compatible with Christianity but also vital to its discernment. "Dualists" offer another option, which holds *Christ and Culture in Paradox*. Like the radicals, dualists envision a dichotomy, but they locate it within human hearts and between a righteous God and sinful humanity. Niebuhr finds precedent for this as a Christian response in the Puritans, Luther, and Paul's epistles.

Niebuhr's final type, *Christ Transforming Culture*, is his favored one. This type offers a blend of the two synthesizing types, combining the dualist's dichotomizing with the synthesist's optimism about culture. These "conversionists" stress the real power of God to redeem all things and thus expect Christians to be involved in the cultural work of the "present permeation of all life by the gospel."[42] The Gospel of John provides a biblical source for this type with its conversion motif through its partial translation of the gospel into the terms of Hellenistic culture. Though Calvin is mentioned briefly, Niebuhr's great exemplar is Augustine, whose life, theology, and historical context testify to the transformation of persons and society writ large toward devotion to Christ.

While Niebuhr clearly prefers the transforming model, he concludes by deeming the question of the proper relationship between Christianity and culture "inconclusive" and denies that any of these types are "*the* Christian answer" (emphasis in original).[43] Instead, Niebuhr invites readers to embrace a "social existentialism" that accepts the fragmentary nature of human knowledge and nonetheless proceeds to make historically informed and culturally relative decisions in the faith that "the world of culture . . . exists within the world of grace."[44]

The second towering ecclesiological typology of the twentieth century is the work of Avery Dulles, already mentioned. Dulles, a Jesuit priest made Cardinal, first published *Models of the Church* in 1974, and followed up with an additional chapter in 1987. In it, he seeks to typologize five dominant modern ecclesiological models that help to broaden the repertoire available for developing the contours of the four paradigms discovered among new Seattle churches.

As *Institution*, the church is visibly unified by hierarchical governance, shared doctrine, and member-only sacraments. As a "perfect society" the church stands among but above the political kingdoms of the world.[45] According to Dulles, while the institutional model finds strong support in church history and generates a strong sense of corporate identity, it lacks scriptural endorsement, produces passive laity and stagnant theology, and is out of step with the times.

The church as *Mystical Communion* is in stark contrast to the Institution, existing as an interior, interpersonal community of mutual love inclusive of the faithful and God. Often conveyed via images of the People of God or Body of Christ, the Mystical Communion model has a good basis in Scripture and Catholic tradition, tends to vivify the spirituality of the faithful, and resonates with the longing for community in the modern world. As weaknesses, this model runs the risks of making the organizational church out to be superfluous and offering no compelling sense of identity or mission.

The third model of church identified by Dulles seeks deliberately to bring together elements of the Institutional and Mystical Communion models in the theologically rich metaphor of the church as *Sacrament*. Composed of both an outer and an inner aspect, the church as Sacrament is an efficacious sign of the grace that is realized in its concrete reality. The chief strength of the Sacrament model is its ability to resolve several of the problems inherent in the Institutional and Mystical Communion models: balancing the importance of the visible church with allowance for divine grace at work beyond its borders, fueling devotion to the church while making room for genuine critique. The key weaknesses of this model, according to Dulles, are not chiefly theological but functional. Simply put, the model has proved difficult to convey compellingly in either congregational or ecumenical settings.

Dulles identifies two dominant models of Protestant ecclesiology, the first of which is the church as *Herald*. Giving pride of place to the Word above sacrament, this kerygmatic model of church is essentially bound to its mission to "proclaim that which it has heard, believed, and been commissioned to proclaim."[46] The herald model recognizes the local congregation as the full church on the basis of Christ's presence among them,[47] and distinguishes itself and the world from the Kingdom of God, an eschatological reality.[48] Unity in this model is found in faith in a common gospel rather than a shared structure. The strengths of this model include strong biblical foundations, a compelling sense of identity and

mission—especially on the local level—a humble and obedient spirituality, and a rich theology of the Word. However, in its word centricity it
too easily underappreciates "the incarnational aspect of Christian revelation," which, Dulles asserts, is expressed in the historically continu-
ous institutional church.[49] This weakness of incarnational imagination is
also expressed in an overly pessimistic view of the possibilities of a better
human society that can be realized and to which the church is called to
contribute.

Unlike the four preceding models in which the church mediates
between God and the world from an elevated intermediate position, the
church as *Servant* exists in solidarity with the world. As a church for others, it takes up mission in the forms of fostering reconciliation, alleviating
poverty, promoting peace, and in all ways contributing to human flourishing. The key unity of this model is not exclusive to believers but, rather,
encompasses all who join the "brotherhood that springs up among those
who join in Christian service toward the world."[50] The greatest strength
of the servant model, Dulles suggests, is its consonance with the times;
promising to reform an inward-looking church and offering hope for the
realization of the Kingdom of God and its values in society. On the other
hand, while the Bible extols service, it does not advance the idea of the
church's mission as service to the world, according to Dulles, nor does it
assign it responsibility for making the world a better place. The Servant
model with its stress on solidarity, Dulles warns, threatens to overlook the
distinctive mission and identity given to the church.

Nearly a decade after publishing *Models of the Church*, Dulles released
an expanded edition with an additional chapter proposing the *Community
of Disciples* as a master model with the potential to provide a basis for a
comprehensive, systematic ecclesiology.[51] The discipleship model casts
the church as a contrast society. With its distinct Jesus-following way of
life, the Community of Disciples witness to the Kingdom through "self-
abnegation, humble service, generosity toward the needy, and patience in
adversity."[52] Worship and mission are complementary centripetal and cen-
trifugal forces in this model, which envisions mission as both evangelization and service. Envisioning church as a contrast community of disciples,
Dulles believes, has a special utility in an environment in which the general culture "gives little support to Christian values."[53]

The types developed by Niebuhr and Dulles by no means provide an
exhaustive ecclesiological catalogue. Indeed, both typologies have been
targets of critique—sometimes important—for decades.[54] Still, combined

with the New Testament models, they will suffice to provide this project with a sufficient palette of theological constructions of church from which to begin to paint comparisons and identify key points of contrast with the ecclesiological variety discovered among new Seattle churches. Before turning to an elaboration of my practical ecclesiological models, attention to key sociological typologies is in order.

Sociological Models of Church

Whereas theologians have tended to focus on the nature of the church (its relationship to the world, the Reign of God, and Godhead), sociologists have considered its human constitution. As such, they have attended to a particular set of questions, such as: "By what manner do people join the church?" "How does this organization interact with society?" "What organizational processes are at work within congregations?"

Church-sect theory developed in response to the question of how people join and is arguably the most important interpretive tool the sociology of religion has developed.[55] As a mid-level theory, church-sect analysis is more useful in understanding varieties of denominations than particular congregations. Still, the various iterations of church-sect theory are illustrative of the questions typical of sociologists. For Max Weber, the most salient difference between denominations is their "mode of membership." That is, whether new members join by being born into it (church) or by personal decision (sect). Ernst Troeltsch, a theologian, utilized Weber's analytical tool of the ideal type, but instead of focusing on mode of membership—a concrete attribute—he regarded the pivotal distinction to be the degree to which the church had accommodated (or compromised) to worldly ways, an attribute determined by theological assessment. H. Richard Niebuhr's presentation of church-sect theory, which popularized it in the United States, shared Troeltsch's more normative posture, and proposed the powerful insight that denominations *progress* from sect status to churchly institutionalization over time.

In the Weberian sense, the status of new Seattle churches as either church or sect typically depends on their institutional and demographic ages; many new churches initially draw single young adults who get married within several years. Thus, most churches in the first few years primarily acquire members by recruitment (sect), whereas churches passing the five-year mark often enter a season of rapid biological reproduction (church). By comparison, many new churches are more active in biological reproduction (and thus more churchly) than their long-established counterparts, in large part because of their younger demographic composition. However, the majority of new Seattle churches are sectarian in the Troelstschian sense, in that they are self-consciously countercultural.

Congregational Typologies

Since the early 1980s, sociologists have given considerable attention to congregations themselves. This interest has produced valuable work ranging from the particular congregation to the national scene.[56] In addition, several important congregational typologies have emerged. Here, four typologies of particular relevance to this project are considered, and they are referenced in chapter 4 for their usefulness in understanding the variety of new Seattle churches. The first three typologies are concerned primarily with the congregation's posture toward its environment—that is, its mission. The fourth typology focuses on congregational identity and culture by integrating a broader set of core tasks with congregational processes for decision making.

The earliest and one of the most influential contributions came from Roozen, McKinney, and Carroll in *Varieties of Religious Presence: Mission in Public Life*.[57] As the subtitle suggests, the project had a primary focus on congregational mission and thus its typology sought to "classify congregations in terms of the dominant way each congregation defines its relationship to its community or neighborhood."[58] Researchers distributed a questionnaire to pastoral leaders in Hartford, Connecticut. The survey questions themselves pertained to the congregational emphasis placed on twenty-three potential community-engagement activities constructed from the insights of Dulles, Niebuhr, church-sect theorists, and others.

The fourfold typology of mission orientations that emerged from factor analysis of the survey responses hinges on two axes. The first axis distinguished this-worldly churches from otherworldly ones. The former regarded "this present world as an important arena for religiously motivated service and action," while churches with an other-worldly orientation tended to minimize the importance of the here and now and elevate "salvation for a world to come."[59] The second axis divided publicly proactive churches—those who publicly enact their sense of mission—from member-centered ones that resist such action. Roozen et al. summarize the resulting fourfold typology in table 3.1.[60]

The fivefold typology offered a decade later by Carl Dudley and Sally Johnson in *Energizing the Congregation: Images that Shape Your*

Table 3.1 Mission Orientations in *Varieties of Religious Presence*

	Membership-centered	Publicly proactive
This worldly	**Civic Orientation**	**Activist Orientation**
• Stress the establishment of the kingdom of God in society • Concern for the welfare of all people • Ecumenical cooperation • Membership involvement in public life • Educate members on social issues	• Stress civil harmony and avoidance of confrontation and conflict • Individual members making their own decisions on moral and social issues • Affirmation of existing social structures	• Stress justice and critical posture toward existing social structures • Affirmation of member and congregational involvement in social action, including the expectation that the pastor/rabbi will be a leader in this regard • Openness to confrontation, conflict and civil disobedience
Otherworldly	**Sanctuary Orientation**	**Evangelistic Orientation**
• Stress salvation in a world to come • Sharp distinction between the religious and the secular • Accept existing structures • Opposition to "sinful" lifestyles	• Accept ones status in life • Congregation as refuge from this world • Tradition and doctrine • Oppose congregational involvement in social change • Patriotism and adherence to civil law	• Stress personal witnessing to and sharing one's faith with others • Strong openness to the Holy Spirit • Conversion of everyone to the "one true faith"

Source: David A. Roozen, William McKinney, and Jackson W. Carroll, *Varieties of Religious Presence: Mission in Public Life* (Cleveland, OH: Pilgrim Press, 1984), 87, figure 5.1.

Congregation's Ministry also focuses on congregational mission, but is different from the *Varieties* approach in three important ways. First, it emerged from qualitative analysis of member narratives rather than factor analysis of pastoral surveys. Second, its types are presented as congregational self-images that provide metaphors for the church's sense of identity. Third, these images are developed in service of the authors' hopes for helping ministers mobilize congregations into community outreach ministries.[61] Despite these differences, there are notable overlaps with two of the *Varieties* types. Churches with a *Prophet* self-image know themselves to be called by God in a time of crisis to challenge systematic evil and readily engage political and social issues (resembling the "activist" mission orientation). *Pillar* churches imagine themselves as key institutions in their neighborhoods—an image often linked to the concrete historical presence of a stately building (similar to the "civic" orientation in *Varieties*). Churches with a *Pilgrim* self-image have a sense of responsibility to a people, rather than to a place, and interweave the cultural and ethnic identities of immigrant groups with their Christian faith. *Survivor* churches share the Prophets' sense of crisis, but tell stories of relentlessly weathering hardship. The final image Dudley and Johnson offer is that of the *Servant* who is committed to faithfully helping individuals in need, beginning with those in the congregation.[62]

A third relevant typology of congregational mission was developed more recently by Heidi Unruh and Ronald Sider in *Saving Souls, Serving Society*, specifically to challenge the widespread notion that publicly proactive mission takes shape in only one of two ways in a congregation. That is, either through social action or through evangelism. Unruh and Sider protest the implication of the dichotomy that these forms of mission are, if not mutually exclusive, in some necessary or fundamental way in tension with one another. While their critique amounts to little more than a lament regarding the limitations of typologies shaped by a two-by-two table, the gradients they offer do provide useful categorization of the churches that "are springing up in the cracks between the *Varieties* mission types."[63] These types are summarized as follows.

Dominant Social Action churches focus on meeting practical needs and/ or working for social justice; their programs involve minimal religious elements, though they may see their good works as an implicit witness. *Dual-Focus* churches include both evangelism and social action as important, but independent aspects of their outreach mission. Churches with a *holistic* mission consider witness and service to be inseparably linked. A *Holistic-Complementary* subtype conceptualizes these as congruent facets of the same seamless mission, while the *Holistic-Instrumental* subtype envisions social outreach as a portal to the primary objective of winning converts. *Dominant Evangelism* churches focus primarily on sharing their faith, though a this-worldly variant sees individual conversions as a pathway to social change.[64]

The Dominant Social Action and Dominant Evangelism types map to Roozen et al.'s activist and conversionist orientations, respectively.[65]

However, Unruh and Sider made a valuable contribution by articulating the reasonably sophisticated logic animating the three evangelism-plus-social-action orientations as more than combinations or strains of two conflicting orientations; instead, they are internally coherent responses to the pluriform biblical call to Christian mission.

Sociologist Penny Becker developed the fourth congregational typology worth considering here in her study of conflict among twenty-three congregations in Oak Park, Illinois. The novelty and value of her approach are in large part due to a twofold broadening of scope. First, rather than placing a primary focus on congregational mission as the aforementioned studies have done, Becker offers a typology of congregational *cultures*. Second, unlike the three above-mentioned typologies that showed clear preference for outward, community-engaging forms of congregational mission, Becker focused on congregational approaches to, and prioritization of, the institutionalized imperatives that congregational studies have found embedded in the field.[66] These core tasks, as noted in chapter 2, include religious reproduction, religious community, and religious witness.

The result of these two broadenings of scope was four congregational models, which Becker describes as "distinct cultures that comprise local understandings of identity and mission."[67] As Becker notes,

> The term "model" implies that ideas about a congregation come in bundles and are institutionalized in ways that broadly affect congregational life. It also implies the idea of moral order. Because congregational models are ideas about core tasks of the congregation and legitimate ways of achieving them, they are an "is" that implies and "ought."[68]

The *House of Worship* model prioritizes religious reproduction above the other congregational tasks; providing religious worship, education, and rituals to individuals are the paramount duties. Experiences of close community are possible in these churches, but so is anonymity. Decisions are largely made by designated leaders: clergy, staff, and committee members. House of Worship churches understand their worship itself to be an act of public witness, testifying to the presence of the faithful in the wider community.[69]

Becker's *Family* congregations consider providing close, family-like relationships to be as central to their identity as the likewise important tasks of worship and religious education. Thus, the coffee hour is regarded as "part of the Sunday morning worship" rather than an addendum.[70] In Family churches, people know each other and share close, caring bonds, a fact reflected in the time these churches allot for public prayers for members.[71] Authority in Family churches is vested more in those with tenure and personal connections than in formal positions. As in the House of Worship model, their religious witness is performed chiefly through their public presence in the community, but family churches regard their visible presence as a tight-knit community to be as important as their public worship.

The *Community* model shares with the Family model a valuing of worship, religious education, and widespread experiences of belonging, but adds to it a distinctive commitment to express the values of the membership in the policies and programs of the church. This gives these congregations more democratic decision-making processes open to all members. Their unique mode of witness is embedded in their practice of open and inclusive processes that maintain community cohesion. This is likely why these churches typically favor ministries of compassion and shun overtly political or potentially divisive action.

Finally, the *Leader* model prioritizes worship, education, and expressing members' values, but—like Houses of Worship—deemphasizes the importance of intimacy. More distinctively, Leader churches have an activist approach to witness, and are compelled to apply the teaching of their denomination or tradition not only to the life of the congregation but also to the wider world. This priority on outreach takes shape in a variety of ways—compassion ministry, political involvement, denominational action—all of which contribute to a sense that the congregation is an important actor in these realms. Clergy in Leader churches often function as public figures in the community. In the church, they oversee congregational processes that are fairly open, but with authority bolstered by their commission as "stewards of the denominational, ritual, and doctrinal traditions of the congregation."[72]

Synthesizing the Typologies

The preceding sample of theological and sociological models of church provide an abundant set of constructions that illuminate the varying ways that ecclesial identity, spirituality, and mission can be conceived, combined, and embodied. Table 3.2 summarizes these. Many of the models mentioned explicitly reflect a primary concern for the church's posture and mission

Table 3.2 **Synthesizing Important Theological and Sociological Models**

Mission	Spirituality	Identity
• Evangelism	• Mission-centered	• Ethnic
• Contributing to society	• Worship-centered	• Place/City
• Socially embodied witness	• Community-centered	• Ecclesiastical Institution
• Preservation		

in the world. Mission is expressed in four primary ways across the various models. First, some stress an evangelistic mission: for example, the Lukan followers of Jesus, Dulles's Herald, classic sects, *Varieties'* Evangelistic mission orientation, and Unruh and Sider's Evangelism-dominant model. Second, others stress the role of the church in contributing to society, as a stabilizing force, social service provider, or social change agent; for example, consider Niebuhr's Christ transforming culture and Christ of culture types; Dulles's Servant model; *Varieties'* Civic and Activist orientations; the Prophet, Pillar, and Servant images of Dudley and Johnson; Becker's Leader; and the social action–dominant model in Unruh and Sider. A third and often overlooked approach to ecclesial witness is found in the models that understand the primary mission of the church to be enacted in the unique social practice of the church community itself. This is true of Paul's People of God, Dulles's Sacrament, and Becker's Community models. That this approach is not adequately represented in Niebuhr's typology is one of the most warranted critiques. A fourth group of models lack a clear sense of mission in the world and they are relatively inward looking for the sake of preservation. These include *Varieties'* Sanctuary, Dudley and Johnson's Survivor and Pilgrim images, Niebuhr's Christ Against Culture, and the Johannine Beloved Embattled Community.

In addition to these four approaches, it is important to note that several typologies—including Niebuhr's and that of Unruh and Sider—have built-in points along a spectrum between the extreme ends. This reflects the reality that concrete churches reflect multiple logics and can be seen engaging in the same practices of mission from their varying postures. Indeed, the four practical ecclesiological models developed in chapter 4 represent combinations of these approaches that, while they may favor one above the others, are not adequately described by any single approach.

The preceding sampling of models also present three primary understandings of the relationship between church and God or spiritualities.
First, some models have a broadly defined "missionary" spirituality. This
includes both those who understand mission primarily in terms of evangelism and those who prioritize contributing to society. These models tend
to represent their relationship with God as centered on the experience of
being commissioned and empowered: God calls the church to act in the
world and energizes it to do so. This describes the spirituality of many of
the models surveyed, including the Evangelist, Activist, Servant, Herald,
Prophet, Leader, and the Lukan Followers of Jesus.

Other models foreground the church's unique experience of God's
love and power in worship, as in Becker's House of Worship and Dulles's
Institution. A third set of models convey a significant connection
between their experience of deep and mutually edifying human community with their fellowship with the divine. These include the Johannine
Beloved Embattled Community, Paul's Body of Christ, Dulles's Mystical
Communion, and Becker's Family model.

The primary centers of ecclesial identity found in the various typologies include ethnic identity (as with the Pilgrim and Sanctuary models),
geographical and municipal entities (as with the Civic and Pillar models),
and ecclesiastical institutions/denominations (as with the Institution and
Leader models).

While none of the surveyed theological or sociological typologies—nor
even the combined catalog—offers a sufficient representation of the varieties of ecclesial presence discovered among the new Seattle churches, the
major contours in mission, spirituality, and identity do provide a means of
relating this field of new churches to the rich theological and sociological
literature.

4

Models of Practical Ecclesiology Among New Seattle Churches

WHAT IS THE most interpretively useful conceptualization of the variety present among the new churches started in Seattle? This is the central question this chapter seeks to answer. Chapter 2's survey analysis revealed four paradigmatic combinations of significant patterns in spirituality, mission, and identity dimensions. These statistical paradigms offer basic skeletons for four of the most evident ecclesial options in the field: the Great Commission Team, the Household of the Spirit, the New Community, and the Neighborhood Incarnation. This chapter offers thick descriptions of these prime ecclesial options.[1] Drawing on qualitative research and analysis, I elaborate, nuance, and add "flesh" to these skeleton paradigms, as well as relate them to the prominent theological and sociological models of church considered in chapter 3. The resulting models, as the previous chapter asserted, are properly understood as practical ecclesiological models.

In this chapter, each practical ecclesiological model is developed in the three ecclesial dimensions of spirituality, mission, and identity—though the order in which the dimensions are treated varies according to the model's cultural logic. By "cultural logic" I refer to the shared sense among those within the model regarding which ecclesial dimension is of primary importance and how the others flow from that fundamental priority.[2] The interpretive models developed here are not simply illustrations of the survey findings. Instead, they unpack themes that emerged from thematic analysis of the data collected from churches that stood out as clear exemplars of the paradigm. The data came from a variety of sources, including interviews with sixteen pastors and informal conversations with fourteen more, eight focus groups, participant observation in twenty-six churches, and a collection of bulletins, brochures, websites, and social media pages. Distinctive practices and characteristics of each model are illustrated by examples from churches that exemplify that model. As such, the models point toward genuine, coherent theological modes of ecclesial culture and praxis. If Dulles is correct that within a given context, a limited number of models achieve dominance on the basis of psychological, ecclesiastical, cultural, and historical factors, then one could conclude that these four practical ecclesiological models are among the best suited to the present moment in the Seattle context. Inasmuch as Seattle embodies important trends characteristic of the United States more broadly—the argument advanced in chapter 1—it follows that the four models can be expected to rise in national prominence. These four models are taken as representative of some of the primary types of ecclesial life likely to present themselves as key options for the church in the United States—and other Western nations—as the cultural context becomes increasingly urbanized, progressive, technological, and post-Christian. Therefore, it will become increasingly important for theologians, sociologists, and practitioners alike to give careful attention to each of these practical ecclesiological models.

Church as Great Commission Team

Perhaps the most visible and securely institutionalized model of church plant in Seattle is the Great Commission Team (GCT), accounting for approximately 25% of the field of new churches. Churches in this model reflect a mission-centered spirituality and an evangelism-centered mission. In important ways, these churches are not new but, rather, a fresh iteration of the neo-evangelicalism that began to emerge in the United States mid-twentieth century. As such, they embody—sometimes in exaggerated ways—beliefs and practices typical of Evangelical congregations more broadly.[3]

These Evangelical churches are heirs to the modern missionary movement, now aimed back at the "home front." GCT churches find their raison d'être in fulfillment of Jesus's charge to "Go and make disciples of all nations" (Matt. 28:19–20). Among these churches, this "Great Commission" is repeatedly referenced and consistently interpreted as a mandate for evangelism and discipleship. For this model, however, evangelism is not only a missiological priority but also essential to their ecclesiology; they embrace and embody a mission-driven ecclesiology. These churches affirm in word and practice the idea that mission is not simply something the church *does* (or ought to do) but, rather, is essential to what the church *is*. Among churches in the Great Commission Team model, mission is understood as basic to the ecclesiality of the church.[4] That is, the church is, in a fundamental way, understood as a task force; it is a group that exists because there is a job to be done. More specifically, in this model the church exists as a disciple-making mission team. As a team, the central unity in this model is a unity of purpose. New Testament precedents for the church as a mission team can be found in the seventy-two disciples Jesus sent ahead two by two (Luke 10) and Paul and his missionary companions. Paired with Jesus's assurance that "when two or three gather in my name, there I am with them,"[5] these texts provide a rudimentary foundation for asserting the ecclesial nature of the mission team.[6]

GCT churches echo the commitment of Lukan ecclesiology to participation in the extension of the gospel to the ends of the earth. However, they do not consistently foreground the Spirit's activity or empowerment. This evangelistic zeal is paired with a sense that the wider culture and society are hostile to the gospel and with a commitment to being a countercultural movement. While they emphasize learning from the incarnational/relational approach of Jesus and discipleship as a key ministry priority, they do not stress imitation of other characteristic features of Jesus's way of life and ministry, such as healing, pacifism, eschewing of crowds, and inclusive table fellowship (this, despite pervasive "all about Jesus" and "Jesus-follower" rhetoric). In their commitment to exist as messengers of the gospel, GCT churches fit comfortably within Dulles's broadly constructed Herald model, sharing its kerygmatic essence and prioritization of the local church over institutional bodies. Indeed, many are nondenominational, and the most-represented denominations emphasize local autonomy. The GCT model holds a zealously countercultural identity, resembling Niebuhr's Christ Against Culture type, though they employ a rhetoric of cultural transformation more aligned with Christ Transforming Culture. Despite their evangelistic intentions, GCT churches fit less well into Roozen et al.'s Evangelistic mission orientation, since most are actively engaged in works of this-worldly service and speak frequently of city transformation, as well as "changing the world." Unruh and Sider's Holistic-Instrumental orientation better describes these churches that see service as a vital means of establishing a "credible witness" and opportunity for building relationships with non-Christians.

Mission Among Great Commission Team Churches

Great Commission Teams are highly conscious of Seattle's post-Christian status, progressive values, urban character, and technological culture; and they engage with each of these characteristics with intentionality. GCT churches describe their context as an urgent and strategic mission field. Seattle is regarded as a strategic context for mission because it is recognized as a culturally influential city and as a city with international reach.[7] Seattle's post-Christian condition is regarded as both a challenge and an opportunity. Perry Burkholder, pastor of Every Nation Church, which meets in a movie theater and focuses outreach efforts on college and international students, described Seattle as "a place that's ripe for the gospel" and in which "the needs are vast." It is precisely because Seattle is "highly post-Christian" that many GCT planters chose the city.

Andrew Arthur, pastor of The Hallows Church, a collegiate-focused church in Fremont launched by a prominent megachurch in Alabama,[8] described intentionally trying to lower the expectations of potential recruits who were considering moving from Alabama to join the planting team; he warned them that "the receptivity to the gospel isn't going to be as widespread. . . . Seattle's not Birmingham." Far from dissuading them, it was clear from conversations with these transplants that the challenge was a major part of the attraction.[9] The challenge Seattle presents is, for mission-minded evangelicals eager to make heroic decisions for God, a significant part of the appeal.

Wes Moore, one of the members of planting team for The Hallows and later the associate pastor, told me that before deciding to join the Seattle team, their sending church in Alabama had presented two additional options. The first church plant was going to be somewhere in North Africa. Church leaders would not say exactly where in order to protect the missionaries and converts from persecution. The presentation to the congregation included photos with "blacked-out faces" and "code names for their people group." This thrilled Wes, who told to his wife with excitement, "this is awesome. . . . Let's go there, like, there's a chance that we could get shot for our faith!" He reasoned, "[We have] no kids, we might as well do it!" His wife, understandably, wasn't biting. The second location presented was Kansas City, which seemed more sensible for the family-minded newlyweds. "They need Jesus, too! Let's go there," she suggested. Wes was decidedly unenthused. It was "basically the exact same place that we were living," he told me. When Seattle was announced as the third location, they were both interested because, as Wes put it, Seattle offered "kind of a combo of both." Like Kansas City, it was safe, and like North Africa, it had "no real religious presence" and was in desperate need of the gospel. After some prayer and exploratory meetings, the two "were kind of like, I think this is where the Lord is leading us."

Much of the rhetoric of the city as a place desperately in need of the gospel is crafted in the process of generating financial support to start these churches. Churches in this model often represent Seattle as an urgent mission field in "desperate need of the gospel" through use of "alarming" statistics about how few Seattleites attend Evangelical churches.[10] Such depictions are a means of motivating financial support and recruiting team members to the cause. But even after these startup needs have been left behind, the image of Seattle that has been constructed remains useful for generating financial giving among members and bolstering the sense of embattlement that Christian Smith has argued helps Evangelicals to thrive.[11]

This countercultural identity is also apparent with regard to Seattle's progressive values. Those in leadership of GCT churches might never use the language I heard from one man on the fringes of a GCT church who described Seattle as "the Sodom and Gomorrah of the West," but there is nonetheless a strong sense of moral objection to sexual practices that are widely accepted in Seattle culture. One pastor characterized the average person on the streets of Seattle as operating with a definition of "love as sex." Another boldly declared to his congregation that he would never perform a gay marriage and that the church should anticipate slanderous persecution as a result.

GCT churches may be in tension with Seattle's sexual culture, but they fit its technological enthusiasm perfectly. They are especially eager and adept users of technology in service to their mission. Taking advantage of the latest and most popular tools is understood as a means for recruitment and ongoing connection (read evangelism and discipleship). Mark Noll has noted that Evangelicals tend to be "culturally adaptive," and Seattle GCT churches stand out as early adopters when it comes to the digital revolution.[12]

Churches in this model engage with the urban dynamics of Seattle in several ways. GCT churches often choose where to plant by identifying newly gentrifying neighborhoods, seeing these as strategic locations.[13] Conscious of the neighborhood centricity of Seattle, several large churches in the model have adopted a multisite strategy, while most others have formed neighborhood-based small groups called "missional communities." Several GCT pastors noted the "Seattle freeze" and widespread loneliness and see their missional communities as presenting to these neighborhoods a faithful offer of belonging.

The keystone mission priority of the Great Commission Team model is "making disciples."[14] Disciple-making language is drawn from Matthew 28:19–20 ("make disciples of all nations, baptizing them . . . and teaching them to obey everything I have commanded you") and serves as a mantra that combines the call to evangelism with the task of Christian education. While their commitment to evangelism is by far the most distinctive mission priority for this model, it is understood best as a part of a broader commitment to discipleship that includes the process beginning in conversion and ongoing toward maturity as a "radical" disciple of Jesus.[15]

The prime evangelistic strategy among GCT churches is the cultivation of missional relationships—friendships with the unchurched that GCT members hope will provide opportunities for evangelistic witness. Most of the other mission practices in GCT churches are subordinate to this overarching strategy of relational evangelism.[16] Many churches host community events such as carnivals, block parties, and neighborhood barbecues a few times a year, intending to bolster the church's "credible witness" (their public profile as a benefit to the community). But the events are also important ways these churches create settings in which members can forge missional relationships with neighbors. As Pastor Andrew Arthur told me,

> Block parties are heavy for meeting people and going from acquaintance to friendship with those in our neighborhood. So we host these block parties at the park. They have been really well attended and its—again, there's no microphone gospel. It's let's just—as a community—hang out, be with one another, get to know each other. Because, you know, some people have suspicions of a church. . . . So I think just being present and showing that we're normal people, living in the same world as you, in the same neighborhood as you. Let's have common ground with which we can relate and move from acquaintance to friendship and over the course of that see what the Lord might bring about.[17]

Discipleship in GCT churches is understood as the process of Christian growth by which individuals deepen in their understanding and application of "the Gospel."[18] Pastor Micah Dodson put it this way: "When we talk about discipleship, we're not talking about information primarily. We're talking about information and imitation and innovation." Concretely, this means that GCT churches stress deepening one's knowledge of the Scriptures (and ability to interpret them Christocentrically), growing in humility and holiness, and—in response to "the Gospel"—growing in one's identity and activity as a missionary.

Though preaching is highly emphasized and GCT churches often offer a few classes such as Gospel 101, their primary venues for discipleship are mid-week, neighborhood-based, mixed-gender "communities" or "missional communities" of between six and twenty people. GCT leaders frequently suggest that these groups are the basic unit of the church and the primary communities in which Acts 2:42ff is lived out ("They devoted themselves to the apostles' teaching and to fellowship, to the breaking of bread and to prayer"). Respondents to the congregational survey at The Hallows rated "being part of a small group/bible study" as the most important practice for their personal way of life from a list of thirty-four choices.[19] Often these churches structure their group gatherings around certain monthly rhythms in such a way as to habitualize the priorities that the church deems most central to Christian living. These rhythms include a monthly pattern of study, prayer, relationship building, and—for most—community service. As Pastor Perry Burkholder, of Every Nation Church, told me:

> In the Community Groups . . . the Word is always central. Relationships are key. We say, "Hey, you're going to eat meals together. It's Acts 2 . . . we're going to eat together . . . we're going to pray, we're going to do the Word and real life discipleship and you're going to shift and try to put the focus on your neighbor."

Study times in missional communities are often focused on a recent sermon and the Bible passages cited in it. For some GCT churches the relationship-focused gatherings are not intended to be occasions for member-only fellowship but, rather, opportunities to practice Christian hospitality and deepen missional relationships. For example, a community at Lux initiated a regular margarita night at a local Mexican restaurant. They invite their friends, including those at the local Trader Joe's with whom they have forged missional relationships. For Lux and others, the intention of this monthly rhythm is to create "Great Commission environments" in which Jesus followers are in a minority.

While missional communities do offer participants an important experience of belonging, they are not intended to host the deepest levels of
intimacy, lest they become unwelcoming to newcomers. For the deepest
relationships, GCT communities often divide into smaller same-gender
groups of two to five people. About half of the survey respondents at The
Hallows indicated that they meet regularly with "a discipleship, accountability, or prayer partner." These micro-groups have a more intentional
focus on growth through confession and confrontation of personal sin.
GCT churches understand the gospel as confrontational in nature and
stress the importance of "calling others out." This was expressed clearly in
the sermon I heard at Mars Hill's University District campus:

> [T]he reality is that love . . . is dirty and it is messy, and it is grimy
> and it is not a pat-on-the-back type of love. It is a love that confronts
> at times. Sometimes confrontation is the most loving thing you can
> show somebody else. It is a love that isn't just surfacy in commu-
> nity. Where somebody is struggling with something and you say,
> "You know what?—I'm just going to let them sit in that." No! It
> pursues them. It is a love that cares. It is a love that sacrifices.

Sometimes that sacrifice is jeopardizing friendships by calling out sin;
other times the gospel calls for more tangible sacrifices in the form of
service. GCT churches are active participants in what has been called the
"new Evangelical social engagement."[20] In contrast to the prevalent stere-
otype of Evangelicals as concerned only with evangelism, GCT churches
prioritize and program service in various ways. Several have partnerships
with the Union Gospel Mission, a large Christian ministry that serves the
homeless. Others have built relationships with public schools, and a handful have also started their own social justice initiatives, like Unbound, an
anti-human-trafficking ministry initiated by Mosaic Community Church.[21]

What is distinct is how these service activities are viewed: primarily as
a vehicle for missional relationship. Service among GCT churches is seen
as instrumental in advancing the foundational mission practice, which is
evangelism. David Parker is executive pastor at Downtown Cornerstone,
an Acts 29 church started by former Mars Hill Church staff. He describes
the rationale for service in his church:

> [We serve] cause we believe we've been loved and served by a
> great God and so really [we're] just continuing to keep that on the

forefront and in a way, too, it also creates space for wanting to build relationships around the organization or the people that are going through the program, and/or . . . to create space to invite folks to join with us as we serve, say, Fair Start or [Union Gospel Mission]. And that's been really awesome because who would say "No" to "Hey, [do] you want to come serve and volunteer with us at a soup kitchen?" You know? Like, it's such an awesome opportunity that you don't just like [say] "Hey, you want to come to church with me?"

Pastor Parker stressed that the central reason they serve is in response to God's love, but he also notes how serving facilitates opportunities for forming missional relationships with people in the for-benefit organizations they partner with, as well as among the non-Christian friends whom they invite to serve alongside them.

Though GCT churches typically coordinate a few church-wide service events each year, they expect the primary external service efforts of the church to occur through missional communities as part of their monthly rhythm. Group leaders are tasked with the responsibility of forging service partnerships and coordinating regular opportunities for their group to serve.

Their commitment to "making disciples" is also expressed in eagerness and intentionality around planting more churches—a vision often expressed with the language of "multiplication."[22] The now-dispersed Mars Hill Church was the most prolific in this respect, having at one point established fifteen multisite campuses. But even brand new GCT churches regularly launch, as they say, with multiplication in their DNA. That is, they begin one church with a view toward starting additional churches in just two or three years, and it is not unusual for them to do so successfully, as I observed.[23] A thriving missional community in a neighborhood fifteen to twenty minutes away from the church's gathering place typically serves as the core for a new plant.

While GCT churches work locally to "multiply the Gospel" by planting new churches, they are also active in reaching out internationally—following the Great Commission's call to "all nations." Some Great Commission Teams financially support mission work overseas. Mars Hill Church leveraged its extensive production and media resources to stream a weekly "global online [worship] service." Others participate directly in short- and mid-term mission trips to extend their disciple-making efforts overseas.

Every Nation Church participates in one or two international mission trips facilitated by their network each year. Pastor Burkholder described the nature of these trips:

> They're word and deed, service and evangelism, and . . . whatever we do is tied to a local church that's going to be doing discipleship follow-up and either planting something or already planted and going to help move that along so we're just trying to find meaningful ways where what we're coming in to do really fits the local culture and really helps the local church do what they've got to do.

Pastor Burkholder mentioned several specific international projects including a water-filter project in Nicaragua, an orphanage built in Haiti, and anti-sex-trafficking work as well as church planting efforts in Nepal.

While these mission trips seek to contribute meaningful Christian ministry overseas, international projects and connections also play an important role in the life of the church back home. Their international partnerships foster the sense that GCT churches are part of a divine mission of global proportions, and thus strengthen corporate identity. As Pastor Burkholder put it with pride: "for a small church—we got our hands in some stuff." In addition, mission trips serve as crucibles for the formation of missionary culture and spirituality and—along with international links of all types—provide focal points for the church's fundraising efforts.[24] Several GCT churches have deliberately made connections with ministries in places where Christians are persecuted, in hopes that these relationships will "kinda rub off on our experience" and create a "global mentality" in their own congregation.[25]

Spirituality Among Great Commission Team Churches

GCT churches relate to God through "the Gospel," a phrase many use repeatedly to point to a cluster of emphases including Christological readings of Scripture, Jesus's atoning death on the cross, and the total life transformation called for by God's grace. GCT spirituality is deeply and characteristically Evangelical. They stress the importance of the whole Scriptural canon—and preach from both Testaments—but interpret all texts with a strong Christological lens. Jesus is presented and worshiped as an obedient scapegoat that satisfied God's wrath toward human sin. In response, GCT churches invite people to respond by accepting Jesus as Lord and Savior, but also recount "second conversions" among the saved to deepened missional identity. The importance of responding to "the Gospel" by becoming a missionary makes sense in the midst of contexts where nominal Christianity is an important foil for GCT churches. As missionaries, members of GCT churches actively respond to God's grace by seeking evangelistic opportunities, and not only experience the consolation of a "personal relationship with Jesus" but also celebrate personal experiences of God's call and provision for their missionary endeavors.

Many GCT churches frequently describe themselves as "Gospel-centered" churches and their recurrent invocation of "the Gospel" demonstrates the importance of the designation. This language has become popular in recent years among conservative Evangelicals, particularly those influenced by the Acts 29 church planting network and The Gospel Coalition.[26] The term suggests two important questions: What is "the Gospel"? and How does this understanding of the central Christian message function at the center of these churches? GCT churches are highly intentional about clarifying their understanding of "the Gospel," especially in view of their assessment that shockingly few people—even churchgoers—can clearly articulate it. Among new Seattle GCT churches, "the Gospel" is an atonement-centered message about human sinfulness that warrants divine wrath and led to Jesus's excruciating, substitutionary death, which (1) merited undeserved forgiveness, (2) calls for a total-life response of humble discipleship, and (3) commissions the redeemed as missionaries. Mars Hill's University District Campus Pastor Drew Hensley elucidated this atonement-centered message in a Sunday evening sermon:

> We don't deserve to be shown love and we're in our sin and we're rebellious and we've rejected God but what God says is this: he says, "You know what? I still love you, and I want you to be my children." And so what God does is he devises a plan. This is the gospel. He sends Jesus. He sends Jesus the God-man to live a perfect life that we could not live. He sends Jesus to give himself for us. Literally, as this passage says, to be the "propitiation for our sins." Super-simple—what does that really mean? It means that the wrath of God that I deserve—that I deserve to be the one on the cross, that I deserve to suffer the penalty for my sin—Jesus took that on himself. That he suffered the wrath of God on our behalf. That's how much he loves you. That's how much he wants you to know he loves you . . . this is the amazing love that Jesus would die this bloody death, that he would die, that God would say, "that is a good sacrifice," and he would be raised from the dead.[27]

In other words, "the Gospel" is that, as the billboard from Mars Hill Church proclaims in figure 4.1, Jesus saves.

Endorsing this atonement-centered message, however, is not all that is entailed in being a "Gospel-centered" church. For GCT churches, "the Gospel" is not something simply to believe but also a reality that "changes everything" (a popular phrase in the field, especially common among GCT churches). "The Gospel" is believed to have ramifications for all of life, which Christians are called to continually seek to discover and apply. Learning about these implications is important spiritual work in GCT churches. Indeed, members at The Hallows Church indicated that they feel closest to God when learning something new about God.[28] Pastor Arthur declared:

> We want to be a Gospel-centered community—not just in language, because that seems like a trendy language nowadays—but we're really seeking to explore the comprehensive claims that the Gospel makes on our lives. So we want to grow deep in our apprehension of the Gospel and then wide in our application of the Gospel, seeing

FIGURE 4.1 Mars Hill Church's "Jesus Saves" Easter 2014 billboard.

that the Gospel really does affect every aspect of our personhood and every aspect of our livelihood.

The undeserved nature of grace demands a total response—humble, obedient discipleship that includes not only moral living but also a commitment to personal evangelism. In an Easter sermon, Pastor Arthur celebrated how the resurrection gives purpose to life that is rooted in a call to witness. The result of "the Gospel" in our lives is that

> we fill our bucket lists with people groups around the world who've never been told that there is a God who loved them enough to send their son to die on the cross and to rise from the grave. People we get to share the gospel with. People we have the privilege of discipling . . . all of a sudden . . . we begin talking to our waitresses and waiters a little differently. We begin engaging our professors a little differently. We begin treating our bosses a little differently. We begin treating the homeless in Seattle a little differently.

"The Gospel" leads believers to reorient their ambitions around evangelization, inviting them to see those they encounter in daily life as potential converts. In other words, one of the most important differences that "the Gospel" makes is how it awakens believers to missional vocation. This awakening results in what Nancy Ammerman calls "sacred consciousness," a spiritual outlook that gives ordinary life extra-ordinary meaning.[29] The sacred consciousness characteristic of GCT churches amplifies their everyday human interactions, giving them eternal significance as opportunities to participate in God's work of human salvation. Pastor Arthur concluded his Easter sermon with an oft-quoted line from C. S. Lewis: "There are no ordinary people. You have never talked to a mere mortal. . . . [I]t is immortals whom we joke with, work with, marry, snub and exploit—immortal horrors or everlasting splendors."[30]

Being "Gospel-centered" significantly shapes the church's central spiritual practices. Pastor Arthur described corporate worship as a multisensory experience of the atonement gospel: "We want to speak the gospel every week. We want to sing the gospel every week. We want to see the gospel every week." Preaching in GCT churches is organized into sermon series that most often move through a book of the Bible, but sometimes focus on a topic or theme. The sermons themselves are typically expository and often last forty-five minutes or more. While preaching normally advances through the books of the Bible chapter by chapter, passages across the canon are interpreted through the Cross, and sermons almost always conclude with reference to Jesus's death. On this basis, these "Gospel-centered" preachers can draw a distinction between themselves and mere "Bible-centered" expositors who may preach the text exegetically but do not share their Christocentric hermeneutic.

Sermons typically begin after a couple opening songs, so that the rest of the service—songs, giving, and Communion—are structured as responses to the Word. Their singing emphasizes human sinfulness, the bloody nature of Christ's death, and expressions of gratitude for God's love, forgiveness, and personal transformation.[31] Communion is celebrated weekly in many GCT churches and serves as a symbolic dramatization of the atonement. It is how they "see the Gospel." Members commonly take the elements back to their seats and bow, praying for God's forgiveness while nonbelievers are discouraged from participation. Typically, services reach an emotional climax with (ritualized) spontaneous standing and hand-raising during the singing that immediately follows communion. This moment is often punctuated with a repeated short lyric that encapsulates their understanding of "the Gospel," such as, "Oh, praise the One who paid my debt and raised this life up from the dead."[32] Worship leaders offer unscripted prayers several times during worship, most consistently expressing gratitude for Jesus's death, inviting nonbelievers into relationship with Jesus, asking God for help in hearing and applying what is preached, and requesting God's blessing on mission efforts. The time for tithes and offerings is often framed as an opportunity for participating in mission through giving and/or as a matter of faithfully responding in discipleship.

While corporate worship gatherings are important, GCT churches often stress that their "missional communities" are the most basic units of the church's life. In these mid-sized missional communities the central spiritual practices include study, prayer, fellowship, and service, while in smaller single-gender subgroups practices extend to confession, accountability, and prayer. In addition, GCT churches emphasize the importance of the personal spiritual practices of Bible reading, prayer, and to a lesser degree, fasting.

In keeping with their understanding of the gospel, GCT churches know God chiefly as Father, Savior, and Lord. The Father and Savior are the two prime characters in their atonement gospel. As Father, God is a simultaneously stern and generous figure, whose justice demanded punishment but who willingly sacrificed his son. As Savior, Jesus is the heroic example of humble, obedient sacrifice that earned righteous standing for humanity.[33] Similarly, the Father and Son are represented as the two prime actors in the present. Most prayers are addressed to the Father or Lord, and a majority of contemporary divine action is attributed to Jesus, or simply "God." Comparatively little is said about the Spirit and feminine language for God was not observed.

Theirs is "a living, active God," experienced as one who calls, guides, provides, and effects personal transformation.[34] GCT members' stories about starting and joining the church consistently hinged on personal experiences of God's call. Frequently, they spoke of divine action in the advancement of mission efforts. They see God as a provider of formative experiences, financial means, strategic partnerships, and relational openings with non-Christians.[35] God is also experienced as one who changes hearts. In several cases these changes of heart involved becoming willing to make personal sacrifices for mission, such as relocating to Seattle. They also name God as the key actor in their stories of personal transformation, commonly shared as public testimonies in worship services and especially common during baptisms. These testimonies characteristically follow a familiar evangelical conversion formula highlighting: (1) the emptiness or sinfulness of life before conversion; (2) a profound experience of Christ as God's love, grace, and call; and (3) the joy and fullness of new life in Christ.

Those regarded as spiritual exemplars embody central GCT priorities and values. They are illustrations of God's transforming grace, as well as instruments of it. As in all models, pastors in GCT churches are looked to as exemplars. What is unique, however, is how GCT pastors are identified as champions of a gospel that confronts sin and demands mission. These men—and they are all men—were repeatedly praised by participants in the congregation for how God had used their words to convict and issue God's call to discipleship and mission.

The lay saints in GCT churches are living examples of humility, personal transformation, and relational evangelism. What the New Seattle Churches Survey found for Conservative Protestants more broadly holds true for GCT churches: they regard "living missionally in relationships with friends and neighbors" as an important mark of Christian maturity.[36] The following stories told by Pastors Perry Burkholder and Micah Dodson, respectively, about exemplary individuals illustrate the uniquely missional nature of their transformation.

We had a couple who had been through two miscarriages . . . you think about the couple you had thought could probably never do something missional, you would probably go, "Nah, these guys, never." And especially through their darkest hour of pain . . . God moved in their heart and showed them that through their pain they could actually love others. Not waiting 'til they're out of their pain, but in their pain. And so they began to do barbecues to get to know their neighbors. They live in Capital Hill and in an apartment block and nobody knows each other and hardly anybody ever speaks to each other. [That's] Seattle. . . . We preached the book of Acts and as we were doing that we were really encouraging this whole out-ward oriented focus of life and as we did that they began to plan barbecues and they invited their [community] group to come join them, to meet their neighbors and they were going to invite them in to this thing called The Story of God that we do . . . we invite non-Christians in to learning the Gospel . . . they began big with some big barbecues and they began to meet different people and they began to pray over who they should invite to dinners, privately in their home. They began to invite them privately in their home and do dinners with them, getting to know them. And then they began to discover their spiritual story, their spiritual journey, and they began to talk about Christ. And as they began to do that . . . they invited them in to do The Story of God as a community there and one guy that was an atheist came to faith through that over about a six-month period. He'd been way over here [far from faith]. And another girl is this close to coming to faith . . . it takes a long time with people as unchurched as they, it's just slow . . . another guy's been impacted—he's still . . . an atheist but, man, it's just, they've created a community. People want to be together. They've actually transformed that whole area. And they want to actually know each other. They're in each other's apartments. So, neat stuff happening.

One of the guys who is our church planting resident ["Matt"] . . . he's done this really well where he's engaged people that don't know Jesus, worked in a coffee shop, and met someone there. Had a dodge ball night with a bunch of guys. One of this guy's roommates . . . they started spiritual conversations, started meeting regularly together. This guy ["Rich"] eventually takes a step of faith to trust Jesus and so they meet on a weekly basis with a group of guys. . . [where he is] being discipled regularly. And then [Rich] begins to see that his house that he's living in is his mission field and starts praying for opportunities to connect with different roommates and share Jesus with them. To me, that's kind of like a full evolution of so [Matt] engages this person who doesn't know Jesus. [Rich] begins following Jesus. He's being discipled. And now [Rich is] looking for people, in turn, to lead to Jesus to then disciple. That's, to me, . . . what we're aspiring to . . . the life of the mature Christian would be that they're reproducing.

These two accounts feature several shared elements—each of which illustrate the important GCT priorities embodied by their celebrated saints. In each, the central characters experience an awakening of missional identity; they come to see themselves as ambassadors of Christ, called to their context. They pray for God's guidance as they pursue missional relationships. They create "Great Commission" environments in order to establish new relationships. They look for opportunities for more intimate conversation in which to share their faith. Finally, both stories highlight the fruit of their efforts. These include, most importantly, conversions—but also ongoing community and a new cycle of missional identity.

Identity Among Great Commission Team Churches

The New Seattle Survey produced no statistically significant identity pattern correlations among GCT churches. That is, none of the identity patterns found in the field (denominational, ethnic, neighborhood) are linked with the spirituality and mission patterns that make up the statistical paradigm upon which the GCT model was constructed. However, my qualitative analysis of exemplar GCT churches suggested several identity themes and offers insight into this survey result. The mission-focused nature of GCT churches makes them deeply pragmatic; whatever is expected to advance their mission is adopted, whatever is presumed to encumber it is shed. Potential identity markers are filtered through this pragmatism, and by and large, visible denominational affiliation, ethnic identity, and neighborhood rootedness are deemed counterproductive.

The most common denominational affiliation among churches in the GCT model is with the Southern Baptist Convention through the Seattle Church Planting Network. Though many of the other GCT churches are nondenominational, few are without significant partners. More important than denominational affiliations is participation in various networks, some of which function like denominations in providing centralized resources and oversight.[37] Also important are connections to evangelical megachurches that function as, or house, church planting networks.[38]

GCT churches are city focused, though they situate this urban focus within a threefold sense of their mission context as composed of the concentric circles of neighborhood, city, and world. This is a deliberate parallel to Jesus's declaration in Acts 1:8 that his disciples would be his witnesses "in Jerusalem, and in all Judea and Samaria, and to the ends of the earth." They tend to regard these circles as of escalating importance and commonly present themselves as churches "for the city." While GCT churches often do serve within their immediate neighborhood contexts, their sense of relationship to their neighborhood (and city) is more as a launching pad than as a parish. The Hallows Church's mission statement expresses this clearly: "We exist to magnify and multiply the gospel through Seattle to the ends of the earth." Anchor Church similarly announces: "We have been sent by Jesus to proclaim His Gospel to the people of Seattle. We're Seattleites who love our city and want to see it renewed by Jesus and His Gospel."[39] GCT churches reflect a trend in the last decade of increased Evangelical interest in cities as centers of cultural influence, as well as venues for mission where "all the nations" are present in one place.[40] The city, for GCT churches, is a place of strategic importance for a global mission. As previously mentioned, the international dimension of their mission efforts facilitates a sense of worldwide identity and purpose.

Their strategic relationship to place is matched with a similarly mission-driven sense of space. Pastor Burkholder explains why he decided to relocate his church from a church building in the Green Lake neighborhood to a movie theater in Northgate:

It was a brand new building . . . very central in the north . . . right by the mall, and the bus depot is right here. So 10,000 people come through that bus depot in a day. A thousand buses a day will come through there and it's the hub. It's the hub of the north . . . it's ten minutes from U-Dub [University of Washington]. The buses come straight here. We care about students. It just made sense. That's pragmatic. The other thing . . . we chose theaters particularly because they're not associated with the church building. . . . I still believe that a lot of folks when they think of church, go to an old building, whatever, may not necessarily fit whatever they are hungry for, and so we thought, "this is more neutral." It's a neutral ground. They're used to walking into a theater.

All three of the new Seattle churches that worship in movie theaters are squarely within the GCT model, and the choice of venue epitomizes the GCT relationship to space.[41] In addition to offering the strategic mission advantages of a neutral, highly visible environment, plentiful parking, and eliminating the need to stack chairs, cinemas offer the new churches room to grow from smaller to larger theaters.[42] While lighting and decor options are limited, the venues are nonetheless well suited for GCT churches' evangelical style of worship with its focus on extended biblical preaching (comfortable seating, facing front, house lights up for note-taking and personal Bible use), passionate, personal worship (large projection screen for lyrics/images, good acoustics for immersive music, lights down for privacy/intimate feel), and casual atmosphere (food-friendly floors, cup holders—for coffee, and an implied jeans-and-tee-shirt dress code).

GCT churches do not identify with particular ethnic groups, but college students are a common demographic target. They seek to channel youthful enthusiasm for making a difference in the world into mission. Some GCT churches place a special value on a multicultural composition and see this as a fulfillment of the "all nations" commission. They pursue this identity through mission efforts aimed at international students.

As mentioned earlier, "Gospel-centered" is a key identifier for GCT churches. This moniker is used by GCT churches to distinguish themselves from the liberal, social-justice churches in their religious ecology. Pastor Parker described the Downtown area as lacking any "gospel works" (i.e., Gospel-centered churches) except for the video venues run by Mars Hill and City Church: "[in] every other church—whether it's Plymouth Congregational, Gethsemane—[the] Gospel is almost nonexistent . . . a lot of great social justice happening, but not a lot of Gospel Word," suggesting that other downtown churches (those he mentioned were UCC and ELCA) were serving the poor, but not preaching "the Gospel." When a member of a missional community that I visited prayed for me and my research project, she asked God to use it to bless, specifically, "Gospel-centered, Jesus-focused churches." GCT churches sense a critical division among churches between those that are faithfully proclaiming "the Gospel" and those that are not, and they have a strong sense of affinity with the former.

Summary

The Great Commission Team model is a mission-driven ecclesiology. They understand their context as a spiritually dark and urgent mission field in need of their life-giving atonement-centered message. Driven by desire to fulfill the task to which they have been commissioned, they strive to make disciples through missional relationships, serving, church planting, and international efforts. Their spirituality centers on obedient response to "the Gospel" in both humble acknowledgment of personal sinfulness and awakening to one's missionary identity and call. The twin centers of their corporate spiritual life are missional communities—with rhythms of study, relationship, and service—and worship services that prioritize Christocentric, exegetical preaching, and emotionally intense singing. Their affiliations, partnerships, and relationships to space and context are strategically determined on the basis of their potential to advance mission. Great Commission Teams present the church as task force—a missionary team called and aided by God to make disciples.

Church as Household of the Spirit

The Household of the Spirit (HS) model enacts the church as a family of faith who experience the power and presence of God's Spirit in a foreign or unfriendly environment.[43] They reflect a worship-centered spirituality, an evangelism-centered mission, and—often—identities connected to ethnic and denominational groups. The New Seattle Churches Survey found this cluster of churches to be characterized by Spirit-filled spirituality, distinctive commitments to "building a refuge from the world," and "witnessing to and experiencing God's miracle-working power," along with significant identifications with an ethnic minority and Pentecostal or Charismatic denomination. These churches, predictably, have much continuity with the wider fields of Pentecostal, Charismatic, and ethnic congregations.[44] The HS model developed in this section has interpretive utility for roughly 30% of new Seattle churches.

"Household" language offers both relational and spatial connotations, presenting the church as both family and home. Relationally, the household evokes the identity of the church as an extended family—something especially important among the ethnic minority and immigrant congregations that exemplify the model. Spatially, the household represents an environment of safety and security in which to take shelter from the dangers of the outside world—a fortress. Importantly, this place of safety is regarded as filled with spiritual potency. It is, like a sanctuary or temple, approached as an environment for transformative spiritual encounter. For these churches, however, the "place" of spiritual encounter is not limited to a physical place. Instead, potency for spiritual encounter is linked to people—especially charismatically gifted leaders, but also the community as a whole. This practical ecclesiological model, then, brings together elements of well-established, biblically rooted ecclesiologies of the church as family and the church as temple of the Spirit. This model embodies the church as an extended family with whom one can take refuge and experience God's miracle-working presence.

With their emphasis on the endowment and exercise of "spiritual gifts," HS churches frequently invoke 1 Corinthians 12, in which Paul not only speaks of various Spirit-given empowerments (verses 4–10, 28–30), but also describes their unity and interdependency by way of the Body of Christ metaphor (verses 12–31). Echoing this vision, the HS model understands the church as comprising Spirit-gifted persons whose supernatural empowerments are intended for the upbuilding of the church. They also embody aspects of Johannine ecclesiology, including its sectarianism. Their sectarianism is evident in both their insistence that they teach the full gospel (unlike other Christian groups) and their sense of embattlement. While HS churches are far different from Dulles's description of Servant churches that seek to improve society, they share with it a sense of existing in the world as God's agents of healing—specifically, in this model as Christ's Spirit-empowered healing hands.

The HS model overlaps in important ways with prominent sociological models, as well. Like the Sanctuary type, it is typically characterized by a predominant otherworldly orientation, suspicion of the world, and an emphasis on the Spirit. Numerous churches in the model, like the Pilgrim self-image, share a cultural or ethnic identity that marks them as distinct from the wider environment. Like Becker's House of Worship model, HS churches prioritize religious reproduction—and specifically spiritually charged worship gatherings—above other congregational tasks. However, an important minority of these churches do not fit the parameters of these prominent sociological models. A number have decentered worship services, and stress a this-worldly, proactive mission orientation by regularly challenging members to pray for physical healing for others beyond the bounds of church gatherings and spaces. These same churches, moreover, embody belief in the church as extended family but without connection to a specific ethnic or cultural identity. In sum, the Household of the Spirit is the Spirit-empowered family of God, experiencing God's miraculous healing and offering it to others.

Spirituality Among Household of the Spirit Churches

Worship gatherings are the central spiritual practice for HS churches. God's presence is regularly invoked, and times of corporate song are foci of spiritual experience as worshipers sing loudly, raise hands, and close their eyes. Applause—for God, for worship leaders, for members—is also common; City Church's University District campus clapped a total of nineteen separate times during the Sunday worship service I attended. Prayers during worship often include repeated mention of the immediate time and place, with such locating phrases as "in this place" and "right now." Pastor Serena Wastman at The Journey of Faith prayed, "May your presence invade this place. This is a place, a holy place, filled with the Holy Spirit of God and his people." Bishop Ray Hampton's benediction at Seattle International Church included, "I anoint every individual in this place, right now in Jesus's name." One of the pastors at Community Dinners prayed, "Thank you for your presence in this place. It's moments like this that we taste and we experience you." This rhetoric of immediacy serves to heighten the sense that the event—this time and place, right here, right now—is a key node of God's presence and activity, and that this ought to be perceptible. The palpable immanence of God in worship is perhaps the most basic and essential element of HS spirituality. Figure 4.2, an image of Seattle International Church in worship, captures several key aspects of HS worship, including raised hands, the invitation for the Spirit to be present, and the rhetoric of immediacy ("in this place").

This God who comes near in worship is known as an omniscient and omnipotent interventionist who cares passionately about individuals. Pastoral prayers regularly attest to God's personal knowledge of "the circumstances and situations of everyone in this room" and God's ability to "speak to each one of our hearts."[45] In addition to these private interactions, God is most characteristically celebrated as "the Great Physician," an eager and proven Healer. Indeed, these churches are animated by their belief in and experience of miracles. In addition to accounts of physical healing, the miraculous is linked to profound, emotional moments of God's loving, guiding presence and to fortuitous circumstances that are interpreted as clear evidence of God's involvements in daily life. At The Journey of Faith,

FIGURE 4.2 Worship at Seattle International Church.
(Image courtesy of Seattle International Church)

in the midst of a chorus declaring "The lost are found / The blind will see / The lame will walk / The dead will live," the young worship leader offered her own testimony to the reality of God's healing work:

> These miracles still happen today. I have a scar on my hand that you can't even find any more because I asked for healing and it was gone. I have things in my heart that used to hurt me and take me down and I asked God for that healing and he's taken that.

Similarly, the co-pastor at City Church's University District campus offered a litany of testimonies to God's healing power and personal interest in the middle of a song declaring God's benevolent power.

> Even as we receive this song and we're reminded of a flood of the various people that I have been praying for week in and week out, year in and year out, even in this congregation of amazing people. From people that are battling their lives with cancer and have gotten clean bill of health from the doctor . . . to . . . a family in our church [that] recently got in a . . . car accident and the father was fighting for his life but it looks like he's coming out on the other side. To people that are battling just the deepest prayer and desire

of their heart, desiring to . . . get pregnant, yet all a sudden we have their baby showing up; we got the family checking their baby girl in . . . this morning. I just see the fight of our lives, but . . . all a sudden we see a God who holds the universe, who holds the world in the palm of his hand, but it is the same God that delights—the Bible says he delights in every single detail of our lives. And today I want to declare . . . this song again: "He holds the universe." That he's the same God, he delights in every detail of our lives, he's fighting for us, but the victory is gonna be won—Amen?

As both of these attestations to answered prayer illustrate, HS churches believe deeply in the power of prayer and God's willingness and ability to intervene in human affairs when God's people ask in faith.

The preceding quotation also points to the centrality and function of the Bible among HS churches. The Bible is to be both obeyed and revered as a vehicle for God's personal revelations. Leaders in these churches regularly pepper sentences with "the Bible says" and proceed to either cite memorized verses or paraphrase texts (sometimes quite loosely) for direct application. The Bible is believed to be not only the final authority on matters of doctrine and practice but also a "living and active" agent capable of cutting to the heart and demanding an immediate response of faith. The acts of faith proposed often include social or financial risk. Experiencing God's personal revelation through the Word is prized. Following the examples of biblical characters is considered more important than scholarly study of the Bible or theology. Pastor Wastman prefaced her church's shared dinner of shepherds' pie and lemonade by explaining,

> Most of us here have not been to Bible college, so we're not a bunch of theologians. We're just simple people that have just read our Bibles. . . . [W]hen I read the Bible, Jesus was eating with his disciples and he said: "When you break this bread, remember me. When you drink this drink, this wine, remember my blood." So . . . we're going to have a meal and it's going to be Communion.

Just as the church seeks to apply the Bible directly to its practice, personal Christian maturity is measured by a distinctive emphasis on obedience to God's will. This obedience includes both moral living and commitment to practices of devotion. Bishop Ray Hampton attributed the "sickness" of several of his members to their failure to "finish the prescription" they had been given by God.

> If you would have just kept remaining in your Word, and if you just would have kept fasting, if you would have kept coming to church, if you would have kept giving your tithes, if you would have kept giving your offering, if you would have kept loving people, giving an encouraging word, then you would have not had to start all over again.

Bishop Hampton's mention of giving tithes and offerings in this litany of prescribed Christian practices is indicative of the way churches in this model put distinctive emphasis on financial giving as a basic part of Christian faith and discipleship. Even at The Journey of Faith, a church composed primarily of high-school-age youth without substantial means, contributions were strongly admonished, both as an avenue for personal financial blessing ("Rob and I are abundantly blessed . . . because whatever He gives us is like a conduit—we give it away") and as a spiritual duty ("When you don't give that 10% to the church, you're robbing Him").

Mission Among Household of the Spirit Churches

HS churches respond to and reflect the trending characteristics of the Seattle context in unique ways. HS churches reflect the urban character of Seattle, both by virtue of where they can be found (largely in Rainier Valley—the poorer, less-gentrified, more ethnically diverse part of Seattle) and their generally weak sense of identification with a particular neighborhood.[46] With regard to technology, HS churches are less likely than the three other models to have a substantial web presence. This digital lag is largely because a significant percentage of HS churches exist among ethnic immigrant populations for whom access to technology is somewhat less prevalent than in the general population. Moreover, whereas dominant-culture individuals (especially in post-Christian contexts) readily use internet searches to find a church and typically scan church websites before attending, members of immigrant groups are more likely to rely upon family and in-group referrals.[47]

HS churches view their context as a foreign environment—both spiritually and, for ethnic minority congregations, culturally—but also as a place in need of God's miraculous touch and healing. Like GCT churches, they lament Seattle's progressive and post-Christian character, but they take a somewhat less proactive posture toward these realities. Rather than rallying around cries of world changing, they instead fortify their resolve to remain faithful despite the winds of dominant culture. Bishop Hampton, an African American, asserted a fundamental division between the church and the world: "There's only two races. Either you're a believer or you're an unbeliever." The preacher when I visited The Journey of Faith spoke of the waywardness of surrounding culture as a whole, and the need for Christians to resist conforming to its decaying trajectory.

> Unless you've been living under a rock someplace, you can't help but notice that there is a certain climate in the world today of sin being pushed on us. It's flagrant. It's aggressive. It's everywhere you turn. Sin. Sin. Sin. It's "accept this sin" and "accept that sin." . . . I've never, in the sixty years that I've been walking on this earth, seen anything like it . . . what the world is trying to push on you now is not normal. The world right now is not normal.

Such a dualistic vision and sin-sick sense of the context are certainly cause for guardedness among HS churches, but they are not taken as grounds for total withdrawal and disengagement. Rather, in such an environment members take a countercultural posture of resisting temptation while accepting a call to serve as personal agents of God's healing and rescue, seeking to save as many lost and desperate souls as possible. While this priority on evangelism is shared with GCT churches, churches in the HS model are less likely to prioritize relational approaches and more likely to invite "unsaved" friends to worship services and special events. This "come and see" approach makes sense given the heightened spiritual experiences that the HS events facilitate. Moreover, worship gatherings are understood as mission contexts because of the evangelistic invitations that typically conclude the events. These appeals are often made in the form of altar calls or invitations to pray along with the pastor and to raise a hand afterward ("while every head is bowed and every eye is closed") in order to indicate you have made a decision for Christ. The somewhat public character of these conversions enact the socially risky faith these churches aspire to.

In addition to invitational evangelism, some HS churches engage in mission by taking their most characteristic spiritual practice—prayer for God's miraculous intervention—out into the world. This most often takes place as prayers for physical healing. Both from the pulpit and in an interview, Pastor Verlon Fosner cited David Lim, a Pentecostal pastor in Singapore. According to Pastor Fosner, Lim's assessment is that Western Pentecostals' obsession with speaking in tongues has left them with "a gift you can't use in the street and cannot use in evangelism," whereas Asia and Africa had embraced the Pentecostal gift of healing—a much more evangelistically useful tool. One Sunday morning, Fosner concluded the service with Lim's typical benediction: "Remember you are Pentecostals: go heal somebody!" For Fosner and other HS leaders, being a Pentecostal is not only about how one experiences God in worship but also what kind of life and mission God has called one to. As Pastor Fosner told those gathered for worship, "I'm a Pentecostal—I breathe healing upon people. I breathe courage. I breathe life. I breathe boldness, but I breathe healing upon people." Leaders model this ministry in their prayers during worship, asking that members receive from the riches of God's blessing and healing.[48]

This posture of seeking to dispense the miraculous in everyday life is the central spirituality and mission for Church of the Undignified. Pastor Benji Rhodes teaches his flock to "just go and live and bring light, bring life, bring healing, bring miraculous [power to] . . . whomever you encounter . . . in normal day-to-day stuff, [like at the] grocery store." In the course of my fieldwork, I witnessed this mission in action firsthand as I was the beneficiary of prayers offered by pastors of three different HS churches.[49] On two occasions, the prayers I received included prophetic visions and words of encouragement—that is, apparent manifestations of spiritual gifting. In one case, a pastor assured me the book that would result from my project "will definitely sell into Lifeway [bookstores] . . . I just feel in my Spirit . . . if I'm a man of God, which I know I am." Another shared a vision of me as an old, well-respected professor carrying an "amazing satchel" containing all my published works. In both cases, these prayers—in a way characteristic in HS churches—forecasted my personal success and invoked supernatural power to provide me with personal encouragement and blessing.

Identity Among Household of the Spirit Churches

Identifying with a particular ethnic or cultural group is important to a majority of HS churches, including numerous and diverse Spanish-speaking, Asian, and African American congregations. As such, these churches are what sociologists refer to as "specialist" or "niche" congregations.[50] However, my fieldwork did not include sufficient field-work among such churches to gain insight into the role of their ethnic/cultural identity within their practical ecclesiology. This remains a task for further research.

HS churches are affiliated with Pentecostal or Charismatic denominations far more often than churches in other models, but a significant number of HS churches are nondenominational. Even among those affiliated with a denomination, informal networks seem to be at least as important as denominational ties.

Summary

Households of the Spirit gather to experience the presence of a miracle-working God in a foreign and fallen land. Their spirituality centers on emotionally charged worship events that proclaim and produce experiences of God's sensible immanence and miracle-working power. They stress the need to live obedient lives of biblical faith in holiness, devotion, public witness, and financial giving. While they seek to foster an environment and community safe and set apart, they also actively invite others into the sanctuary community, and some stress going out to offer supernatural blessings and healing prayers to others. This practical ecclesiological model presents the church as a temple of God's powerful presence and an extended family of faith called and empowered by the Spirit to offer supernatural healing in a sin-sick world.

Church as New Community

About 10% of new Seattle churches share key features of the New Community (NC) model. These churches reflect an approach to spirituality that is worship and community centered, strong denominational identity, and a socially embodied approach to mission. This practical ecclesiology brings together eschatological and institutional hopes for renewal and sets its community-centered progressivism in contrast to dogmatic, countercultural, exclusivist, and proselytizing expressions of Christianity. Commonalities among NC churches include progressive cultural and spiritual values, sacramental-liturgical worship practices, identification with mainline Protestant denominations, and a core mission commitment to creating a community of belonging that—along with their practices of contemplation and advocacy—witnesses to their values.

The majority of the churches within this model are recognizable as "emerging churches." This designation and movement arose, in the U.S. context, near the turn of the millennium, primarily among youth-focused Evangelicals, and was the topic of a flurry of publishing.[51] More recently, many Evangelicals eschewed affiliation with the more progressive "emergent" label, and often with the broader "emerging" brand as well.[52] As a result, in the United States today, self-identified emerging churches are predominantly theologically progressive. Recent social scientific research among emerging churches has highlighted key traits and practices, such as deconstruction, inclusivity, participatory-experiential worship, conversation, nonhierarchical leadership, and nontraditional gathering spaces.[53] While many NC churches are emerging churches, the model also includes a small number of new mainline congregations for which "emerging" does not quite fit.

NC churches fit most comfortably within the Community model identified by Penny Becker. They share with it a high valuation of worship and widespread experiences of belonging, as well as a distinctive commitment to expressing the values of its membership in the everyday life of the church. They typically make decisions through open, democratic, or consensus-building processes that facilitate community cohesion and function as a distinctive mode of visible witness.[54] Adult religious education in NC churches often takes place in nontraditional formats that prioritize "deep listening," conversation, cultural engagement, and/or the arts.[55] In keeping with Becker's Community model, most NC churches are not involved in extensive political action. However, the reason for this among NC churches is not an attempt to maintain community cohesion as with Becker's model. Indeed, few NC churches shy away from advocating for progressive positions on divisive political issues. Rather, their lack of political action is better understood as a factor of their limited size and influence, as well as the logic of their approach to religious witness, which is explored in a later section.

Paul's People of God ecclesiology echoes in New Community churches, but without the emphasis on the multicultural dimension of the new humanity that Paul envisioned in the union of Jew and Gentile. Instead, they claim the eschatological and social dimensions of People of God as a vanguard of the new creation. NC churches seek to embody God's coming social order through inclusion, and they believe their unique community practice itself is its primary enactment of witness.[56] There are also traces of the diversely gifted Body of Christ and Johannine Community of

Equals that come to expression in a priority on democratic and participatory culture. While unlike the countercultural posture of John's Beloved Community, the model shares with it a critical posture toward the other Christian groups in its local ecology.

The "newness" of New Communities is not merely descriptive of their recent establishment. They are "new" in at least four ways. First, NC churches assert that their gospel and practice are a refreshing departure from old, dogmatic, and culture-condemning expressions of Christian faith.[57] They identify themselves with progressive social trends, and pronounce sacred the culturally new. Like Niebuhr's Christ of Culture liberals, NC churches find substantial harmony between their Christian ideals and those celebrated in Seattle's progressive milieu. Second, churches in the NC model are "what's new" within their denominational ecologies. They are self-consciously celebrated instances of mainline institutional renewal and innovation.[58] Third, and relatedly, in their practice, NC churches intentionally recover and renew ancient liturgical and sacramental spiritual practices by adapting and integrating them with contemporary technology and culture.[59] Fourth, as already suggested, they can be represented theologically as sacraments of the new humanity; they are communities that celebrate their ordinariness but also view themselves in an eschatological light. Though their eschatological identity is typically expressed in muted terms (they describe themselves as a "progressive" community moving "forward" or "onward"), there is nonetheless a subtle prevailing sense that their fellowship offers a foretaste of what God intends for human community as a whole.

As "communities," NC churches exist primarily as a web of relationships.[60] Though resembling Dulles's Mystical Communion in the interpersonal nature of their unity, NC churches—unlike Dulles's model—readily include within the fellowship those without explicit Christian faith. Like Dulles's Servant model, belonging within these churches is not for believers only but, rather, is actively inclusive of all who participate (in any way) in the life of these communities. This focus on relational intimacy also inclines NC churches toward a relative smallness in size that matches their distaste for proactive evangelism, recruitment, and church growth efforts.

Spirituality Among New Community Churches

New Community churches combine progressive sensibilities with liturgical and sacramental practices, forging a spirituality that embraces mystery and ritual while standing in stark contrast to the dominant Evangelical pattern. The most distinctive aspect of NC spirituality is its high regard for the ambiguous and mysterious dimensions of life and faith. The service I attended at Valley & Mountain concluded with this quote from poet Rainer Maria Rilke as a blessing:

> Be patient toward all that is unsolved in your heart and try to love the questions themselves, like locked rooms and like books that are now written in a very foreign tongue. Do not now seek the answers, which cannot be given you because you would not be able to live them. And the point is, to live everything. Live the questions now. Perhaps you will then gradually, without noticing it, live along some distant day into the answer.[61]

Those regarded as exemplars of spiritual maturity among NC churches are at peace "living in the tension," authentic, transparent about their own weaknesses, and relationally open to others.[62] Respondents to the congregational survey conducted among Wits' End Church identified "humility, listening, and openness" and "embracing ambiguity and divine mystery" as the top two markers of Christian maturity from a list of eleven. Mystery is ritualized in the frequent celebration of the Eucharist, but their embrace of ambiguity, indeterminacy, and non-propositional, embodied, collectively discerned truth is a thread that runs through the whole of their practice.

Worship gatherings are at the heart of NC spirituality. While their worship follows a liturgical calendar and incorporates traditional liturgies, it is also deeply intentional in its *ressourcement*.[63] NC churches filter and adapt traditions with their own context and congregation in mind in order to ensure that they are "life-giving" and "make sense to us."[64] At Wits' End Church and Church of the Apostles, this is accomplished by inviting groups to "curate" a liturgical season—that is, to take responsibility for the worship aesthetics and practices that will mark that part the Christian calendar for the year. When I visited during Ordinary Time, Wits' End invited people to "bring an item from their lives and tell of its sacred significance" and then to leave these "ordinary icons"—a teapot, framed picture, toys— on the altar for the duration of the season. In these and innumerable other ways, NC churches creatively collaborate to facilitate participatory experiences of worship.[65] Some emerging NC churches not only adapt the shared liturgy but also make space for individuals to disperse and engage with one of several available practices, such as walking a labyrinth, meditating before an icon, beautifying a sidewalk with chalk, or packing a lunch for the homeless. Pastor Helmiere at Valley & Mountain described this practice whimsically as a "choose-your-own-adventure kind of liturgy."[66]

Corporate song among NC churches serves as a key site of intersection between Christian tradition and local culture. Traditional hymns are common in each of the four models, but in uniquely nuanced ways in each. While for churches in the GCT model hymns lend historical language and authority to "the Gospel" as the orthodox faith, among NC churches hymns provide those who have been burned by negative church experiences (in which hymns were also sung) with the opportunity to experience continuity with the fondly remembered aspects of their childhood faith, as well as to reclaim these powerful symbols by situating them within a progressive faith community. For example, at Church of the Apostles, worship included singing of the traditional hymn "Immortal, Invisible God Only Wise," which not only echoed with stalwart tradition but also affirmed their embrace of divine mystery "in light inaccessible hid from our eyes." More distinctive for this model, however, is the use of songs from the Taizé community. Taizé is an ecumenical monastic community in France whose simple, contemplative songs have become popular internationally.[67] With repetitive, chant-like melodies and lyrics often in Latin and commonly drawn from the Psalms and other Scriptural texts, Taizé singing provides NC churches with another point of connection to an aesthetically ancient Christian tradition.

Weekly celebration of Communion or Eucharist is the norm among churches in this model.[68] Eucharist is endowed with multiple layers of meaning, but most fundamentally it is regarded as a sacred meal that mysteriously provides spiritual nourishment. Instead of dramatizing "the Gospel," as among GCT churches, Communion in NC churches is itself a manifestation of the gospel they embrace—it is God's unqualified welcome and blessing. Receiving Communion is, thus, receiving the gospel itself. Participants at Wits' End indicated that celebrating Communion was far and away more important for their personal way of life than any of the thirty-three other options, including personal Bible reading and attending worship. Declaring the openness of the table to any who would come is also characteristic and illustrative of the inclusive nature of these communities. The openness of Church of the Apostles' Communion table has been proclaimed in neon (figure 4.3). As Ivar Hillesland, pastor of Church of the Apostles, announced, "All are welcome to draw near and share these holy mysteries of God's love and forgiveness." This wide-openness is further practiced via the gluten-free and nonalcoholic elements that are commonly made available.

Sermons among NC churches are shorter than in other models— typically about fifteen minutes. They are delivered in a conversational tone and are offered by non-clergy members of the community with some regularity. However, preaching is not the only mode by which they encounter the Word.[69] In addition to multiple Scripture readings, several NC churches make space for shared discernment of God's Word for the community, sometimes described as a "communal sermon." At Wits' End, the sermon is followed each week with discussion around tables, which Pastor Phil Nellis believes "kind of asserts that the preacher does not have the last word. But the gospel, as we've heard it, rumbles in the dialogue and the community and we take it with us." Such worship practices—as well as the

FIGURE 4.3 Church of the Apostle's "Open Table".
(Image courtesy of Church of the Apostles, Seattle)

"theology pub" conversations that several NC churches host—enact their characteristic belief that dialog and conversation are the proper responses to life's ambiguities and the mystery of God.

It is within this framework that the Bible functions as a normative conversation starter rather than as an authority in the traditional, decisive sense. On the one hand, NC churches are free to critique and express discomfort with the Scriptural texts, but on the other hand, they are committed to wrestling with them when they come around in the lectionary schedule. As Pastor Hillesland stated before reading from Hosea, "The first reading tonight is from a book I find troubling and I don't like it a lot, but it's in Scripture and as we go through Scripture we have to encounter these passages and deal with them." Moreover, NC churches believe that these unsettling encounters can provoke them, expose truth, and lead them back to God. Becca Shirley, a Covenant Participant (member) at Wits' End, captured this relationship with Scripture in a reflection on Psalm 15, posted to the church's blog: "I am enraged and want to dismiss the words as futile . . . even in saying so . . . I find that Scripture has brought the despair that I so often hold well-concealed within myself out in the open, into conversation with God."[70] The Bible is often disturbing, but it must be grappled with, for in that disruption, NC participants encounter the mysterious God.

Corporate prayer among NC churches includes scripted prayers, as well as, occasionally, spontaneous ones. Language for God is diverse and regularly draws upon creative and feminine metaphors. The Lord's Prayer is the most prevalent form of communal prayer, but corporate prayers of confession are also common. These practices of communal prayer invite the congregation to speak in one voice, uniting those present in posture and purpose before God and thus creating of those gathered a true, spiritual community. At Valley & Mountain, a time of petitionary prayer was introduced with these words: "Join me now as we seek the healing power of community and the liberating power of God our source through the act of communal prayer." In addition to praying for their own needs, NC churches regularly include in their petitions prayers for the needy and hurting, along with concerns for local or national situations in need of peace and justice.

The "sacred consciousness" characteristic of this model is one in which the ordinary stuff of life—bodies, emotions, matter, nature, people, conversations, the arts—are regarded as sites of God's mysterious presence.[71] This sacramental-incarnational spirituality not only shapes their worship but also provides a theological cornerstone for other practices that honor the embodied nature of human life, celebrate the ordinary, and find expression through various artistic media.

Use of labyrinths is rare in the other models but common among NC churches. However, their most distinctive practice of embodied spirituality is yoga.[72] Some emerging NC churches include yoga as an occasional option during their liturgical free time, but more often it is offered as a class open to the community in hopes that it can serve as a point of connection with body-and-spirit-minded Seattleites. NC churches show little concern about the connections between yoga and Eastern religions—reflecting a characteristic openness to interreligious engagement.[73] Still, they are sensitive enough to the novelty of yoga as a liturgical practice that they do offer rationales for its compatibility with Christian spirituality: Columbia City of Hope describes their practice of yoga as "going through the body to quiet the mind and listen to the Spirit"; All Pilgrims includes yogic movements in a class they have called "Body-Praying the Gospel Story."

In addition to the importance of weekly celebration of Communion—a sacred token meal with a bit of bread and sip of drink—NC churches are also distinct for the regularity and intentionality with which they share more substantial meals. While these range in form and theological framing from community suppers for the needy and potlucks to dinner churches and agape feasts, these shared meals address the basic need of embodied persons to eat, while at the same time the ordinary table becomes a holy place of conversation and community.

The arts have an especially important place among NC churches.[74] Original music and artwork are often present in worship and contain multiple layers of meaning.[75] Pastor and artist Phil Nellis's description of the large crucifix made by "many hands" at Wits' End (figure 4.4) exemplifies this.

[I]t's modeled after the Cross of San Damiano where Saint Francis received his conversion and his call in this dilapidated old church that was falling apart and he heard Christ speak to him to rebuild the church . . . that's a big part of Wits' End's legacy: imagining the church to be a different place and then rebuilding that. There's a lot of particular imagery on that icon that we brought in that was unique to Wits' End. . . . On the sides there's two waves and those are styled after . . . our original logo that I drew . . . the boat is on these waves from Psalm 107 where we get our name . . . there's a

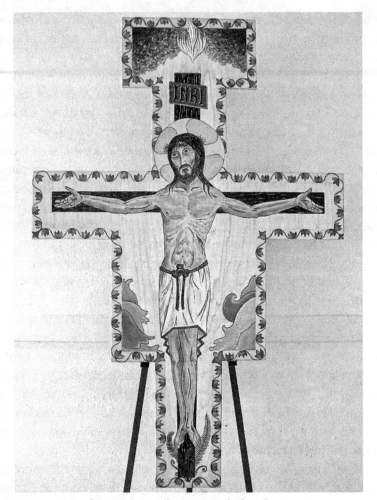

FIGURE 4.4 Cross of San Damiano by Wits' End Church.
(Image courtesy of Wits' End Church)

fern at the bottom which is a desire to contextualize [to] the Pacific
Northwest a little bit. And the fern in Christian symbolism is an
image of humility. So it's down there at the feet of Christ. And the
waves are on either side of Christ which is kind of . . . the Exodus
is a huge narrative, core narrative for us in terms of through the
waters and into freedom. The Exodus, and baptism.

As Pastor Nellis indicates, this central piece of communal art weaves
historical and biblical threads (St. Francis, Ps. 107) with unique features of

the community's identity (waves), sense of mission ("rebuild the church"), and local context (fern).[76] The musical arts are especially important to Church of the Apostles, a commitment expressed in their patronage of a performing arts group called The Opiate Mass.[77] When I visited Church of the Apostles, they were considering launching a music school as a ministry of the church. In addition, several NC churches have close partnerships with nonprofit art groups.[78]

Decision making, like worship, is a participatory endeavor in the NC practical ecclesiology. In most, the whole community is invited to participate in the church's important moments of decision. At Valley & Mountain, they describe their approach as "a modified consensus." Wits' End has a board, officially designated as "The Troublemakers," but on important matters they serve to make proposals for a congregational vote after "a process of deep listening to the community, to each other, and to the Spirit." All Pilgrims, reflecting the statehouse architecture of its historic building, is governed by democratic principles. When their newest pastor was hired, he purposefully went about "disorganizing" the community so it could "become a little more flattened as an organization."[79]

Identity Among New Community Churches

Nearly all NC churches are affiliated with mainline Protestant denominations, and they evidence a self-consciousness regarding their place within their denominational ecologies by taking on roles as celebrated examples of institutional innovation and renewal.[80] They are often featured in denominational reports and promotional videos as sterling specimens of what the denomination aspires to be. Their primary partnerships and affiliations are with other pastors and churches in their own denominations. Emerging NC churches regularly have significant relationships with emerging churches in other denominations, but these partnerships rarely extend beyond mainline Protestantism. In addition to providing relational and resource support, denominational identities offer an institutional sense of the rootedness they embody in their liturgical and practices. NC churches, though innovative, identify themselves as part of a larger church with a longer history. Their leaders and participants often express a certain attraction to Catholicism and Orthodox Christianity. Mainline Protestant denominations, while of more recent vintage, provide both centuries of tradition and, importantly, affirmation of their progressive and democratic values.

Even though their denominational affiliations were found in the survey to set them apart, equally important is the strong distinction they draw between themselves and self-conscious distinction from the dominant players in the new church field—conservative Evangelicals, most especially the now-defunct Mars Hill Church. This polarizing multisite GCT church—and its charismatic, cussing pastor, Mark Driscoll—had been a consistent target for critique in the local media, especially from *The Stranger*, an alternative weekly paper. NC churches—in sync with their progressive context—have looked to Mars Hill as their primary foil. As one pastor told me less than a minute into our phone conversation: "We're fun, liberal, mainline—so we'd be very different than Mars Hill."

The strength of this differentiation is likely related to the high percentage of NC attendees who describe themselves as wounded or disillusioned by fundamentalist or evangelical churches.[81] The accompanying experiences of "deconstruction and deconversion are central" not only to these individuals but also to the corporate identity of these churches as communities of healing and hope for those shipwrecked by bad church experiences.[82] For these communities, Mars Hill functioned as a larger-than-life symbol of all that can and has gone wrong with Christianity—patriarchy, homophobia, violence, shunning, dogmatism, celebrity-worship, and greed.[83] It is likely that the foil has served them fairly well to this point, since research has suggested that evangelical megachurches are a benefit to the vitality of mainline congregations nearby.[84] But the dissolution of Mars Hill Church in January 2015, following months of turmoil and Driscoll's resignation,[85] poses a challenge to NC identity—though Evangelicals will continue to dominate the new church field.[86]

Mission Among New Community Churches

Churches in the NC model describe Seattle favorably as a progressive city with residents who long for meaningful community. The lush and scenic natural environment and LGBTQ-friendly character are commonly celebrated aspects of the Seattle context, and both were mentioned during corporate prayer at Valley & Mountain: one participant gave thanks "for the sunshine that keeps coming back" and another "for the opportunity to be in the Pride parade, and actually be proud about my city and my state and where we're going." The same two issues are interwoven into All Pilgrims Christian Church's efforts to create the "Same Love Garden" on their grounds, in partnership with local pop-artist Macklemore. While

NC churches celebrate Seattle's progressivism, they also sense its need for spaces of meaningful community, and believe this is what the church is called to provide. Drawing a connection between Seattle's grayscale atmosphere and a lonely population, Pastor Hillesland explained the opportunity:

> Seattle—just because of the sheer number of days of darkness—is somewhat of a city where people will look down [at the ground]. People always talk about this "Seattle freeze." And so that actually gives the church a unique place where we can form honest community and create friendships in ways that are not threatening.[87]

This assessment of the context and opportunity syncs with the model's ecclesial self-understanding and mission approach; both point to the ideal of community NC churches seek to live by and, thus, implicitly offer to others.

NC churches practice mission primarily by living out their shared values in community; their witness is enacted foremost by the ways their spirituality shapes their life together.[88] When they invoke the Trinity in describing their sense of mission, it is most often to speak of the divine fellowship they seek to emulate as a community rather than to point to the Father's sending of the Son as a precedent for outreach. Instead of being a church that "does mission," NC churches believe their distinctive culture and practices provide a vital witness and can lead to both extensions of that community and to personal transformation. Greg Turk, pastor of All Pilgrims Christian Church, offered a "classic story of All Pilgrims" testifying to the transformational impact his church had on one member.

> I think in his young adult experience of coming out [as homosexual, he] felt excluded . . . to the degree that he moved away from home and really struggled with his own . . . sense of identity. [His] relationships . . . were stressed to say the least. And then [he] became homeless and drug addicted and out of that, in a process of recovery, found All Pilgrims. And here . . . that was seven years ago. He just bought his first house last year, and is a leader in the congregation who does wonderful healing ministry and is a transformed person. So to hear his story told that: in this community of faith he found that God loves him and found in that new life. And in that new life was able to embrace more fully who he is and the future that God has for him and to live in that. I think that's a story that's told

here so often . . . that folks come wishing and wondering if, in fact, God really loves them and if so, could they maybe find a glimpse of that somewhere, in the look, and the embrace, and the welcome of another. And every Sunday this church does such a wonderful, remarkable, even miraculous job of expressing that.

As this account illustrates, NC churches narrate transformation as attributable to experiences of their extraordinarily welcoming, loving communities, which speak for themselves. That is, their social practices enact their mission. Whereas GCT churches talk about radical discipleship, churches in the NC model are more likely to speak about radical hospitality. Their inclusivism extends not only to those rejected by other Christian groups—such as sexual and gender identity minorities—but also to nonbelievers and anyone else who desires to participate in their communal life in whatever way. This "permeable boundary" of community is ritualized in the open Communion table, but it is also apparent in the way members describe people who may show up only for yoga or be a regular at a local pub frequented by members but not participate in the church's programs; these individuals, too, are "part of our community."[89]

Talk about justice is especially common among NC churches, but their use of the language of liberation is more distinctive. These communities pray corporately for justice and liberation and for specific political and social issues.[90] The most common contemporary justice issue engaged is LGBTQ rights and inclusion, but they also attend to other politically progressive concerns, notably environmentalism and immigration.[91] The most activist example of the model is Valley & Mountain, whose minister, John Helmiere, posted a blog post about being brutally beaten by police at an Occupy protest at the Port of Seattle. By his account, when an officer asked who he was and what he was doing there, he replied, with eschatological vigor, "I'm a minister of the gospel of Jesus Christ; I believe another world is possible!" His story generated nearly 200 responses on the church blog. While celebrated, this type of activism is the exception among NC churches.[92] Though they speak about and pray for justice, most act on the level of compassion, providing opportunities for works of service in the local community. Service takes shape among NC churches much as in other churches, through partnerships. They work with community organizations to provide meals to the homeless, and—more characteristically—opportunities for the arts.[93] Unlike GCT churches who serve in order to build a bridge to evangelism,

NC churches serve primarily as a means of enacting and demonstrating the values of their community.[94]

Summary

Churches in the New Community model embody a practical ecclesiology that is at once eschatological in its underlying vision and institutional in its concrete identity. In stark contrast to the conservative Evangelicals whose countercultural postures have left many participants disillusioned, NC churches celebrate the social progressivism of their context as a foreshadowing of the new humanity they seek to embody in their authentic fellowship. Their community embodiment of inclusive and participatory corporate life is their chief form of witness. At the center of their practice is worship that integrates ancient and institutional liturgical practices with contemporary arts and technology, thus exercising their identity as mainline innovators. The open Communion table at the center of their worship enacts the gospel of God's unqualified welcome into community and reflects their embrace of the mysterious and ambiguous presence of God hidden in everyday, embodied life.

Church as Neighborhood Incarnation

Neighborhood Incarnation (NI) churches are deeply rooted in their local communities and their corporate life is shaped by the proximate needs they discern.[95] They reflect a strong place-based identity, a commitment to contribute to their neighborhoods and make a socially embodied witness, and a spirituality that is both mission centered and community centered. The Neighborhood Incarnation model describes about 25% of the field, including churches from both sides of the wide divide between Evangelicals and Progressives. Like GCT churches, NI churches are proactive in forging new relationships and serving those outside of the church. Like NC churches, they understand their community identity eschatologically, blur the lines of belonging, and practice their belief that God is present in the everyday stuff of life. In addition, among NI exemplars were three instances of the Household of the Spirit model. Like the HS model, NI churches aspire for family-like intimacy and speak easily about the contemporary work of the Spirit. The NI model is not, however, merely a composite of, or middle way between, these other models. While it does include some of the features characteristic of each, it is more sharply defined by its own, distinctive emphases on the local parish, extra-congregational forms of ecclesial life, and an approach to mission centered in hospitality and service.[96]

Neighborhood Incarnation churches bring together important elements of types identified by sociological typologies, but they also represent a genuinely new development that diverges from traditional congregations.[97] Like the Civic mission orientation and the Pillar self-image, they have a strong sense of geographical rootedness paired with eagerness to be good citizens. But unlike Civic and Pillar churches, NI churches—like new churches more generally—rarely have a historic building to serve as a symbol of their community presence or out of which to base their ministry. They are Pillar churches without pillared buildings. Still, having a tangible, public presence in the neighborhood is a central strategy for these churches. Many have expressed this through the creation of "third places"—informal environments that foster bonds among neighbors.[98] Also breaking the Civic mold, Neighborhood Incarnation churches' sense of good citizenship makes them neither membership centered nor content with existing social structures. Instead, like Dudley's Servant churches they embrace an existence "for others" and often make caring for society's least an important practice. In affinity with Dulles's Communion model, they view the church as a web of relationships, but unlike this type, these relations are understood to exist as a visible—rather than invisible—reality in a delimited place.

To identify the church in this model as an "incarnation" is to suggest that the ecclesiological model is rooted Christologically in the incarnation and takes shape in contextualized ways as both social bodies (communities) and material presence (gathering spaces).[99] NI churches look to the Christmas miracle—when "The Word became flesh and blood and moved into the neighborhood"[100]—as the normative example of God's way of going about mission, emphasizing the learning posture and long years of obscurity that preceded Jesus's public ministry. Like the Lukan model of church as Followers of Jesus, NI churches intentionally seek to imitate Jesus, especially in his ministry of hospitality and care for society's sick, poor, disenfranchised, and outcast members. With this incarnational framework for ministry, the shape of their organizational life (times, places, and roles) is not limited by traditional congregational practices but, rather, is formed in freer response to local realities. Stressing that the church is the people, NI communities exist as social bodies that strive for such solidarity that their neighbors, too, are "the people" who make up their communities of belonging. These new social bodies incarnate or materialize into new physical gathering spaces "for the community" rather than for Christ followers alone.

Designating these new churches as "incarnations" is also intended to evoke the Body of Christ metaphor. However, for NI churches (as well as many other churches), this fundamental ecclesiological image is less often invoked, as Paul did, to promote internal appreciation for the diversity of giftedness within the body. It is more commonly utilized to stress the church's mandate to serve, the charge to act as "the hands and feet of Jesus." Indeed, NI churches emphasize Jesus's ministry of service and table fellowship and strive for continuity with this way of Jesus by prioritizing the work of creating hospitable space and offering concrete help. For these churches, being the Body of Christ incarnate means being a community that exists and acts in tangible, local, relational ways—through such physical things as neighborhood spaces, warm hugs, and cups of coffee.

Identity Among Neighborhood Incarnation Churches

NI churches are linked to a diverse set of denominations, with the Christian Reformed Church being the best represented. Many are linked in networks with the Seattle School of Theology and Psychology and/or with Parish Collective, both of which have recently become international champions for neighborhood expressions of church.[101] But more important than these institutional affiliations are NI churches' core identification with their neighborhood and their innovation with regard to patterns of corporate life.

The defining feature of this model of church is its deep and guiding identification with its immediate neighborhood as parish.[102] NI churches ground their rationale for embracing bounded-parish ministry by appeals to both theological anthropology—specifically, the inherent sense of scale appropriate to embodied human existence—and the present cultural moment, which they describe as characterized by the failures of modern commuter culture and digital isolation.[103]

NI churches understand themselves as Christian communities in, of, and for their neighborhoods. Not only are their gathering spaces located in these neighborhoods but so, too, are many of their homes. Thus, they are not only neighborhood churches but, in fact, also the people of the neighborhood.[104] When I visited Valley & Mountain, I was greeted with the friendly but nonetheless pointed question: "Are you in the neighborhood?"

Indeed, NI churches stress the value of living residentially within the parish, celebrate church members who relocate into the neighborhood, and even discourage church visitors who attend services while living in other areas.[105] Their parish identity is also foundational for their approach to mission as *for* and *with* the neighborhood (rather than as mission *to* the neighborhood).[106]

Several NI pastors described themselves as chaplains to the neighborhood and intentionally structure their schedules to limit their church responsibilities and free up space for building relationships with neighbors and stakeholders in the life of the community. Such a strong parish identity blurs the lines between insider and outsiders traditionally associated with church membership. As Randy Rowland, pastor of Sanctuary, told me, he often answers questions about the size of his church with this quip: "[my church is] about 17,000 people, of which 6,000 a month come through the Green Bean [church-run coffee shop], and about a hundred or so on any given week come to Sanctuary [worship]. But that's how big my church is, 'cause that's my parish. And I feel like I'm a pastor of that neighborhood."

Neighborhood Incarnation churches diverge from the traditional congregational mold in which church is functionally conflated with a Sunday morning worship hour in a dedicated religious building.[107] Indeed, their *place* (neighborhood) matters far more than a designated ecclesiastical *space*. The reasons for this are both pragmatic (buildings are difficult for new churches to acquire) and theological. They regard the church as the People of God in the neighborhood, wherever they might happen to gather, and whenever they are gathered "in Christ's name."[108] As Andy Carlson, a pastor at Awake, told visitors,

> We sort of identify by our spaces but also we met in a backyard last week, we met in people's houses in the past, we jostle back and forth here [between the storefront "neighborhood living room" and Chinese restaurant]. We—if you need to know what Awake Church is—it is us as a people and so please just spend some time getting to know one another.

As the authors of *The New Parish* have noted, when the followers of Christ in a neighborhood start to see themselves (rather than a building) as the church, "every building becomes a potential 'church building'" because it is a building in which the church—the People of God—may be present and attentive to God.[109]

In the NI model, the spaces in which the people (the church) ought to gather and the proper patterns of shared life together are not treated as fixed or handed down. They seek to forge a contextually Christian way of life together as followers of Jesus in the neighborhood. They do not feel constrained by the congregational template. Neither are they rigid in their appropriation of their theological traditions, although these are often retained in creative ways as they adapt them to parish-centered ministry.[110] As Verlon Fosner, pastor of Community Dinners, writes: "We believe [dinner churches are] what it looks like when God's kingdom is happening in a neighborhood." Even while they break the congregational mold, NI churches assert the ecclesiality and historical validity of their nontraditional Christian communities. "Community Dinners . . . are not a feeding program or an outreach; they are dinner churches modeled after the Agape Feasts of the first century." Like other NI churches, Community Dinners has found a way to give authentic expression to their theological and spiritual tradition within a neighborhood-centered embodiment. As an Assemblies of God church whose Pentecostal tradition emphasizes the palpable presence of the Holy Spirit in worship environments, Community Dinners intentionally prays for God's restoring presence at its meals in the belief that this is the best gift they have to offer their neighbors. Multiple attenders told me that this gathering did, in fact, have an intangible warmth atypical of a "homeless feed." When local artist Joshua Boulet showed up for the neighborhood meal he noted both the unique atmosphere and the family-likeness also typical of HS churches (see figure 4.5).

> When I stumbled upon Community Dinners I immediately recognized the community there: the warmth, the kindness, the sharing, the love. That is what made me come back and eventually [do] the drawing. I tried to capture the "family" feeling the dinners provided, and I wanted to include the people that make it so special.

The combination of church-as-community and neighborhood-as-parish seems to free up NI churches to make innovative departures from some of the features typical of U.S. churches: they are markedly less likely to identify as "congregations," more likely to identify with some other designation such as "missional community"; and they are more likely to gather in nontraditional spaces and at times other than Sunday morning. Sociologist Stephen Warner's definition of the "congregational form" highlights how NI churches diverge from it: a congregation is "(1) a voluntary membership association, whose identity is (2) defined more by the

FIGURE 4.5 Sketch of Community Dinners in Greenwood, by Joshua Boulet.
(Image courtesy of Joshua Boulet)

people who form it than the territory they inhabit (cf. the "parish" form of organization)."[111] As will be explored in the following sections, the extra-congregational identity pattern among NI churches has significant implications, including a decentering of worship and reorientation of church spaces around mission.

Mission Among Neighborhood Incarnation Churches

Churches that embody the NI model reflect and engage with Seattle's nationally trending characteristics in a variety of ways. Like most Seattle church plants, they are very conscious of Seattle's unchurched majority, and are hopeful that their unique approach to church might draw in some who are disinterested in more traditional congregations. However, the degree of ambition and urgency with regard to growth and conversion varies. This largely depend on whether a particular NI church's spirituality is more rooted in evangelical or in progressive patterns.

NI churches describe Seattle as a city of neighborhoods, revealing a fairly sophisticated understanding of its urban character. Thus, the primary context in which they locate themselves is not the city qua city but, rather, their own neighborhood with its particular corners, cafés, and characters. NI leaders are fluent in the language of urban dynamics—gentrification, walking villages, mixed-use zoning—and interpret their environs with the help of such frames. More saliently, they describe their parishes with a refreshing blend of idealism and realism, as sites of beauty, need, and hope.[112] Aware of the low levels of social cohesion among Seattleites, NI churches (like NC churches) prioritize offering community to neighbors. While typically led by a core of young, hip professionals who are comfortable in Seattle's technological milieu, NI churches do not rely heavily on social media for community building or recruitment. This reflects their central commitments to neighborhood relationships and human-to-human interactions that do not depend upon technological tools, though they are augmented by them. NI churches celebrate certain aspects of Seattle's progressive culture while holding no single position on others. They generally share a common interest with the wider urban population in improving the plight of the poor, supporting increased minimum wages, and pursuing environmental sustainability. Though NI churches stress welcoming all neighbors into community, among NI churches there are a diversity of views on formal LGBTQ inclusion.

Their approach to mission arises from their parish identity, is understood as a spiritual practice in itself, and takes shape as mission for the neighborhood. They believe that the church ought to be a catalyst for their neighborhoods' becoming better places to live, work, and play. Thus, mission takes shape as they discern neighborhood needs and sense the prompting and resources of God to respond. Respondents to the congregational survey at Community Dinners indicated how closely intertwined spirituality is with their service; they reported feeling closest to God when "serving the needy, the poor, the sick, or the imprisoned." Their mission is also intertwined with their local identity. Pastor Ben Katt indicated that mission for Awake is driven by "whatever is in our neighborhood." Such an unspecified mission requires these churches to invest considerable time and attention to listening to neighbors and seeking to understand the dynamics and forces at work. For Awake, located in Seattle's "redlight district," "the main themes that continue to emerge are mental health issues, homelessness, sexual exploitation, and substance abuse . . . so we're trying to grow [our mission efforts] . . . in each of those areas." Indeed, engagement with urban challenges through compassionate service is common among these churches. Community Dinners provides meals in a "family dinner table" atmosphere five days a week in Seattle neighborhoods and is working toward building low-income housing to assist some of the members of the communities they have formed.

Not all churches in this model have a primary mission of helping those on society's fringes, however. What is universal among NI churches is a commitment to facilitating relationships among residents of the neighborhood. Similar to NC churches, the contextual need that NI churches most consistently address is the longing for community; they offer humanizing relationships. Many began developing the church by hosting neighborhood gatherings like barbecues and block parties. Union Church aims "to be a viable expression of God's love and truth by being an asset to the South Lake Union Neighborhood," and they enact this mission through "an active chocolate and coffee café that serves as a place of connection and community for the residents and workers in a new developing neighborhood."[113] This focus on building relationships reflects a need characteristic of Seattle as a whole. As noted earlier, Seattle's "social cohesion" is among the lowest among similar communities in the country, with Seattle ranked as 48th out of 51 for the frequency of residents talking to their neighbors.[114]

Aware of this need for community in their neighborhoods, many churches in this model have responded by opening "third places." Third places are comfortable spaces for neighbors to experience belonging and enter into conversations beyond their homes and workplaces (first and second places, respectively).[115] The buildings that NI churches talk about most are not their worship spaces but their third places. In Seattle, church-based third places have materialized primarily as coffee shops, event venues, community gardens, community meals, coworking spaces, and "neighborhood living rooms."[116] These community spaces are intended to function much as the stately church building does for the Pillar self-image; NI churches actively embody their intention to be good neighbors and citizens by creating spaces for the benefit of the community. These community spaces are paired with a strong commitment to hospitality as a mission priority. Indeed, the spaces themselves are often crafted to evoke and facilitate the home-like experiences of kitchens and living rooms. They are places intended to foster a sense of belonging and ease of conversation, and they are lubricated with food and drink—meals, home-garden–grown produce, and, as you would expect in Seattle, plentiful coffee.

The success of these third places is measured largely in the depth of relationships they facilitate. Lisa Carlson, the program director of Awake's third place, the Aurora Commons, shown in figure 4.6, spoke with an emotional quiver when she described it as "one of the only places I've ever been where I feel like people really, truly live as if they belong to one another in the world."[117] Those NI churches that are unable to muster the resources needed to establish these kinds of venues instead intentionally plan gatherings in public places—especially cafés and parks. In every case, NI churches intentionally infuse these shared environments with hospitality in the form of food and conversation.

After an arson fire destroyed The Green Bean, a coffee-shop run by Sanctuary, the church leadership considered retiring the project, which had never been profitable. They debated instead trying something else like a laundromat that could get them more connected to the poor of their community. One of the pastors told me what happened next:

> We were thinking about closing The Green Bean. The community said, "You can't!" So they went around and collected money for us. Gave us this check for like $4000. Just, "we want you here." The radio and TV stations all pursued us, followed everything we did. It was amazing. And that really justified us being here.

FIGURE 4.6 Aurora Commons: A Neighborhood Living Room.
(Image courtesy of Aurora Commons)

In addition to this important endorsement from their community,[118] Sanctuary came to terms with the reality that they had already invested a lot in learning the coffee business, in the equipment, and that their organizational identity as a church had become intertwined with the coffee shop as particular expression of local mission. "The Green Bean—that's our thing. It's what we do. It's how we love our neighbors; how we know our neighbors."

Several NI leaders spoke of designating laity with intentional roles amid their third spaces, commissioning them as "ministers of presence." These lay ministers of presence are encouraged to intentionally develop missional relationships without the evangelistic urgency that attends the GCT approach to forging new friendships.[119] This role reflects an understanding of mission that some describe as "faithful presence."[120] Whereas GCT churches emphasize the need to establish relationships to create opportunities to speak God's Word *to others*, NI churches distinctively recount experiences of hearing God's Word spoken *to them* through neighbors, even atheist and addicted neighbors.

In keeping with their organic, relational ethos, churches in the NI model shy away from marketing approaches to recruitment through flyers and advertisements, relying instead on word-of-mouth. In fact, some NI churches are extremely discreet, if not somewhat secretive, about the affiliation between their third place and church community. The apparent disparity between how third places were sometimes described, for example, by Sanctuary as "our 7-day lobby and flashing sign board," and the reality of the understated connection to the church evident in these third places may reflect some of the diversity of thinking within NI churches who draw members from both evangelical and progressive quarters.

Spirituality Among Neighborhood Incarnation Churches

The NI paradigm had no statistically significant correlations to any of the four predominant spirituality patterns found in the survey.[121] This is noteworthy, and results in part from the fact that among NI churches can be found strong examples from each of the other three models; a handful of GCT, NC, and HS churches simultaneously embody the features of the Neighborhood Incarnation model. This raises the question of whether strong neighborhood identification has the potential to relativize differences of theology and spiritual practice that have been and remain primary points of division and distinction among U.S. congregations.

In contrast to New Community churches, whose spirituality is tightly bound with its worship services, NI churches have a spirituality in which worship is clearly decentered. Indeed, the statistical paradigm on which the NI model was developed is negatively correlated with an emphasis on "passionate worship" as an important church practice. Pastor Ben Katt's description of his thinking when he planted Awake illustrates this decentering.

> My vision for what a church would be like was not based on, like, a vibrant, lively Sunday worship service. I didn't want to start a worship service, do the launch, and then do it every week after . . . that would drive me crazy. But I did have the sense [of] clear calling to a neighborhood or to a particular place. And so the question then was, "What does it look like to be the church along Aurora?"

As Pastor Katt's comment reveals, the decentering of worship among NC churches actually goes along with a recentering of Christian spirituality around everyday life in the neighborhood and openness to taking an extra-congregational form in order to "be the church." The "sacred consciousness" of these churches is summarized in their belief that God is present and active in the neighborhood. Thus, like NC churches they seek God in the ordinary stuff of life—conversations and circumstances—but especially among places and faces that are part of their parish.

Their practices of prayer follow this same move away from a primarily devotional practice for private edification and toward life in the parish. Prayer in these churches has a distinctive emphasis on bringing local concerns before God.[122] NI churches, like those in the New Community model, generally include a prayer of confession within worship, but unlike NC churches, they have no increased propensity to include Communion hymns, the Lord's Prayer, or other liturgical traditions.

NI churches, like GCT churches, experience God as intimately involved in their story and mission. Emmanuel Bible Church's annual report locates their ministry in place and testifies to God's activity.

> Here on the corner of 50th and Dayton—God has been doing all sorts of inexplicable and unpredictably exciting things to propel us on our way. He has brought new ideas; fresh resources and some highly gifted people to foster, clarify, and advance our mission.[123]

In recounting their origins and how their ministries evolved, NI leaders frequently describe sensing God's call to a particular neighborhood. In that context, they experience God as actively facilitating beneficial relationships and pointing them toward particular forms of mission engagement and community life. As Pastor Katt describes, this divine call seems to typically emerge from the interplay of context and the church community: "When I see a need or a hope in the neighborhood or we see one together, and then there's, like, this passion and gifting of someone in our church . . . it feels like God's calling us to do something in our area." Their spiritual exemplars are, like Pastor Katt, capable of bringing together a spiritual sense of call with practical action as good neighbors and good Samaritans. They are those who have become "characters" in the neighborhood. Their celebrated saints are known around town and are agents in shaping local life. Moreover, they have made caring and building community among and for neighbors a way of life.

Summary

The Neighborhood Incarnation model is anchored in a fundamental identification with the local neighborhood as a God-given parish. It is within their immediate contexts—understood as sites of beauty, need, and hope—that these followers of Jesus seek both to experience God's presence and to join in God's mission. NI churches practice their neighborhood-rooted spirituality and mission through significant personal and corporate commitments to local hospitality. They seek to exist as an asset to their neighborhood, often by creating third places that facilitate meaningful relationships among members of the local community. NI churches are incarnations of Christian community in, of, and for their neighborhoods. They manifest as social bodies (Christian community) and material presences (spaces for hospitality).

Interpretive—Not Prescriptive—Models

The four models presented in this chapter—the Great Commission Team, the Household of the Spirit, the New Community, and the Neighborhood Incarnation—constitute the clearest, most prevalent varieties of new ecclesial presence in Seattle. Not all new Seattle churches fit exclusively or comfortably into one of these four models, however.[124] Several churches are suitable examples of two models, others of none. In addition, it seems that at least two additional models may exist and could be developed with further research.[125] Nonetheless, these four dominant models offer robust descriptions that account for roughly 80% of the field of new Seattle churches. The Great Commission Team, Household of the Spirit, and New Community are fresh, contextual embodiments of familiar players in the U.S. congregational field—Evangelicals, Pentecostals, and emerging churches, respectively. The Neighborhood Incarnation, however, is a fairly novel model that calls for further study.[126]

These four models, it is worth stressing, are not offered merely as illustrated sociological types or idealized theological constructs. They are practical ecclesiologies, reflecting an integration of disciplinary methods infused with an overarching belief in the presence of God among the churches and an orienting intention that their explication may serve the church, both in its doctrinal self-understanding and in its task of faithful contextual witness. Inasmuch as the models are representations of what the church *is*, they contain doctrinally constructive hints regarding *the nature of the church*. In and of themselves, however, the models developed in this chapter do not necessarily advance the cause of faithful contextual witness. While they might be construed as several approaches to church that "work" in a post-Christian context like Seattle, effectiveness is no measure of faithfulness.[127] To be clear, the work of identifying and developing these models was not undertaken to directly translate them into strategies for successful church planting. Rather, these models were discerned and defined in large part in order that they might be subjected to theological and missiological scrutiny. This kind of evaluation is needed in order that churches of each model be able to guard against the dangers inherent in their approach, as well as to capitalize on the promise they hold for faithful and vital Christian witness. It is the task of chapter 5 to move from what *is* to what *ought to be* by offering theological assessment of the four practical ecclesiological models.

5

Missional Theological Assessment

CHAPTER 4 DREW ON theological and sociological sources to describe the four dominant practical ecclesiological models in the field. Having developed these practical ecclesiologies informed by "critical analyses of the concrete church and its context," it is now time that the models be analyzed and challenged so that churches reflecting each model may see the way to more faithful ecclesiopraxis.[1] It is the task of this chapter to provide a theological assessment of each of these models, discerning the strengths and weaknesses inherent in each in order to promote increasingly faithful ecclesial forms of Christian witness.[2]

I have chosen missional theology as the theological perspective from which to evaluate these practical ecclesiological models. This chapter begins with a synthesis of the core ideas of missional theology, developed with the help of insights from key contributors—most notably, Lesslie Newbigin. Missional theology is one of the most important theological developments of the twentieth century. It emerged largely as the theological fruit of the modern mission movement and the ensuing ecumenical soul searching. In the 1960s, missionary efforts became the object of serious criticism, with accusations that missionaries were little more than "cultural imperialists" in league with failing Western colonialism.[3] Even earlier, Western churches, in large part through the influence of their missionaries, had begun haltingly to take more seriously the voices of the "young churches" they had established and overseen in non-Western cultures. The rise of Global Christianity fostered a growing recognition of the appropriateness of diverse cultural expressions of Christian faith and led to a remarkable upsurge in ecumenical openness, dialogue, and hope. As the heritage of Protestant missionary work, fresh theological ideas were cultivated in the early decades of the World Council of Churches and crystallized in influential assertions of the "missionary nature of the church" that eventually found a place in mainstream works of ecclesiology and even played a notable role within the documents of Vatican II. Enriched by various theological and ecclesiastical traditions, as well as diverse cultural embodiments of the gospel, this missionary ecclesiology emerged offering fresh insights into the nature of the church and its relations to the Triune God, the mission of God, the Reign of God, and the world. More recently, since the 1998 publication of *Missional Church: A Vision for the Sending of the Church in North America*, a flood of Protestant literature utilizing the neologism "missional" has been published.[4] Currently, the "missional conversation" is a discourse largely about the theology and practice of mission in the post-Christian West. As such, it is a natural fit with the aims of this project.

While missional theology has made and continues to make a significant contribution to ecclesiological, ecumenical, and missiological reflection, I am conscious of the fact that it is only one of a number of theological and critical perspectives that could provide fruitful analysis of the models of practical ecclesiology embodied by new Seattle churches. My choice to use missional theology is based, in part, on the popularity of "missional" rhetoric among new church developers. It is my hope that the critiques emerging from the following analysis will be more seriously considered by practitioners because they spring from a theological discourse that is broadly affirmed, even though "missional" verbiage it is widely misappropriated and the implications of the discourse for ecclesiopraxis are scarcely considered.

It should be clarified at the outset that the purpose of this chapter is not simply to crown a "most missional" model and make a plea for the others to be abandoned. While this chapter will argue that Neighborhood Incarnation practical ecclesiology most clearly embodies the insights of missional theology and, thus, deserves increased theological and practical consideration, this project shares with Dulles's the conviction that the mysterious and complex nature of church requires it be manifest in a multiplicity of expressions.[5] Rich ecclesial diversity is the testimony of both the New Testament and Christian history up until today. The church that is "one," "holy," and "apostolic" has always been the church that is also "catholic." That is, the universal church has, from its origins, been understood through a vibrant array of metaphors and has taken shape in diverse ways, in particular social and cultural settings. This irreducible ecclesiological pluralism is why good ecclesiologists are not bound to a single model of

church.[6] Just as theologians must entertain multiple formulations, practitioners ought to be familiar with multiple forms, if only to better understand the ecclesiopraxis of their preferred expression. In recent years, the
Fresh Expressions movement in the Church of England has championed
the practical imperative of diverse forms of church in calling for a "mixed
economy" of churches.[7] This chapter's survey of the missional theological
strengths and weaknesses of the models lays the groundwork for the practical proposals in the concluding chapters.

Missional Theology

The following section highlights four key ideas that form the core of missional theology and considers vital implications for the faithful missional
practice of church planting. The heart of the chapter brings these core
ideas into conversation with the practical ecclesiological models. Whereas
the ancient and Reformed marks of the church both arose from historical contexts characterized by intense conflict between competing forms
of Christianity (as means of distinguishing "our" faithful churches from
"those" heretical ones) and most traditional ecclesiology has originated
from focused reflection on specific church practices such as celebration of
the sacraments, ordination, and preaching, missional theology emerged in
the midst of ecumenical missiological reflection on the experience of missionary endeavor and an increasingly global and multicultural Christianity.[8]

Missionary Trinity

Missional theology is not, in the first place, about the church. Rather, the
fundamental ground for missional theology lies in the doctrine of God.
In missional perspective, God is understood fundamentally as a sending,
missionary Trinity.[9] Karl Barth is generally credited with pioneering this
theological paradigm in the middle of the twentieth century, rooting mission in the very nature of God and thus situating it in relation to the doctrine of the Trinity rather than in its traditional contexts of ecclesiology
and soteriology.[10] In contrast to predominant understandings of mission
as the church's act of obedience to Christ's Great Commission, missional
theology asserts that mission is more fundamentally an attribute and
activity within God's own self. The divine relations are characterized in an
essential way by sending (*missio*)—"God the Father sending the Son, and
God the Father and Son sending the Spirit."[11] These divine emanations

are the result of God's other-loving nature that always results in the exten-
sion of goodness, blessing, and welcome into the Trinitarian shalom.
Thus, creation is seen as a divine act of other-blessing mission, reflecting
God's essential character. Redemption, too, as well as the formation of the
People of God, flows from this same missional origin in God's nature.
The redemptive mission that sent the Son and the Spirit was "expanded
to include yet another "movement": Father, Son, and Holy Spirit sending
the church into the world."[12] Missional theology is Trinitarian theology in
which God is known as a missionary God.

Missio Dei

A second and closely related core missional idea is commonly referred to
in the Latin, *missio Dei.* Meaning "mission of God," the doctrine of *missio
Dei* includes three important elements. First, it means that God—not the
church—is the primary agent of mission. The recognition that mission
emerges from the nature of the Godhead leads to the further implication
that the mission belongs to and is enacted by God. The mission is not ours
but God's. God is the originator and key actor in mission.[13] As Newbigin
put it, "The Church is not so much the agent of mission as the locus of
mission. It is God who acts in the power of the Spirit, doing mighty works,
creating signs of a new age, working secretly in the hearts of men and
women to draw them to Christ."[14] The church is a product of God's mission rather than producer of it. Thus, Jürgen Moltmann asserted, "it is
not the church that has a mission of salvation to fulfill in the world; it is
the mission of the Son and the Spirit through the Father that includes the
church, creating a church as it goes on its way."[15]

This understanding is a paradigm shift from traditional mission
approaches that have emphasized the church's agency in responding to
their missionary obligation. The agency of the church is not, however,
erased in missional perspective but, rather, re-envisioned as the agency
of participation in God's ongoing mission, and indeed in the very life of
the Trinity.[16] As Newbigin wrote, "we are not engaged in an enterprise of
our own choosing or devising. We are invited to participate in an activity
of God that is central to the meaning of creation itself. We are invited to
become, through the presence of the Holy Spirit, participants in the Son's
loving obedience to the Father."[17] The People of God are participants in
this mission, but the mission has thus far been and will finally be accomplished by the efficacy of Father, Son, and Spirit.

The second element of *missio Dei* regards the holistic scope of the mission God has undertaken. The Christian canon casts a meta-narrative in which God's good created world is marred by human sin and God works graciously and cooperatively with human partners over millennia not only to redeem humankind to right relationship with God's self but also to restore a groaning creation. This narrative arc finds consummation in a new heaven and new earth, a renewed home for a redeemed humanity to dwell with God.[18] The *missio Dei*, then, is the holistic renewal of all things and within its scope are included human redemption and restored creation. The mission of God is comprehensive renewal of the cosmos. God's sending—of the Son, of the Spirit, of the church—aims to restore perfect and peaceful harmony, which is God's loving will.

The holistic scope of the *missio Dei* is consistent with the central focus of Jesus's ministry, the Reign of God. Jesus's ministry was fundamentally proclamation and demonstration of the Reign of God. While his teaching clearly heralded God's Reign, he also demonstrated the nature and nearness of God's Reign in physical and spiritual healings, miraculous provisions, mastery of the natural world, and honor for social outcasts. In such practices, Jesus enacted the availability of God's shalom and in his teaching he invited his contemporaries to enter and receive it.[19] The Reign of God that Jesus pointed to is precisely of the same holistic, harmonious character as that toward which the *missio Dei* moves. Indeed, the *telos* or goal of the *missio Dei* is the Reign of God. God's missionary purpose is the restoration of all creation within God's good will and care. There is basic scholarly consensus regarding the simultaneously "already and not yet" nature of the eschatological Reign of God. It is this present but not fully present reality that Jesus announced and enacted and to which he pointed as a reality destined for the whole of creation in the renewal of all things. The *missio Dei* is God's purpose and activity toward the actualization of the Reign of God "on earth as it is in heaven." Thus, it is the Reign of God, rather than the church, that defines the scope of the *missio Dei*. The church participates in God's mission and dwells within God's Reign, but God's mission is not limited to the expansion of the church, nor is the Reign of God coterminous with the church. The church is a telltale fruit of God's mission, but God's mission will produce not only a redeemed human community but also the renewal of all things.[20]

These first two elements of the *missio Dei* are evident in the most cited passage of the 1998 book that popularized "missional" language, *Missional Church*:

The ecclesiolocentric understanding of mission has been replaced in this century by a profoundly theocentric reconceptualization of Christian mission. We have come to see that mission is not merely an activity of the church. Rather, mission is the result of God's initiative, rooted in God's purposes to restore and heal creation. "Mission" means "sending" and it is the central biblical theme describing the purposes of God's action in human history.[21]

Mission, in missional perspective, belongs to God, and God's mission moves toward the holistic renewal of the cosmos.

A third element of the *missio Dei* stems from the first two. If God is the primary agent of a mission to restore all creation, then the church can anticipate that God is at work in every context in which it might find itself. God's mission is not only logically and chronologically prior to the church but also geographically prior. This was an important shift in mission thought as international missionaries began to move away from describing their mission contexts in sweepingly negative terms—as spiritual wastelands inhabited by immoral heathen. Instead, they came to recognize that in all the lands to which they had been sent, God had already been at work, planting seeds of goodness, beauty, and truth in local contexts, cultures, and religions.[22] Indeed, wherever Christians may find themselves—in whatever place or relationship—they may rest assured God has long been there working toward the renewal of all things.[23] Thus, the church must recognize that its task is not to bring God's mission to a place but, rather, to seek to participate in God's already-in-motion mission, a work of the Spirit that began before they arrived and will continue after they leave.[24]

Jesus as Paradigm for Mission

A third core missional idea identifies Christ's life and ministry, and specifically the incarnation, as the paradigmatic expression of the *missio Dei*. It is with respect to this point that missional theology is decidedly Christocentric.[25] The incarnation, in missional discourse, invokes not only the Christmas miracle but, more broadly, the life and ministry of Jesus as God-with-us. Jesus's life and ministry reveal God's nature and characteristic way of mission.[26] Darrell Guder has defined "incarnational mission" as "the understanding and practice of Christian witness that is rooted in and shaped by the life, ministry, suffering, death, and resurrection of Jesus."[27] The *missio Dei* took the form of God becoming one of us, living among us, moving into the neighborhood, taking a self-emptying posture of radical solidarity. "The incarnation is a profound, concrete act of God's participatory presence."[28] In Christ, we discover that God's way of mission is personally, humbly, sacrificially stepping into the middle of God's beautiful-broken-beloved world. God, in Christ, kenotically shed the privileges of divinity and willingly accepted the limitations and vulnerabilities of human existence, took the form of servant, and submitted even to death.[29]

Jesus's contextually immersive, self-emptying posture not only demonstrates *God's* way of mission but simultaneously exemplifies *human* participation in the *missio Dei*. Thus, Christ is seen not only as a divine agent of redemption but also as paradigmatic for the church's agency through cooperative participation in God's mission. Guder suggests that "the incarnation of Jesus that constitutes and defines the message and mission of the church [has] concrete significance for *the way in which* the church communicates that message and carries out the mission" (emphasis mine).[30] Stuart Murray clarifies the nature of God's missionary means: "If mission originates in the character and activity of God, the means by which God engages in mission are paradigmatic for those who participate in this mission."[31] This focus on the *means* of God's mission draws attention to Jesus's life and ministry as an expository counterpart to the doctrine of the *missio Dei*, discussion of which tends to focus on the *ends* toward which God's mission precedes. Without this counterpart, emphasis on the *missio Dei* can unwittingly serve as justification for the use of coercion—whether violent, legislative, or apologetic.[32] As the Crusades and colonial mission illustrate, the pursuit of the universal reign of peace can become implicated in the violent means of empire building. By contrast, the *missio Dei* is properly understood as God's future Reign of Shalom "breaking in" to the present exclusively via the use of peaceful means, exemplified in the life, ministry, and death of Jesus. The coming Reign of God is present and available because the means of the *missio Dei* are consistent with its *telos*. Human participation in the *missio Dei* is itself part of life within the Reign of God. The means of Christian witness are only virtuous inasmuch as they are faithful to its peaceable ends. Christ did not enter the world in power but as a helpless infant. He did not rally his disciples and the angels of heaven to exercise judgment and wield coercive power but instead suffered a violent death at the hands of political and religious authorities. Jesus's way is not the way of control. On multiple occasions, when his disciples sought to exercise coercive power, he rebuked them.[33] Illustratively,

Jesus did not teach in such a way as to compel obedience to the will of God. Rather, his most characteristic manner of teaching, in parables, purposefully created the conditions under which hearers could understand and respond—or not—as they sincerely desired in their heart of hearts.[34] The character of the *missio Dei* was made known in the way of Jesus; he arrived as a child, grew as a student, lived a servant, and died as a martyr.

From this fundamentally noncoercive position, Jesus nonetheless boldly proclaimed and subversively demonstrated the Reign of God and its contextual implications. The nearness of the Reign of God has material, tangible repercussions. As Murray notes, "it is important to affirm that both *word* and *flesh* are involved in incarnation."[35] The Reign of God is made known in deed, but also in word. Not only did the Word become flesh but the Word-become-flesh also *spoke* with authority. As Newbigin put it, "words without deeds are empty, but deeds without words are dumb."[36] This holism reflects the full scope of God's mission. Jesus's ministry was characterized not only by a radical solidarity with humanity but also by a radical call of discipleship. In Jesus, God paradigmatically gave utterance to God's good news for a particular culture "in its own speech and symbol" speaking "the word which is both No and Yes, both judgment and grace."[37] Even as God is present and active in all cultures, the gospel judges all cultures. The significance of the incarnation must be seen in double perspective, as both the affirmation of culture and its intelligible critique.[38]

The Missionary Nature of the Church

The significance of the three core ideas just discussed for the church has been touched upon in several ways, but to state it plainly as a fourth, the church is missionary in its very nature. The church is born of God's mission and exists as the first fruits of renewed human community. This renewed humanity, however, is not merely a harmonious society but more so one whose pattern originates in the Trinitarian society of love. As Michael Moynagh puts it, "What constitutes the church is participation in the perichoretic dance of the triune God."[39] And the love of this divine society extends beyond the Godhead, becoming known to humankind through its activity as a missionary society. Thus, the church's identity as a first fruit of God's Reign is linked intrinsically to its participation in the ongoing mission of God. The church in its essence is a sharing in the life and mission of the Triune God. As such, the congregation that is not participating in God's mission is not merely an unhealthy church but also has forsaken its own nature and purpose.[40] This is a point stressed repeatedly by Newbigin, who located the church's very existence "in the act of being the bearer of that salvation to the whole world."[41] Mission, he suggested, even has soteriological import, for "apart from participation in Christ's mission to the world, there is no participation in Christ."[42] As Johannes Blauw, author of *The Missionary Nature of the Church*, concluded in 1962, "the church is a missionary Church or it is no Church."[43]

The missionary nature of the church is the basis for what the authors of *Missional Church* call a "missional ecclesiology." Three noteworthy implications follow from this understanding of the church's essential missionary nature. The first regards the nature of the relationship between the church and God's Reign. Newbigin famously formulated this eschatological relation, describing the church "as a sign, instrument, and foretaste of the reign of God."[44] As a *sign*, the church points beyond itself to the fullness of God's coming shalom, simultaneously confessing its own partial character.[45] While the church is not the Reign of God in its fullness, it is an authentic *foretaste* of the new humanity that is to come. The function of a foretaste, like that of an appetizer, is "to make us long ardently for that which is yet to come."[46] The church is an *instrument* of the Reign of God, Newbigin asserted, primarily through its active participation in various forms of Christian mission. The church is instrumental in God's work of salvation, but it must be emphasized, God is the agent whose hands wield this instrument. Thus it is that the church can be said to be participating in God's mission inasmuch as its life reflects the noncoercive character and way of God in mission revealed in Christ.

The missionary nature of the church does not, however, point only to the church's call to Christ-like participation in concrete mission actions such as evangelism and work for social justice. A critical dimension of the church's witness to the Reign of God lies in the character of its communal life together.[47] This second implication is the practical significance of the church's identity as a foretaste of the Reign of God. As *Missional Church* contributor Lois Barrett asserts, the church is to be "an alternative community" in the world marked by a distinct political identity, as well as an alternative culture, allegiance, economics, and understanding of power.[48] Its public worship is one prominent expression of the missional church's alternative culture.[49] Providing a foretaste of God's Reign means that the church ought to be distinguishable from the world in which it dwells. This difference stems from the church's identity as a socially-embodied anticipation of the new redeemed humanity.[50] The church's "life will necessarily be different from the life of the neighbourhood, but the important thing is that it be different in the right way and not in the wrong way."[51] What makes the church unique should not be its language or style but its life, its way of being and behaving in the world, its animating principles, social character, and core practices. The quality of these points of difference between the church and the world ought to point to the eschatological new humanity rather than flow from a strident countercultural posture that condemns the world in which God is present.

The missional church functions as a foretaste, most centrally, through particular local churches, for it is in contact with the persons who make up a local Christian community that the world is invited to sample the flavors of the Reign of God.[52] Even as the mission of God in Christ took shape in a manner appropriate to a particular time and place, so too does the church's participation in that mission. Thus, as Newbigin stressed, the "basic form of Christian witness is a company of followers of Jesus called by God's Spirit and joined together as God's people in a particular place."[53] It is the local church "in which the reality of the new creation is present, known, and experienced."[54] Encounters with Christians-in-community make the good news of the Reign of God both comprehensible and plausible. This is the meaning of Newbigin's dictum that "the only hermeneutic of the gospel is a congregation of men and women who believe it and live by it."[55]

The phenomenological priority of the local church in the universal church's witness to the Reign of God has an important impact on the main structural concerns of missional ecclesiology.[56] Dominant European ecclesiologies—Catholic, Orthodox, Reformed—had been concerned, in the first place, with asserting the legitimacy of various ecclesiastical bodies and movements as authentic manifestations of the universal church. As a result, the ecclesiality of local churches has been understood as derivative in nature.[57] In this view, local gatherings of Christians are regarded as churches on the basis of their inclusion in the properly ordered institution of the universal church. Missional ecclesiology, by contrast, roots ecclesiality in witness to the Reign of God as it occurs in every place. As a result, it asserts the ecclesiological priority of the primary vehicle of this witness—that is, the local church.[58] Missiologist David Bosch described this remarkable shift—notable even in the documents of Vatican II—as the "discovery that the universal church actually finds its true existence in the local churches; that these, and not the universal church, are the pristine expression of church."[59] Thus, the "church-in-mission is, primarily, the *local* church everywhere in the world."[60]

The church's missionary nature, to summarize, has three key implications. First, it situates the church in vital relationship to the Reign of God as a sign, foretaste, and instrument. Second, it calls for the church to exist in the world as a distinct community that foreshadows the new humanity. Third, and finally, the missionary nature of the church prioritizes local churches as the elemental ecclesial and evangelistic unit.

Missional Theology and Church Planting

The preceding four core missional ideas constitute the key tenets of missional theology. In review, they include God's nature as a missionary Trinity, the *missio Dei* as God's renewal of all things, Jesus as paradigm for divine and human mission, and the church as missionary in nature. Despite the obvious relevance of these theological assertions for the practice of new church development, disciplined reflection on the practical implications of these core ideas is remarkably rare. This is so, notwithstanding the frequency with which church planting books use the word *missional*. An important exception to this trend, *Starting Missional Churches: Life with God in the Neighborhood*, was co-edited by Mark Lau Branson, a chaired professor at Fuller Theological Seminary and missional church consultant, and Nick Warnes, a church planter and coach for the Presbyterian Church (USA).[61] In chapter 2, Branson, drawing substantially on the work of Alan Roxburgh, offers four priorities for starting churches that develop upon the core insights of missional theology and provide a highly serviceable additional rubric for missional theological assessment of the practical ecclesiological models.

The first priority Branson names is of principal importance: "a priority on discerning God's initiatives."[62] This priority follows directly from the doctrine of the *missio Dei*, which asserts that God is the prime agent in mission and is always, everywhere out ahead of the church seeking the renewal of all things. This comprehensive vision has a poignant, local corollary: "God is on the ground in neighborhoods and communities."[63] The church's call with respect to this on-the-ground *missio Dei* is to cooperative participation. However, before the People of God can participate in the activity of God they must work to discern what God is doing locally.[64] In order to discern God's proximate activity, there is need to cultivate a particular form of attention—a disciplined, local, and spiritual attentiveness.[65] Because God is at work in every context, practices of attention to, discernment of, and participation in that work are foundational to church planting that is truly missional.[66] As Branson puts it, "if God is living and active, then . . . church planting should attend to discerning God's initiatives in . . . lives and context."[67]

This priority on discerning God's initiatives is in stark contrast to pragmatic marketing approaches that rely upon clever human agents capable of tapping niche markets, developing desirable religious goods and services, and having skills in the arts of prediction, management, and control.[68] Rather than apprenticing themselves to such trades, missional church planting teams ought to cultivate habits and engage processes that cultivate attention to what God is doing and facilitate cooperative, experimental participation in that work as part of an ongoing practice of discernment. Branson names a host of corporate activities and personal practices in this vein, including conversation, research, Bible study, listening prayer, experimentation, hospitality, worship, and generosity, all of which, he suggests, "are needed for a planting group to be vulnerable to God, sensitive to the Spirit's initiatives, constantly reflecting and learning, and ready to be engaged in God's initiatives."[69] Those who would be missional church planters must prioritize the spiritual and communal practices that "tune our lives to God" lest it be the case that their well-intentioned mission efforts be out of sync with the Spirit's action and empowerment in that place.[70]

Branson's second priority for missional church planting stresses the need to approach the neighbor as subject rather than object. Too often, Branson observes, church planters arrive on the scene assuming they know what is needed and proceed to set up their proscribed style of church and deliver their "version of the gospel's provisions to them."[71] Informed primarily by demographic profiles and so-called effective tactics for growth and multiplication, many church planters fail to reverently attend to the persons and unique communities to which God has called them. Not only is this approach strategically unwise, it is dehumanizing because it treats others as objects, as holes that need to be filled, rather than as subjects and actors with their own God-given agency. This is the legacy of colonizing mission, which approached the missionized as subhuman, as beasts and children in need of a gospel and civilization that could justifiably be forced upon them for their own good. This coercion is precisely what is restricted by missional theology's recognition of Christ's paradigmatic way of mission.

In contrast, Branson calls for a postcolonial approach to others fundamentally shaped by hospitality—a practice that "that brings us into a missional engagement we cannot control."[72] Echoing the mission of the seventy commissioned by Jesus in Luke 10, Alan Roxburgh advises the missional People of God, "Like strangers in need of hospitality who have left their baggage behind, enter the neighborhoods and communities where you live, sit at the table of the other, and there you may begin to hear what God is doing."[73] Newbigin, too, stressed hospitality as a practice not only essential to spiritual discernment but also full of soteriological import:

> God's saving revelation of himself does not come to us straight down from above—through the skylight as we might say. In order to receive God's saving revelation we have to open the door to the neighbor who he sends as his appointed messenger, and—moreover—to receive that messenger not as a temporary teacher or guide who we can dispense with when we ourselves have learned what is needed, but as one who will permanently share our home. There is not salvation except one in which we are saved together through the one whom God sends to be the bearer of salvation.[74]

In setting a priority on engaging the neighbor as subject, Branson invites church planters to seek "genuine, human encounters, which are always life-on-life," for it is in these relationships that it becomes possible to discern how God is present and to imagine "how a church can participate in healing, beauty, trust-building, belonging, and witness."[75]

Boundary-crossing is the third priority Branson identifies for starting missional churches. This priority challenges the theological integrity of Donald McGavran's homogeneous unit principle—still popular among church planters. This principle asserts the effectiveness (and defends the theological validity) of forming Christian communities of people who are the same in terms of race, culture, or social class.[76] Branson acknowledges the human tendency toward seeking comfortable communities of sameness, but claims that "the border-crossing love of God doesn't give us that kind of consumer option."[77] As a missionary in India, Newbigin confronted the reality of separate missions among each level of the caste system. Such mission defended itself on the basis of effectiveness and the homogenous unit principle, but Newbigin decried it as perpetuating a fundamental disunity in the Body of Christ along class lines and thus presenting a public contradiction to Christ's gospel of reconciliation.[78] Instead, he called for churches to be communities "in which men and women of very different social and ethnic backgrounds live together in harmony."[79] Branson acknowledges the discomfort and challenge that attend such mixed communities, but stresses that, while challenging, "boundary crossing . . . is key to participation with God."[80] Roxburgh points to the discovery of the church in Acts whose prototypical experience of participation with the Spirit called them into boundary-breaking fellowship.[81] The early church was led to join the Spirit's work precisely by crossing the very boundary that delimited their primary sense of identity—the boundary that separated Jews from Gentiles.[82] So too, Branson suggests, missional church planters should expect that participation in the contemporary *missio Dei* will involve crossing one or more of the deep-rooted social boundaries present in their local context.

Finally, Branson urges a fourth priority on "plural leadership that shapes an environment."[83] The call for multiple leaders—rather than a single pioneering authority—provides a reflection of the Trinitarian fellowship of equals whose mission church planters seek to join. Planting churches with a community of leaders also testifies that the missionary nature of the church lies primary in its corporate call *as a community* to witness to Christ. *Missional* is a more fitting adjective for churches than for individual Christians because the practice of Christian witness belongs most fundamentally to the People of God collectively and takes place primarily through local Christian communities. Individual Christian witness is derivative. God's mission, Branson notes, "is shaping a people (a church)" and "the Spirit is inspiring, forming, motivating and teaching a cluster of people who are to provide leadership on the ground."[84]

This community of leaders is diversely Spirit-gifted, but shares a common purpose of equipping the ordinary People of God—the saints—for "the work of ministry."[85] The work of ministry is, theologically speaking, cooperative participation with God in the *missio Dei*. The equipping task of leaders, then, is to assist the community's discernment of their identity and vocation as participants in the *missio Dei*. This is precisely what the Spirit has empowered them to do through *charismata*, Branson suggests. Offering a fresh interpretation of spiritual gifts, he presents them as diverse empowerments for helping churches to discern and participate in God's activity in the concrete realities of their context.[86] Missional leadership, then, is primarily the work of facilitation, cultivating environments in which God's people "can come together in shared life to discover their participation in God's mission."[87] Such environments, Branson notes, are marked by relationship, imagination, questions, experimentation, learning, hope, and holiness.[88]

In summary, Branson brings substantial insights of missional theology to bear on the concrete practice of church planting by urging four priorities: (1) discerning God's initiatives, (2) the neighbor as subject, (3) boundary-crossing, and (4) plural leadership that shapes an environment. It is with these priorities, as well as the four core ideas of missional theology developed earlier (God as missionary Trinity, the *missio Dei* as God's renewal of all things, Jesus as paradigm for divine–human cooperative mission, and the church as missionary in nature) that the remainder of this chapter turns to missional theological assessment of the four practical ecclesiologies.

Great Commission Team in Missional Theological Perspective

The Evangelicals whose practical ecclesiology casts the church as Great Commission Team are compelled by Jesus's parting words in the Gospel of Matthew: "go, and make disciples of all nations." Consequently, their spirituality and community life reflect a thoroughgoing evangelistic orientation. In a missionary context that they perceive as hostile to "the Gospel," they proclaim Jesus's obedient submission to the Father's just wrath as he endured death on the cross, offering a substitutionary sacrifice that makes a total demand on the lives of all people.[89] The requisite life transformation and missional vocation called for by "the Gospel" is nurtured in long sermons, mid-sized missional communities, and smaller, same-gender accountability groups. This prominent model not only calls the church to obey Christ's missionary mandate but also asserts that the church is constituted as a disciple-making force.

The Great Commission Team model has several noteworthy strengths and points of resonance with missional theology. Foremost among these is an abiding commitment to proactive mission as an essential practice of the church. GCT churches understand themselves as the sent people of a sending God. Indeed, envisioning the church as a missionary team highlights the missionary purpose and nature of the church. In their stress upon evangelism, as well as their involvement in mercy and justice ministries, they affirm and give witness to the missionary nature of the church.[90] The church is not—and cannot be—a holy huddle of self-congratulating saints apathetic to the spiritual well-being of the rest of humanity. The church is a missionary people united with Christ, whose mission was "to seek and save the lost."[91]

The centrality of mission to the church's nature is also born out in the lives of participants of GCT churches. Among churches in this model, individual Christians evidence a stronger sense of personal missional identity than was observed among participants in other models. They frequently present the Christian life as a missionary life and revere fellow church members who exemplify missional identity. Among GCT churches there is widespread agreement that every believer ought to live as a missionary and there is a commitment, especially among church leaders, to faithfully witness to Christ in daily life and relationships.

Closely related to their commitment to personal evangelism, members of GCT churches spoke more frequently and naturally about the activity of God in their daily lives than in churches of other models. GCT narratives frequently attest to God's agency, describing God as a provider of formative experiences, financial means, strategic partnerships, and relational openings with non-Christians.[92] God was also credited with effecting personal transformation toward salvation, holiness, and sacrificial mission. This kind of God-talk was unexpectedly rare in other churches, and its frequency among GCT churches points to their genuine, and commendable, appreciation for God's agency in their lives, personally and corporately. Furthermore, it suggests that the central practices of these communities—missional relationships, missional communities, "Gospel-centered" preaching, and so on—have served to tune the attention of members to a certain slice of God's initiatives, those that involve personal transformation and evangelistic endeavor.[93]

Finally, the GCT model takes seriously the call for the church to be a holy community, a "contrast community" distinct from the cultural context in which the church is located. This is the corporate expression of their commitment to personal holiness. GCT churches recognize that the gospel's word to their culture includes a "No" and they are willing (even eager) to suffer or sacrifice in order to remain true to Christ.

The Great Commission Team practical ecclesiology, however, is beset by a number of serious weaknesses in missional perspective. Inasmuch as the model is an iteration of the classic approach of modern missions, and inasmuch as missional theology represents a paradigm shift away from this approach, representations and embodiments of the church as Great Commission Team represent a failure to grapple seriously with missional theology, despite the prevalence of "missional" rhetoric in these churches. Several specific points of weakness in missional perspective can be enumerated.

First, the central emphasis among GCT churches on the Great Commission of Matthew 28 as a duty that the church is called to fulfill serves to exaggerate the role of human agency in mission and concurrently intercept recognition of God as its prime agent.[94] In GCT spirituality, God supplies the opportunity and power to the church as it obediently seeks to share "the Gospel." This is an unfortunate reversal of the missional understanding; God is envisioned as participating in the church's mission instead of the church participating in God's mission. In practice, this reversal undercuts the need for the church to discern God's initiatives in context. GCT churches are convinced that they already know what they are to do—make disciples—so there is no need to look to God for anything other than empowerment and evangelistic opportunity. Missional discernment is forfeited when missionary obedience is the order of the day.

The Great Commission is a relevant text to include in theological reflection on mission, and many have judged it to be a succinct statement of the church's mission, with good reason. However, it is important to note that the passage came to exert such influence on missionary imagination only after 1792, when a Baptist minister in England named William Carey published *An Inquiry into the Obligations of Christians, to Use Means for the Conversion of the Heathens.*[95] Since its release, teaching on the Great Commission (and mission in general) has been largely framed as a matter of obligation and duty. In critique of this framing, Roland Allen and Lesslie Newbigin have both pointed out that Paul is nowhere found offering "exhortations to missionary zeal."[96] The driving focus of Paul's teaching was not that the early churches must be obedient to fulfill the Great Commission mandate. Rather, Paul insisted that they needed to attend to the quality of their lives and life together so that the Christian community might provide a winsome testimony to the gospel. Paul was, of course, very concerned with Christian witness—a fact evident whenever he explained the purpose of his household codes.[97] Paul is, without question, personally and wholeheartedly invested in missionary endeavor, but even so he does not indicate any anxiety about whether the churches he has planted will be obedient to an evangelistic obligation. Mission, Paul's letters would seem to suggest, is not the sort of thing best motivated by guilt-ridden appeals to dutiful obedience. Indeed, what could possibly be a less winsome act of witness than anything done from a spirit of coerced duty?

Perhaps a significant contributor to the misapplication of the Great Commission results from a difficulty of translation. Champions of the Great Commission from William Carey to today have laid emphasis on that first little English word, *go*, presenting it as a prerequisite injunction to the command to "make disciples." While the doctrines of *missio Dei* and incarnation alone are ample justification for an approach to mission that purposefully "goes" to the ends of the earth, that first word of the Commission adds nothing to it, since in the Greek it is better understood to mean "as you are going."[98] Jesus commissioned his disciples for ministry on the way, not overseas missions per se.[99]

This conceptualization of mission as on-the-way draws a connection between the first and final lines of the Commission text: "All authority in heaven and on earth has been given to me" asserts Jesus's power for mission and, "surely I am with you always, to the very end of the age" promises his ongoing involvement in it (Matt. 28:18, 20). Jesus's power and presence are promised to his disciples wherever and whenever they find themselves, regardless of whether they have been driven there by missionary zeal or, alternatively, by persecution—as was more commonly the case. Both Jesus's claim of authority in the opening sentence and his assurance of ongoing presence in closing serve to relativize the strength of faith and the courage of obedience required of the disciples. These framing words of Jesus's provide the context for how the disciples are to receive the intervening verses—with faith in God not a spirit of anxious duty. Great Commission theology's accent on human agency overlooks the crucial fact that the bookends of the oft-cited text point squarely to the primacy of God's agency in mission.

Furthermore, the GCT model's narrow focus on the Great Commission text as the basis for mission correlates with an elevation of Christology at the expense of the robustly Trinitarian missiology at the heart of missional theology.[100] As Dwight Zscheile and Craig Van Gelder observe, a super-exalted practical Christology produces three negative results.[101] First, it typically goes hand in hand with downplaying the role of the Spirit. As noted in chapter 4, GCT representations of "the Gospel" lift up the Father and Son as the dominant characters in both "the Gospel" and Christian living and, thus, they rarely speak of the Spirit. When they do, the Spirit is not so much an agent who "blows where it will" but is imagined impersonally as a power source fueling the mission activity determined by the church's agenda.[102] The inflated Christology among GCT churches also results in a tendency to "focus attention on our responsibility to emulate the example of Jesus—a perspective not wrong in and of itself, but insufficient for disclosing the fullness of God's intent in sending God's Son."[103] The example of Jesus that these churches seek to emulate is precisely his humility and obedience to the Father's will in submitting to a sacrificial mission.[104] Indeed, humility and mission are the very attributes churches in this model praise among their spiritual exemplars. While this humble-sacrifice vision of Jesus's example has theological and practical value, when it functions as a church's primary image of Jesus through ritual repetition and is not adequately balanced with representations of the mutuality of the Trinitarian persons, it misrepresents the Christian God and distorts the nature of Christian mission (as obedience vs. participation).

Moreover, Van Gelder and Zscheile suggest, this Christological image functions to legitimate "hierarchical patterns of authority and decision making."[105] Quite obviously, the power arrangements in the GCT model, which locate nearly all authority in pastoral offices, are in strong tension with Branson's priority on plural leadership that shapes an environment for communal discernment. GCT leadership is restricted to the few and regards its task primarily as setting the agenda for the church—vision-casting—rather than fostering corporate practices and processes whereby the whole church can discern and step into God's call. Despite language of "servant leadership," GCT churches attempt to fulfill the pastoral task of "equipping of the saints" primarily by exercising authority, determining strategy, delivering doctrine, and motivating the church to fulfill the Great Commission via personal evangelism.[106]

The mission practices of this practical ecclesiological model are unfortunately driven primarily by a sense of missionary duty. The result is a prevailing tendency to view neighbors as targets. Non-Christians are subconsciously approached as objects by participants in GCT churches—as "God-shaped holes" that need to be filled with "the Gospel."[107] The nature of these relationships, while ostensibly oriented toward the other, is fundamentally about the spiritual status of the evangelist. If evangelism is (primarily) conceived of as a duty, then the goal of the practice is satisfaction of the evangelist's personal obligation before God. Evangelism in this context is essentially oriented toward the spiritual improvement of the evangelist rather than toward the benefit of the evangelized. Moreover, because the evangelist herself has been compelled to missionary action on the basis of appeals to divinely ordained duty and Christ-like obedience, it does not seem inappropriate to use similar, subtly coercive means in evangelistic encounters. If God calls disciples to mission via invocations of duty and demands of obedience (for their own good), then it only seems reasonable that the church's mission would deal in the manufacture and use of guilt and fear to move sinners toward salvation (for their own good). This is quite obviously at odds with the decidedly noncoercive approach set forth in the paradigm of Christ's incarnation and ministry.

This theological and spiritual error is somewhat mitigated by the centrality of missional relationships and missional communities, given that these GCT practices are often exercised in relational contexts—environments of genuine hospitality that incline toward life-on-life mutuality. As Roxburgh suggests and as I observed in my fieldwork,[108] hospitality is a practice that interrupts dehumanizing subject–object relations and challenges the deeply held assumptions that drive them.[109] That is, the relational/hospitable practices at the core of GCT praxis have the potential to subtly trouble GCT theology at some points of weakness and thus provide fertile soil for the work of the Spirit. This dynamic is explored further in chapter 6.

Though GCT churches speak of their approach to mission as "incarnational," they tend to conceive of the incarnation primarily as a strategy for effective mission.[110] Rarely is the incarnation appreciated for its larger significance as revelatory of how the *means* of God's mission manifest the nature of God's Reign. Consistent with their belief that Scripture offers a playbook for effective mission, churches in the GCT model take from Jesus's example a relational, culturally relevant approach but do not give heed to how the life and ministry of Jesus reveal the noncoercive character of God's mission in Christ. God's way of mission fundamentally honors human dignity and freedom: "Nowhere is the theme of reciprocity in relationships more evident than in the incarnation."[111] GCT churches often approach the ministry of Jesus as a tactical exemplar for effective evangelism. Their hermeneutic of effectiveness belies a productionistic logic of mission that overlooks the fact that Jesus's earthly mission was strikingly ineffective in terms of "multiplying" disciples.[112]

A further important weakness of the GCT model is that while its churches tend to be involved in noteworthy ministries of compassion and service, they do so instrumentally as a means of gaining credibility and relational contacts for the purpose of personal evangelism. As Roxburgh notes, "if the basic intent of our engagement in the neighborhood is to attract and get people into our church, then we will, no matter how much we might want it otherwise, treat our neighbors as the objects of that goal, as ends to a strategy."[113] This instrumental logic of service not only reinforces the objectification of neighbors but it also reflects a poor understanding of the *missio Dei*'s holistic scope. God seeks not only the salvation of human souls but also the renewal of all things within the Reign of God. Indeed, substantive reflection on the central focus of Jesus's ministry—the Reign of God—is very limited in these churches. When it does enter conversation—as the "Kingdom of God"—it is often in the context of stressing the church's mission to "build" or "extend" the Kingdom. Such language betrays a misunderstanding regarding the nature of the Reign and the nature of mission. In fact, Jesus never spoke of human agents building or extending the Reign of God. Rather, Jesus presented his listeners with the possibilities of entering, receiving, seeking, and inheriting the Reign of God.[114] The Reign of God's peace is not and will not be the product of human agency; it is God's coming shalom for the whole of creation, now breaking in and being freely offered as a gift.

Typical GCT churches are driven by the idea that God's ambition is to save people from hell and for heaven, and that God has largely delegated this task to the church, and given them the Spirit so they can get it done. But when you begin to see that the *missio Dei* is bigger than getting some people into heaven, that it is the renewal of all things, the massiveness of this scope starts to undermine the credibility of the notion that God has commissioned the church to accomplish such an overwhelming task. Recognizing that God's mission is cosmic renewal drives the church to stop trying to muster its strength to "get it done" and to start asking God: "What is our part to play in this? How might we participate?"

The thin understanding and representation of the Reign of God typical of GCT churches is further reflected in a lack of hopefulness or curiosity about God's activity in the world beyond the church. This is closely bound up in their understanding of "the Gospel" which—in its representation of the Christian meta-narrative of creation-fall-redemption-*eschaton*—lays heavy emphasis on fall and redemption but gives little attention to creation and the *eschaton*. The result is a diminished anthropology. Their stress upon human sinfulness nearly overwhelms celebration of the *imago Dei*. In addition, their celebration of God's accomplished work of human salvation dwarfs their attention to God's inbreaking renewal of all things. By contrast, missional theology insists that the present be understood in an eschatological light: the God who will bring to pass the renewal of all things is already, always, and everywhere out ahead of the church. "God is," as Branson says "on the ground in neighborhoods and communities."[115]

This missional perspective is not reflected in GCT descriptions of their Seattle context, which are filled with overwhelmingly pejorative terms: unchurched, post-Christian, spiritually dark, lost, sinful, rebellious. As Newbigin stressed, the gospel does speak a "No" to every culture, but also a "Yes." The truly missional church is not only a contrast society but also a community that names and celebrates the inbreaking Reign of God as it is currently reflected in their context. Missional churches echo Jesus's own witness: the Reign of God is among you! By contrast, an overdrawn "ecclesiology of the church as a contrast society tends to limit the ability of the church to actively discern God's work through the Spirit within the larger world in order to more fully participate in it."[116] Van Gelder and Zscheile aptly summarize this theological weakness: "[A]ny discussion of the reign of God is either very limited or absent in defining God's redemptive work in relation to the church and world, which makes the church the primary locus of God's redemptive activity."[117]

Finally, this inadequate eschatology is paired with a functionalist ecclesiology. While the church is missionary in nature, the missional church is considerably more than a mission team. Whereas the church in missional perspective is a participation in the life of the Triune God—a seed of the new humanity with an eternal quality—the church as missionary task force is a temporary, purely instrumental group. The church as mission team does not hold up well in eschatological perspective. When the redemptive mission is complete, what then is the church? Missional theology would suggest the church's nature will continue to be what it always has been–human community in cooperative fellowship with the Triune community whose life is a never-ceasing overflow and extension of goodness and blessing.

In summary, Great Commission Team practical ecclesiology is more properly regarded as a mission-driven model of church rather than a genuinely missional one. It should be affirmed for its proactive commitment to God's redemptive work in the world, its affirmation that the church has a key role to play in God's mission, its ability to cultivate strong missional vocation, its cognizance of God's activity in the lives of its members, and its commitment to offering substantive cultural critique. However, at multiple key points it lacks authentically missional character. It tends to circumscribe the scope of God's mission to evangelism, to exaggerate the role of human agency and the church in its fulfillment, to view the context in godforsaken terms, and to present an inadequately Trinitarian vision of God. These weaknesses compound to produce a deeply duty-bound mission spirituality that bears bad spiritual fruit in the lives of Christians and reinforces hierarchically ordered leadership structures. Moreover, this spirituality of missionary obedience fosters inattentiveness to the Spirit, as well as to persons, while fostering subtly coercive and ultimately dehumanizing forms of evangelism.[118] For these reasons, theologians and practitioners in GCT contexts have ample reason for critical self-reflection (and repentance) as they seek to make the best of this prominent model of ecclesial witness.

Household of the Spirit in Missional Theological Perspective

The Household of the Spirit practical ecclesiology is lived out among Pentecostal and Charismatic churches that gather in worship to intimately experience and testify to a miracle-working God. HS churches band together as extended families seeking refuge, feeling that their environment is spiritually hostile and, for the numerous immigrant and minority churches in the model, culturally foreign. In addition to inviting others into their spiritual sanctuary, members are encouraged to be conduits of God's supernatural healing and encouragement to others through personal intercessory prayer.

This practical ecclesiological model has several notable strengths in missional perspective. Most clearly, this model revels in the agency of God—through the Spirit—at work in the contemporary sphere.[119] God is routinely credited for personal experiences of healing and provision. Just as important, HS churches know the present action of God through *feeling*—that is, through intimate emotional, physical, and spiritual sensations, most typically in the midst of worship gatherings in times of song or prayer. HS churches not only affirm that God is active in the world, they also experience God's presence in an immersive, visceral way.

Second, the practice of testimony, often present in HS worship, serves to further attest to the reality of God's agency and power as they have been encountered through experiences of conversion or of miraculous healing. Declaring the spiritual and physical transformations that God has wrought among them is an important way these churches give witness to the Reign of God. The gospel, according to churches in this model, is not merely news about the salvific work of Jesus accomplished 2,000 years ago but, additionally, news about the Spirit's contemporary work in their lives. While HS churches would not be likely to frame the Spirit's work as "the first fruits of the inbreaking Reign of God," this is precisely how missional theology would interpret that to which they testify.

Third, like churches in the Great Commission Team model, HS churches nurture within their ranks a strong sense of personal missional identity and vocation.[120] While this includes the GCT drive to personal evangelism, it is more characteristically expressed through offers of personal, intercessory prayer. HS leaders admonish community members, as Spirit-filled agents of God's power, to "bring light, bring life, bring healing."

Fourth, and relatedly, the most distinguishing mission practice within the HS model—prayer for healing—is intrinsically and explicitly intended as a human–divine cooperative one. Intercessory prayer, rightly understood, is entering into the Trinitarian conversation in which the Father speaks, the Son intercedes, and the Spirit groans.[121] As such, it is fundamentally a participation in the Trinitarian mission. For even as God is working for redemption and renewal, intercessors join their voices and wills to God's redemptive purpose as it relates to a specific situation, so that through their partnership God might graciously allow the Reign of God to break through in those particular circumstances. Intercessory and healing prayer invite God's comprehensive work and eschatological promise to be made manifest in the particular concerns that Spirit-filled Christians find incongruous with God's coming shalom. Offering to pray for another person (often with the laying on of hands), as a primary form of HS mission, functions to create spaces for giving witness to the gospel as they experience it. Prayer for others embodies their belief in God's personal knowledge and concern for every individual's concrete circumstances, as well as God's presence (as real as the hand laid upon the one receiving prayer) and power to intervene "right here, right now."

Moreover, the primary orientation of HS prayer toward physical healing suggests a somewhat holistic understanding of the *missio Dei*. God, healing prayer reminds us, cares about bodies and intends not only to "forgive all your sins" but also to "heal all your diseases."[122] In addition to prayers for healing, HS prayers frequently invoke supernatural resources as they seek to offer prophetic words of encouragement—as I experienced myself on two occasions during this research.[123] This simultaneous concern for physical and psycho-spiritual well-being is consistent, as well, with major foci of Jesus's own ministry. In addition to healing of physical ailments, Christ was known for his ministry of exorcism and speaking prophetic words of blessing, especially among the poor and marginalized.[124] As such, this key HS practice reflects resonance with the incarnation as a paradigm for God's way of mission.

The significant number of HS churches composed of minority cultural groups offers another strength in missional perspective: their presence as a nonmajority Christian group in the midst of a population that tends to regard Christianity as an (outdated) Anglo tradition testifies to the boundary-crossing work of the Spirit and the rich human diversity included within the Reign of God. They can also offer a sorely needed witness to Christians who are part of the majority Anglo culture. As Newbigin argued, "the only way in which the gospel can challenge our culturally conditioned interpretations of it is through the witness of those who have read the Bible with minds shaped by other cultures. We have to listen to others."[125] HS churches (and minority culture congregationsmore broadly) can play a critical role in helping majority culture Christians begin to recognize how their interpretations of the gospel are culturally tinged and to consider more seriously and concretely the points of tension that exist between the Reign of God and "the way things are." This understanding, in turn, promises to enhance the faithfulness of the whole church's witness.

Several of the missional critiques of the Great Commission Team also apply to the Household of the Spirit model. First, despite their emphasis on the agency of the Spirit, HS churches demonstrate a lack of imagination and hopefulness for God's activity beyond the church. The HS model tends toward an underdeveloped appreciation for God's work in the world and a correspondingly overdeveloped view of the role of the church within God's mission that manifests in various ways. One way this is evident is that HS churches—like GCT churches—describe their cultural and social context in overwhelmingly disparaging terms ("Sin. Sin. Sin."). As a result, they inhibit rather than cultivate attention to the inbreaking Reign of God "on the ground in neighborhoods and communities."[126] The centrality of worship services in this model—while not a weakness in itself—reflects weak apprehension of God's presence and activity in the wider world.[127] The Spirit is, for the most part, expected to act in surprisingly predictable places and through a predictable and limited number of individuals.[128] It should be noted, however, that their emphasis on daily, personal interaction with the Spirit offers a point at which God can (and often does) break through this weakness offering revelations of divine presence in the world that unsettle the dichotomous paradigm.[129] Thus, the HS model contains within its practice resources for mitigating this characteristic weakness.

The exaggerated role for the church as a whole is matched with exaggerated individual self-images, the unfortunate flip side of cultivating strong missional identity. Individual Spirit-filled Christians sometimes slip into regarding themselves as God's (only) instruments in interactions with neighbors and strangers.[130] In these encounters they aspire to bring supernatural light, life, healing. A noble intention, certainly, but often grounded in the understanding that the other is basically an object in need, a person defined by his "God-shaped hole." A posture of *I'm-bringing-the-kingdom* inhibits discernment of the Spirit's unexpected initiatives and undermines the mutuality of relationships commensurate with Christ's way. While praying for the Spirit's blessing in the lives of others can be a divine–human cooperative act par excellence, it can also function to reinscribe a vision of the prayer relationship as facilitating a one-way flow of blessing from the Spirit-filled subject to the objectified person in need.[131] Proposals for mitigating this danger inherent to intercessory prayer as a mission practice are considered in chapter 6.

A further weakness that the HS model shares with GCT churches is a penchant for hierarchical leadership structures and practices. While the ministry of women is somewhat more welcome among HS churches than in the GCT model, HS churches do not exemplify plural leadership. Although an emphasis on spiritual gifts and the Spirit ("who gives to each one for the common good") has the potential to provide a rationale for distributed forms of leadership, in practice HS churches tend to structure leadership around individuals or couples perceived to have apostolic and teaching gifts along with, as a bonus, empowerments to prophesy and heal.[132] Moreover, their teaching on gifts tends to focus on the miraculous nature of (certain) gifts, rather than the missional purpose underlying all the empowerment the Spirit gives for participation in the *missio Dei*.[133]

Multisensory worship services, as noted earlier, facilitate valuable spiritual encounters and foster an important sense of God's presence and agency in worship. The danger, however, when emotion-filled worship gatherings are the focal center of a church's life is that leaders feel a pressure to produce such experiences and under such pressure may resort to un-Christ-like manipulation in order to achieve it. This manipulation can take place in myriad ways, including rhetorically (through guilt-laced financial appeals or heart-wrenching stories) and aesthetically (through powerful visual images, swelling music, and psychologically savvy lighting). The judgment of when such practices have become manipulative is a complex and contextual one that hinges on the *effect* of the practice on the agency of those present (rather than its espoused intent). When such techniques overwhelm the free choice of persons—to whatever end—they fail the test of Jesus's noncoercive way. The *missio Dei*, in contrast, honors human agency and heightens rather than diminishes the power of human will as persons confront the choices that stand before them. To repeat, even when manipulative techniques are used to produce "good" ends—conversion, charitable giving, repentance, forgiveness, service—they are not participations in the *missio Dei*. This is because, as Jesus has demonstrated, legitimate means of the *missio Dei* are always consistent with its end—the peaceable Reign of God.

The previous paragraph considers the ethical liability for leaders of HS worship, but a danger lies also on the side of worshipers. It is this: a focus on a heightened emotional-spiritual experience risks reducing the Spirit of God to a supernatural reality whose primary function is to provide satisfying spiritual consumer experiences. The Spirit of God is no psychedelic drug, and Christian worship does not share the same *telos* as a feel-good movie. If the Spirit is not sought as an agent capable of disrupting consumer expectations of worship and leading the church into disquieting realizations, unfamiliar relationships, and other-oriented lifestyles, then it is dubious whether the spiritual highs experienced in this context are genuine works of God. Worshipers gathered for heightened spiritual experiences must be wary that they are not worshiping the gratifying experiences themselves and in so doing partaking of a synthetic spirit.

To summarize this assessment, the Household of the Spirit model has a unique set of strengths and vulnerabilities, as well as several that overlap with those of the GCT model. HS strengths are found in their witness to God's active agency in their lives and in testimonies to the inbreaking of the Reign of God though miraculous healings and provision, as well as personal, multisensory experiences the Spirit's intimate presence. The model cultivates personal missional vocation and encourages members to actively engage in the divine–human cooperative work of intercessory prayers for healing, blessing, and insight. Unfortunately, HS churches share with GCT churches an impoverished apprehension of God's presence in the world beyond the church, an overwhelmingly critical assessment of their social-cultural environment, and hierarchically ordered structures of leadership. In addition, the model is in particular danger of resorting to emotional manipulation and warping the worship of God into a consumer experience. For these reasons, HS theologians and practitioners have reason both to celebrate the missional potential and to contemplate the model's inherent vulnerabilities as they work to utilize and develop it is as a popular form of ecclesial witness.

New Community in Missional Theological Perspective

The New Community practical ecclesiology is found among emerging churches and mainline congregations whose spirituality is sacramental and liturgical in form and reflects progressive values and thoroughgoing critiques of Evangelicalism. Their primary mission is to be and to witness as a participatory and inclusive worshiping community. Their newness is fourfold inasmuch as they represent (1) a departure from Evangelicalism, (2) innovation within the mainline, (3) affirmation of progressive cultural changes, and (4) an intention that their corporate life would model the new eschatological humanity.

This practical ecclesiological model of the church features some considerable strengths in missional perspective. Foremost among these is the way that the model reflects an understanding of the church as sign and foretaste of the Reign of God. NC churches seek to be socially embodied hermeneutic of the gospel in their manner of shared life and practice.[134] They grasp that the way they structure their life together—their practices and culture—are a chief part of the witness they are called to offer to the world. Thus, their central mission practice is living out their values of inclusive and participatory spiritual community in their worship and corporate life.[135] Their socially embodied witness points to the inclusive and participatory Triune fellowship, as well as to the new redeemed humanity.[136] They give and receive the sacrament of Christ's body weekly that they might become a sacrament of Christ's body in the world.[137] Churches in this model strive to exist as "contrast communities" marked by social practices that are reflective of the way of Jesus.[138]

Even while they seek to order their shared life together in ways that foreshadow the eschatological humanity, members and leaders openly and frequently speak of their personal failings and doubts. This vulnerability enacts the church's identity as a *sign* of the Reign of God, confessing that the church and the people who compose it are not yet whole; they have not yet arrived at the fullness of the Reign of God.[139] Personal expressions of humility echo a corporate sense that the renewal of all things is a task beyond the church's power and scope. It is a work of God that is manifest not only in the church but also in the world. With this eschatologically rooted humility, NC churches are relatively unencumbered by the burdens of evangelistic duty and spiritual anxiety that characterize GCT and HS communities.[140]

New Community churches embody Branson's missional priorities in several ways. First, NC churches strive to see God at work in the wider world and testify to the inbreaking of the Reign of God as they discern it. This most characteristically takes place in their use and support of the creative arts and their endorsement of progressive social movements. Second, the NC model has a distinctive emphasis on shared models of leadership that create spaces for participatory decision making and spiritual experiences. Third, these churches are sensitive to the dangers of colonial, coercive, and dehumanizing mission approaches and are therefore deeply committed to treating others as subjects.[141] Many NC participants have been wounded by and are wary of religious coercion and exclusion. This is reflected in their inclusive welcome, the centrality of conversation and dialogical modes of communication, "open space" for self-guided practice in worship, and distain for proselytism and evangelistic appeals.

NC churches are predominantly homogenous, but they do reflect Branson's priority of boundary-crossing in a certain way as they blur the lines between the sacred and secular. In worship, this blurring occurs in such practices as the use of "ordinary icons" and blending of traditional songs and liturgies with contemporary art, culture, and technology. The centrality of the Eucharist, and meal sharing in general, points to the sacramental nature of such blurring. Their penchant for gathering in nontraditional worship environments further complexifies the division between sacred and secular.[142] Their everyday spirituality reflects their belief that God is at work beyond the confines of the church. They approach the ordinary stuff of life—bodies, emotions, nature, people, conversations, beverages, the arts—as sites of God's mysterious presence. Also important are the porous community boundaries that blur traditional lines between church insiders and outsiders. They describe even those who have relational ties to the fellowship as "part of our community" whether or not they participate in official church activities. In their practice of sacred–secular boundary blurring, NC churches implicitly testify to multiple missional perspectives. Among these are (1) the incarnation's key implication that the sacred can be found in the midst of the profane; (2) the Spirit's free-ranging character, in that its domain can neither be tied down to a specific place or time nor tied to a single cultural or religious group; and (3) the holistic scope of God's mission as the renewal of all things.

These promising resonances with missional theology notwithstanding, New Community practical ecclesiology also has some notable weaknesses in missional perspective. Several of the critiques in the following paragraphs are similar in kind to those that Evangelicals have directed toward mainline and progressive Christians for decades: they accommodate to culture, lack evangelistic zeal, have a low view of Scripture, and so on. Here, however, these criticisms are developed explicitly from the perspective of missional theology, which—as the previous section demonstrated—can be equally harsh in its critique of certain forms of Evangelical theology and practice.

A significant flaw of New Community practical ecclesiology stems from the negatively constructed nature of its identity and practice. The NC model is, in a basic and unfortunate way, anti-Evangelical.[143] Marti and Ganiel describe emerging Christians as reactive, noting that they "*react* primarily against conservative/evangelical/fundamentalist Protestantism but also against other forms of traditional Christianity that they have experienced as stifling or inauthentic."[144] An identity rooted so deeply in distinction from other churches is at odds with an authentically missional identity. By consistently defining themselves in contrast with Evangelicals—both corporately and in personal accounts—churches in this model implicitly limit their frame of reference to the ecclesiastical scale rather than grounding their identity in the work of the Triune God.

The result of this negative identity construction is the rejection of Evangelical perspectives and practices without adequately considering the practical wisdom they may carry.[145] Among the babies that NC churches ingloriously throw out with the Evangelical bathwater are intentional, proactive practices of evangelism and discipleship.[146] While GCT churches are too often compelled by an ethic of duty, and while they often practice evangelism and discipleship in subtly dehumanizing ways, evangelism and discipleship are, nonetheless, basic forms of human participation in the *missio Dei* that NC churches largely eschew. To put this weakness in Newbigin's terms, while on the whole churches in this model self-consciously serve as *sign* and *foretaste* of the new humanity, they are conspicuously inert when it comes to being an *instrument* for it by proactively joining in God's redemption of human souls. While GCT churches typically assert *too much* agency in the realization of the Reign via evangelization, churches in the New Community model typically assert *too little* and, thus, embody a diminished sense of mission.

This diminished sense of active, personal participation in the actualization of God's Reign is most clear in their disdain for evangelism. NC churches, on the whole, do not encourage members to try to share their faith, but as an alternative, try to cultivate agenda-free friendships with diverse persons. This approach is attractive for its apparent humility, but it rests on a false dichotomy between evangelism and friendship. As a result, these communities ultimately over-correct for the productionistic logic and dehumanizing evangelism practices of some Evangelicals. To set this in the incarnational frame, consider that Jesus did not come merely to fellowship with sinners but, rather, as he claimed, "to seek and save the lost." This "seeking and saving" ministry was a matter not only of forming a new community of disciples, not only of performing healings, not only of inclusive table fellowship, but also of public preaching and private conversations about the Reign of God, its demand for repentance, and its offer of salvation. In terms celebrated by GCT churches and that make NC churches uneasy, proclamation of the gospel and personal evangelism were key elements of Jesus's ministry. Thus, followers of Christ are called to actively pray for, discern, and seize opportunities to participate in God's work via personal, evangelistic conversations with others (whom they love and whose agency they honor).

Their evangelistic malaise might seem less egregious if it were paired with zeal for ministries of compassion and justice. On the whole, however, they are not. While NC churches talk and pray comparatively more about justice and mercy than GCT churches, few practice it with as much intentionality as the typical GCT church.[147] Together, these data suggest that NC churches fail to recognize that the eschatological humanity they seek to embody in their social practices is missionary not only in nature (i.e., by virtue of its social embodiment) but also in its engagement with the world. The new humanity, like the divine community, is and ever shall be a missionary fellowship. Just as the church is a fruit of the sending Trinity's desire to extend blessing and to welcome others into its fellowship, missional churches actively seek to extend blessing and welcome so that others, too, may enter into the divine community. Evangelism is intentional extension of this welcome. The focus among NC churches on witness through social embodiment reflects a tendency to envision the Trinity primarily as an ideal community without sufficient reflection on the essential sending that characterizes the relations of the divine persons.[148]

Moreover, the gospel of the Reign of God, as Jesus spoke of and demonstrated it, issues both an inclusive welcome and a costly summons to repentance.[149] The *missio Dei*, as it is bringing about a new redeemed humanity, necessarily calls for conversion. Jesus modeled this paradigmatic divine–human cooperative practice. Following his example, the church's participation in this divine work includes heralding the need for conversion among "sinners" and "saints" alike. Evangelism and disciple-ship call people to turn away from all forms of sin and idolatry and to radically reorient their thinking and living around the near-and-here Reign of God.

Such reorientations, however, can only seem necessary if a meaning-ful difference is seen to exist between the Reign of God and the culture in which a person or community dwells. The overly negative view of progres-sive culture espoused by GCT and HS churches has a counterpart in the overly positive view held by NC churches.[150] Even as God is present and active in all contexts and cultures, the gospel also critiques all cultures and contexts. H. Richard Niebuhr's critiques of liberal Christ of Culture Christians apply; NC churches underestimate the conflicts present between the gospel and the progressive culture they embrace.[151] Newbigin warned of the dangers of syncretism, even confessing to have discovered his own modern, Western Christianity "profoundly syncretistic."[152] In view of this dilemma, Newbigin stressed the imperative of "listen[ing] to the witness of Christians from other cultures."[153] The reality that most of Seattle's NC churches are (1) homogeneous, comprising young, white, well-educated, and politically liberal individuals; and (2) typically not in significant relationships with Christians of other cultures (who could offer needed perspective), no doubt contributes to this weakness.[154]

Prominent missional authors have accused many emerging churches of reflecting little more than a "postmodern attractional" approach.[155] There is certainly nothing new about churches adapting their worship, programming, and message to appeal to certain demographic and ideolog-ical categories. Churches across the theological spectrum are engaged in such well-intentioned, sometimes "successful" efforts, but very rarely do they spring from the deep wells of missional theology. Lighting candles, integrating the arts, and endorsing progressive theological positions may be "relevant," but they are not necessarily missional.

Their approach to Scripture as conversation starter, while intriguing and generative, can also be construed as further evidence of an apparent unwillingness to place their own cultural values and personal practices under divine judgment. God, according NC churches, may be saddened that you are making self-destructive choices and invite you into a more life-giving path, but this God would never get angry about or judge you for them. (Though God is quite free to frequently get angry at and judge their conservative Evangelical foils.) This is what Niebuhr points to when he accuses liberals of distorting the figure of Jesus.[156]

Perhaps the most salient and overarching cultural value to which churches embodying the NC model have tended to accommodate may be summed up as "tolerance." Tolerance, as a core progressive virtue, calls for the acceptance of all forms of difference—cultural, ethnic, religious, sexual, political, lifestyle, and so on—without expressed judgment of their relative validity, truthfulness, or morality except, it should be noted, those forms of diversity that make such judgments. "It seems tolerance acts as a break to any constructive action. . . . [It] reduces us to silence and inactivity, because to add to and seek to change what others think is by definition intolerant."[157] Eager to honor the subjectivity of others, NC churches risk failing to relate to others as Christ did, with a love manifest in a presence and words that not only embraced but also convicted.[158] Hospitality, not modern tolerance, is the ultimate practice for treating others as subjects.[159]

The central place of the worship gathering among NC churches presents a missional liability. Though NC worship is very different from that of Household of the Spirit worship, both risk worship being constructed and received as custom consumer experiences.[160] In NC churches, worship experiences offer a number of consumer goods—moments of individual spiritual inspiration, a sense of personal empowerment, spaces for healing via quasi group therapy, and feelings of belonging. When a church's life is so centered on its unique form of worship, proactive practices of mission are often relegated to secondary, nonessential status. Communities whose operative identity is as consumers with shared tastes in worship experiences are not missional churches. Missional churches are communities whose identity rests in a shared intention to discern and participate in the *missio Dei*—in worship, community, and witness. Whereas a consumer identity centers on personal preferences, a missional identity centers outside of those gathered, in the will and work of God in the world of which the church is a part.

To summarize, the New Community practical ecclesiology embodies missional theology in some vital and unique ways, but it lacks the proactive posture appropriate to intentional participation in the *missio Dei*. It enacts the church as a sign and foretaste of the Reign of God, but not as an instrument purposefully working toward its realization. Their negatively constructed identity, defined in contrast to Evangelicals, is a key factor contributing to several weaknesses. Although the model resonates with each of Branson's missional priorities for church plants, its mode of boundary-crossing rarely fosters the kind of cross-cultural relationships that could challenge their naïvely sanguine assessment of the progressive milieu of which they are gladly a part. Practitioners and thought leaders within this practical ecclesiological model will be wise to grapple with these weaknesses and further develop these strengths as they strive to live into the wisdom of missional theological insights.

Neighborhood Incarnation in Missional Theological Perspective

Among the four practical ecclesiological models discovered in Seattle, the Neighborhood Incarnation model most thoroughly embodies a missional vision. NI identity, mission, and spirituality generate considerable resonance with both the core ideas of missional theology and Branson's missional priorities for church planting.

NI churches recognize God as the prime agent in mission in a way akin to New Communities, but without slipping into their typically passive posture. When they speak about the origins of their churches, they commonly point to God's call and guidance as determining the parish in which they planted and the particular mission efforts they are involved in. Once in place, they deliberately seek to discern the Spirit's initiatives so that they might participate. Their participation in the *missio Dei* includes both specific mission efforts and, more fundamentally, the character of its communal life together. That is, like NC churches, NI churches understand that their social practices and material spaces are critical aspects of their witness.

Like GCT churches, NI churches understand themselves as the sent people of a sending God. Both have the strength of a deep-rooted missional identity that drives proactive engagement in their communities and forming new relationships. However, whereas the GCT model identifies chiefly with the evangelistic purpose for which Jesus was sent—"to seek and save the lost"—the NI model identifies most strongly with the placed nature of Jesus's sentness—"The Word . . . moved into the neighborhood." NI churches reflect the sending nature of the Trinity as communities that believe they have been sent to dwell within their local parishes. Even as the Father sent the Son to the people and place of Palestine, NI churches believe they have been sent by God to their neighborhoods.

Their definitive identification as Christian communities *in, of,* and *for* their neighborhoods yields several strengths in missional perspective.[161] First, it results in a holistic concern for the neighborhood that testifies to the holistic scope of the *missio Dei*. The contrast with the Great Commission Team model is illustrative. Whereas GCT churches believe they have been sent with a limited task on a comprehensive scale (evangelization . . . of all nations), NI churches believe they have been sent with a comprehensive task on a limited scale (renewal of all things . . . within the parish). Even as God's mission is the renewal of all things, NI churches seek to participate in this manifold work within the bounds of their parish. As they do so, they practice the wisdom of Newbigin: "[T]he congregation must be so deeply and intimately involved in the secular concerns of the neighbourhood that it becomes clear to everyone that no one and nothing is outside the range of God's love in Jesus."[162] NI involvement in the "secular concerns" of their neighborhoods points directly to the holistic scope of God's mission.

A second key strength stemming from the model's parish identity is the way that it gives focus to a core task of missional churches: discernment of the Spirit's initiatives. NI churches give concentrated attention to their own local environment as the place where they are to find God. In their particular focus, they affirm that God is present in every context. While it is true that "God is everywhere," this truth is easily invoked by those who seek to justify undisciplined inattention to God's presence in particular places and practices.[163] A parish focus can help to guard against this dispersal of attention.[164]

Closely related to their affirmation of God's local presence is their refreshingly balanced assessment of their context. Whereas GCT and HS churches hold a starkly negative view, and NC churches evidence an overly positive assessment, NI churches more closely approximate the "Yes" and "No" that the gospel speaks to all cultures. While the specific points of affirmation and critique vary from one church to another, the balance of celebration and criticism is considerably more even than in other models. This reflects their understanding that their parishes are places of beauty, need, and hope.[165] The beauty of the neighborhood testifies to God's provenience. The needs reveal the results of sin and brokenness that call for healing and conversion. And the hope is grounded in the belief that God is not finished there yet; God's Reign is yet to come in its fullness.

A third strength related to their neighborhood identification is how it postures church members in relation to those who do not participate in the life of the church. Rather than regarding others primarily through a lens of us/them, churched/unchurched, or Christian/non-Christian, NI participants relate to neighbors, first, as neighbors. That is, as fellow members of the community of foremost importance, their primary reference group is the neighborhood. The key "others" whom they encounter—their neighbors—are persons with whom they share a fundamental solidarity. Moreover, neighbors are simultaneously regarded as those to whom God has sent the church and those whom God has sent *to the church*.[166] Neighbors are not only a mission field for the church but also God's evangelists to the church (even if inadvertently).[167] Hospitality is the natural and essential practice when you believe strangers might be divinely ordained ambassadors of truth, and it is the central mission practice for the model. The positive result of such a fundamental neighborhood identity is that it promotes vital missional vocation while avoiding the dehumanizing liability inherent in GCT conceptions of sentness. NI churches, in short, embody Branson's priority on relating to others as subjects.

NI churches are also in step with Branson's other three missional priorities. They discern neighborhood needs and sense the prompting and resources of God to respond. A primary task of NI leadership is to facilitate this discernment via engagement with God, one another, and neighbor.[168] Their leadership structures are somewhat flattened and distributed, though not as consistently as among NC churches. Also, like NC churches, they engage in boundary-crossing through a blurring of sacred and secular in their everyday spirituality, use of nontraditional gathering spaces, porous community boundaries, and, uniquely, their creation of third places. In addition to this sacred–secular boundary-crossing, NI churches actively seek to connect with persons across the socioeconomic, generational, and cultural barriers that are present within their neighborhoods.[169] Indeed, a neighborhood orientation is much better suited to diversity than a network approach.[170] Their elemental identification with their parish and the full spectrum of its people asserts that the neighborhood is a sacred place and that God has ordained that they be in community with their neighbors. These boundary-crossing practices witness to their neighborhoods as places where the free-ranging Spirit is on the move, where the incarnation is reverberating on street corners and in coffee shops, and where the inbreaking Reign of God can be discerned in the stories and faces of neighbors.

Many of the aforementioned strengths could also be described in the incarnational frame. More than the other models, NI churches embody a holistic mission based on the paradigm of Christ's incarnation. NI churches both practice radical solidarity and speak to the cost of discipleship. They relate to others as neighbors, extending belonging and offering humanizing relationships that are free of coercion. Their mission is enacted in word and deed as proclamation and demonstration of God's good news for the neighborhood. NI churches underscore Jesus's ministry of service and table fellowship and strive for continuity with this way of Jesus by prioritizing the work of creating hospitable space and offering concrete benefits to their neighbors. Following the paradigm of the incarnation, they seek to be the Body of Christ by existing as a community that acts in tangible, local, relational ways through such physical things as neighborhood spaces, hugs, and cups of coffee. Their incarnate, material presence in third places and public gatherings opens up spaces for the kind of mutuality and care that characterized Jesus's ministry.

The NI model champions the missional primacy of the local church while simultaneously and subtly challenging traditional congregational theology. While the operative ecclesiology in most congregations ecclesiology identifies the local church with a local group of believers who gather,[171] the Neighborhood Incarnation practical ecclesiology envisions the local church as the neighborhood People of God—as all the followers of Jesus who dwell within a given parish.[172] Traditional congregational ecclesiology emphasizes the practice of *gathering in a place of worship*; Neighborhood Incarnation ecclesiology puts the primary accent on *witness in a place of dwelling*. Congregational ecclesiology focuses on where and how believers *worship*; incarnational ecclesiology focuses on where and how believers *live*. This decentering of worship guards against the danger that gatherings for the worship of God would devolve into consumer-oriented, synthetic spiritual experiences. Their geographically defined ecclesial vision resonates with the longstanding practice of parish, as well as with early Christianity and Scripture in which the one church was divided into churches on the basis of geography—the church in Corinth, or Ephesus, and the like.[173] This raises intriguing questions to be considered in the final chapters about the nature of the church vis-à-vis gatherings, memberships, relational networks, and geography, and may yield promising proposals for ecumenical collaboration in neighborhood mission and even—if one can dare imagine it—the possibility of reunions of the church on the local scale.[174]

These strengths touch on virtually all aspects of missional theology. However, like all practical ecclesiological models, the church as Neighborhood Incarnation also contains some inherent liabilities. One danger is that NI churches would function in isolation from the wider church to their own detriment and to the detriment of Christian witness. This risk flows from both their parish focus and its extra-congregational form. Their intense parish identity has the potential of discouraging meaningful, mutually beneficial, and even necessary connections with these churches' wider contexts. Similarly, developing and defending arguments for noncongregational forms of Christian community can easily degenerate into overly harsh criticisms of more traditional models, fostering distain for the congregations that dominate the religious ecology, as well as the denominations and ecclesiological traditions of which they are a part.[175]

These are real dangers, and churches within the model would be wise to take them seriously. At the same time, I believe the resources for transcending these liabilities are present within the practical ecclesiological model itself. NI churches that listen carefully to neighbors and discern prayerfully the issues present in their parish will predictably discover their complexity and how they are wound up in the cultural, legislative, and political systems at work on the city, state, national, or even global scale. For example, learning the story of a neighbor living in poverty has the power to ignite questions about a range of issues that are best understood within wider contexts, such as access to quality education, health care, and employment opportunities, as well as connected economic and legislative realities such as the local economy and housing regulations. Seeking to participate with God in the renewal of all things within the parish can drive them to understand the complex relationships that exist between the parish and its wider contexts—cities, states, ecoregions, and so on. In their devotion to acting locally, NI churches will ultimately be driven to think globally.[176] This process was evident in myriad ways among the NI churches in the study.[177]

Similarly, within almost every parish are to be found multiple expressions of Christianity, including churches and individuals of various denominational and ecclesiastical traditions. NI churches that devoutly seek to know their neighbors and who conceive of the church as the neighborhood followers of Jesus are primed for ecumenical relationships and partnerships. If they approach fellow Christians in traditional congregational settings with the same posture of listening and respect they take with neighborhood atheists and addicts, they can avoid becoming isolated from the wider church in its diverse expressions. While ecclesial isolation is, in theory, a danger of the model, I found that in practice Seattle's NI churches are overwhelmingly affiliated with national denominations in addition to various networks.

A further liability of the model relates to a strong parish identity; neighborhoods vary considerably with regard to their diversity. Some neighborhoods are more or less homogenous and relatively isolated from the issues that face neighboring communities and the wider contexts of which they are a part (city, state, nation). Consider an affluent suburban community with good schools, housing prices that prohibit poorer residents, and policing policies that drive out "undesirables." A nearsighted NI church that is not intentional about raising its gaze beyond parish borders would likely fail to reflect and participate meaningfully in the Spirit's boundary-crossing work. In such settings, missional churches must call members to intentionally engage with diverse residents of other communities.[178]

The extra-congregational form is, organizationally speaking, both an asset and a liability. While it may be attractive to those who are disenchanted with traditional expressions of Christianity but nonetheless remain interested in following Jesus in community, its novelty poses an obstacle to others. To put it plainly, unchurched people are often wary that unfamiliar, noncongregational churches are cults. Thus, while traditional forms of church are off-putting to many among "the Dones," they are the most legitimate and least suspect form of Christianity for many among the larger much category of the unchurched.[179] A significant number of the unchurched in post-Christian contexts went to church as children, stopped attending as adolescents because of lack of interest rather than disillusionment and will, at some point, become interested in being part of a church again. Typically, this return to church takes place when people get married or have children.[180] These "returners" typically seek out churches that resemble—at least in form if not in theology—those they recall benignly attending as children. That is, many will be in the market for a congregation that gathers in a religious building on Sunday mornings for a sermon and singing, and that provides Christian education classes for children. For the most part they will not be looking for what NI churches offer. They will seek a congregation, not a group of Jesus followers in their neighborhood who focus on practicing local hospitality and service.[181] This presents an organizational liability, though not a theological shortcoming in missional perspective.

A final danger of this model—perhaps the most severe—is the possibility that NI churches would lose their distinctively Christian and/or ecclesial identity and become little more than social service or community development agencies. Constructing and rehearsing rationales for deep engagement in the "secular concerns" of the neighborhood raises the liability of ceasing to give adequate attention to "sacred concerns" such as worship, prayer, personal holiness, and proclamation. Listening to neighbors can be a life-giving practice for discerning the Spirit and witnessing to Christ, but without intentionality this potent practice can become unmoored from its profound spiritual significance. Likewise, the eschatological and Trinitarian practices of service and hospitality can function as powerful witnesses to the Reign of God, but they can also be enacted merely as human efforts to be good people and make a better world.

While churches in this model speak in comparatively balanced ways about their context as both beautiful and broken, the brokenness should be conceived and described not only in its social dimensions but also in its spiritual ones. NI churches need to practice naming not only the social sins such as inequality and racism—critiques that will be largely welcomed in the liberal milieu—but also those of personal sin. As Newbigin cautioned, "The church ought not to fit so comfortably into the situation that it is simply welcomed as one of the well-meaning agencies of philanthropy."[182] The churches in this study may be too new to reveal the extent of this danger. The NI churches I found in Seattle all maintained a strong sense of ecclesial and Christian identity.

In sum, the NI model strongly resonates with missional theology, but nonetheless contains certain noteworthy liabilities. This thoroughgoing missional ecclesiology attests to the primacy of God's agency in mission, attends to the local initiatives of the Spirit, and seeks to follow the model of Christ's incarnational ministry. In addition, representative churches proactively strive to participate holistically in the renewal of all things within their neighborhoods. NI churches engage neighbors as subjects, favor plural models of leadership, and seek to overcome boundary lines that divide neighbors. They exist as communities of Jesus followers (and friends) witnessing to the new redeemed humanity and extending the Trinity's wide welcome into a community of human belonging. Their considerable strength in missional perspective is paired, however, with several vulnerabilities including the potential to lose Christian/ecclesial identity in the midst of engaging in less obviously spiritual matters. In addition, intentionality is required so that NI churches do not become isolated from wider church bodies or succumb to such a strong parish focus as to be guilty of nearsighted ignorance of the connections between the parish and larger contexts. As the most robustly missional practical ecclesiology in the field, this model deserves increased theological and practical consideration by practitioners and theologians alike.

The Neighborhood Incarnation Model in the Seattle Context

One of the central affirmations of missional theology (and the discipline of missiology) is that when it comes to Christian witness, context is key. In view of the importance of context, it must be admitted that the above assessment of these models on the basis of theological priorities and principles alone—while providing insight—is incomplete. The context in which these models of ecclesial witness are functioning is critical for their evaluation. Rather than evaluating at length the various ways each model engages with each of the four characteristic features of the Seattle context, I will, in this section, instead make a case for the Neighborhood Incarnation model as contextually superior for Christian witness in Seattle, as well as, by extension, other urban, technological, progressive, and post-Christian contexts.

The NI model is particularly appropriate for Christian witness in the urban environment for several reasons. First, as noted in chapter 1, urban environments like Seattle are brimming with transplants and lonely individuals who are longing for community. While all four models consider the offer of belonging an important mission priority, the NI model gives focus to this offer within the residents of the parish. This focus increases the likelihood that this community will be more diverse than the affinity-based, homogeneous communities most common in the field. Inasmuch as NI churches reflect the diversity of their parishes, they witness to the boundary-crossing work of the Spirit and to the new redeemed humanity.

A second reason the NI model is especially appropriate in the urban environment stems from the reality of the challenges typically present in the urban context—poverty, homelessness, crime, pollution, and the like. Their driving interest in creating community among neighbors is good for the life of these communities because, as Robert Putnam and Lewis Feldstein note, "the crime rate in a neighborhood is lowered when neighbors know each other well."[183] Beyond the creation of a safer community and generation of social capital through relational means, NI churches engage directly in compassionate service and justice-oriented action as a key mission priority. While GCT churches also practice service in a routine way, they do so instrumentally as a preliminary step (of secondary importance) before the "real" mission of evangelism can occur. In contrast, NI churches recognize that their service is itself participation in the *missio Dei* and thus a practice of the highest order, with intrinsic value on par with that of evangelism (without negating the need for it).

Third and finally, the NI commitment to localism reflects wider urban trends; urban dwellers are becoming increasing disenchanted with commuter lifestyles and are attracted to living in urban walking villages. There are also environmental and health benefits that serve to mitigate some urban challenges; when city-dwellers can live, work, shop, and recreate within a relatively small radius, they are more likely to walk and bike and less dependent upon gas-guzzling and polluting modes of transportation. They are also more likely to forge community-strengthening "weak ties" from a sidewalk vantage than from inside a vehicle.[184] Even when not located in parishes that have been designed or developed by urban planners as urban villages, NI churches promote values such as mixed-use zoning, public spaces, and shopping local that help to create the kinds of neighborhoods more and more people are seeking and that witness to God's mission of seeing human societies flourish as part of the renewal of all things.

The NI model is also uniquely positioned for Christian witness amid an increasingly technological society. As noted in chapter 1, the rapid increase of internet connectivity, hand-held internet devices, and social media use have led to increasing reflection on the human impacts of these pervasive technologies. Various commentators and scholarly studies have raised concerns about how new technologies are distracting, addicting, and ultimately diminishing the quality of human relationships. NI churches have been less eager to exploit these technologies than some other models and more cautious of their negative effects. As digital culture continues to expand, there will be an increasing need for churches to offer theological and practical wisdom for utilizing new technologies in ways that honor the embodied nature of human existence, as well as enhance, rather than diminish, the life-giving bonds between persons. As Andrew Sullivan has written in his revealing personal reflection on "our civilization's specific weakness," "if the churches came to understand that the greatest threat to faith today is not hedonism but distraction, perhaps they might begin to appeal anew to a frazzled digital generation."[185] Key NI practices of hospitality, disciplined attention to place, and focused listening to the people around them seem destined to become increasingly important aspects of the witness the church can offer as an "alternative society" in the midst of a distracted, displaced, and disconnected digital culture.

The naïve might presume that Seattle's progressive values suggest that the most contextually appropriate (and effective) model of church would, itself, be similarly progressive, but this is not the case.[186] Certainly, the progressivism of churches in the New Community model provide a valuable witness as they celebrate points of perceived resonance between Seattle's culture and the eschatological Reign of God. However, it could also be said that Great Commission Team churches provide a valuable witness to the points of discontinuity between the gospel and culture. Counter-intuitively a strongly countercultural posture is correlated to numerical strength.[187] But faithful Christian witness cannot be assessed on the basis of numerical success. As has been previously suggested, faithful contextualization of the gospel requires, on one hand, affirmation and resonance with the culture and, on the other, critique and dissonance. The appropriate Christian witness in a progressive cultural context, then, is—as in all contexts—a witness that is both celebratory and convicting. Neighborhood Incarnation churches model this tension better than the other three models. In so doing, they witness to a new humanity, a new way of life, and a new creation, that—like Jesus—does not submit to yes/no, either/or dichotomies but instead proposes a third way, a better question, a different narrative.[188]

Not only do NI churches model the proper tension of contextualization better than the other models, they also provide a faithful witness to a contextual feature closely related to Seattle's progressivism. That is, although Seattle is a progressive context, it is also (like the nation as a whole) a context that is deeply polarized along liberal and conservative lines. This is true politically as well as religiously, as is so evident in the tension between GCT and NC churches. In a social context defined by division and antipathy between liberals and conservatives, most new churches identify strongly (even if not publicly) with one label and against the other. GCT (as well as HS) churches are predominantly theological and political conservatives decrying their hedonistic liberal environment, as well as the accommodations of liberal churches. NC churches are predominantly theological and political liberals celebrating their progressive context and distancing themselves from the dogmatism and abusive practices of conservative churches. While these models are in polar opposition, they are nonetheless locked in the same culturally defined dichotomy. As a result, the ecclesial identity of each is, in large part, negatively constructed in contrast to the other. GCT churches functionally declare: "We are a Gospel-centered church (not one of those liberal, pick-and-choose your morality, activist churches)" while NC churches take the opposing position, asserting that "We are a progressive, inclusive community (not one of those oppressive, proselytizing, Bible-thumping churches)." Faithful ecclesial witness in a polarized context, however, prohibits identification with either side of such dichotomies. The boundary-crossing Spirit does not lead churches to be defined in such antithetical ways. The best alternative to this either/or deadlock is a model of church that breaks out of the dichotomy by refusing to root its identity within the parameters of the conservative/liberal binary. In such a setting, strong identification with *either* "conservative" or "liberal" factions does a disservice to Christian witness and hampers discernment of the Spirit.

Unlike the other models, NI practical ecclesiology cannot be quickly boxed into the pervasive liberal/conservative dichotomy. This is perhaps because the model does not rest on a particular pattern of spirituality or theology. Indeed, for NI churches, neighborhood solidarity is the preeminent and model-defining identity marker.[189] While some churches in the NI model reflect strong evangelical or progressive spiritualties, the logic of the model itself tends to relativize these commitments, downgrading them to levels of secondary importance. This opens possibilities for NI churches to more freely shape their theology and practice without being constrained by the stark division entrenched in the political context and reified by the predominant ecclesiastical landscape.[190] As such, NI churches can more naturally include persons who may themselves identify as either liberal or conservative. Crafting such diverse, alternative communities can provide a dramatic witness to the gospel in a polarized context. This witness is precisely the kind that results from the boundary-crossing work of the Spirit that the missional church seeks to join.

Fourth and finally, the post-Christian character of Seattle has tremendous implications for Christian witness. In a setting where levels of church participation and affiliation are markedly low, and in which religious institutions and leaders have a negligible role in the public square, Christians must learn to practice Christian witness from the margins of power via practices that neither require nor seek the cultural dominance held by the church during Christendom. Attempts to leverage public institutions for Christian formation though such things as school prayer or to promote Christian morality via devout politicians and legislation are neither faithful to the noncoercive way of Jesus nor can they any longer hope to be effective. In their own way, each of the models highlights distinct and valuable post-Christendom practices of witness. Of note, Great Commission Team churches prioritize personal, relational faith-sharing; Household of the Spirit churches practice personal, intercessory prayer for others; New Community churches strive to witness via a participatory community; and Neighborhood Incarnation churches accentuate mission in the forms of hospitality and service.

While each of these forms of witness is valid and potentially faithful and fruitful, hospitality is unique as a simultaneously proactive and humble practice of Christian witness. As Catholic spiritual writer Henri Nouwen has written:

182   CHURCH PLANTING IN POST-CHRISTIAN SOIL

> Hospitality means primarily the creation of free space where the
> stranger can enter and become a friend instead of an enemy.
> Hospitality is not to change people, but to offer them space where
> change can take place. It is not to bring men and women over to our
> side, but to offer freedom not disturbed by dividing lines.[191]

Giving and receiving hospitality brings a listening posture together with
a serving posture, and sets up a mutual relationship with the other. As
such, it is the premier form of Christian witness in post-Christian and
post-Christendom contexts. GCT and NC models do practice hospitality in
significant and vibrant ways, but in the NI model hospitality permeates all
dimensions of the practical ecclesiology, shaping its spirituality, mission,
and identity. Evangelism, intercessory prayer, and service, while needed,
have too often been practiced within Christendom patterns of unequal
relations in which Christians regard themselves as benevolent evange-
list-intercessor-helpers condescending to assist the other, a lost and needy
recipient. Such power dynamics fail to honor the subjectivity of the other
and inhibit discernment of the Spirit and presence of Christ as it is mediated to the Christian through the other. While the NC practice of modeling
participatory community commendably avoids the trap of unequal relations, when it is not accompanied by more proactive practices it represents
an over-correction for abuses and yields a largely inert practice of witness.
Hospitality, however, as NI churches practice it, is both a proactive form of
witness and one that intrinsically inclines toward relationships of mutuality. It also has a sound pedigree as a central and early Christian practice.[192]
As Christians in post-Christian settings strive to offer and receive hospitality, they model both proactive participation in the *missio Dei* and humble submission to marginality and dependence that is in concert with the
witness of Jesus and the early church. The NI model's distinctive priority
on hospitality commends it as a preferred practical ecclesiology in post-
Christian contexts.

In conclusion, Neighborhood Incarnation practical ecclesiology is not
only the model that most thoroughly embodies missional theology, it is
also (and perhaps consequentially) especially well suited for Christian
ecclesial witness in urban, technological, progressive, and post-Christian
contexts like Seattle—contexts in which U.S. church planters will increasingly find themselves.[193] Inasmuch as the nation continues to follow
Seattle's trajectories, the NI model will take on increasing relevance. In
light of these trends and the preceding assessment, focused efforts to

further develop the NI model and plant new NI churches are practically savvy and theologically wise.

This endorsement of the NI model should not be construed as grounds for the rejection of the others. Faithful ecclesial witness in our complex and diverse settings calls for a "mixed economy" of ecclesial expressions. Multiple practical ecclesiologies are needed not only so that we can provide "all kinds of churches for all kinds of people" but also because a variety of forms of church provide unique and needed witness to the multiple dimensions of the nature of the church, the gospel, and the Reign of God.[194] Dismissing models—even those with serious theological weaknesses and practical flaws—would be both misguided and futile, since churches in each of these models will continue to be started. Instead, this project aims to utilize the theological and contextual critique of this chapter toward the development of proposals for how practitioners and theologians working with each model might mitigate its weaknesses and maximize its strengths, thus increasing its potency for faithful and vital Christian witness. The strengths and weaknesses of each model will be taken into consideration in the following chapter, in proposals for capitalizing on the former and mitigating the latter.

6

Renewing Practice in the Models

THE AIM OF this book is to assist the U.S. church in its pursuit of faithful and vital ecclesial witness. The preceding chapters have identified and assessed the most prominent practical ecclesiological models in the future-trending city of Seattle, Washington. This penultimate chapter draws upon the missional theological critiques of the previous chapter to propose concrete steps that practitioners in each of the four models can take to minimize the characteristic weaknesses of their models and amplify their unique strengths. Offering these proposals is itself an exercise in Christian witness. With the previous chapter, the proposals testify to the eschatological and ethical disjunctures between the church in its concrete manifestations and a vision of the Reign of God. They confess the church's imperfection as a sign of God's coming Reign while also affirming the church's nature as a foretaste of the Reign, a nature that is made manifest inasmuch as the church authentically participates in the life and mission of the Trinity.

More central to this project, however, is the witness that can be made in the ongoing transformation, renewal, and reimagining of ecclesial life. The need for ongoing ecclesial change stems from the church's own frailty, as well as the nature of its missionary task. As John H. Yoder wrote,

> If the church is to be missionary, change and faithfulness must not be alternatives. We must find ways of defining both of them so they belong together. Faithfulness must not be conceived of as timeless rigidity. Change must not include a blank check for all kinds of adaptation, but rather modification within the original mandate.[1]

The development of new churches and new forms of church is part of this ongoing witness. New churches implicitly testify that previously existing churches were not sufficient to embody the full diversity and beauty of God's Reign in all contexts. The renewal and redevelopment of existing churches and models of church also testify to the unrealized dimension of the Reign of God. As Darrell Guder has put it, the renewal of congregations is "really a question of their conversion, their own evangelization."[2] In fact, the willingness of the church to be evangelized is a key aspect of its witness to a living Christ and a Reign more beautiful than the current reality of church represents. The visible reformation of the church offers a public testimony. Thus, Guder writes, "the essence of the church's credible witness is its own ongoing evangelization."[3] That is, a missional church must not only faithfully evangelize but also faithfully be evangelized, welcoming the ongoing converting work of the Spirit in its midst. If evangelism is also directed at the church, then conversion is an appropriate way of talking about the requisite response. Indeed, the Spirit's evangelism among the people of God calls it to repentance, to conversion, and to live in ways that are more at home with the Reign of God.

A missional church is not a static entity but, rather, a community that is endlessly being reformed by the Spirit of God—*semper reformanda*. This "continuing conversion" happens as a "congregation hears, responds to, and obeys the gospel of Jesus Christ in ever new and more comprehensive ways."[4] The church's response to the gospel is its witness. Indeed, the totality of its authentically ecclesial life is response to the gospel. If the church is a "hermeneutic of the gospel" it is not because it is ever a perfect embodiment of the Reign of God but precisely because it is not—and yet it receives God's grace to become ever more so. Therefore, the church's willingness to relinquish and repent, to repeatedly convert its practice toward greater harmony with God's Reign, and intentionally allow its form to be reshaped for more integral participation in the *missio Dei* may be the missional mark par excellence. William Cavanaugh puts it plainly, "the visibility of the church lies in its repentance."[5] It is in the hope that new and renewing churches and forms of church may faithfully make this visible witness that the following proposals are offered.

Guidance for Practitioners

The proposals developed in this section are offered to practitioners who identify with one (or more) of the practical ecclesiological models this project has discovered and analyzed. These proposals are relevant to established churches and developing churches within each model. As practical ecclesiologies are lived, socially embodied, and operative ecclesiologies, the proposals call, first and foremost, for renewed practice. They do not directly call for thoroughgoing reformulations of the doctrinal ecclesiologies espoused by churches in each model in order to bring them into alignment with the insights of missional theology. This is not, however, because these doctrinal ecclesiologies are free from theological weaknesses, as chapter 5 has demonstrated. Rather, these proposals are primarily of a practical nature, for three basic reasons. First, practitioners, as a group, are typically more open to concrete suggestions than to unsolicited theological critique of their convictions about the nature of the church. Second, and relatedly, it is renewed practice that has the most potential for exposing the inadequacies of doctrinal formulations and fostering the imagination necessary for more robust articulations. As Father Richard Rohr has noted, "We do not think ourselves into a new kind of living. We live ourselves into a new kind of thinking."[6]

The third reason for the practical, rather than doctrinal, nature of these proposals is grounded in the belief that God has been and is at work among these Christian communities. As indicated in this book's introduction, the ecclesial communities included in the sample were limited to those that would be regarded as fellow members in the Body of Christ by the majority of other Christian churches. Thus, inclusion was determined on the basis of their Trinitarian doctrine and baptismal practice. While it is beyond the scope of this project to prove the ecclesiality of these Christian communities, I join the ecumenical church in recognizing that even in their typical, current forms, which manifest various theological and practical weaknesses, the communities that embody each of these models, are composed of members of Christ's Body through baptism. These communities are made up of the church (the people) even if not all Christian traditions would recognize the particular communities themselves as churches in the fullest sense. Inasmuch as Christ is present in a special way wherever two or three are gathered in Jesus's name, as the ecumenical church would agree is the case in all these communities, I presume that they have been and continue to be special loci for the presence and mission of God.[7] As such, I regard these communities as stewards of God-given practical wisdom. These traces of God's handiwork include not only kernels of spiritual truth but also practices capable of mediating genuine engagement with God. Among the characteristic patterns of each model, therefore, are practices that are capable of opening the community to transformative encounters with the evangelizing, converting Spirit of God. The net result of the ecclesiality of these bodies, then, is that each practical ecclesiological model contains within its constellation of core practices resources for its own spiritual and missional renewal. As a result, among the proposals offered for practitioners in each model are included those for renewed engagement with particular practices already embedded within the model and its cultural logic.[8]

For these three reasons, the proposals offered to practitioners are of a practical rather than doctrinal nature. These proposals are intended to strike a balance between practical coherence within the model and constructive subversion of it. While they explicitly aim to mitigate weaknesses, they do so by calling for practices intended to resonate within the model's cultural logic so that they might actually be received by practitioners who are invested in retaining the characteristic strengths of the model. The proposals are developed in order to walk a fine line between maintaining the status quo and subverting it. These "tweaks" in practice are calibrated to enhance the models' characteristic strengths and to shrewdly, over time, erode problematic theology and practice.

In multiple cases, the genesis for particular proposals is found in practices I encountered among churches in the model who reflected a more missional quality than was typical of the model as a whole. Often, missional exemplars among GCT, HS, and NC churches were simultaneously instances of the Neighborhood Incarnational model. I found these NI+ churches to be ripe sources for best practices within the additional model. The missional excellence of the NI model suggests that practices for renewal within NI churches be considered first.

Renewed Practice for Neighborhood Incarnation Churches

Neighborhood Incarnation churches are Christian communities in, of, and for their immediate neighbors who exercise hospitality as a practice of spirituality and mission, seeking to discern God's presence and initiatives in the midst of everyday parish life. Its varied embodiments among new Seattle churches are vibrant and promising. The overall missional and contextual strength of this model has important implications for the other models.

Structure Local Discernment

The first set of proposals for NI practitioners builds off of one of the model's key strengths—its characteristic sacred consciousness—and seeks to guard against its most threatening liability, loss of distinctively Christian and/or ecclesial identity. One of the principal tasks of missional churches is the discernment of the Spirit's initiatives. The conviction that God is everywhere—emphasized by both NC and NI churches—risks diffusing attention, and therefore diminishing consciousness of the sacred rather than heightening it. Neighborhood rootedness is one powerful way of focusing attention, and it is thus a key strength of the NI model. But the mere assertion that God is present in the neighborhood can still leave the average community participant uncertain as to how it might actually go about trying to discern the divine presence. While the parish gives *focus* to this task, specific patterns of practice and contexts for discernment are still needed to realize the full potential of disciplined attentiveness.

I propose practices and contexts of three basic types for structuring local discernment in a way or rule of life. First, practices of *neighboring, conversation and meal sharing*, can give form to NI intentions to discern God as they listen to and build community among neighbors. While conversation is a universal human practice, it should not be assumed that all who aspire to NI ideals are comfortable or adequately skilled in its art. As Roxburgh has observed, many in our society—perhaps especially Christians—have seemingly forgotten or failed to learn how to have a conversation about the normal stuff of life.[9] By contrast, Jesus was an excellent conversationalist, as can be seen in various texts, most notably his conversation with the Samaritan woman at the well in John 4.[10] NI leadership can fulfill its call to equip the saints by recommending several questions that members of the community might ask neighbors in everyday conversation, train them in attentive and reflective listening skills, and provide contexts for reflection on these conversations.[11] Further obstacles to conversations are lifestyles and built environments that inhibit opportunities for them to arise organically.[12] NI practitioners have offered various suggestions, including increasing use of the front yard and porch, building a bench or free little library, regular walks, and frequenting neighborhood parks and coffee shops.

Meal sharing is an elemental human practice of solidarity that nonverbally expresses trust and forges social ties. Vitally, meals provide contexts for deeper, extended conversations with neighbors in an environment of warmth. Hosting neighbors for a meal not only conveys a basic interest in their nourishment but also shows a desire to know them and a willingness for them to know you, enacted in the opening of the private space of the home. As a rule of thumb, NI practitioners may find it helpful to encourage participants in the church to seek opportunities for conversation with neighbors on at least a weekly basis and to share a meal with a neighbor at least once a month. Promoting these two neighboring practices as basic to the way of life among Neighborhood Incarnation churches can give structure to their intention that the whole of their fellowship would participate in discerning God's presence and initiatives in the midst of relationship with their neighbors.

A second proposal for giving concrete form to efforts of local discernment is to highlight two forms of *prayer for discernment*.[13] One commendable practice of discerning prayer is neighborhood prayer-walking—that is, simply going for a walk in the neighborhood with a spiritual intention. While among some Christian groups prayer-walking is practiced assertively as a way of "claiming" a neighborhood for Christ or engaging in spiritual warfare, I recommend it to NI churches as an active but more receptive than assertive practice of discernment. Prayer-walking as a discernment practice can weave together attention to God and availability to neighbors. It is particularly suited to the walking lifestyles celebrated by NI churches. Prayer-walking is praying with eyes open to the world in which God is present. It is an embodied form of praying "with your feet," as well as a sacramental practice fostering recognition of the sidewalks underfoot as hallowed ground. Prayer-walkers should pray silently and unobtrusively (so as not to appear mentally unstable), but may do so in a variety of manners. They might silently recite short, memorized petitions such as "Thy kingdom come, thy will be done, in [neighborhood] as it is in heaven" or "Grant me eyes to see and ears to hear." Alternatively, prayers of intercession might be offered for particular persons or neighborhood issues.[14] More positively, prayer-walkers might offer up to God spontaneous thoughts of gratitude for signs of beauty and hope or silently direct the Aaronic blessing, "May the Lord bless you and keep you . . . ," toward all persons and residences on which their eyes fall.[15] Whatever type of prayer is used, prayer-walkers should also eagerly anticipate interruptions—especially opportunities for conversation—and receive these as divine responses, invitations, and gifts.[16]

In addition to prayer-walking, I recommend that NI practitioners encourage use of the prayer of examen. Examen is a practice popularized by Saint Ignatius of Loyola that invites daily reflection upon the events, encounters, and emotions of the day seeking to notice God's graces and invitations. Regular examen can provide NI followers of Jesus with a structured context for personal retrospection and prayerful discernment.[17]

A modified practice of examen might proceed through several movements: expressing gratitude for God's blessing and presence; a petition for discernment; calling to mind moments of strong emotion (both positive and negative), encounters with others who offered a presence of Christ, and experiences of God's invitation to act; reflecting on how these moments were received and responded to; and making a resolution for how one will act in the coming day.

In addition to the inclusion and emphasis of these neighboring and prayer practices within the daily habits of NI participants, I propose a third practice for structuring local attentiveness: the *formation of small discernment groups*. These groups, of approximately six to twelve people, can provide a key context for forming missional attentiveness.[18] These communities would gather to share a meal and to tell stories of their experiences with the neighboring and prayer practices. Under the overarching question "What do you notice God doing in and around you?" they would carry these experiences into engagement with Scripture and prayer. Roxburgh describes the intended form of Scripture engagement as "dwelling in the Word." This engagement remains with a single, evocative text for a season, entering it imaginatively and drawing connections to personal experiences.[19] A simple two-hour schedule might devote the first hour to sharing experiences with the practices and identifying themes over a meal, and the second hour to scripture engagement and prayer. Limiting meetings to no more often than every other week would avoid infringing upon the availability needed to be present to neighbors.

These neighboring practices, forms of prayer, and small groups promise to help Neighborhood Incarnation churches live into their ideals of discerning God's presence and invitation to cooperative action in the parish. Together they offer a rudimentary rule of life for NI communities that establishes life-giving and interwoven rhythms of attention to neighbor and attention to God. In addition, they offer NI churches concrete means of habitually grounding their shared neighborhood life and work within a spiritual frame, providing a bulwark against the potential threat of diminishing Christian or ecclesial identity.

Foster Local Ecumenism

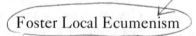

A second set of proposals for renewed faithfulness and vitality in Neighborhood Incarnation churches is that intentionality be given to *forging bonds with all the churches present in the neighborhood*. This includes primarily those churches that gather for worship in the neighborhood (i.e., have a building within the parish), but also those churches beyond the neighborhood whose worship services are attended by a significant number of parish neighbors—especially if they gather in small groups, formally or informally, within the parish. These churches, their leaders and members, are potential sources of discernment regarding the initiatives of the Spirit in the neighborhood—as well as potential partners for missional action.[20]

Building relationships with the churches who hold worship services in the neighborhood is a straightforward task that can begin by making a face-to-face connection with the pastor at worship and requesting a lunch or coffee appointment. Identifying the other churches who are present in the neighborhood in small groups and residents can be accomplished by contacting staff of nearby churches over the phone. If there are large churches within a twenty-minute drive, it is worth finding out if they have a small group that meets in the neighborhood. Small group leader contact information is sometimes available on the websites of large churches.

Initial interactions with local church leaders should help to set the stage for ongoing relationships and collaborative partnerships in the neighborhood. New planters should be aware that leaders of established congregations often feel threatened by the prospect of a new church being started nearby. Speaking directly to this potential anxiety can be helpful: "We have no interest in recruiting people from your church. We intend to discourage any potential transfers. We're just hoping to get to know all of our neighbors so we can make the neighborhood a little more like God intends it, and we figure that getting to know the other Christians living here would be a good place to start." In these initial conversations, NI practitioners should offer a simple articulation of their parish mission, but primarily engage the conversation from a learning posture.[21] The level of curiosity and the kind of questions practitioners ask can lay a good foundation for a collaborative—rather than competitive—relationship. The questions posed should make clear your interest in "scouting the divine" rather than conquest and empire building. For example:

· What can you tell me about the history of this neighborhood?
· Could you tell me any stories about some of the people who live here?
· What are your hopes and prayers for this neighborhood?
· What are some of the challenges facing this community?
· How is your congregation, corporately and through individuals, involved in the life of this community?

- · What is your sense of what God might be up to in this neighborhood?
- · What wisdom might you offer us as we try to get to know the people of the neighborhood and discern what God is calling us to do and be?

Once initial contacts have been made with other churches and ministerial associations in the neighborhood, which are often divided along ethnic, theological, and political lines, NI practitioners would be wise to convene all who are willing for a time of relationship building, meal sharing, and prayer for the neighborhood. The degree of freedom that NI churches have from the polarized liberal–conservative ecology makes them promising brokers of ecumenical relationship. Similar meetings can be scheduled on a monthly or quarterly basis, and responsibility for hosting can rotate among the various churches, and may evolve into a more formal neighborhood ecumenical community. These meetings are ideal contexts to seed (and harvest) the discernment of the whole people of God in the neighborhood with questions such as:

- · What stories do we have to share of noticing God at work in the lives of our neighbors and in the neighborhood as a whole?
- · What might God want to do in our neighborhood?
- · How might we—as Christ's church in our neighborhood—pray and act in order to join God's initiatives?[22]

The collected insights can be invaluable to NI leadership, as well as help to cultivate missional vitality among all the participating congregations. The third question may lead to opportunities for partnership in concrete acts of service or even collaboration toward creation of a third place. NI practitioners should also consider inviting these Christian leaders to participate in events that they host for the whole neighborhood, such as block parties and barbecues.

The purpose of intentionally building substantial relationships with the other churches and followers of Jesus in the neighborhood is not merely to advance the development of a NI church and to improve life in the neighborhood, but also to head off several of the dangers of the NI model. While NI churches often have to work fairly hard to legitimate the novel form of their ecclesial life, intentional relationships with other congregations can help prevent them from becoming disconnected from the wider church. These relationships can also provide implicit accountability for attending to spiritual and ecclesial practices—worship, prayer, Scripture, discipleship, evangelism, and so on.

These two sets of proposals can contribute to the flourishing of churches in the NI model, equipping practitioners with concrete actions for capitalizing on the strengths of the model and tempering two of its potential weaknesses. Giving structure to NI ideals of attending to God and neighbor through specific neighboring, prayer, and group practices can accentuate the advantages of a parish focus and head off loss of Christian or ecclesial identity. Intentionally developing partnerships with the other churches in the neighborhood follows the trajectory of NI ecclesiology, extends the circle of spiritual discernment, and guards against the danger of isolation from the wider church and context.

Renewed Practice for Great Commission Team Churches

Chapter 5 identified the key weaknesses and strengths of the Great Commission Team model in missional perspective. Two strengths of particular note are the model's effectiveness in cultivating missional identity and its deep commitment to relational evangelism or missional relationships. Two weaknesses that are particularly concerning are the model's propensity for fostering duty-bound spirituality and generating dehumanizing forms of Christian witness. It might be asked whether it is possible for a church to be an authentic expression of the GCT model without its succumbing to serious theological, practical, and missiological errors in such a way as to nullify the model's value for faithful ecclesial witness. In short, the answer is yes. The proposals that follow are intended to suggest how these churches might retain a distinctively GCT character, with its signature strengths, while also sufficiently mitigating the model's most significant missional deficiencies.

Adapt Missional Community Rhythms

Perhaps the most remarkable strength of the Great Commission Team model is its ability to cultivate vigorous missional identity among its members.[23] This is accomplished through the whole life of the church, but missional communities play an especially critical role. The monthly rhythms of these well-attended mid-size groups powerfully shape the collective "sacred consciousness" of GCT participants. Unfortunately, the theological weaknesses of the GCT model significantly imprint the character of the missional vocation formed on many GCT churches. As a result, church members take on an oversized vision of their role in God's mission, prioritize evangelism in contrast with the renewal of all things, view their context (and non-Christians) in starkly negative spiritual terms, and are motivated to missionary action by a spirituality of duty. The first proposal I offer seeks to correct for this constellation of shortcomings while retaining the genius of missional formation via missional communities.

I propose that practitioners among GCT churches adapt the rhythms of missional communities in several ways. As a reminder, missional communities typically structure their weekly meetings around a monthly rhythm that incorporates practices of study, prayer, relationship building, and community service. I propose a monthly rhythm with similar elements, but somewhat adapted emphases.

First, while many missional communities include service in their monthly rhythms, these monthly serving opportunities are predominantly in partnership with Christian organizations and/or done independently in the home of a group leader.[24] While it makes sense within GCT logic for churches qua churches to partner with Christian agencies—so that the services they render will be credited to Christians and build "credible witness" for the church as a whole—I propose that GCT practitioners urge missional communities to partner with secular service agencies that are active in their immediate community.

The advantages of this approach to the service rhythm are twofold. First, it makes sense within the GCT cultural logic, given their deep commitment to relational approaches to mission. The opportunity to serve alongside non-Christians can create new missional relationships and build credible witness among unchurched staff and volunteers. Moreover, seeking out local nonprofit groups in which to participate will increase the likelihood that contacts created through the service partnership will lead to serendipitous encounters in the neighborhood. A strong rationale for this proposal can emerge authentically from within GCT values and core strategies.

Second, joining in the service work of nonreligious agencies has potential for sparking needed missional renewal in GCT theology and spirituality. Serving alongside non-Christians and building ongoing, mutual relationships with them are two potent ways of delegitimizing the disparaging portrayals of non-Christians and the culture at large that are characteristically present in the GCT model. Serving only through Christian agencies, by contrast, can reinforce a Christendom paradigm of mission in which Christians benevolently sacrifice their time and resources for the material and spiritual benefit of others, whose identities are constructed on the basis of their material and spiritual need. Serving jointly with, and under, non-Christians relinquishes the control endemic in Christendom forms of mission. Moreover, serving alongside "Nones," Buddhists, and others can also disrupt the problematic tendency of the GCT model to view all non-Christians as targets of God's mission, and therefore as sub-persons they are called to evangelize. By collaborating with these religious others, GCT members may be awakened to the reality that participation in God's mission is not the exclusive province of the church. The unchurched are neither devoid of good nor intended only to be on the receiving end of the *missio Dei*. Rather, God invites all people to join in the renewal of all things, with whatever spiritual awareness or confession they might have. Indeed, GCT members may even come, through their mutual relationships with non-Christian others, to recognize that those who choose to serve, and thus to participate in the renewal of all things, are enacting a form of conversion to the Reign of God. In their service, then, non-Christians can become ambassadors of God—sources of revelation and conviction—to those who had previously envisioned such a title as only befitting church members.

A second proposal for adapting missional community rhythms is that they devote regular time to intentional enjoyment of their natural and cultural context. The Hallows Church already includes "play" as one of their monthly rhythms, although in practice it seems these gatherings take shape as enjoyment of one another's company in members' homes rather than communal immersion in the goodness and beauty to be found in their environment. Experiencing the goodness of the context could mean spending an afternoon at a local park; a bonfire at the beach; an evening at a local theater production or art gallery; an outing to the zoo, aquarium, or professional sporting event; or a visit to a local coffee shop or micro-brewery. This proposal, too, can be supported on the basis of core GCT ideals; it would provide these missionary teams with deepened personal knowledge of their missionary context, allowing them to experience what some of their unchurched friends and neighbors experience, and create points of conversation and understanding.

More important, for the purposes of missional renewal, intentionally celebrating the natural beauty and cultural vitality of the context can serve as a corrective for the several GCT weaknesses. This practice would provide experiential encounters with the vibrant goodness present in a context which GCT churches typically paint in a spiritual gray scale. Delighting in the cultural assets of the context—art, food, sports, and the like—can bring to life to the Reformed doctrine of common grace as GCT members experience firsthand the goodness and spiritual value of cultural products, even those produced by a post-Christian culture. Additionally, enjoying the natural environment can begin to subtly expand "the Gospel" of GCT churches to include the goodness of Creation and the renewal of all things in the *eschaton* as bookends and context for the Fall and Redemption. Finally, deliberate enjoyment of life as a core spiritual rhythm may ease the typically duty-heavy spirituality characteristic of the model. Cultivating a picture of God as not only Lord and Savior but also as gracious giver of life and unbounded Spirit. Indeed, this practice of delighting in the context is at root a practice of identifying and celebrating the inbreaking of the Reign of God in its manifestations beyond the walls of the church, and it can sow seeds for more robustly missional expressions of GCT practical ecclesiology.

A third and final proposal for renewing rhythms among missional communities seeks to lean into the potential for the practice of hospitality among GCT churches. Lux Communities, a church representative of both GCT and NI models, includes hospitality in its rhythm of monthly practices. As Pastor Dodson told me, on these weeks the missional communities throw parties and facilitate events that he described to me as "Great Commission environments" because the Christians are purposefully outnumbered by non-Christians by roughly four to one. While this is obviously a means of developing missional relationships—and is thus utterly coherent within GCT culture—it also holds great promise as a practice that can mitigate the model's characteristic weaknesses.[25] Like serving with non-Christian agencies, creating (or joining) social contexts in which Christians are significantly outnumbered can be a way of shedding the managerial ethos characteristic of Christendom missionary efforts. The margarita nights that one Lux Community participates in is an example of hospitality as a practice that facilitates relational encounters beyond their control.[26] Even if missional communities practice hospitality by hosting parties in their own homes, such environments, furnished with food and unstructured conversation, naturally include unpredictable moments and role-switching in which guests become hosts and hosts become guests.[27] The space created by the practice of hospitality inclines relationships toward mutuality, and can thus serve as a corrective for the lamentable tendency of the GCT model toward dehumanization of non-Christians as missionary targets.

These three "tweaks" to missional community rhythms—serving with non-Christian agencies, delighting in the context, and practicing hospitality—are each justifiable on the basis of the GCT model's own cultural logic. In fact, each is already being practiced fruitfully in one or more GCT church. In addition, they hold promise as practices that can begin to organically transition churches within this model away from some of the model's most common and egregious weaknesses.

Appreciative Practice in Missional Relationships

In addition to these recommendations for renewed practice among missional communities, I propose that GCT practitioners encourage members to refresh their practice of missional relationships. Missional relationships are the central mission strategy among GCT churches. As part of this strategy, GCT leaders regularly spur members to initiate and nurture friendships with neighbors and co-workers and to pray for them. I propose altering these central practices in two ways. First, in group and private prayers for non-Christians, begin by offering thanks to God for the goodness, creativity, and love evident in their lives and for the blessings that friendship with them provides. As I suggested in an article titled "Missional Acuity," prayers for the conversion of non-Christians ought to be "paired with a disciplined devotion to seeing and celebrating their virtues as well as the recognition that these are Christ himself incarnate. As these persons are held before the mind's eye, they should be imagined (and thus seen truly) not only as those to whom Christ appeals through us, but also as those through whom Christ appeals to us."[28] Second, and flowing from this renewed prayer practice, Christians should deliberately speak words of affirmation and gratitude to their non-Christian associates for the beauty of their virtues and the encouragement found in relationship with them.[29] While affirming speech can be practiced as a disingenuous and manipulative evangelistic tactic, inasmuch as it emerges from habits of genuine gratitude, it will prove to be an authentic and spiritually formative practice for both those who give affirmation and those who receive it. These nuances to the practice of missional relationship not only support GCT hopes of demonstrating God's love for others but can also help GCT members to conceptualize their non-Christian friends in ways that more faithfully honor the *imago Dei*. In this way, these prayer practices can disrupt the propensity to view non-Christians in dehumanizing ways as targets of missionary endeavor.

These proposed changes to core GCT practices of missional communities and missional relationships offer leaders and pioneers practical steps they can take to address the model's problematics while retaining its inner logical and unique potency.

Renewed Practice for Household of the Spirit Churches

The Household of the Spirit practical ecclesiology has a unique set of strengths and weaknesses. HS churches profoundly witness to God's active agency in their lives, giving testimony to the inbreaking of the Reign of God as they experience it in miraculous healings and intimate encounters with the Spirit in worship. They foster a sense of missional empowerment and encourage members to participate in the divine–human work of prayer for healing, blessing, and insight. Unfortunately, HS churches typically share with GCT churches an impoverished apprehension of God's presence in the world beyond the church, a bleak assessment of their social-cultural environment, and hierarchical leadership structures. In addition, the model is in particular danger of resorting to emotional manipulation and turning worship into a consumer-oriented production. The two proposals that follow seek to maintain the character and strengths of the model but instigate missional renewal and ease characteristic weaknesses by suggesting changes to central HS practices of worship and prayer.

Enrich Worship

Worship is the central hub of HS spirituality. These multisensory worship environments facilitate moving personal encounters with the Spirit and serve as the primary formational context for HS churches. The characteristic "sacred consciousness" of HS participants is shaped largely in the worship environment. Thus, my proposals for missional renewal begin with recommendations for renewed worship practices. While several of the HS churches in the field had moved toward a more decentralized practice of worship, a shift of this magnitude is more ambitious than the proposals advanced here.[30] This is both because it would be unrealistic to imagine that such a drastic proposal would be adopted by HS practitioners and because it would jeopardize the integrity of the model both practically and ecclesiologically.[31] Instead, I offer a number of thematic suggestions and practical examples for how HS practitioners might adapt worship in order to mitigate some of the theological shortcomings typically evident among HS churches. The proposals that follow intend to keep intact the multisensory and spiritually potent character of HS worship while nonetheless suggesting some particular worship practices that are not commonly utilized by churches in the model.[32]

First, I propose that HS worship leaders enrich worship by exploring ways of *heightening worshipers' consciousness of fellow worshipers.* HS worship is typically characterized by practices of personal disengagement including darkness, closed eyes, and spontaneous, independent movements such as hand-raising, kneeling, and bowing. These can serve to intensify the sense of direct, individualized spiritual encounter. However, the purpose of this proposal is to highlight the potential of the gathered community as an additional conduit for profound spiritual experience. In addition, this proposal can help to head off the temptations of individualistic and consumeristic worship.

One common HS practice already exemplifies the power of being sensitized to the presence of the fellowship in facilitating intense spiritual encounters, the laying on of hands. In continuity with this practice, I propose the use of hand-holding as a counterpart to hand-raising. Holding hands with fellow worshipers is a visceral, intimate experience, but one funded by awareness of others rather than disengagement from them.[33] Similarly, HS churches may consider rearranging their worship space so that worshipers may face one another rather than face a stage. In addition to heightening awareness of the community, this practice can disrupt problematic dynamics seen in some HS churches in which stage-centered performances seem to coincide with cultures of fame and show.[34] Having one's gaze directed toward fellow worshipers may also very subtly encourage HS churches to practice more plural forms of leadership such as are consistent with the texts on spiritual gifting they prize.

A second theme for missional enrichment of HS worship pertains to use of song and sound. HS worship environments are characteristically immersive and loud, thanks to impassioned congregational singing and rock-like instrumentation, as well as, in some settings, spontaneous eruptions of prayer, praise, and *glossolalia.* The song selections among HS churches are often replete with praise choruses written by Hillsong, Chris Tomlin, and Matt Redman. While the lyrics of the songs HS churches sing affirm broad evangelical themes such as redemption, God's loving desire for relationship, and God's miracle working power, it is important to consider the mental scenes they conjure. HS songs overwhelmingly situate the spiritual encounters that they seek to facilitate in numinous or idyllic settings. That is, as HS worshipers sing, the songs draw their imaginations to lofty planes—sanctuaries awash in God's Spirit, heaven's throne room, majestic natural vistas.[35] Spiritual encounters are thus consistently located away from the mundane, local context (in which God's Spirit is also present and active).

I propose that HS worship leaders *incorporate songs that can help the congregation to recognize God's presence in the everyday contexts in which they live*. Worshipful singing that evokes such everyday contexts such as the home, workplace, highway, neighborhood, restaurants, and sporting events can help to bridge the gap prevalent in HS (and GCT) churches between church and world. Songs centered on petitions for spiritual discernment of God's everyday presence can have a similar impact and help to correct for the model's typically disparaging assessment of the social-cultural environment. Admittedly, songs of these types are not mainstream.[36] For this reason, it may be necessary—and would certainly be powerful—to commission gifted members of the community (or other local churches) to write songs for use in worship that incorporate local elements.[37] Fortunately, the centrality of worship music among HS churches means that many are equipped with able musicians, presumably some of whom could write original songs. The use of images of local scenes as backgrounds on the screens containing songs lyrics could also prove fruitful.

In addition to making changes to song selection, I propose HS worship be enriched by the use of *extended moments of silence in worship*.[38] Silence is typically absent in HS worship, characterized as it is by multiple layers of sound.[39] While silence may be an unfamiliar practice for churches in the model, it is not inconsistent with a Spirit-filled spirituality nor Pentecostal tradition. As Philip Pruit writes of the early Pentecostal movement:

> periods of silence in corporate and private prayer—called "tarrying," and "waiting on the Lord"—were an important part of the fabric of developing Pentecostal spirituality, as was the "holy hush," as worshipers waited in reverent silence, with an overwhelming sense of God's presence, to "hear a word from the Lord.[40]

Corporate silence offers HS churches several advantages. First, as Pruit suggests and early Pentecostal writer J. T. Boddy said, "God's presence and direction can be discerned amid silence."[41] Their openness to the voice of the Spirit is one of the unique strengths of HS spirituality. Creating moments that are stripped of all music and speech—the tools HS leaders typically use to craft the worship environment (and sometimes use to manipulate)—is designating openings for God to interject. It is the silence of a pause in conversation that signals it is the other person's turn to speak. In silence, worship leaders can surrender the control that sometimes seduces and worshipers can relinquish the consumer gratification that sometimes intoxicates. Moreover, in these moments of silence the unruly Spirit may make its evangelistic appeals, leading them into disquieting realizations, unfamiliar relationships, and other-oriented lifestyles. In silence, the Spirit of the Household may seize the opportunity to call the church to conversion.

The proposals offered for heightening other-consciousness and adapting use of song and sound in worship offer multisensory practices that are rich with potential for mediating encounters with the Spirit. At the same time, these proposals can help to mitigage the individualism, consumerism, and synthetic gratification that too often attend their worship.

Practice Missionary Prayer

In addition to these proposals for increasing missional vitality through worship renewal, I propose that HS practitioners attend to their central practice of prayer as another node for effecting missional revitalization. As has been noted in chapters 4 and 5, intercessory prayer for others in daily life is a distinctive practice of HS mission. This practice was especially pronounced in two HS churches that are among the model's exemplars of missional identity and practice. These same churches reflected important characteristics of the Neighborhood Incarnation model. It is for this reason that I urge HS practitioners more broadly to imbibe and convey the conviction I heard among these churches that spiritual encounters and empowerment are to be carried forward into everyday extensions of God's power and will through prayer and Spirit-inspired words of encouragement. *Seeking God-given everyday opportunities to pray for healing and offer encouragement* has several benefits. First, it violates the perceived boundary between church and world. Second, with respect to the ecclesiology of the church as household, this practice provides needed balance by developing the family (personal) aspect alongside the sanctuary (spatial) aspect.

Third, missionary prayer can help HS participants and their churches to break out of the cul-de-sac of me-centered, consumeristic spirituality by making a priority of blessing others.

While beneficial, these modes of missionary prayer alone will leave unaddressed other problematics in the model. Praying God's will and blessing upon others can be a divine–human cooperative act par excellence, but it can also function to reinscribe objectifying forms of relationship.[42] Too often in healing prayer and speaking "words of knowledge," the Spirit-filled Christian is represented as blessed benefactor deigning to offer help to a spiritually impoverished and physically needy soul. Thus, missionary prayer, as typically practiced, while useful in some respects, will not help HS churches overcome impoverished imaginations for God's activity beyond the church and desensitization to virtue among non-Christians. One small remedy I suggest to address this weakness is that in preparation for this missionary prayer practice, practitioners *pray for divine empowerment not only to heal or receive special knowledge regarding the past or future of those they encounter but also for perception of goodness within them*, that practioners would become aware of the desires within those they are praying for that are pleasing to the Lord, the contributions they make to renewal of all things, signs of the *imago Dei* and the prevenient grace of God at work in their lives. Seeking spiritual inspiration of this kind will serve to sensitize those who pray to the human goodness around them and charge them with spiritual fervor to name it.

Pastor Rhodes, a proponent of praying for supernatural healing in grocery stores, also recounted offering "natural" encouragement in a coffee shop. After overhearing a mother and daughter nearby, he interrupted them to say: "you're a really good mom—it just brought so much joy to me just seeing and overhearing you guys interact." In this, and more supernaturally inspired ways, HS churches can give witness to the unruly Spirit's active agency in the lives of others even as they characteristically do so often in testimonies to God's action in their own lives. This revised missionary prayer practice holds promise for awakening HS communities to the reality of God's work beyond the church, in the lives of everyday people, by calling into question their vision of the social context as a spiritually hostile environment. Ultimately, it may serve to disrupt the dead end of subject–object missionary relations.

The proposals advanced above for enriched worship and prayer practices are illustrative rather than comprehensive. By accentuating the strengths of the model and seeking to minimize its weaknesses, they provide a means for HS practitioners to lead their communities toward greater missional faithfulness and renewal.

Renewed Practice for New Community Churches N C

The emerging and mainline churches within the New Community model offer a vivid, contextual approach and embody missional theology in some unique and important ways. Most notably, they bring into strong relief the eschatological nature of the church as sign and foretaste of the new human-ity, while integrating historical Christian practices with elements of contem-porary culture in participatory worship experiences. While the model offers a needed and profound appreciation for the witness of the church's social practice, NC churches too often lack the proactive disposition appropriate to joining the *missio Dei*. This is, at least in part, a result of their negatively constructed identity over against Evangelicals. Finally, the model's commit-ment to boundary-crossing between sacred and secular spheres rarely leads to the kind of cross-cultural relationships that could help to trouble their overly optimistic assessment of their progressive context.

Communally Discern Mission Focus

The first proposal I offer is for NC practitioners to *lead communal processes of discernment toward developing a greater clarity of mission focus*. This focus ought to arise from corporate discernment regarding contextual opportu-nities (to participate with God), as well as the church's unique, God-given gifts. Facilitating processes for intentional, inclusive conversation is a key strength of NC churches and one that makes this proposal feasible. Some rough guidelines for such a process would include several months of con-versation, in various forums, including worship, working with questions such as:

· What is happening in the lives of those around us—what are their sto-ries, hopes, and challenges?
· Who has God gifted us to be?
· How might God be inviting us to actively join in the renewal of all things?

The themes emerging from these conversations could provide direction for missional experiments, which would in turn fuel further conversation and reflection, and eventually lead to corporate commitments to new or renewed forms of proactive engagement in mission.[43] Such an inclusive, participatory, experimental, and iterative process of decision making promises to produce broad-based buy-in.

This proposal intends to mitigate several of the weaknesses prevalent among NC churches. Most obviously, it would directly address a common lack of engagement in proactive forms of mission engagement. Not only do NC churches typically eschew personal evangelism but they are also, on the whole, less active in ministries of compassion than their GCT and NI counterparts. This is inconsistent with their prayers and rhetoric of justice and liberation. Second, a clearer mission focus can provide NC churches with a healthy source of identity that is rooted in the church's participation in the *missio Dei* rather than in counter-distinction with Evangelicalism. Third, and finally, such a process can bring focus to the sometimes diffuse spiritual attention that attends emphasis on the truism that "God is everywhere." That is, designating particular mission contexts and efforts as of particular importance can encourage more disciplined attention to the presence and activity of God in that particular arena.

Wits' End is an example of a NC composed of persons whose disillusionment with evangelism has left the community without a concrete sense or practice of mission beyond itself. While providing a safe community in which those wounded by bad church experiences can be healed is needed, valuable work, such churches run the risk of self-consumption. Indeed, if missional theology is correct that human life flourishes when it participates in the Triune life and mission, then it may be that mission beyond the church community will prove an important contributor toward the healing of its members.

The heightened mission focus might take various forms, including resolving to shape mission in response to the needs of a particular neighborhood or people group, or to make a commitment to a particular social issue, such as immigration, or to focus on leveraging particular community assets, like a building or specialized skill-set.[44] Among churches in the NC model, those that evidence the most vibrant sense of mission are those that overlap into the Neighborhood Incarnation model.[45] These NC exemplars embrace a neighborhood identity, operate as "third places," and are invested in either ongoing relationships with the poor and marginalized or significant partnerships with nonprofit groups.[46] Each of these churches is also involved in advocacy on behalf of immigrants. These are suggestive of best practices for churches in the NC model.

Cultivate Cross-Cultural Church Partnerships

The second proposal that I offer to NC practitioners is the *intentional development of significant relationships with Christians of other cultures.*[47] This could build from intentional engagement in advocacy for and mission with immigrant populations or from local or institutional connections. It would be preferable that these partnerships be formed locally rather than internationally for the sake of meaningful, regular interaction, though local cross-cultural partnerships may lead to meaningful international links. If it is difficult to forge such relationships in the immediate neighborhood, denominational structures may provide avenues for these, since most mainline Protestant denominations are home to ethnic minority and immigrant communities that hold somewhat conservative social and theological views.[48]

The nature of these relationships and the forms of partnership would naturally depend on the congregations themselves but should touch on practices of worship—given the central nature of worship in NC life, but could also take shape in intentional fellowship and mission efforts.[49] Connections in the worship context might include, for example, celebrating worship jointly on a biannual basis in alternating venues, switching preachers a couple times each year, as well as having members of the other church share personal testimonies in the context of worship on a monthly schedule.[50] Community connections might involve a buddy system or creating mixed small groups or dinner groups. The paired congregations could partner in mission to host events that benefit the wider community, like a sports camp or service day. Before any such formal programs are put into place, the NC leaders should approach leadership of the minority culture congregation with a posture of humility and eagerness to learn and inquire about opportunities the NC might have to join in and support the life of the minority culture congregation.[51]

The promise of cross-cultural church partnership for NC churches is twofold. First, it would provide a means for churches in the NC model to pursue greater authenticity in their core commitments of inclusive community and honoring the subjectivity of others. Second, these relationships would provide NC churches with the opportunity to "listen to the witness of Christians from other cultures," a witness which would presumably include critique of dominant cultural norms and commitment to proactive practices of evangelism and discipleship.[52] Receiving this critical witness in the context of personal relationships with Christians within cultural minorities will, presumably be more agreeable than receiving it from white American Evangelicals.

These two proposals—for mission-clarifying processes and cross-cultural partnerships—provide concrete directions for NC practitioners to consider as they seek greater missional vitality. Though they do not address every weakness of the model, they do leave intact the practical coherence and ecclesiological character of the model while also promising to create new contexts, conversations, and relationships in which the Spirit might effect continuing conversion among this vital sector of new churches.

To repeat Darrel Guder's incisive assertion, "the essence of the church's credible witness is its own ongoing evangelization."[53] The proposals developed here are offered as means of evangelizing new churches across the range of their practical ecclesiological positions. They are not a promised cure for what ails each model. They are not miracle drugs, but are more akin to customized exercise and diet plans. They promise to advance the overall health of these churches and thereby to contribute toward their continuing conversion, through shades of glory, as they move toward more faithful ecclesial witness and in so doing come increasingly to exist as signs, foretastes, and instruments of the Reign of God.

Practical Wisdom from
the Frontier of Faith

WHAT BROADER INSIGHTS does this study offer to the church in its evolving context? In this final chapter I identify the five threads of practical wisdom I discovered in the field. Each is ripe with implications both for theologians reflecting on the lived experience of the church and for church administrators, leaders, and coaches who seek to support the work of new church development. From these threads of practical wisdom I offer to theologians some potentially fruitful trajectories for theological development. To practitioners and leaders in church planting initiatives, I offer practical proposals.

The doctrinal possibilities I sketch in this section are meant to be expressive rather than definitive. As Pete Ward, drawing on the work of Nicholas Healy and Rowan Williams, puts it: "[S]peech about the Church does not take the form of a 'blueprint' rather it is itself crucially influenced by and located in the lived. Theology of all kinds, and particularly theologies of the Church, arise from the 'middle.'"[1] This is certainly true of the dogmatic writing about the church included in this section. It arises from the middle of this research. While the doctrinal trajectories that are charted in what follows are knowledge inasmuch as they point to what is true regarding the church in its concrete forms and essential nature, they are also "products of theological creativity." As such they are not, in and of themselves, normative. Instead, they are "approximations of normativity."[2] This is the nature of ecclesiology as a discipline. Ecclesiology is, according to Ward, "both a journey into that which holds the Church to account, while also holding that expression itself to account."[3] The practical ecclesiological models developed in chapter 4 witnessed to concrete manifestations of ecclesial life that call doctrinal formulations to account. The doctrinal formulations offered in this section arise from the dynamics and features of the field of new churches as a whole, and are taken as grounds for promoting certain practical implications for church planting leaders. Thus, the ecclesiological journey comes full circle: having begun with sociological description, it concludes with doctrinal constructions arising from the experience of new Seattle churches.

What follows is an explication of what I have called five "threads of practical wisdom" that I discovered were woven through the field of new churches. Practical wisdom, or *phronesis*, has been an important topic among practical theologians, especially since the publication of Don Browning's *A Fundamental Practical Theology*.[4] As the authors of *Christian Practical Wisdom* describe it, practical wisdom

> is morally attuned, rooted in a tradition that affirms the good, and driven toward aims that seek the good. It is not a package of pre-planned rules but stays open and adaptive to new situations. It is nimble and at times even self critical. Most of all, this knowledge is practical, grounded in ordinary experience, and learned over time in the company of others for the sake of others.[5]

The threads of practical wisdom explored in this final chapter emerged from analysis of the overall tendencies in the field as matters for critical reflection grounded in missional theology. As such, these threads point to theologically sound and contextually relevant focal considerations for shaping ecclesial practice. They are suggestive of best practices, but not in the way that best practices are typically conceived. They are not secrets to effectively planting churches that are destined for exponential growth and multiplication. These threads of wisdom arise not as the most effective strategies of a select group of numerically successful churches but as faithful, missional practices emerging from the field of new churches as a whole. As such, they offer insights toward ecclesial *viability* and ecclesiological *fidelity* in places like Seattle.

Given the superior missional vitality and contextual relevance of the Neighborhood Incarnation model, it should not come as a surprise that the key insights that emerge from the field as a whole resonate with this practical ecclesiological model. As chapter 2 concluded, the New Seattle Churches Survey revealed a broad consensus among new Seattle churches on a number of practices and priorities. Several of these points of general consensus will be revisited in this chapter.[6] While the fact that there is majority agreement on these priorities and practices may be suggestive of their utility for church planting, consensus alone would not serve as sufficient theological or missiological grounds for promoting these as best practices. However, having already developed practical ecclesiologies and subjected them to missional theological analysis, what I offer here are the consensus currents filtered through a missional theological lens. I will highlight those with the most value to ecclesiological and missional faithfulness.[7]

The five threads of practical wisdom that emerged as points of convergence between the currents in the field and missional theological reflection are:

- Embracing local identity and local mission
- Cultivating embodied, experiential, everyday spiritualities
- Recognizing community life as both witness and formation
- Prioritizing hospitality as a cornerstone practice
- Discovering vitality in a diverse ecclesial ecology

In addition to describing each of these themes, I explore the contributions each one offers to dogmatic understandings of the nature of the church, and, for each, propose practical implications for leaders among church planting efforts.

Embracing Local Identity and Local Mission

New Seattle churches are embracing their local identities and engaging in local forms of mission. Two-thirds of those surveyed indicated that "identifying with our neighborhood" was an extremely or very important priority. Nearly a fourth of new churches include their neighborhood location in their church name. While neighborhood-rooted identity is especially pronounced among churches in the NI model, it is also strong among NC and GCT models, and also among HS churches that do not identify with a particular ethnic or cultural group.[8] This new cohort of urban churches suggests that the ecclesial future includes the "return of the neighborhood church."[9]

The practical advantages of a neighborhood identity and mission, as well as its strengths in missional theological perspective, have already been enumerated in the chapter 5 assessment of the NI model, so I will only briefly repeat several of the most salient here. Neighborhood identity provides a human-size scope of attention in which to discern the Spirit's initiatives; echoes the incarnational paradigm; fosters Christ-like solidarity with church outsiders; promotes boundary-crossing; encourages a holistic understanding of the *missio Dei* as inclusive of evangelism and social action; cultivates longer-term, relationship-based approaches to mission; affords a helpful corrective for the dislocated, disembodied habits that accompany technological society; and is well suited to the increasing localism of urban environments.[10]

Church as Neighbors, Neighborhood, and City

The lived ecclesiology of these new neighborhood-identified churches offers promising directions for dogmatic ecclesiological construction. First, these new neighborhood-identified churches press for an understanding of the church as a foretaste of the new humanity dwelling in neighborhoods that God is determined to renew. They offer a vision of the *church as neighbors*. As neighbors, the persons of the church are citizens of the future Reign of God living in the midst of the present neighborhood. The eschatological difference between the church and the world is a temporal not a spatial one despite what popular Christian piety and heavenly hymnody would seem to suggest. The church's neighborly nature points to its enduring solidarity with places—its people, history, and material form. The eschatological newness of the church as neighbors points to the "future," not merely in the general sense but also to the future of its particular neighborhood. These neighbors are eschatological in as much as they are alert to the presence of the neighborhood's future, and inasmuch as they are responsive to this inbreaking of the Reign of God on the local scene. The church as neighbors attends to the presence of God in the neighborhood (which will one day permeate it in a palpable way). They pattern their lives in the ways of the Reign of God, training themselves to live in its approaching reality. In so doing they make the future manifest. It is in this way that they join God in the renewal of the neighborhood. As the NI model posits clearly, the local church may be framed in geographic rather than denominational or congregational terms in order to envision the church as the followers of Jesus in the neighborhood.

The church as neighbors coincides with a new theology of the parish. Classic Christendom theologies of the parish functioned most often and practically as rationales for ecclesiastical dominion, in parallel with the divine rights claimed by feudal lords and landholders. The ecclesiology underlying the "new parish," however, is a post-Christendom one. New parish ecclesiology is disabused of illusions of control and, therefore, is focused more squarely on the spiritual task of discernment of God's local initiatives, so that the church—a band of neighbors—might participate in this grassroots work. In the parish, neighbors are authorized in their mission neither by ecclesiastical institutions nor municipalities but, rather, by the eschatological neighborhood itself. They are empowered by the Reign of God as it is already present there, arriving from the future. As such their task is neither one of recruitment nor of ensuring contentment with the status quo, but instead to discern the cracks through which the future is already visible and join God in widening these cracks. Neighboring in this eschatologically shaped way is a non-anxious but proactive and potentially disruptive activity.

Several biblical sources can enrich a vision of the church as neighbors. I briefly note four especially fruitful sources. The People of God in exile—a popular theme for ecclesial reflection over the last several decades as Christians in the United States have become aware of their post-Christendom context—dwell in the midst of their exilic home as neighbors.[11] While they are foreigners in terms of their allegiance and the narrative that most profoundly shapes their identity, the People of God are to enter into a profound solidarity with the context in which God has placed them. They are to buy homes, form deep and abiding relational ties through marriage, and invest labor and prayer in its flourishing. They are to "seek the welfare of the city," YHWH declares, for "in its welfare, you will find your welfare."[12] This theme of the neighborly life of the People of God in exile is developed considerably in 1 Peter, which calls for God's scattered elect to be good neighbors, show proper respect, do good deeds, and live such exemplary lives as to point visibly and verbally to God's coming Reign.[13] Jesus straightforwardly declared that love of one's neighbor as self should be set alongside the great commandment to love God with all of one's heart, soul, mind, and strength. On these two commandments, Jesus asserts, "hang all the Law and Prophets."[14] The parable of the Good Samaritan clarifies the scope of neighboring and invites Jesus's disciples to envision themselves as neighbors to whomever they happen to encounter in the daily events of their life. They are to act accordingly with compassion and generosity.[15]

A second trajectory for doctrinal development is to explore an understanding of the *church as neighborhood*. Whereas the church as neighbors expands upon the social metaphors of the church as new humanity and family, the church as neighborhood is a variation on the multiple spatial-social metaphors for the church found throughout the New Testament. There, the church is compared to a household, city, and nation.[16] Each of these metaphors indicates strong social dimensions, but locates the human community within, and binds it to, a geographical and material context—within a home, inside city walls, upon the land.[17] As these metaphors illustrate, we can faithfully speak of the church not only as a group of persons but also holistically as a redeemed society that includes both its human members and the environment in which they dwell. The church is not only a redeemed human community—a group of spirited bodies who have received salvation—but also, inasmuch as it is a foretaste of the new creation, a redeemed society that includes its material, social environment.[18]

The church as neighborhood sounds many of the same notes as the aforementioned spatial-social metaphors but expands them in various ways. The church as neighborhood carves out a middle place and middle society between the church as household and the church as city. The neighborhood includes more than the personal property of the household, but is on a smaller, more human scale than the city as a whole. Neighborhood corners and cafes are known by many without being owned by them. In space, the neighborhood is made up of places that are simultaneously "mine" (my street, my local park, my favorite café, my grocery store, my library) and "not mine." Though they are not owned in a legal sense, they are deeply identified with them and one may feel a strong psychological sense of ownership of them.

The middle place that the neighborhood represents is paired with a middle society, a social space of belonging between intimate relations and the masses. Whereas the bond within the family is personal and direct, the bond to one's fellow city-dwellers and co-nationals is one of shared affiliation.[19] The neighborhood evokes both personal and affiliational solidarity, but also introduces the importance of a third variety—recognitional solidarity. Recognitional solidarity is the sense of unity one shares with acquaintances and familiar strangers. The neighborhood is a space filled with the faces of persons that while not known intimately are nonetheless familiar. The neighborhood is the context in which one's daily life is interwoven with others—the clerk at your grocery store, the neighbor who walks her dog down your street, the panhandler by your freeway exit, the janitor at your child's school, your mail carrier. Certainly, modern life has disconnected many people from significant experiences of neighborhood life, as they live in one neighborhood, work in another, and shop in a third.[20] In such a setting we may not recognize our mail carrier, even if he has delivered our mail for years. Nonetheless, neighborhoods offer a rich metaphor for understanding the church's nature as a social-spatial reality. As a social-spatial metaphor, it has a parallel in the experience of the average church-goer whose belonging to the church is tied in intertwined ways to the built environment (the building), to close friends, and to the wider community of "familiar strangers" with whom he or she worships.[21] Sixty-nine percent of U.S. congregations have a regular worship attendance of less than 150, a size that suggests that while not all fellow church participants can be known well, all can be familiar faces.[22]

Neighborhood ecclesiology envisions the church as both a human community *and* the concrete places it inhabits. This community of belonging includes solidarity of three types: personal, recognitional, and affiliational. The church is a people that lives out its life in multiple, but not infinite, places—in homes, workplaces, public venues, and worship spaces. Just as neighborhoods provide environments for the various activities that make up the life of human communities, the church nurtures social and material spaces for human life to flourish. A healthy church is like a healthy neighborhood. The church as neighborhood is a "place," a habitat in which all the aspects of life can take shape and flourish. Members may work, sleep, eat, play, and socialize all as part of ecclesial life. That is, the church as neighborhood invites reflection on the various elements of daily life—relationships, activities, places—as intrinsic parts of the life of the church. This removes ecclesiological reflection from its sometimes overwrought rootedness in worship and also from a sense that the People of God are only being the church when they are doing practices that are transparently churchly, such as sacraments, prayer, and evangelism. In fact, the church as neighborhood presses for an understanding of ecclesiality that is rooted in God's dream of all human life and community—not just special religious practices—as ecclesiologically relevant. Inasmuch as labor, recreation, sex, and commerce are practices common to the neighborhood, they are ecclesial practices.

A third promising trajectory to develop is seen in *church as a city* of neighborhoods—that is, a city composed of many neighborhoods, each of which represents one of the many diverse Christian traditions within one ecumenical church. The new churches in Seattle invite renewed reflection on the nature of the church as they highlight the character of contemporary U.S. cities as formed by numerous neighborhoods.[23] The church as city is an ecclesiological metaphor deeply rooted in biblical understandings of Jerusalem—as a center of Jewish worship, as the "city on a hill" emblematic of Jesus's new community, and as the dwelling for a new humanity. The city is the eschatological meeting place of a new heaven and new earth. Throughout Christian history, theologians have worked with this metaphor, exploring the ecclesiological implications in connection with their own urban environments. Seattle's new churches, by virtue of their neighborhood identities, create new possibilities for developing the church-as-city that reflects the contemporary, urban reality that cities are made up of discrete and interconnected neighborhoods. These neighborhoods, for city-dwellers and churches alike, are primary places of identification. Many Seattleites do not identify as "from Seattle" but, rather, as from one of its constituent neighborhoods—Greenwood or Capital Hill or Queen Anne. If the church is a city like Seattle is a city, then the church is a city of neighborhoods. The Seattle context invites reflection on the church as a single municipality that includes multiple, unique communities.

The church as city of neighborhoods is an ecumenical reality. The one church is made up of numerous distinct communities that are interconnected not only spiritually through baptism but also by their proximity and shared environment. That is, the whole church is materially and geographically related to its constituent parts as a city is materially and geographically related to its constituent neighborhoods.[24] The distinct character of each neighborhood is of great importance, but so, too, is the integrated whole that comprises the city. The same is true of the distinct denominations and traditions in the church in relation to its ecumenical whole.

Each of these theological insights arises from the "local turn" in ecclesial identity and mission found among new Seattle churches, and each points to the fruitfulness of ecclesiological engagement with the human disciplines that contribute to understanding and enriching life in the urban environment—discourses such as urban sociology, urban planning, new urbanism, community development, and place studies. As the preceding paragraphs have sought to illustrate, conversation with these fields of study can stimulate fresh dogmatic articulations regarding the nature of the church.

Implications for Leaders

Among the new churches in Seattle, those that best exemplify this local turn in identity and mission are those embodying the Neighborhood Incarnational model.[25] Its missional theological strengths and contextual advantages for urban, progressive, technological, post-Christian contexts make it worthy of attention from church planting leaders of every theological stripe. The reality that NI churches are not, as a group, growing faster or larger than church plants of other models, is no basis for discounting its preeminence as a viable and faithful expression of missional ecclesiology. The flexibility of this model is a further advantage. The existence of GCT, HS, and NC churches that are also NI churches testifies to its relevance and compatibility across the theological spectrum. The fact that these dual-model churches stand out as some of the most vital and missionally vibrant examples within their respective models further demonstrates the promise of this relatively new form of practical ecclesiology. So, whether church planting leaders are at home within mainline, Evangelical, or Spirit-filled traditions, they should seriously consider experimenting with, learning from, promoting, and developing tradition-specific theological rationales for the Neighborhood Incarnation approach.

Church planting leaders might respond to this missiologically promising current not only by adopting the NI model but also more broadly by encouraging urban church plants to reach clarity regarding the parameters of their context—whether that be a school district, Zip code, city limit, or, alternatively, a specific ethnic or subcultural group in the city.[26] A clearly specified focus can provide church plants with many of the advantages of a neighborhood identity—though a geographic focus has advantages over ethnic or subcultural identities that tend to inhibit, rather than promote, boundary-crossing. Neighborhood-focused approaches should be paired with modest expectations regarding the size of the church at full maturity. As a result, creative approaches to leadership and financial sustainability are critical.[27] Several concrete practices that church planting leaders can encourage include naming churches after a specific neighborhood; designating a specific community as the context in which hospitality and mission efforts will be focused; gathering for worship in a well-trafficked site near the center of the chosen parish; hosting special church and community events in nearby public spaces and third places like parks and community centers; partnering with a local school, nonprofit, or business that provides an asset to the community;

holding pastoral office hours at cafés within the parish; patronizing local businesses; displaying a map and images of the context in the worship setting; and requiring staff and encouraging members to live in the neighborhood. Church planting leaders, additionally, may find it advantageous to plant several neighborhood-focused churches in nearby neighborhoods in short succession or simultaneously, as this can promote collegiality and reinforce neighborhood identity.

Cultivating Embodied, Experiential, Everyday Spiritualities

Seattle's newest cohort of churches practice forms of Christian spirituality that reflect the experiential culture of the postmodern, emerging adults they seek to reach. Several survey findings point toward this reality. The number of churches that identify with "sacramental" theology is six times that of those located within classically sacramental traditions.[28] This shift in theological identification corresponds with similar shifts in practice. Eighty percent of survey respondents celebrate Communion "often" or "very often or always." While Communion is celebrated with variations in meaning, the frequency with which it is celebrated across the field as a whole reflects a turn to more embodied and experiential forms of Christian practice. The participatory worship of NC churches and the multisensory, visceral character of HS worship also reflect the popularity of experiential spirituality.

The *everyday* character of the spiritualities predominant in the field is evident in their meal practices, as well as in theory-laden practices of place and community belonging. The importance of the ritual meal of Communion is matched by the centrality of common meals.[29] Eighty percent of new churches indicated that "sharing meals together" is "extremely" or "very important" to their church culture. A significant number of churches deliberately blur the lines between sacred and mundane community meals by deliberately and consistently connecting their community lunches and dinners with Communion or the agape feast tradition.[30] Those in the NI and NC models deliberately blur the lines between sacred and secular spaces, as well as the distinction between church community insiders and outsiders. These forms of blurring are, in fact, the sacralization of everyday life, and it is a noteworthy tendency. This turn to the spirituality of everyday life syncs well with Elizabeth Drescher's recent study of "Nones." She found that the four most "spiritually meaningful" activities among America's "Nones" are what she calls "'The Four Fs of Contemporary American Spirituality": Family, Fido, Friends, and Food."[31]

Churches in the NC, GCT, and NI models each—in their own way, and with varying degrees of efficacy—seek to cultivate "sacred consciousness" that infuses everyday experiences, relationships, and places with spiritual significance. NI churches stress that God is on the move in the neighborhood and seek to discern and cooperate in this action. GCT churches alert members to everyday opportunities to build relationships in which they might shape eternal destinies. NC churches emphasize broadly that God can be found in the ordinary stuff of life, connecting social change with the inbreaking of God's Reign. In addition, a select number of HS churches adamantly encourage members to follow the prompts of the Spirit to be conduits of supernatural healing and blessing for those they cross paths with in daily life. These tendencies coalesce into an overarching embrace of embodied, experiential, and everyday forms of spirituality that have both doctrinal and practical significance.

Church as Engaged Parent

The spiritualities of new Seattle churches invite fresh doctrinal reflection on the nature of the church. Roman Catholic and, more recently, Protestant ecclesiologies have described the church as sacrament and ongoing incarnation.[32] While these formulations have value for describing the church's mission, their weakness lies in the suggestion that experiences of the divine must be mediated through the church. In this vision, the church and its practices distribute God's grace. In contrast, the embodied, experiential, and everyday forms of spirituality among new Seattle churches cast a vision for a church that cultivates, but does not contain, encounters with God. This church is an incubator, sensitizing people to encounter the sacred in all of life. This is closer to the Orthodox traditions that celebrate Christ's incarnation as an event which confirmed the goodness of ordinary created matter and exalted it to a new status as holy substance.[33] The church's life and practice do, of course, include spaces for experiences of God, but at their best they provide these with a wider aim: to awaken persons to the sacramental character of all of life.[34] Thus, the church is not the ongoing incarnation itself but, rather, partners with the Spirit in facilitating discoveries of the ongoing incarnation in all of life. These incarnational encounters can take place in mundane meals and places and faces, as well as in sacred spaces and rituals.

These forms of spirituality invite exploration of the ecclesiological metaphor of *church as engaged parent*.[35] While ecclesiological tradition has long envisioned church as mother, for my purposes the gendered character of this tradition is more problematic than helpful.[36] As an engaged parent, the church actively nurtures and guides its members toward maturity, recognizing the evolving phases of the parent–child relationship. The trajectory of relationship between parent and child moves from one of utter dependence through various stages of increasing independence until the nature of the parent–child relationship achieves a certain interdependence and mutuality. Engaged parents hope and intend that their children will eventually feed themselves, as well as others. Indeed they may in fact feed their parents in their old age. Engaged parents teach not only so that that their children will learn what is taught but also so they will learn to teach themselves and others. These changes in dependence do not constitute the conclusion of the parent–child relationship but, rather, signal its development toward maturity.

The church, likewise, in its practices, creates environments in which spiritual nourishment is available, incrementally providing figurative infant bottles, purees, and solid foods. But the practices of the church also cultivate within maturing believers a taste for wild game and berries, and apprentice them in how to hunt and scavenge. The church does this not so the individual can set off alone but so that she may be well-nourished and also so that the whole church and wider community might share in the harvest of her developing expertise and labor. The fact that these sources of nourishment come from holy encounters in both sacred and secular realms does not signal a weakening of the vital relationship between the Christian and church; rather, it is maturation, and this is to the credit of the parent, not shame.

Implications for Leaders

The key practical implications of this overarching propensity for embodied, experiential, and everyday forms of spirituality for church planting leaders are quite straightforward. Church planters should be trained and encouraged to shape corporate worship as a context for experiential, embodied spirituality, while framing such experiences as orientation toward the presence of God in all of life, rather than as sufficient in themselves. The frequent celebration of Communion is one obvious and rich practice in the tradition for cultivating such a spirituality, and it is one that is part of the life of many new Seattle churches. A vital, experiential spirituality can also be cultivated by means of creative practices that invite attendees to actively engage rather than passively observe and curate multisensory experiences of the gospel. Crafting these kinds of worship environments has not been the traditional focus of seminary education, so church plant-ers would benefit from specialized training. Field trips will probably be especially useful.

Beyond worship, church planters ought to be trained and coached in other central—but taken for granted—skills for cultivating embodied, experiential, and everyday spirituality. For example, practitioners might be encouraged and coached to pursue expertise in facilitating meaning-ful shared meals, holding gatherings in public spaces, hosting conversa-tions about contemporary issues, and integrating elements of everyday life into the whole spiritual praxis of the church.[37] Everyday spirituality can be encouraged in the worship context, but its cultivation depends on the whole pattern of the church's corporate life, and especially upon the social practice of its community.

Recognizing Community Life as Both Witness and Formation

New Seattle churches do not practice community merely as fellowship—as the simple practice of friends enjoying the company of fellow believers. Rather, they recognize the profoundly missional and formational charac-ter and potential of Christian social practices. Perhaps this is why more than a third of new Seattle churches surveyed designate themselves as a "missional community." The ways in which Seattle church plants prac-tice community reflect both a consciousness of corporate witness and an intentionality toward forming disciples via social practice. They embody the practical wisdom that it is our shared rhythms of practice that both show us (witness) and make us (formation).

Several survey findings point to the community-as-witness character of these new churches. By far the most common approach to "mission, social action, and evangelism" among new Seattle churches is neither evange-lism nor social action, nor even a combination of the two, but being "pres-ent and modeling different values to the community." This syncs with the third most highly rated priority from a list of seventeen: 87% of respon-dents indicated that "modeling God's intentions for humanity" was an "extremely" (57%) or "very" (30%) important priority. This eschatological, communal modeling is also a highly ranked priority in terms of the time and energy churches devote to it.[38] Together, these indicate a strong thread of practical wisdom regarding how the corporate life of the church—its practices and values and social embodiment—provide a key part of their witness.

While intentionality with regard to the witness provided by the social practices of the church is distinctive of the New Community model, it is strong across the board, manifesting in unique ways in each model. NC churches seek to provide a corporate witness to the new humanity primarily through participatory and inclusive forms of worship, community, and leadership. HS churches strive to offer a worship atmosphere that prefigures heaven, both in its immersive sense of God's nearness and in the availability of supernatural healing. Churches in the NI model shape their corporate life toward the renewal of all things in the parish—presenting themselves as a social body that is making incarnate God's intentions for their neighborhood. GCT churches form missional communities that provide intermediate, invitational contexts that welcome outsiders to observe Christian community and undertake significant churchwide service projects with the intention of building a credible witness. While these approaches are distinct, they are informed by a common sensibility. They reflect the conviction that the corporate life of the church—its public, community life—provides a "hermeneutic of the gospel" and a "foretaste" of the Reign of God. New Seattle churches exemplify the practical wisdom that the church's socially embodied witness rings out in the public display of its unique values.

In addition to the function of the community as corporate witness to the wider world, new Seattle churches reflect serious intentionality regarding how their community life shapes the sense of identity, attention, and vocation held by individual church participants. That is, they reveal how important corporate social practices are in shaping how participants perceive and act in the world. The significance that new churches place on this formational task was evident in several survey findings. "Forming Christians into Christ-like character" was the fourth most highly rated priority and the fifth most highly ranked priority in terms of resource allocation. Many of the same community practices that provide a corporate witness to the world simultaneously function to form disciples. This tendency toward community-as-formation is strongest and most evident among GCT missional communities that live by shared monthly rhythms such as study, conversation, service, prayer, fellowship, and hospitality. These rhythms, as they are lived out in the context of Christian community, structure a powerfully formational praxis of discipleship and produce individuals with a strong personal sense of missional identity and vocation.

While GCT missional community rhythms provide the clearest and most instructive example of community-as-formation, the community life of churches in the other models is also transparently formational. The NI model elevates hospitality as the critical community practice that leads to their designation of third places and dinner parties with neighbors as prime contexts for discerning the Spirit's local initiatives. Community practices among NC and HS churches are no less formational, though centered as they are in worship, they are less oriented toward the cultivation of missional vocation. Community practice in the NC model centers on worship and is formative via the very practices they point to as providing their corporate witness—through inclusive and participatory forms of worship, community, and decision making. Notably, the NC practice of conversation as a primary mode of communication and discernment forms and reinforces that model's characteristic spirituality, marked by openness to finding God in the ordinary, the other, the ambiguous, and the mysterious. HS churches also locate their primary community practice and formation in the worship context. In these environments they cultivate disciples with a vivid sense of the Spirit's miraculous power and presence. These diverse approaches all attest to the formational power of community practice. GCT and NI models, especially, leverage their core community practices toward the cultivation of missional identity.

Church as Conversion Community

Corporate witness and personal formation are twin fruits of the community life of the church. This practical wisdom is rich with significance for dogmatic formulations of the nature of the church. The socially embodied witness of the church has been a focus of neo-Anabaptist, missional, and emerging church movements in recent decades, sometimes speaking of the church as a "contrast" or "alternative" society. New Seattle churches are evidence of the impact of such discourses and their relevance for contexts like Seattle. The church's social practices preach without words, ringing out at precisely their points of difference with the social practices of the wider cultural context. The significance of these points of difference, as they are noticed by the watching world and felt by the church itself, suggests that the distinctive social practices of the church are, in large part, what gives the communities that practice them a truly ecclesial character.[39] Eucharist, baptism, confession, healing prayer, witness, and the like, properly understood, are peculiar social practices that order human relationships in ways that foreshadow the new humanity. What is significant about this insight is that not just any contrast will do. The contrast practices of the church with a truly ecclesial character are those that are not merely countercultural but also mark out a trajectory toward the abundance, impartiality, mutuality, forgiveness, joy, and peace that characterizes the Reign of God that Jesus proclaimed and demonstrated. A proper contrast to the world is how the church serves as a sign and foretaste of God's Reign. Unfortunately, ecclesiologies that emphasize contrast have sometimes been used to justify expressions of the church that self-righteously condemn the world and, thus, misrepresent the character of the Reign of God.

In addition, the church's life is a context and cultivator of personal formation. Church is a context in which the habits and identities of individuals are reoriented toward the ways of God's Reign and toward intentional participation in the *missio Dei*. As such, the church can be understood as a *conversion community*.[40] The church provides what conversion theorists Arthur Griel and David Rudy call an "encapsulation."[41] Encapsulation can take place socially, ideologically, and/or physically.[42] As a conversion community, the church is a sphere of influence that provides the would-be disciple with a (new) primary social reference group, designates and utilizes certain physical spaces as orienting environments, and offers an ideological/theological system for interpreting life outside the social and physical borders of the community. In conversion, the church functions as both mentor and peer group, ushering individuals into a way of life in the Reign of God.[43] Liturgical scholars have written volumes on the formative impact of worship.[44] More important to disciple formation, however, than the elements that fill an hour or two on a Sunday morning, is the total pattern of social habits and activities among the people of the church—official and unofficial. The church as conversion community attends to this whole.

The post-Christian cultural context of the U.S church, as many have noted, has notable resonances with the context of the early church.[45] Without addressing the many intriguing parallels observers have drawn, I wish to consider only one: the imperative that the church facilitate holistic conversion. The church in a post-Christian context cannot rely on predominant culture to nurture people even halfway toward a way of life consonant with the Reign of God. The church in such an environment must be, and is, a conversion community. Precisely because of the early church's marginal status, it gave considerable attention to initiation practices. The foremost example of this is the three-year-long, mentored transformation process called the *catechumenate*. It was behaviorally demanding, socially immersive, and intellectually challenging.[46] The extensiveness and intensiveness of this process give some sense of how important it was to the early church to facilitate holistic, personal conversions. The early church was, and new Seattle churches are, conversion communities.

The central witness provided by the social practices of new Seattle churches has a key implication for missional theology. Namely, it challenges the disproportionate emphasis in missional theological discourse on the economic, sending Trinity and calls for missional theological reflection on the relational, social Trinity. Missional ecclesiologies have tended to root ecclesiality exclusively in the church's participation in the Trinitarian *mission*, without sufficiently considering what it might mean for the church to participate in and mirror the Trinitarian *community*. Van Gelder and Zscheile identify this as one of the major areas in which the missional conversation needs to deepen, and I concur.[47] As Zscheile writes:

> The God we know in salvation history, in Jesus Christ, and in the community of the church is a communal, relational God *for* and *with* us. Such a theology must take into view not only the *sending* concept of the Trinity so characteristic of Western theology but also the *social* doctrine of the Trinity that has been so richly developed in Eastern theology and, more recently, by contemporary Western theologians.[48]

Jürgen Moltmann is one of the Western theologians Zscheile points to as having explored the rich implications of *perichoresis*—the Trinitarian dance of mutuality, equality, openness, and mutual participation—for ecclesial life.[49] While the social practices of the church imperfectly provide a foretaste of the new humanity, the Triune relations reveal the true fellowship of equals toward which the *missio Dei* draws history. The Trinitarian fellowship provides an eschatological horizon for the church's practice of community. Inasmuch as missional theology calls for a church in the image of the Trinity, it has much to learn from reflection on the unity-in-diversity and mutual indwelling of the Godhead. The centrality of social practices in ecclesial witness suggests that for missional churches to be truly Trinitarian, they must not only attend to mission but also learn to reflect the perichoretic dance in their social practices.

Reflection on the social Trinity has already born significant fruit in missional theology and practice, as is evidenced in Branson's priority on "plural leadership." Here, Branson is echoing the perspectives of Roxburgh, Van Gelder, Zscheile, and others who discern a connection between the mutuality of the divine community and forms of church leadership characterized by plurality, diversity, partnership, and a shared effort to facilitate the discernment of the whole People of God. Not all who write and speak under the "missional" banner reflect this commitment, however, demonstrating the ongoing need for missional theology to engage with Eastern conceptualizations of the Trinity and their implications for ecclesial life. Van Gelder and Zscheile link the "underfunctioning" of Trinitarian understanding to "patriarchal and dominating patterns of social and ecclesial life and leadership [and] . . . the problematic legacies of colonial missions."[50] For these reasons, it is important that missional theological discourse pair its enthusiasm for the *sending* Trinity as grounds for mission with robust reflection on the *social* Trinity as a norm for the ecclesial character of the church's mission.

Implications for Leaders

In addition to these implications for doctrine, there are several implications of a practical nature stemming from this missional current of community as a core witness and incubator for missional discipleship. The first proposal stems from the importance of the community-as-witness theme: church planting leaders would be wise to provide the church planters under their care with basic training in congregational sociology. Theological education and church planting training typically offer theology and strategy, respectively, but rarely does either provide the critical interpretive tools needed for analyzing the socially embodied testimony of a community. As new Seattle churches—and a significant body of literature—attest, a church's way of life together, its leadership structure, decision-making processes, and social habits offer an implicit but potent witness, for good or for ill. Church planters with the tools of congregational sociology will be better equipped to understand what implicit witness their churches are making, and to respond accordingly. By attending to the stories, practices, and processes of their local Christian communities, church planters will become more alert to the subtle ways that the life of the church itself "proclaims" its gospel. With this understanding, they will be in a better position to provide theological and practical leadership in the day-to-day decisions that impact a church's calendar and budget—documents that often reveal more about a church's life than its official mission statement. The complex task of leading churches into renewed forms of socially embodied witness calls for leaders capable of holding the comprehensive community practice of the church in view. Practically speaking, while reading may be of some use, hands-on congregational study projects are strongly recommended. Prospective church planters will benefit greatly from being led through the process of "exegeting" the socially embodied witness of existing churches.[51] Church planting leaders might group church planters under their charge into trios and have each provide some outside perspective on the implicit witness offered by the social practice of each other's church.

If congregational sociology can illuminate the socially embodied witness of the church to the world, social psychology can help church planters to understand how community practice forms the identity and vocation of individuals. The key implication here is that discipleship and Christian formation are not solitary endeavors but social ones. Churches that are eager to cultivate "sacred consciousness" and missional iden-tity among members, therefore, will find it useful to analyze their core, shared practices, for these are the basic elements of the formation the church is facilitating. Regardless of how often church leaders stress the importance of discipleship and witness, if these are treated as parts of the Christian life that individual Christians ought to pursue on their own time, then church leaders are unwittingly implying that they are of sec-ondary importance. Worship gatherings—while they play a key role—cannot bear the full weight of Christian formation. The practices that are done together and regularly are those that the church is teaching its members (and the watching world) matter most. Serving others, loving your neighbor, authentic Christian community, and sharing your faith will never be regarded as important habits for following Jesus if they are merely the punch line of sermons. If they are to become normative activ-ities, they will have to be woven into the fabric of the church's shared practice. A church's rhythms of practice and conversation are its basic ways of forming "sacred consciousness" and missional identity. Church planters who understand this will be better equipped to awaken God's people to the presence of God in daily life and their identity as welcome participants in God's renewal of all things.

Supporting this vision of discipleship via corporate practice is an often overlooked implication of the Great Commission in which Jesus links making disciples with "teaching them to obey everything I have commanded you" (Matt. 28:20). While churches often interpret these words as an injunction to *preach* obedience to Jesus's commands, Jesus's own pedagogy with his disciples was via an extended, relationally intimate cohort of apprentices. In this perspective, it is clear that Jesus was eager that his disciples would actually create the social conditions whereby such formation could take place, so that future disciples would be able to obey his commands. Again, Jesus's own formative work with his disciples (rather than preaching-centric churches) provides the model.

Churches that are truly missional—that are filled with persons who know themselves as participants in God's renewal of all things—are marked by practices that cultivate this awareness. Concretely, to achieve this, church planting leaders can highlight approaches to church planting that integrate mission into the core rhythms of the community rather than focus exclusively on launching a worship service.[52] Notable examples of these include the missional communities strategy common among GCT churches as well as the community dinner church model, which combines hospitality, service, and worship into a single, meal-centered event. By drawing attention to such models, church planting leaders can shape the imaginations of new church planters and provide them with templates of good practice that prioritize the formation of missional disciples over measures such as worship attendance.

Prioritizing Hospitality as Cornerstone Practice

New Seattle churches highlight the importance of hospitality as a key practice of Christian mission. Even as the community life of new churches offers a prominent dimension of their witness, a central aspect of mission among new churches is welcoming others into the community via relational means. Several survey findings point to this thread of practical wisdom. "Offering a community in which to belong and be loved" was the second most highly rated priority, as well as the second most highly ranked priority in terms of time and energy use.[53] In addition, "Welcoming all—especially those excluded—as an inclusive community" was rated the seventh most important priority overall and among roughly three-fourths (74%) of new churches was rated as "very" (15%) or "extremely" (59%) important. Two-thirds of new church pastors see small groups as "very" or "extremely" important to the culture of the church. Strong majorities of Seattle church plants have avoided traditional marketing strategies for recruitment, such as door-to-door (84%), direct mail (71%), and advertisements (69%). Rather, 51% sponsored community events as a way of building relationships and credibility. Nearly a fourth of respondents opted to write in an open-ended "other" outreach strategy that indicated a relational, word-of-mouth approach.[54] Together, these numbers paint a picture of new churches that understand their community of belonging as a core aspect of what they have to offer, and who extend welcome through personal, relational ties.[55]

When the missiological and contextual reflections of chapter 5 are brought into conversation with these reports, it becomes apparent that new churches reveal the preeminence of hospitality as an ecclesial practice for post-Christian contexts. Not only is hospitality widely emphasized and practiced in the field, the practice has an orienting function for the life of the church. Much like a cornerstone squares a building, hospitality brings the ecclesial dimensions of mission, spirituality, and identity into proper alignment. Hospitality disciplines *mission* to take shape as a simultaneous proactive and noncoercive activity. The *spirituality* that naturally accompanies a robust practice of hospitality is one that seeks God in the midst of the other and the ordinary. The forms of ecclesial *identity* born of hospitable practice locate the church in its proper solidarity with the world and its diversity without collapsing the church into the world. Far from being a strategic mission gimmick, hospitality orients missional ecclesiopraxis.

Hospitality, as forging new friendships and creating spaces and communities of conversation and belonging, is the most elemental missional task of ecclesial witness in places like Seattle.[56] Framed by hospitality, mission is seen not as the transmission of a particular set of ideas, goods, or behaviors but, rather, as a practice of entering into relational webs that transform us even as we shape others. In this hospitality-oriented mission, the agencies at play are God's, ours, and our neighbor's, all at the same time.

When the general population is not interested in attending a religious event or affiliating with a religious institution, no amount of marketing is going to get them to show up on Sunday.[57] Personal relationships have always been an important bridge between the church and the world, but in post-Christian contexts they are indispensable. Proactively building genuine mutual friendships with people at work, next door, in third places, or through local events and welcoming them into a community of friends, some of whom are seeking to pattern their lives in the way of Jesus, is the most basic and essential practice for ecclesial vitality and witness in places like Seattle. This is true regardless of whether that community's main entry point is a neighborhood third place, a dinner party, a missional community, a service project, a block party, or a worship gathering.

Hospitality, however, should not be thought of as a relational recruitment strategy—though in numerous churches, especially Evangelical ones, it is conceived in precisely this way.[58] In missional perspective, hospitality is a spiritual practice, as well as a mission practice. Hospitality creates contexts for mutual relationship that strip Christians of the comfortable positions of benevolent superiority that characterize Christendom-shaped expressions of mission in evangelism and service. As Keith Anderson observes, "when we make ourselves open and vulnerable by entering these third places we do not manage or control, we are more open to the unpredictable ways the Spirit moves in us, in others, and in our world."[59] In these contexts of mutuality, followers of Jesus are well positioned to attend to the sometimes surprising initiatives of the unruly Spirit of God who intends the renewal of all things and invites human participation in its realization. Moreover, it is from within the contexts of mutual hospitality that faithful, Christ-like expressions of evangelism and service can emerge that are unencumbered by the fraught power dynamics of Christendom and are, thus, vibrant, vital practices of participation in the *missio Dei*.

Church as Guest and Host

This vision of the practice of hospitality as an ecclesial cornerstone in post-Christian and post-Christendom contexts recasts the *church as guest and host*. This ecclesiological identity is thoroughly mixed and cyclical, encompassing both the church's spiritual orientation and its mission efforts. As *guest*, the church humbly accepts that it dwells within a wider community, as a guest in its context, seeking to find and forge life there, dependent on the hospitality of others. As *host*, the church intentionally seeks to build new relationships and invites others into spaces for conversation and belonging. As *guest*, the church confesses that it dwells in God's world, seeking to find and forge its life in partnership with the Spirit's local initiatives. As *host*, the church invites, welcomes, and attends to God's presence in the midst of their communities of belonging. These overlapping and interwoven postures of guest and host to the world and to God express the true nature of the church.

The Emmaus road account in Luke 24:13–35 grounds this hospital-ity-shaped ecclesial vision of church as guest and host. In this account, a demoralized pair of disciples extend hospitality to a stranger on the road, insisting that he dine and stay with them; they host him for dinner. At the dinner table, their guest becomes host, and offers the blessing. At that moment, the stranger is revealed as the risen Christ himself. According to Luke, the church's first encounter with the resurrected Christ arose from their practice of hospitality, in an exchange of conversation and food with a stranger, who became their teacher, who became their host, and finally who was revealed as the presence of Christ among them. The church as guest and host resonates with the experience of these bewildered disciples who began as hosts to a stranger but became guests at Christ's table. At the same time, the church strives to follow in the way of Jesus who, in this passage, appeared as a foreigner, asked his fellow travelers what they were talking about, listened to their emotion-filled story of loss and confusion, offered a new perspective, received hospitality, and spoke words of blessing.[60] The church as guest and host humbly yet eagerly moves toward relationship with neighbors and strangers and fellow travelers. It is open for new conversation partners, eager to "set the table" for a shared feast, and filled with spiritual expectation in the hopes that their guests may become their teachers and hosts and might awaken them to the presence of Christ in their midst.

Implications for Leaders

The preeminence of hospitality as a practice of post-Christendom ecclesial witness has numerous practical implications for church planting leaders. First, the time has come for church planters to abandon traditional mar-keting approaches in post-Christian contexts. These practices are not only theologically and contextually problematic but unnecessary, as the viability of Seattle's new churches that have discarded them demonstrates.[61] A web presence is important but it ought to be developed from a logic of hos-pitality rather than one of marketing. Church websites and social media presence ought to serve as "front porches" for the church, creating digital narthexes that allow guests to explore at their own discretion, allowing out-siders to explore the community and its practices without requiring them to enter an environment they fear will be coercive (i.e., worship).

Second, church planting leaders can make the practice of hospitality a key matter of discussion and training, asking potential planters how, and in what spaces, they intend to practice it. Popular and authentic forms of hospitable practice in the field include hosting block parties, barbecues, and community events, as well as creating third places. Practitioners formed in worship-centric churches will naturally tend to assess potential gathering spaces for their utility for worship gatherings. However, it is equally critical that practitioners learn to identify spaces conducive to large and small gatherings, to formal and informal conversations, to parties and meals. Indeed, places of residence are prime sites for hospitable practice. In addition to these concerns for space, church planting leaders can, and should, urge practitioners to integrate practices of hospitality into personal and group habits, and to highlight hospitality as spiritual practices on a par with prayer, and a missional practice on a par with serving.

Third, because hospitality is the basic, and preliminary, expression of ecclesial life in places like Seattle, potential church planting teams will benefit from living in communities and practicing hospitality for a year or more before seeking to formally initiate a new church in that place. During this year, the planting team could find jobs that facilitate develop-ing multiple, meaningful relationships with colleagues and/or clients.[62] This time can be devoted to developing friendships and creating spaces for community with neighbors and co-workers, learning their stories, hopes, and challenges. These relationships and communities would provide the primary context for the team's discernment of the Spirit's local initiatives, and thus set the stage for developing the rhythms of community practice and local service partnerships that would largely determine the character of the new church.

Discovering Vitality in a Diverse Ecclesial Ecology

Perhaps the most straightforward finding of this study is among its most important: 105 churches were active in Seattle in 2014 that were planted after 2000. This is a sign of ecclesial vitality in a context with a reputation for rejecting church. As noted in chapter 1, the vibrancy of religious life in the Pacific Northwest comports with the openness of a religious environ-ment that favors creative and nontraditional religious communities. That is, counterintuitively, the non-religiosity of the context is boon to ecclesial innovation and thus provides fertile soil for the Spirit's wildest initiatives. The church in the None Zone may be numerically small and institution-ally weak, but it is nonetheless full of life, and its life takes many shapes.

The field of new Seattle churches offers the practical wisdom and hope that ecclesial vitality can be found in ecclesial variety.

New Seattle churches provide a lesson that ecclesiologists steeped in Christendom assumptions need to take seriously: the church's nature does not lie in its cultural strength or numerical expansion. There is a critical distinction between the church and the Reign of God; the institutions of the church may decline and its members may lose faith, but God's Reign is unwavering and undaunted. While ecclesiologists in the last century have increasingly admitted this distinction, the mistaken assumption that ecclesial fidelity and vitality are inextricably linked with institutional growth and cultural influence largely remain. Seattle's new churches stand as a concrete demonstration that diminishing numbers and cultural power need not be regarded as a threat to the vitality of the ecumenical church. For, as missional theology asserts, the life of the whole People of God rises and falls, ultimately, not with environmental factors but by the Spirit and the faithful persons who collaborate with her divine initiatives.

While the context has yielded significant ecclesial innovation and diversity, these 105 new churches do not represent 105 utterly unique approaches to ecclesial life. To the contrary, a second key finding of this research has been the identification of four dominant practical ecclesiological models that describe 80% of the churches surveyed. While there is diversity among new churches, these pioneering Christian communities are far from idiosyncratic. Rather, this diversity coalesces into a limited number of dominant bundles of understandings and practices of mission, spirituality, and identity. Moreover, these four models exist in significant relationships with one another, forming an ecology of practical ecclesiologies. This is most clearly seen in the stark contrast between the Great Commission Team and New Community models, whose defining characteristics are, across the board, counter-indicated. This ecological relationship entails a mutual sense of critique and identity in distinction, as well as a noteworthy flow of disillusioned Evangelicals from GCT and HS churches to those in the NC model. While transparently somewhat antagonistic, this relationship is also semi-symbiotic.[63] More broadly, the GCT and NC models establish the dominant poles in the field between and around which the life of the church flows. Household of the Spirit churches lay in close proximity to the GCT model on this spectrum, in several cases overlapping with it, with a fairly free and amiable exchange of practices and participants. Neighborhood Incarnation churches, however, exist virtually everywhere along the polarized spectrum. Some NI

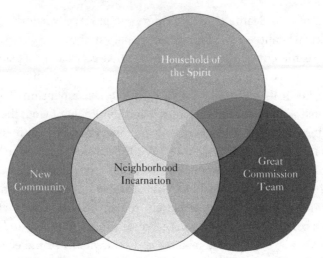

FIGURE 7.1 The ecological relationships between models of new Seattle churches.

churches are also strong evangelism-focused GCT churches, others are among the most progressive NC churches, and still others reflect the most supernaturally oriented of HS churches. Even more interesting, some NI churches seem to have forged a home for themselves between the extreme poles, as evangelically originating churches that retain a zeal for proactive mission but also reflect certain progressive spiritual sensibilities. In other words, the NI model fills out the middle of the ecology by confounding the dichotomy between liberal and evangelical Christianity that dominates not only the field of new churches but the broader field of U.S. congregations as well. The relationships between the models is illustrated in figure 7.1.

As mentioned in chapter 4, my research pointed to the likely existence of two additional models among the 20% of churches that do not clearly fit into the four models that have been the focus of this study. This omission may be attributable to underrepresentation of these churches in the survey sample or, perhaps, to the inadequacy of the survey instrument to indicate their types.[64] These two possible models are made up of, on one hand, several multisite campuses of somewhat progressive Evangelical megachurches and, on the other, a handful of ethnically specific congregations in sacramental traditions.[65] As figure 7.2 suggests, these two additional models fit quite nicely into niches between the confirmed models. The Sacramental Ethnic model would echo the cultural identity of the HS model and the liturgical/sacramental practice of the NC model. The

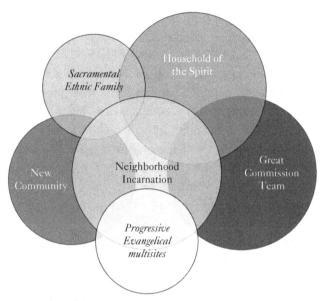

FIGURE 7.2 Possible additional models among new Seattle churches.

progressive Evangelical multisite model would resonate with the proactive mission posture and pragmatism of the GCT model and the culture-affirming stance of the NC model. The relationship of these models to the NI form is also interesting. The multisite model itself represents a shift toward the local, especially in contrast to the commuter-culture of many megachurches. The ethnic identity of the Sacramental Family model would, presumably, preclude a significant overlap with NI characteristics except in cases where the relevant ethnic populations are concentrated in particular neighborhoods.

Church as Family System
and Noah's Ark

The ecology of practical ecclesiologies that this research has brought to light offers a fresh context for doctrinal reflection. In recent decades, congregational sociologists have advanced an "ecological frame" for studying churches. This perspective approaches congregations in a given context as interdependent, even apart from any direct interaction, on the basis of "their physical proximity, and by virtue of common environmental factors, for example, economic, educational, or infrastructural changes."[66] An ecological frame attends to both competition and cooperation between churches, as well as to the unintended ways they affect one another, as they navigate their shared—and often changing—contexts.

Change in an ecclesial ecology, as Nancy Eiesland observed, "happens less through adaption and more by organizational replacement. . . . [N]ew organizations with a better "fit" come in to fill their place."[67] "Religious groups will continue to go where the people are, planting congregations and buttressing the ideals of community life that families want when they move to these particular places."[68] The four (or six) models discovered indicate not merely what pioneering missionaries are creating but also—to use the ecological metaphor—where the sun is breaking through the canopy and bringing new life to the jungle floor. In theological perspective, the ecology of models point not only to human action but also to divine agency; the models are what the Spirit is planting in northwestern soil.

A handful of sociological studies have offered rich ecclesial ecological portraits.[69] While a few church practitioners have plucked applications from these studies, theologians have largely failed to consider what these ecumenical and contextual portraits of ecclesial life reveal about the nature of the church itself. It is, of course, beyond the scope of this book to remedy the dearth of robust theological engagement with congregational studies.[70] However, this study has brought to light the ecclesial ecology among Seattle's new churches, highlighting both major environmental features (urban, progressive, technological, post-Christian) and interrelationships between prevalent models. Thus, while these new churches are not the only congregations in Seattle's ecclesial ecology (they are roughly one-fifth), I will briefly consider the following question: *What might be the shape of an ecumenical ecclesiology rooted in Seattle's ecology of new churches?* Here, I sketch two contours that further ecclesiological construction might explore.

First, the interrelationship between new churches in the Seattle context invites reflection on the *ecumenical church as a family system.* Family systems theory, developed by psychiatrist Murray Bowen, suggests that "families are systems of interconnected and interdependent individuals, none of whom can be understood in isolation from the system."[71] Family systems theory has been usefully applied to particular congregations, most notably by Edwin Friedman, but here I propose drawing on its interpretive concepts for understanding the relationships between predominant ecclesiological models.[72] The four (or six) models are what the Spirit is giving birth to in Seattle.[73] Like siblings, they interrelate in myriad ways, sometimes as adversaries, sometimes co-dependently, often as playmates, role models and identity foils, but always in ways that deeply affect one another.

Two concepts within family systems theory are suggestive of the promise of understanding the ecumenical church—on the local or global scale—as a family system. The first, self-differentiation, refers to the ability of individuals to separate their feelings from their thoughts, and further, to distinguish one's own feelings from those of others. Those who are differentiated are "able to have different opinions and values than [their] family members, [while] being able to stay emotionally connected to them."[74] Applied to the ecumenical church through the lens of the field of new churches in Seattle, it is clear that some models are more differentiated than others. The identity in distinction that characterizes the dynamic between GCT and NC models points to a lack of differentiation on both sides.[75] Moreover, the capacity of the NI model to integrate harmoniously with the other dominant models suggests strong differentiation.

"Triangles" are a second useful concept of family systems theory. Bowen noted the tendency within families toward the formation of three-person relationship systems. Triangles emerge when conflict between two individuals draws in a third party. This third person is typically recruited by one of the individuals in conflict to help "reduce [his] anxiety and take action, or calm [his] strong emotions and reflect, or bolster [his] beliefs and make a decision."[76] This triangle dynamic of relationships can be seen in the conflicted relationship between GCT and NC churches that also includes HS churches in a two-against-one antipathy. The size disparity between the allied GCT and HS models (more than half of the field) compared to the NC model (one-fifth of the field) is dramatic. This may mirror an opposite disparity between the dominant cultural progressivism compared to the zealous conservative minority that includes Evangelical and Pentecostal Christians.

As a family system, the nature of the church is revealed to be one of emotionally charged and often fraught relationships, stemming largely from the undifferentiated personalities of individual church leaders, particular congregations, and ecclesiastical groups or models. The ecumenical church is a typical and somewhat dysfunctional family. This should come as no surprise, as it is in perfect continuity with the families that come to us in the pages of the scriptural canon. The People of God throughout redemptive history—from Abraham's family, to the tribes of Israel, to the disciples and early church, through the rise of Christianity and into today—have always been fraught with conflict, filled with emotionally reactive movements and leaders, and seasoned with other leaders and movements that are quite differentiated and contribute greatly to its overall health and development. The one, holy church is also a community rife with internal tension and identity confusion.

Second, the ecological relations among new Seattle churches might lead to imaginatively constructing the *ecumenical church—locally and globally—as Noah's Ark*.[77] Here, I do not intend to retrace the classic church-as-ark-of-salvation metaphor.[78] Instead, I wish to evoke the diverse and interdependent web of life that the Ark account says was hosted aboard for forty days and forty nights. Genesis specifically mentions that the Ark was home to both ravens and doves—that is, to predators and prey alike.[79] Moreover, it held "birds of the air" and "animals," as well as "every creeping thing," each "according to its kind." That is, it contained creatures whose distinguishing features are best appreciated in contrast and comparison to like and unlike others. Specifically, the Ark's passengers are distinguished from one another on the basis of their characteristic forms of movement. That is, their unique ways of interacting with their environments—flying, walking, and creeping.

Likewise, the ecumenical church in the local context is a biome whose organisms (models and congregations) exist simultaneously in conflict and symbiosis, in proximity and distinction, and who act in their environments in distinctive ways (i.e., mission orientations). The nature and vitality of this ecumenical ecosystem, like that of the Ark, rests in two features: its comprehensive diversity and the reproductive capacity of each species. Noah was to preserve seven mated pairs of every "clean" creature and one mated pair of every "unclean" animal. The ecumenical church, like Noah's floating biome, is not entirely "clean," theologically speaking. This is conveyed explicitly as God's intent. Indeed, Noah's task was to preserve the whole creative work of the divine *ruach* (translated variously as "spirit," "breath," and "wind") that brooded over the waters of chaos and was exhaled in God's originating speech. In creation, God birthed not individual creatures, not singular species, but a whole, living system. The Ark was to be the biosphere in microcosm. In creation, and in the ongoing creation of the church, the Spirit is doing many things at once, some which may seem to be at cross-purposes with each other, but all of which play a role in the created whole. As the Ark was filled with "pairs of all creatures that have the *ruach* of life in them," so the one, holy, catholic, and apostolic church is composed of all self-propagating churches to whom the Spirit has given breath. It comprehensively includes all congregations and practical ecclesiological models that have arisen by the action of the Spirit and reproductive capacity of its progenitors. The ecumenical church as Ark is an ecosystem replete with all varieties of Spirit-given life, preserved by God in order to be released to find viable habitats across the face of the earth, to adapt, to find food, and to reproduce.[80]

Implications for Leaders

The ecclesial vitality and ecological diversity found in this research are suggestive of several practical implications for church planting leaders. First, the vitality of new Seattle churches challenges predominantly negative characterizations of the context used for recruitment and fundraising that paint Seattle as a spiritual wasteland and a hostile environment for the gospel. Church planting leaders, as overseers of recruitment and training, can equip on-the-ground practitioners with more faithful and life-giving narratives that honor God's presence and work. They can bear witness to the natural and cultural beauty, the social impulses that they recognize as harmonious with the Reign of God, local stories of renewal and restoration. Orientations to context should include not only statistics about the high percentages of unchurched people and sparse church attendance but also stories about the panoply of ecclesial expressions that the Spirit has planted in native soil.

A second practical implication for church planting leaders stems from the insights of the ecological frame. Because these four (or six) practical ecclesiological models are what the Spirit is giving birth to in the future-trending city of Seattle, church planting leaders intent on joining in and synchronizing their efforts with the initiatives of the Spirit should eagerly seek to build and encourage harmonious relationships across the whole diverse ecclesial ecology. The ambition of church planting leaders should not be limited to the advancement of their denomination, network, or preferred model but, rather, to contribute to the flourishing of the whole ecumenical church. While particular local congregations may be more or less aligned with the tenets of missional theology, the ecumenical church is most missional when it is finding incarnational expression in wide ecclesial diversity and consistent reproduction into new communities. It is for this reason that I recommend that church planting leaders embrace and promote diverse ecclesial forms, as well as meaningful relationships between practitioners in various models in order to smooth their rough edges without blunting their cutting edges.

Achieving such relationships will require that these leaders seek a degree of self-differentiation, and learn to recruit and coach practitioners toward the same. The basic lessons of the family system for the church are straightforward: church planters should strive for differentiation and beware of triangles. The whole church will be strengthened as the models and their constituent churches more thoroughly ground their identities in practical theological reflection, as opposed to operating from emotional reactions to the values and practices of others, based on past experiences. This will require that practitioners reflect on personal church experiences—positive and negative—that have shaped their vision of what the church is and ought to be. In particular, this is necessary so they can identify and work through any unresolved emotions that would threaten productive ecumenical relations across the whole ecclesial ecology. I recommend that potential practitioners be advised that "The fact that you're angst ridden and don't like the church you're in is not necessarily a sign that God has called you to plant a church."[81] Indeed, it is more likely a sign that such a church planter would be disruptive of ecumenical harmony in whatever context he or she settled. The overarching implication of the ecclesial vitality and ecological diversity evident in the Seattle context is that church planting leaders, both those working in similar contexts and those whose contexts are only beginning to reflect these national trends, should celebrate, seek to learn from, and be in relationship with the other ecclesial expressions being born of the Spirit.

Final Words

According to news headlines, Christianity in the United States is on the decline.[82] It is true that the falling numbers of church-goers and self-identified Christians can tell this story. But the place this story has in media and public discourse as the dominant religious narrative has resulted, too often, in implied suggestions that these numerical declines signal decay and irredeemable irrelevance. Too many assume they signal a trajectory toward an inevitable day, not far off, when the last demoralized church will finally close its doors.[83] The decline narrative is often overdrawn into an extinction narrative that envisions Christianity quietly fading into historical memory, like the mythologies of the Greeks and Romans millennia before. If, however, as this project has argued, Seattle's new churches provide a glimpse into the future of church in the United States, those who anticipate its demise are in for a surprise. As several more careful observers have noted, Christianity is not dying—it is changing.[84]

This is nothing new, as careful students of church history can attest. For nearly two millennia, Christianity has—with God's help—sought fresh connections between the resources of Christian tradition and new historical situations, navigated challenges from within and without, and forged fresh, contextual ways of practicing faith in Jesus in community. As the United States undergoes a period of dramatic change, the church is once again, engaging in renegotiation and innovation.

That this era of ecclesial change is marked by diminishing numbers of Christian affiliates and worship attenders is not, theologically speaking, necessarily an indication of the church's *decline*. Ultimately, the vitality and integrity of the church cannot be measured by attendance figures or cultural clout but only by the church's fidelity to its Lord. Of course, measuring Christian faithfulness is an exceedingly contested matter, as divergent interpretations of burgeoning numbers of "Nones" illustrate. Some analysts have drawn compelling connections between these numerical drops and the marriage of Evangelicalism with conservative Republican politics, which I judge to be a failure of faithful witness.[85] I anticipate that the strong support Donald Trump received from white Evangelical voters in the 2016 election—according to exit polls, 81% backed him—will propel a continuing uptick in disaffiliation. In this respect, declining numbers of affiliates may be interpreted as corresponding with lapses in fidelity. However, other analysts have suggested that disaffiliation and drops in attendance can be seen as the refining of American Christianity. As nominal and cultural Christians shed rather meaningless labels and practices, the result is that the remaining self-identified Christians and church-goers are becoming, as a group, overall more convicted in their beliefs and more regular in their practices.[86] In this way, the numerical decline can conversely be read as corresponding to an increase in the church's fidelity.

The contested nature of measuring fidelity, on one hand, means that the true vitality of the church is always clouded, known only to God and, perhaps, in partial ways to humans in retrospect. On the other hand, however, assessing the fidelity of Christian doctrine and practice has been and should be a central task of theology. To this end, in chapter 5 I drew on key ideas within missional theology to assess the practical ecclesiologies in the field. This evaluation, broadly speaking, concluded that new Seattle churches, as a whole and in each model, show signs of vitality—in the various ways these churches faithfully embody the missional nature of the church—as well as causes for concern and repentance. This sort of mixed assessment is the proper contribution of normative theology to

reflection on the church's total practice in a given context. Normative theology, when applied to such a broad and diverse field, is wise to speak both
a yes and a no, rather than merely deliver a single, overarching verdict.
This is because the *telos* of the theological enterprise is renewed Christian
practice. Assessment is intended to spur repentance and renewal. To
repeat Healy's claim, ecclesiology's primary function is "to aid the church
in performing its task of truthful witness within a particular ecclesiological context."[87]

It is precisely this purpose that has animated this project from its con-
ception to its completion. The ecclesiological description, interpretation,
assessment, and proposals developed in the preceding pages are offered to
assist the church as it endeavors to fulfill its identity and calling as a witness to the good news of Jesus Christ in a rapidly evolving context. With
Seattle as a proxy for the future of U.S. cities, it has highlighted national
trends in urban population growth, progressive values, technology use,
and post-Christian religious dynamics. By identifying the four dominant
practical ecclesiologies among new Seattle churches, I have signaled these
as viable options for ecclesial life, especially in the coming years. I have
done this in the hope of drawing the attention of practitioners and theologians capable of utilizing, adapting, and improving upon each of these
models. The missional theological assessment of chapter 5 seeks to contribute to the faithful renewal of these living forms of ecclesiopraxis. It also
highlights the Neighborhood Incarnation model as an especially promising option. These final chapters have gone further to propose specific practices, name generative threads of practical wisdom, and suggest doctrinal
trajectories with the potential of spurring the church on in its continuing
conversion.

Inasmuch as Seattle offers the U.S. church a glimpse into its future,
there are grounds not only for hope but also for enthusiasm. The American
church is in the midst of a period of great contextual change, and through
the eyes of faith, believers affirm that God is in the midst, actively engaged
with human history and by the Spirit is inviting the church to join in
the "new thing" that God is doing. As Alan Roxburgh has observed, "in
Scripture, places of unraveling were preludes to God shaping a new future
for God's people."[88] That the new future God is forming would slip beneath
the radar of popular attention is to be expected. Indeed, such seems to be
the pattern with God's renewing work. "Behold . . . now it springs forth, do
you not perceive it? I will make a way in the wilderness and rivers in the
desert" (Isa. 43:9, ESV). Like rivers in the desert, these new churches in the

None Zone are the "new wineskins" into which God has already begun to pour "new wine."[89] They may on the whole be relatively small and institutionally weak by comparison to their Christendom predecessors, but they are also a vital, diverse, and engaged cohort. Through local identity and experiential spirituality, social practices that witness and form, and mission grounded in hospitality, these churches of the future are joining God in the renewal of all things, participating in the *missio Dei* as signs, foretastes, and instruments of God's Reign, and beckoning the whole church on a journey into the ecclesial future God is shaping.

APPENDIX A

Research Methodology

In order to develop the description of the field of new Seattle churches provided in chapter 2, I began by attempting to locate all Christian churches within the city limits of Seattle that had been founded since January 1, 2001, and that remained active through 2014. In the following paragraphs, I offer a rationale for each of these three parameters: (1) Christian church, (2) in Seattle, (3) founded since 2001. First, with regard to specifying *Christian* churches, this project was undertaken in service of aiding the ecumenical Christian church in the United States. In order to heighten the sense of relevance of my findings for their intended ecumenical audience, it seemed wise to limit the sample to communities that would be viewed by most Christian bodies as genuine expressions of the Christian faith. I sought an ecumenically inclusive sample, but also a distinctly Christian, rather than an interreligious, one. To provide a benchmark for this in practice, I looked to the most widely embraced ecumenical document in recent decades, *Baptism, Eucharist and Ministry*. This document is the basis for numerous ecumenical agreements, most notably the recognition by major Christian bodies of baptisms performed in other traditions with the Trinitarian formula (. . . in the name of the Father, Son, and Holy Spirit).[1] Of course, multiple churches reject infant baptism, but on the other side, the baptisms these churches conduct are recognized as valid by the Catholic Church and many major Christian bodies on the basis of their Trinitarian doctrine and use of the Trinitarian formula for baptism. The net result of this choice was the exclusion of one spiritualist community, a Swedenborgian church, and six Latter-Day Saints congregations, all which describe themselves as Christian, but which would not be recognized as such by the majority of other Christian congregations and bodies on the basis, primarily, of their non-Trinitarian doctrines and baptismal practices, their Christology, and/or additional Scriptures. It was not my intention—nor within the scope of this project—to attempt to demonstrate the ecclesiality of the included churches nor to refute the ecclesiality of those not included in the sample. I did, however, seek a sample that most Christians would agree comprised fellow Christians.

Second, the choice of Seattle was based on my knowledge of its status as one of the "least churched" cities in the United States and its counterintuitive emergence as a fertile ground for ecclesial pioneering. Seattle is the birthplace, home, or focus area for several networks and hubs for church planting, including Acts 29, Seattle Church Planting, Northwest Church Planting Network, Metro Northwest, Northwest Anglican, and The Parish Collective, as well as several churches proliferating through the multisite strategy. In addition, this was a location to which I—as a Seattle native—had good access.

Third, the choice of January 1, 2001, as a chronological limit was based on several considerations. Not least among these were concerns about the feasibility of scope. I expected that going much further back could yield a sample too large for me as a solo researcher to handle, while including at least a ten-year span meant that brand-new churches would be joined in the sample by others now fairly well established. In addition, 2001 seemed wise given that the "defining moment" of the first decade of the millennium took place that year, with the 9/11 terrorist attack. This moment is especially significant for the young generations of Americans who most new churches are seeking to reach.[2] One summative consideration came from the American Religious Identification Survey, which found that while the Pacific Northwest had the highest percentage of "Nones" in 2001, by 2008 it had ceded this distinction to New England.[3]

IDENTIFYING THE CHURCHES

Having set the parameters, the next task was to find the new churches. Thorough identification of churches within a geographical area is a challenge well recognized by sociologists of religion. New churches are even more difficult to uncover. This is one reason they have generally been underrepresented in congregational studies research. This difficulty is attributable to several causes. For starters, relatively few new churches have primary rights to their place of worship. As a result, new churches do not always have a sign-laden building to serve as a 24/7 testament to their presence in the community. Even churches that meet in church buildings regularly rent the space from other churches whose signage adorns the building. Accurately identifying new churches is also inhibited by the lag time between when churches are established or relocate and when denominational, network, or web administrators update online information. This difficulty is compounded by a reverse effect: when church starts fold, it may take months or even years for websites to come down and for them to be removed from denominational listings. In addition, house churches, small fellowships, and intentional communities do not always seek 501(c)(3) status, sometimes choosing to operate under the nonprofit status of a host or sponsoring church.

With these difficulties in mind, the identification phase, which began in spring of 2013 and was ongoing through the summer of 2014, sought out churches via multiple means, including extensive internet research, contacting denominational and network offices, and on-the-ground fieldwork. A few qualifying churches were stumbled upon and added after this period of focused investigation. The three most productive sources were internet listings, staff contacts within the denominations identified by city-data.com as present in the county in which Seattle is located (King County), and key informants among the church planting networks in the region. Google keyword searches were very useful. Facebook and Twitter also proved to be valuable research tools, and led to the discovery of more than a few churches. Also helpful was the National Center for Charitable Statistics listings of 501c3-501(c)(3)10 (church) rulings between 2001 and 2014. These listings helped me uncover several churches that other approaches had missed, though the list produced required substantial verification, as many were found to be in existence before the ruling or had gone defunct since that ruling.[4] A few churches identified themselves in response to my personal and research web presence, which included a research website, publication of a preliminary sketch of the field in a regionally focused online ministry journal,[5] and social media accounts. Finally, during my four research trips I engaged in purposeful networking with local informants and at church conferences, and scanned for church sandwich boards and signs while driving around the city. My physical presence in Seattle included four research trips between August 2013 and April 2014, for a total of forty-three days. Onsite research included eighteen days in July-August 2013, nine days in November 2013, eight days in December 2013–January 2014 (including Christmas services), and eight days in April 2014 (including Holy Week). As a result, I identified 105 new Seattle churches that I was able to confirm as fitting within the parameters of the study. I acquired basic information about all identified churches, such as denominational affiliation, founding date, address, web presence, place of worship, and ethnic composition from a variety of sources, including church websites, social media sites, church and denominational staff, and Google Maps Street View.

NEW SEATTLE CHURCHES SURVEY

I constructed the project with the hypothesis that a strong majority of the new churches in the field could be characterized by a limited number of types. This hypothesis was based on the findings of two previous geographically based congregational studies.[6] In order to test this hypothesis and identify the number and character of these types—as well as to surface overall tendencies in the field—I designed a 44-question instrument called the New Seattle Churches Survey. The survey was intended to reveal the culture, theology, and practices of the churches, especially in the dimensions of spirituality, mission, and identity. These three dimensions are, of course, overlapping and integrated aspects of ecclesial life, but were distinguished for the sake of analysis as, respectively, how the church relates to God, what it believes it is to do in the world, and how it understands its uniqueness as a group.

In order to illumine these dimensions and gain a holistic sense of the ecclesiopraxis in each church, I developed, utilized, and adapted survey questions from existing literature in congregational studies, church planting, and missiology.[7] The survey is included in appendix B.

Leaders at all identified churches were invited by email or a social media message to complete the New Seattle Churches Survey online via SurveyMonkey. I was able to locate a means of electronic communication for nearly all the identified churches. One survey was conducted in person. Another was conducted over the phone. These invitations were followed up by a reminder message and/or phone call, and in a few cases by face-to-face connections on church property or during worship. The survey was also promoted via a website www.newseattlechurches.com (active until summer 2014); my personal social media platforms on Facebook, Twitter, and a blog; and a Twitter account named New Seattle Churches with the handle @newSEAchurches. Through this Twitter account I followed and made a list of the Twitter accounts associated with new Seattle churches, their pastors, networks, and denominational bodies.

In all, I received surveys from 57 of the 105 churches identified. Respondents were overwhelmingly Lead Pastors or Founding Pastors. While I had some concern about whether surveys completed by pastors would accurately represent the culture and priorities of their churches, this fear was substantially allayed by the results of congregational surveys conducted in the three focus churches that showed strong agreement with the responses of their pastors. Not all surveys were complete, though on all key questions at least 52 responses were received. The survey was voluntary and thus did not provide a random or representative sample. Conservative Protestants are overrepresented, while Mainline churches are slightly underrepresented, chiefly because of the omission of Mainline ethnic congregations. Still, a solid majority of churches from within each of the various subgroups of white and multicultural churches in Conservative Protestant and mainline traditions did complete the survey. Orthodox churches were absent altogether, and less than a fourth of Seattle's new ethnic churches submitted surveys. Responses were received from just under half of the historically black churches, as well as from the only new multicultural Catholic parish and a lone Messianic Jewish synagogue. As is always the case with online surveys, the respondents were somewhat more digitally connected than the general population in view. Ninety-eight percent of the responding churches have websites, 95% have Facebook accounts, and 63% are on Twitter.

SURVEY ANALYSIS

The results of the New Seattle Churches Survey illuminated both currents and patterns in ecclesial mission, spirituality, and identity. Patterns were determined by grouping survey variables into one of three dimensions (mission, spirituality, and identity) and correlating variables within each group with statistical analysis software. Variables within each dimension that were mutually correlated were grouped together into patterns. If three or fewer variables were included in a pattern, all variables were correlated at the .01 level of two-tailed significance. If more than three variables were included in a pattern, then all variables correlated at the .01 level with more than half of the other variables in the pattern and at the .05 level with the remaining variables. Patterns were then analyzed for correlations across spirituality, mission, and identity dimensions. These correlations clustered so as to reveal four dominant paradigms— four primary configurations of spirituality, mission, and identity patterns among new Seattle churches. Paradigms were constructed exclusively of patterns correlated at the .01 level of two-tailed significance. This statistical analysis provided a framework to structure the interpretive work and direct ongoing fieldwork.

QUALITATIVE RESEARCH

I began qualitative research—participant observation and pastoral interviews—even before the survey analysis had revealed the four paradigms. Once discovered, however, these paradigms were useful for structuring my fieldwork from that point forward. That is, I identified a handful of churches within each paradigm that were exemplary of the paradigm and focused my qualitative research among them. In this way, these survey-based paradigms provided "skeletons" of ecclesiopraxis that the qualitative research built upon in the development of the four practical ecclesiological models. I observed worship in twenty-six unique churches. From multiple *exemplar* churches in each paradigm, in addition to completed surveys, I collected most or all of the following: pastoral interviews, field notes and transcripts from worship gatherings, online recordings, media coverage, newsletters, brochures, web pages, and social media posts for analysis. I conducted interviews with sixteen different pastors. All pastors who were interviewed declined anonymity.

In addition, as a subset of these twenty-five exemplar churches, three *focus* churches were selected for intensive study on the basis of their theological diversity, the feasibility of participant observation among all three on a single Sunday, and my early assessment of their potential contributions to the study. The three focus churches were The Hallows Church, Wits' End Church, and Community Dinners. In each focus church, I was a participant observer at a minimum of nine gatherings (including Christmas and Easter celebrations), conducted two or three focus groups and multiple formal and informal interviews, facilitated a thirty-three–question online congregational survey, and shared early observations with church leadership for feedback.

The qualitative materials from exemplar and focus churches were coded and analyzed using NVivo, a qualitative data analysis software, for themes within each of the four paradigms. These themes in mission, spirituality, and identity compose the major part of the practical ecclesiological models developed in chapter 4.

LIMITATIONS

Two limitations of this study are worth noting. The first pertains to the parameters of the study: churches currently gathering within the city limits of Seattle that were founded between 2001 and 2014. These parameters inherently inhibit the generalizability of findings. While I am convinced—as I argue in chapter 1—that Seattle is a serviceable proxy for the future trajectory of the U.S. context more broadly, no context could provide a *perfect* proxy. Admittedly, Seattle is a better proxy for other major urban, technological, progressive, and post-Christian U.S. settings such as Portland, Oregon; San Francisco, California; Austin, Texas; Boston, Massachusetts; Boulder, Colorado; and Madison, Wisconsin, than for the United States as a whole. The most notable disjuncture between Seattle and major national trends is Seattle's overwhelmingly Euro-American demographics against the backdrop of a nation that is rapidly diversifying in terms of ethnic and cultural demographics. The U.S. 2010 Census projected that non-Hispanic whites will cease to be a majority in the United States in 2043.[8] Choosing Seattle's city limits as a parameter for the study—rather than including the whole Seattle-Tacoma metropolitan area—intensified this disjuncture. While more than 80% of Americans live in what the U.S. Census designates as "urban areas," only 45% live within the city limits of cities with a population over 50,000.[9] For these two reasons, Seattle's utility as a proxy for the future of the U.S. context more broadly, and beyond, should not be overstated.

A second noteworthy limitation is related to the research itself. Survey responses and fieldwork underrepresented the churches composed of nonmajority ethnic, culture, and language groups. As a result, the significance of this study for nonmajority churches is somewhat diminished, and some of the invaluable contributions that nonmajority churches offer the wider church are inevitably missing from its findings and proposals.

New Seattle Churches Survey

A survey using the following questions was conducted online using Survey Monkey.

1. What is the name of your Christian faith community? _____

2. What kind of Christian faith community is it? (check all that apply)
   - ☐ A congregation
   - ☐ A missional community
   - ☐ A new monastic or intentional community
   - ☐ An emerging church
   - ☐ A house/cell/organic church
   - ☐ A para-church group
   - ☐ A multi-site campus of a church
   - ☐ Other (please specify) _____

3. Do you consider it to be a "church"?
   - ☐ Yes
   - ☐ It is an expression of church/ecclesia but not church in the fullest sense
   - ☐ No (please complete the survey with the understanding that "church" will be used throughout)
   - ☐ I'm not sure

4. When was, or will be, the first official gathering of the church? (approximating is OK)

5. How important are these potential priorities for your church?
   [not important / a little important / important / very important / extremely important]
   Offering a community in which to belong and be loved
   Seeking God through prayer and contemplation

Building a refuge from the world's dangers and temptations
Serving the needs of the community
Forming Christians into Christlike character
Identifying closely with our neighborhood
Engaging culture and being relevant
Innovating and experimenting for the sake of the broader church's future
Adding beauty to the world
Witnessing to and experiencing God's miracle-working power
Improving society through political action and community organizing
Teaching and learning about God, the Bible, and our world
Embodying multi-cultural diversity
Giving opportunities to worship God
Speaking out about evil and injustice
Providing an extended family for a cultural group
Proclaiming the gospel of Jesus
Welcoming all—especially those excluded—as an inclusive community
Equipping people to go out as agents of God in the world
Modeling God's intentions for humanity
Other (please specify) _____

6. From among those you identified above as extremely or very important, which does the church spend the most time and energy on in terms of programs and practices? (Rank the top four below)

     Most important: _____

     Second most important: _____

     Third most important: _____

     Fourth most important: _____

7. Which potential indicators of Christian maturity are emphasized most strongly in your church? Please rank the top four (the rest will be disregarded)

     Having Christlike character
     Embracing ambiguity and divine mystery
     Serving those in need
     Living missionally in relationships with friends and neighbors
     Walking in the power of the Spirit
     Humility, listening, and openness
     Standing up against injustice
     Relational closeness with God
     Being obedient to God's will
     Commitment to devotional/spiritual practices

8. In a sentence or two, how would you describe the church?

9. How often does the church gather for worship?
   ☐ Less than weekly   ☐ Weekly   ☐ More than weekly

10. Where does your church have its primary gatherings?
    ☐ Our primary gatherings are at a single location
    ☐ Our primary gatherings are in locations across Seattle
    ☐ Our primary gatherings are across the Greater Seattle area
    ☐ Our primary gatherings are in locations within a specific neighborhood or district (please name) _____

11. In what kind of space does the church have its regular gatherings?
    ☐ Church building
    ☐ School
    ☐ Community center
    ☐ Movie theater
    ☐ Home(s)
    ☐ Other (please specify) _____

12. When does your church gather for its primary time of worship?
    ☐ Sunday Morning   ☐ Sunday afternoon/evening   ☐ Other (please specify)

13. Does your church have a website, facebook page, twitter account, or other social media or web presence? (please list) _____

14. Is your church affiliated (officially or informally) with a church, a denomination, or a network?
    ☐ No   ☐ Yes (please list all affiliations and official/informal)

15. How many worship services, if any, does your church have each weekend? ____

16. How many people, on average, attend your largest, weekly gathering? _____

17. How many people would you estimate consider this to be "their" church? _____

18. Please briefly describe the demographics of your church in terms of: Age, Marital status, Ethnicity/Race, Education level, Occupation, Religious background

    _____

19. How important were these considerations in motivating the development of this church?
    [not important / a little important / important / very important / extremely important]
    A growing population group
    A neighborhood with needs a church could address

Replacing churches that have closed
Offering an alternative to ineffective/unfaithful churches
New housing developments
Reaching unchurched people
Helping new Christians mature
Embodying our convictions about the church
Reaching specific cultures and networks
Creating a different expression of church
Engaging with contemporary society
Other (please specify) _____

20. Who was this church started for?

    The church was started for a specific neighborhood (name the neighborhood below) Y/N

    _____

    The church was started for a specific group or type of person (describe below) Y/N

    _____

    The church was started for those involved in starting it (describe those involved) Y/N

    _____

21. What kind of organization(s), if any, supported or sponsored the new church development?
    (check all that apply)
    ☐ None   ☐ A church   ☐ A denomination or regional denominational body
    ☐ A church planting network   ☐ Other (please specify) _____

22. Who started the church?
    ☐ A solo church-planter or couple
    ☐ A team
    ☐ A group of 20 or more from the sponsoring church
    ☐ The church formed spontaneously
    ☐ Other (please specify) _____

23. Total number of paid staff (full and part-time) in the first year when the church was being started, if any: _____

24. Total number of paid staff currently, if any: _____

25. Did the church start with an official "launch" worship service? Y/N

26. What strategies, if any, has the church used to reach others? (check all that apply)
    ☐ Direct mail ☐ Advertisements (online, billboards, etc)
    ☐ Going door-to-door ☐ Online social media
    ☐ Sponsoring community events ☐ None
    ☐ Other (please specify) _____

27. If your church has a "mission" and/or "vision" statement, please include it/them here:
    _____

28. How would you describe the theology of the church? (check all that apply)
    ☐ Anabaptist   ☐ Baptist   ☐ Charismatic
    ☐ Conservative   ☐ Evangelical   ☐ Pentecostal
    ☐ Progressive   ☐ Reformed   ☐ Sacramental
    ☐ Other (please specify) _____

29. Which statement best characterizes how leadership functions in your church?
    ☐ The pastor is the key leader and final decision maker
    ☐ A core team which includes the pastor(s) makes key decisions
    ☐ The whole church is involved in making decisions
    ☐ Decisions are made through informal processes

30. What roles are open to women in your church? (check all that apply)
    ☐ Leading ministry to women and children
    ☐ Women may lead as volunteers in various kinds of ministry
    ☐ Deacon/deaconess
    ☐ Elders or board members
    ☐ Associate/Assistant Pastor
    ☐ Senior Pastor
    ☐ Other (please specify) _____

31. How important are these practices to your church's culture?
    [not important / a little important / important / very important / extremely important]
    Church retreats
    Creation-care/environmental stewardship
    Fasting
    Living simply
    Mission trips
    Passionate worship
    Personal Bible reading and prayer
    Personal evangelism
    Sharing meals together
    Small groups/Bible studies
    The liturgical Christian calendar

32. Which option below best describes how your church approaches mission, social action, and evangelism?
    ☐ We share the good news of Jesus through evangelism
    ☐ We integrate social services and evangelism
    ☐ We pursue social justice through political/social action
    ☐ We provide social services and do evangelism, but separately
    ☐ We are present and modeling different values to the community
    ☐ We offer ministries of compassion, in part, as a means for evangelism

33. How much are these names for God emphasized in your church?
    [not emphasized / emphasized a little / emphasized / emphasized strongly / emphasized very strongly]
    Father   Jesus   Spirit   Creator   Savior
    Sanctifier   Lord   Teacher   Friend   Almighty
    Healer   Provider   Trinity   Other important names/roles: _____

34. How often are these scriptural passages referenced or alluded to in your church?
    [very rarely or never / rarely / sometimes / often / very often]
    Jesus . . . overturned the tables of the money changers . . . (Mt. 21:12/Mk. 11:15).
    Come to me all you who are weary . . . and I will give you rest (Mt. 11:28).
    By this everyone will know that you are my disciples, if you love one another (Jn. 13:35).

    You will receive power when the Holy Spirit has come upon you; and you will be my witnesses . . . to the ends of the earth (Acts 1:8).

    The Spirit of the LORD is upon me, for he has anointed me to preach good news to the poor . . . (Lk. 4:18-19).

    Go and make disciples of all nations, baptizing them . . . (Mt. 28:19-20).
    Are there other scriptural passages that are most frequently referenced? Please list and indicate how often (very often, often, sometimes . . .).

35. How would you describe the general style(s) and mood(s) of your worship services? (Examples: creative, experimental, casual, informal, reverent, contemplative, energetic, passionate, liturgical, sacramental, etc.). _____

36. How long is a typical sermon at your church? (in minutes) _____

37. How often are these practices included in your worship?
    [very rarely or never / rarely / occasionally / often / very often or always]
    Communion/Eucharist
    Baptism
    Time of Confession
    Charismatic gifts: speaking in tongues, prophesy, healing, etc.
    Church members share personal thoughts or experiences of God

Youth and children are present
Verse-by-verse biblical preaching
Preaching on a topic or theme
Singing hymns
Hand raising during singing
Reciting the Lord's prayer
Opportunity to share prayer requests

38. Please provide your name (it will be confidential unless you give permission below).

39. Would you prefer that your survey responses be anonymous in publications?
    ☐ Yes—please just indicate that the survey was taken by a "church representative"
    ☐ No—it is fine to name me as the one who completed the survey

40. Please provide an email address at which to contact you (it will only be used to contact you if questions about your survey responses arise): _____.

41. What is your role in the church? (please choose one)
    ☐ Founding Pastor
    ☐ Lead Pastor
    ☐ Campus Pastor/Director
    ☐ Assistant Pastor/Minister
    ☐ Church planting team or founding member
    ☐ Elder/Deacon
    ☐ Volunteer/lay leader
    ☐ Staff
    ☐ Member/regular attendee
    ☐ Other (please specify) _____

42. Do you know of other new churches in Seattle who might be willing to take the survey (or to simply be listed and mapped as a new Seattle church)? If so, please list their name and how they might be contacted: _____

Interview Guide for Pastors

INTERVIEW GUIDE FOR PASTORS

1. Ecclesial Narrative
   a. I'd like to hear the story of how and why this church was started and how it came to be what it is today.

2. Characteristic Practices
   a. Could you walk me through a typical week in the life of your church?
   b. Are there other things you do on a monthly, or yearly basis?
   c. What are the most important things your church does? (Activities or Programs . . .)
   d. If I wanted to see this church at its best, what should I show up for?

3. Mission
   a. What do you think God is doing or wants to do through this church?
   b. How do you measure the success of your church?
   c. What are the most important ways you do outreach as a church?
   d. Who is this church for?
   e. Who do you hope to reach?
   f. How many people have joined, been baptized, etc., this year?

4. Spirituality
   a. What are some of the most important signs of spiritual maturity that are emphasized in your church?
   b. What kinds of spiritual disciplines would you say are most common in your church? How do you think most of the people in the church actually practice their faith?

   c. What advice would you give to someone who wants to grow spiritually?

   d. What are you asking or hoping each person in your church will do?

   e. Does your church have membership expectations? What are these?

   f. If I asked you to name a few people in the church that exemplify what this church is all about, who would come to mind? Why?

5. Community

   a. What are the major ways you build community in your church?

   b. Are there different levels of belonging or commitment in the church?

Notes

1. Patricia O'Connell Killen and Mark Silk, eds., *Religion and Public Life in the Pacific Northwest: The None Zone* (Walnut Creek, CA: Altamira Press, 2004).

2. The "Nones" are those who do not affiliate with any religious group, and their number has grown sharply since the 1990s, having reached 23% in 2014. See Michael Lipka, "A Closer Look at America's Rapidly Growing Religious 'Nones,'" *Pew Research Center*, May 13, 2015, www.pewresearch.org/fact-tank/2015/05/13/a-closer-look-at-americas-rapidly-growing-religious-nones.

3. Pew Research Center, "Adults in the Seattle Metro Area," *Pew Research Center's Religion & Public Life Project*, www.pewforum.org/religious-landscape-study/metro-area/seattle-metro-area.

4. Pew Research Center, "Adults in the Houston Metro Area," *Pew Research Center's Religion & Public Life Project*, www.pewforum.org/religious-landscape-study/metro-area/houston-metro-area.

5. Research in 2007 and again in 2015 suggested that church planting had outpaced church closures that year in the United States, with about 4,000 new churches started. Ed Stetzer and Dave Travis, *Who Starts New Churches? State of Church Planting USA*, Leadership Network, 2007, p. 2, www.leadnet.org/wp-content/uploads/2015/04/CP-2007-OCT-State_of_Church_Planting_Report_Who_Starts-Stetzer.pdf. Ed Stetzer, Micah Fries, and Daniel Im, *The State of Church Planting in the U.S.*, Lifeway Research and NewChurches.com, 2015, www.newchurches.com. These new churches are the result, in part, of audacious church planting goals set by multiple denominations in recent years. As important as these denominational initiatives have been, the efforts of non- and interdenominational church planting networks have rapidly become a major engine of new churches.

6. For a helpful proposal on reflexivity in theological method, see Natalie Wigg-Stevenson, "Reflexive Theology: A Preliminary Proposal," *Practical Matters*

Journal 6 (March 1, 2013), http://practicalmattersjournal.org/2013/03/01/reflexive-theology.

7. "The Most Post-Christian Cities in America: 2017," Barna Group, posted May 26, 2017, www.barna.com/research/post-christian-cities-america-2017.

8. An recent exception to this can be found in Stephan Pass's helpful study. Stephan Paas, *Church Planting in the Secular West: Learning from the European Experience,* Gospel and Our Culture Series (Grand Rapids, MI: Eerdmans, 2016).

9. See, for example, the influential work of Ed Stetzer and David Lim, *Planting Missional Churches: Your Guide to Starting Churches that Multiply* (Nashville, TN: 2016).

10. Wide-scale sociological study samples consistently underrepresent new churches and omit noncongregational ecclesial groups. A primary example of this is David A. Roozen, William McKinney, and Jackson W. Carroll, *Varieties of Religious Presence: Mission in Public Life* (Cleveland, OH: Pilgrim Press, 1984), which developed a typology of "mission orientations" through a study of congregations in Hartford, Connecticut. Sociologist Nancy Ammerman, among others, have called for greater attention to new congregations. See Nancy T. Ammerman, *Congregation and Community* (New Brunswick, NJ: Rutgers University Press, 1996), 262.

11. Among qualitative research in congregations, Penny Edgell Becker's *Congregations in Conflict* (Cambridge: Cambridge University Press, 1999) is exemplary and in many ways worth emulating in its inductive typology of congregational cultures comprising "local understandings of identity and mission . . . understood analytically as bundles of core tasks and legitimate ways of doing things" (7). Understandably, the work of social scientists such as Becker is not explicitly theological.

12. Information about The Network for Ecclesiology and Ethnography is available at its website, www.ecclesiologyandethnography.com. This network, convened by Christian Scharen and Pete Ward, hosts conferences and a program unit at the American Academy of Religion Annual Conference and produces the journal *Ecclesial Practices.*

Several notable titles in practical ecclesiology include Pete Ward, ed., *Perspectives on Ecclesiology and Ethnography* (Grand Rapids, MI: Eerdmans, 2012); Christian Scharen, ed., *Explorations in Ecclesiology and Ethnography* (Grand Rapids, MI: Eerdmans, 2012); Christian Scharen, *Fieldwork in Theology: Exploring the Social Context of God's Work in the World* (Grand Rapids, MI: Baker Academic: 2015); Sune Fahlgren and Jonas Ideström, eds., *Ecclesiology in the Trenches: Theory and Method under Construction,* vol. 10, Church of Sweden Research Series (Eugene, OR: Wipf & Stock, 2015); Mary McClintock Fulkerson, *Places of Redemption: Theology for a Worldly Church* (New York: Oxford University Press, 2007); William T. Cavanaugh, *Torture and Eucharist: Theology, Politics, and the Body of Christ* (Berlin: Blackwell Publishers, 1998); Nicholas M. Healy, *Church, World and the Christian Life: Practical-Prophetic Ecclesiology* (Cambridge: Cambridge University Press, 2000); and Pete Ward, *Liquid Ecclesiology: The Gospel and the Church* (Leiden, Netherlands: Brill, 2017).

13. Peter Berger is the most seminal exponent of "methodological atheism"; see Peter L. Berger, *The Sacred Canopy: Elements of a Sociological Theory of Religion* (New York: Anchor, 1990), appendix II.

14. These critiques are found, among other places, in Ward, *Perspectives on Ecclesiology and Ethnography*.

15. The ecclesiology and ethnography discourse has generally critiqued quantitative research in its advocacy for qualitative methods. This approach aligns with an emphasis on the value of learning from the particularity of congregations rather than placing much value in generalizability. While my approach—using mixed-methods to study a religious ecology in a future-trending context—seeks to balance a recognition of particularity with its aim to yield significant insights with relevance beyond the particular congregations and context itself.

16. Ward, *Perspectives on Ecclesiology and Ethnography*, 2.

17. The Latin *missio Dei* means "mission of God." It is a key theme in missional theology, developed especially in David J. Bosch, *Transforming Mission: Paradigm Shifts in Theology of Mission* (Maryknoll, NY: Orbis Books, 1991). Its key elements, along with those of missional theology more broadly, are synthesized in chapter 5 of this book.

18. For the basic outlines of the practical theological method of this project, see Richard R. Osmer, *Practical Theology: An Introduction* (Grand Rapids, MI: Eerdmans, 2008).

19. The rationale for these three parameters—Christian church, in Seattle, founded since 2001—can be found in appendix A along with a fuller discussion of the research methodology.

20. Roozen, McKinney, and Carroll, *Varieties of Religious Presence*; and Becker, *Congregations in Conflict*. The findings of these two studies are summarized in chapter 3 of this volume.

21. Elaine Graham et al. describe the theological method of "Writing the Body of Christ," drawing on sociological and theological accounts, as a corporate activity focused on congregations, examining their sense of corporate identity through central metaphors, and narratives. Elaine Graham, Heather Walton, and Frances Ward, *Theological Reflection: Methods* (London: SCM Press, 2005), 109.

CHAPTER 1: THE LAY OF THE LAND

1. Tracy Simmons, "Ye of Little Faith (in the Pacific Northwest)," *SpokaneFAVS*, November 16, 2011, https://religionnewsspokane.wordpress.com/2011/11/16/ye-of-little-faith-in-the-pacific-northwest.

2. Jan Shipps, "Religion and Regional Culture in Modern America," in *Can Charitable Choice Work?: Covering Religion's Impact on Urban Affairs and Social Services*, ed. Andrew Walsh (Hartford, CT: Leonard E. Greenberg Center for the Study of Religion in Public Life, Trinity College, 2001), 36.

3. Boundless, "U.S. Urban Patterns," *Boundless Sociology*, updated May 1, 2014, www.boundless.com/sociology/textbooks/boundless-sociology-textbook/

population-and-urbanization-17/urbanization-and-the-development-of-cities-123/u-s-urban-patterns-696-8160.

4. The U.S. Census Bureau defines "urban areas" as areas with a population density of at least 1,000 people per square mile and at least 2,500 total people. U.S. Census Bureau, "2010 Census Urban and Rural Classification and Urban Area Criteria," www.census.gov/geo/reference/ua/urban-rural-2010.html.

5. Jean-Paul Rodrigue, "The Burgess Urban Land Use Model," *The Geography of Transport Systems,* https://people.hofstra.edu/geotrans/eng/ch6en/conc6en/burgess.html.

6. Gene Balk, "Seattle once again nations' fastest-growing big city; population exceeds 700,000," *Seattle Times,* May 25, 2017, www.seattletimes.com/seattle-news/data/seattle-once-again-nations-fastest-growing-big-city-population-exceeds-700000.

7. "Seattle, Washington (WA) Profile," *City-Data.com,* www.city-data.com/city/Seattle-Washington.html#ixzz369FBhMOx.

8. Blanca Torres, "Seattle's Urban Villages Strategy Is Working—But More Planning Is Needed in the Next 20 Years," *Seattle Times,* January 29, 2015, http://blogs.seattletimes.com/opinionnw/2015/01/29/seattles-urban-villages-strategy-is-working-but-more-planning-is-needed-in-the-next-20-years.

9. Gene Balk, "Seattle No Longer America's Fastest-Growing Big City," *Seattle Times,* May 21, 2015, www.seattletimes.com/seattle-news/data/seattle-no-longer-americas-fastest-growing-big-city. Gene Balk, "Seattle Growing Faster than Suburbs, First Time in 100 Years," *Seattle Times,* February 24, 2014, http://blogs.seattletimes.com/fyi-guy/2014/02/24/seattle-growing-faster-than-suburbs-first-time-in-100-years.

10. National Conference on Citizenship, *Greater Seattle: King, Pierce and Snohomish Counties Civic Health Index* (Seattle, WA: Seattle CityClub, 2013), 10.

11. Between 2000 and 2013, the percentage of "black alone" in Seattle dropped from 8.3% to 6.8% while the percentage of "white alone" remained quite stable at 67.9% and 67.0%, respectively. "Races in Seattle, Washington (WA): White, Black, Hispanic, Asian," *City-Data.com,* http://www.city-data.com/races/races-Seattle-Washington.html.

12. Naomi Ishisaka, "Changes in the Central District Affect the African-American Community," *Seattle Magazine,* March 2014, www.seattlemag.com/article/changes-central-district-affect-african-american-community.

13. U.S. Census Bureau, "2011-2015 American Community Survey," American FactFinder, https://factfinder.census.gov/faces/tableservices/jsf/pages/productview.xhtml?src=CF.

14. Jason Jurjevich and Greg Schrock, "Is Portland Really the Place Where Young People Go to Retire? Migration Patterns of Portland's Young and College-Educated, 1980-2010," Nohad A. Toulan School of Urban Studies and Planning, Population Research Center, September 2012, http://pdxscholar.library.pdx.edu/cgi/viewcontent.cgi?article=1004&context=prc_pub

15. Gene Balk, "When Can You Call Yourself a Seattleite?" *Seattle Times,* October 2, 2012, http://blogs.seattletimes.com/fyi-guy/2012/10/02/when-can-you-call-yourself-a-seattleite.

16. U.S. Census Bureau, "Seattle QuickFacts," QuickFacts, 2011-2015, https://www. census.gov/quickfacts/table/POP715215/5363000,00.

17. Cathy Grossman, "'Amen' to a Church-Free Lifestyle," *USA Today*, March 6, 2002, http://usatoday30.usatoday.com/life/2002/2002-03-07-church-free.htm.

18. Patricia O'Connell Killen, "The Religious Geography of the Pacific Northwest," *Word & World* 24, no. 3 (Summer 2004): 269–278.

19. Julia Sommerfeld, "Our Social Dis-Ease: Beyond the Smiles, the Seattle Freeze Is On," *Seattle Times*, March 8, 2005, www.seattletimes.com/pacific-nw-magazine/ our-social-dis-ease-beyond-the-smiles-the-seattle-freeze-is-on.

20. Ibid.

21. Gene Balk, "Seattle Freeze: Can We Blame It on the Norwegians?" *Seattle Times*, December 4, 2012, http://blogs.seattletimes.com/fyi-guy/2012/12/04/ seattle-freeze-can-we-blame-it-on-the-norwegians.

22. National Conference on Citizenship, *Greater Seattle* (2013), 10. Social cohesion in Seattle has improved since 2013. National Conference on Citizenship, *Greater Seattle: King, Pierce and Snohomish Counties Civic Health Index* (Seattle, WA: Seattle CityClub, 2017), http://civic-health-index.seattlecityclub.org.

23. Gene Balk, "A Lot of Seattle Renters Live Alone—but Maybe Not for Much Longer," *Seattle Times*, June 17, 2014, http://blogs.seattletimes.com/fyi-guy/2014/06/ 17/a-lot-of-seattle-renters-live-alone-but-maybe-not-for-much-longer.

24. "Sharecare Names America's Top 10 Cities with the Strongest Social Ties," *Sharecare.com*, last modified November 20, 2013, www.sharecare.com/static/ sharecare-names-top-10-cities-with-the-strongest-social-ties.

25. Center for Behavioral Health Statistics and Quality, *Suicidal Thoughts and Behavior in 33 Metropolitan Statistical Areas: 2008 to 2010* (Substance Abuse and Mental Health Services Administration, 2012), www.sprc.org/library_resources/items/ suicidal-thoughts-and-behavior-33-metropolitan-statistical-areas-2008-2010.

26. For reporting on progressive trends in the U.S., see, for example, Peter Beinart, "Why America Is Moving Left," *The Atlantic*, February 2016, http://www.theatlantic.com/magazine/archive/2016/01/why-america-is-moving-left/419112; Janie Velencia, "America's Morals Are Shifting to the Left," *Huffington Post*, May 27, 2015, www.huffingtonpost.com/2015/05/27/socially-liberal_n_7453526.html; and Steve Rosenthal, "American Politics Are Moving to the Left," *Washington Post*, January 16, 2014, www.washingtonpost.com/opinions/american-politics-are-moving-to-the-left/2014/01/16/30161350-7885-11e3-af7f-13bf0e9965f6_story.html.

27. M. Alex Johnson, "Seattle's Only Legal Marijuana Shop Sells out of Pot," *NBC News*, last modified July 11, 2014, www.nbcnews.com/storyline/legal-pot/ seattles-only-legal-marijuana-shop-sells-out-pot-n153971.

28. Sreekar Jasthi, "Most LGBT-Friendly Cities," *NerdWallet* (blog), last modified May 27, 2014, www.nerdwallet.com/blog/cities/most-lgbt-friendly-cities.

29. Pew Research Center, "Changing Attitudes on Gay Marriage," *Pew Research Center's Religion & Public Life Project*, last modified May 12, 2016, www.pewforum.org/2016/05/ 12/changing-attitudes-on-gay-marriage/#public-opinion-on-same-sex-marriage.

30. Ibid.

31. Public Religion Research Institute, *Shifting Landscape: A Decade of Change in American Attitudes about Same-Sex Marriage and LGBT Issues*, February 26, 2014, http://publicreligion.org/research/2014/02/2014-lgbt-survey.

32. Edward I. Dovere and Jennifer Epstein, "Obama Seeks Boost from LGBT Order," *POLITICO*, last modified June 17, 2014, www.politico.com/story/2014/06/obama-lgbt-nondiscrimination-executive-order-107900.html.

33. Hasani Gittens, "Trump Vows to Protect LGBTQ Citizens," *NBC News*, http://www.nbcnews.com/widget/video-embed/730050627538.

34. Ariane de Vogue, "Trump: Same-Sex Marriage Is 'Settled,' but Roe v Wade Can Be Changed," *CNN*, last modified November 15, 2016, www.cnn.com/2016/11/14/politics/trump-gay-marriage-abortion-supreme-court/index.html. Trump's actions and rhetoric since have been hostlie to LGBTQ concerns.

35. Garland Potts and Gene Balk, "Map: Seattle's 'Gayborhood' Is Becoming Less Gay," *Seattle Times*, last modified July 31, 2014, http://old.seattletimes.com/html/localpages/2024202935_seattle-gayborhood-becoming-less-gay.html.

36. Jim Brunner, "Eastside Suburbs Joined Seattle in Strong Approval of Gay Marriage Referendum," *Seattle Times*, December 3, 2012, http://blogs.seattle-times.com/politicsnorthwest/2012/12/03/eastside-suburbs-joined-seattle-in-strong-approval-of-gay-marriage-iniatiative.

37. Gregory Krieg, "It's Official: Clinton Swamps Trump in Popular Vote," *CNN*, last modified December 22, 2016, www.cnn.com/2016/12/21/politics/donald-trump-hillary-clinton-popular-vote-final-count/index.html.

38. Lazaro Gamio, "Urban and Rural America Are Becoming Increasingly Polarized," *Washington Post*, last modified November 17, 2016, www.washingtonpost.com/graphics/politics/2016-election/urban-rural-vote-swing.

39. Lazaro Gamio and Dan Keating, "How Trump Redrew the Electoral Map, from Sea to Shining Sea," *Washington Post*, last modified November 9, 2016, www.washingtonpost.com/graphics/politics/2016-election/election-results-from-coast-to-coast.

40. "List of Current Mayors of the Top 100 Cities in the United States," *Ballotpedia: The Encyclopedia of American Politics*, https://ballotpedia.org/List_of_current_mayors_of_the_top_100_cities_in_the_United_States. Harold Meyerson, "Harold Meyerson: Progressives Take Manhattan and Many Other U.S. Places," *Washington Post*, April 23, 2014, www.washingtonpost.com/opinions/harold-meyerson-progressives-take-manhattan-and-many-other-us-places/2014/04/23/8f727cf0-cb17-11e3-a75e-463587891b57_story.html.

41. Benjamin Anderstone, "Seattle as Liberal Bastion? Think Again," *Crosscut.com*, January 21, 2014, http://crosscut.com/2014/01/political-heat-map-shows-seattle-not-liberal.

42. Pew Research Center, "Majority Now Supports Legalizing Marijuana," *Pew Research Center for the People and the Press*, April 4, 2013, www.people-press.org/2013/04/04/majority-now-supports-legalizing-marijuana.

43. Johnson, "Seattle's Only Legal Marijuana Shop Sells out of Pot."

44. Matt Ferner, "Colorado Recreational Weed Sales Top $14 Million In First Month," *Huffington Post*, last modified May 8, 2014, www.huffingtonpost.com/2014/03/10/colorado-marijuana-tax-revenue_n_4936223.html.

45. "2016 Energy Star Top Cities," *Energy Star*, last modified 2014, www.energystar.gov/buildings/press_room/top_10_cities_2016/about_the_list_top_cities_most_energy_star_certified_buildings.

46. Ibid. The number of Seattle's Energy Star certified buildings rose from 69 to 124 between 2009 and 2014.

47. "U.S. Conference of Mayors Climate Protection Agreement," Mayors Climate Protection Center, www.usmayors.org/mayors-climate-protection-center.

48. "ChargePoint Releases List of Top 10 Cities for Electric Vehicles," *ChargePoint.com*, last modified October 24, 2013, www.chargepoint.com/news/2013/1024.

49. Gene Balk, "Census: Seattle among Five Cities Where Majority Do Not Drive Alone to Work," *Seattle Times*, September 20, 2013, http://blogs.seattletimes.com/today/2013/09/census-majority-of-seattleites-did-not-drive-alone-to-work-in-2012.

50. Bellamy Pailthorp, "Why the Northwest Is a Potential Climate Refuge from Effects of Global Warming," *KNKX 88.5*, last modified August 1, 2014, http://knks.org/post/why-northwest-potential-climate-refuge-effects-global-warming.

51. Seattle was named the nation's most sustainable city in 2014 by STAR Communities; "Seattle, Washington," *STAR Communities: Sustainability Tools for Assessing & Rating Communities*, 2014, https://reporting.starcommunities.org/communities/31-seattle-washington. Seattle was named the fourth greenest city by Siemen's Green City Index in 2012; Siemens Global, "Green City Index," *Siemens*, 2012, www.siemens.com/entry/cc/en/greencityindex.htm.

52. Pew Research Center, "Record Shares of Americans Now Own Smartphones, Have Home Broadband," *Pew Research Center: Internet, Science & Tech*, January 12, 2017, www.pewresearch.org/fact-tank/2017/01/12/evolution-of-technology.

53. Pew Research Center, "Mobile Technology Fact Sheet," *Pew Research Center: Internet, Science & Tech*, last modified January 12, 2017, www.pewinternet.org/fact-sheets/mobile-technology-fact-sheet.

54. Pew Research Center, "Social Media Fact Sheet," *Pew Research Center: Internet, Science & Tech*, last modified January 12, 2017, www.pewinternet.org/fact-sheet/social-media.

55. "Mobile Mindset Study: Technology Habits," *Lookout.com*, June 2012, www.lookout.com/resources/reports/mobile-mindset.

56. "Smartphones: So Many Apps, So Much Time," *Nielsen.com*, last modified July 1, 2014, www.nielsen.com/us/en/insights/news/2014/smartphones-so-many-apps--so-much-time.html.

57. "The Common Sense Census: Plugged in Parents of Teen and Tweens," *Common Sense Media*, 2016, www.commonsensemedia.org/research/the-common-sense-census-plugged-in-parents-of-tweens-and-teens-2016.

58. Wilhelm Hofmann, Kathleen D. Vohs, and Roy F. Baumeister, "What People Desire, Feel Conflicted About, and Try to Resist in Everyday Life," *Psychological Science* 23, no. 6 (June 1, 2012): 582–588. Andrew K. Przybylski and Netta Weinstein, "Can You Connect with Me Now? How the Presence of Mobile Communication Technology Influences Face-to-Face Conversation Quality," *Journal of Social and Personal Relationships* 30, no. 3 (July 19, 2012): 1–10.

59. For examples of viral videos offering a critique of the social impacts of technology, see Gary Turk, "Look Up," 2014, www.youtube.com/watch?v=Z7dLU6fk9QY; and Miles Crawford, "I Forgot My Phone," 2013, www.youtube.com/watch?v=OINa46HeWg8#t=21.

60. Michael Fancher, "Seattle: A New Media Case Study," *The State of the News Media 2011: An Annual Report on American Journalism*, last modified 2011, www.stateofthe-media.org/2011/mobile-survey/seattle-a-new-media-case-study/#fn-7847-7.

61. City of Seattle, Department of Information Technology, *Information Technology Access and Adoption in Seattle: 2014 Report* (Seattle: City of Seattle, 2014), www.seattle.gov/community-technology/technology-adoption-in-seattle-.

62. UBM's Future Cities ranked Seattle as the only U.S city in the top 10 internet cities; Mary Jander, "Future Cities Report: Discover the World's Greatest Internet Cities," August 26, 2013, www.ubmfuturecities.com/document.asp?doc_id=525595.

63. Richard Florida, "America's Leading High-Tech Metros," *CityLab*, last modified June 28, 2012, www.theatlanticcities.com/technology/2012/06/americas-leading-high-tech-metros/2244.

64. Gene Balk, "Study: Seattle Is Top Twitter Trendsetter in the U.S.," *Seattle Times*, October 24, 2013, http://blogs.seattletimes.com/fyi-guy/2013/10/24/study-seattle-is-top-twitter-trendsetter-in-the-u-s.

65. Gene Balk, "Seattleites Are Hooked on Facebook—Can We Kick the Habit?" *Seattle Times*, February 5, 2013, http://blogs.seattletimes.com/fyi-guy/2013/02/05/seattleites-are-hooked-on-facebook-can-we-kick-the-habit.

66. "ReSTART Center for Technology Sustainability," *reStart*, 2009, www.netaddictionrecovery.com.

67. Bruce Katz, "The Challenge of Seattle's Emerging Society," Brookings Institution, last modified May 28, 2010, www.brookings.edu/research/opinions/2010/05/28-seattle-katz.

68. Jennifer Polland, "PRESENTING: The 15 Hottest American Cities of the Future," *Business Insider*, last modified June 26, 2012, www.businessinsider.com/up-and-coming-cities-2012-6.

69. Boyd Cohen, "The 10 Smartest Cities in North America," *FastCompany*, last modified November 14, 2013, www.fastcoexist.com/3021592/the-10-smartest-cities-in-north-america.

70. Richard Florida, *The Rise of the Creative Class, Revisited* (New York: Basic Books, 2014).

71. The waning cultural influence of Christianity is another marker of post-Christian and—more precisely—post-Christendom contexts.

72. The number of those "never" attending religious services increased from 9% in 1972 to 26% in 2014; Association of Religion Data Archives, "Religious Service Attendance," 2014, www.thearda.com/QuickStats/qs_105_t.asp.

73. For a solid study of the unaffiliated, see Elizabeth Drescher, *Choosing Our Religion: The Spiritual Lives of America's Nones* (New York: Oxford University Press, 2016).

74. Robert P. Jones et al., *Exodus: Why Americans Are Leaving Religion—and Why They're Unlikely to Come Back,* Public Religious Research Institute, 2016, www.prri.org/research/prri-rns-poll-nones-atheist-leaving-religion.

75. Joanna Piacenza, "The Three Religious Traditions That Dominate the U.S.," Public Religion Research Institute, March 4, 2015, www.prri.org/spotlight/top-three-religions-in-each-state.

76. Pew Research Center, *The Future of World Religions: Population Growth Projections, 2010-2050,* Pew Forum, April 2, 2015, www.pewforum.org/2015/04/02/religious-projections-2010-2050.

77. Pew Research confirmed this in 2012, but the General Social Survey (GSS) locates the shift in the mid-2000s. According to GSS, Protestants lost 16 percentage points between 1993 and 2010; Pew Research Center, " 'Nones' on the Rise," *Pew Research Center's Religion & Public Life Project,* October 9, 2012, www.pewforum.org/2012/10/09/nones-on-the-rise; "Religious Preference," Association of Religion Data Archives, www.thearda.com/quickstats/qs_101_t.asp.

78. Pew Research Center, " 'Nones' on the Rise," 10.

79. Ibid., 9.

80. Peter L. Berger, "The Religiously Unaffiliated in America," *The American Interest,* last modified March 21, 2012, www.the-american-interest.com/2012/03/21/the-religiously-unaffiliated-in-america.

81. Eighteen percent identify as "religious," 37% as "spiritual but not religious," and 42% as neither; ibid., 22.

82. For an excellent study of the spiritual-but-not-religious, see Linda A. Mercadante, *Belief Without Borders: Inside the Minds of the Spiritual But Not Religious* (New York: Oxford University Press, 2014).

83. Changes in dis/affiliation do not reliably predict changes in belief or practice, as Lim, MacGregor, and Putnam discovered; Chaeyoon Lim, Carol Ann MacGregor, and Robert D. Putnam, "Secular and Liminal: Discovering Heterogeneity Among Religious Nones," *Journal for the Scientific Study of Religion* 49, no. 4 (December 1, 2010): 596–618. Dougherty et al.'s 2007 study found that a significant number of those with no religious affiliation nonetheless have concrete ties to local congregations; Kevin D. Dougherty, Byron R. Johnson, and Edward C. Polson, "Recovering the Lost: Remeasuring U.S. Religious Affiliation," *Journal for the Scientific Study of Religion* 46, no. 4 (December 1, 2007): 483–499. Nearly one-fourth of "Nones" attend church "monthly/yearly," only one-third of the affiliated do; one in five pray daily, 40% pray monthly, according to Pew Research Center, " 'Nones' on the Rise," 49.

Barna reports that 30% of young outsiders to Christianity believe the Bible is "accurate in all the principles it teaches" and have more favorable views of Jesus than either the Bible or Christianity; David Kinnaman and Gabe Lyons, *UnChristian: What a New Generation Really Thinks about Christianity . . . and Why It Matters* (Grand Rapids, MI: Baker Books, 2007), 24. On Christmas and Easter attendance, see "David Kinnaman and Jon Tyson Discuss Millennials, 'Nones' And a Renewed Vision for Church," *Barna.org*, last modified April 1, 2014, https://barna.org/barna-update/faith-spirituality/662-david-kinnaman-and-jon-tyson-q-a.

84. Kinnaman and Lyons, *UnChristian*, 44–45.
85. Nancy T. Ammerman, "Spiritual But Not Religious? Beyond Binary Choices in the Study of Religion," *Journal for the Scientific Study of Religion* 52, no. 2 (June 1, 2013): 258–278.
86. Ibid.
87. Nancy T. Ammerman, "Nones and Spiritual But Not Religious," lecture, Boston University School of Theology, February 25, 2014.
88. Nancy T. Ammerman, "Religious Pluralism in Everyday Life," lecture, Boston University School of Theology, May 1, 2014.
89. Nancy T. Ammerman, "The *Reality Behind* 'Spiritual But Not Religious,'" *Studying Congregations* (blog), July 23, 2014, http://studyingcongregations.org/blog/ask-the-expert-the-reality-behind-spiritual-but-not-religious.
90. Killen and Silk, *Religion and Public Life in the Pacific Northwest*, 9.
91. While the Pacific Northwest has since 2001 been surpassed by New England as the U.S. region with the highest percentage of the unaffiliated, its claim as the "None Zone" remains in view of the fact that the Northeast is home to slightly more Catholics than "Nones," whereas "Nones" are the Northwest's largest "religious" group. In 2014, Washington State ranked third for "Nones" per capita; Seattle ranked as the second most unaffiliated metro area in the nation. See Kosmin et al., *American Nones: The Profile of the No Religion Population* (Hartford, CT: Institute for the Study of Secularism in Society & Culture, 2008, https://commons.trincoll.edu/aris/publications/2008-2/american-nones-the-profile-of-the-no-religion-population; Joanna Piacenza, "How Religiously Unaffiliated Is Your City?" Public Religion Research Institute, last modified March 16, 2015, www.prri.org/spotlight/how-religiously-unaffiliated-is-your-city/#.VoLSG_GpLXn.
92. Killen and Silk, *Religion and Public Life in the Pacific Northwest*, 9.
93. Ibid., 140.
94. Ibid., 14.
95. Ibid., 11.
96. Ibid., 12.
97. Janet I. Tu, "Northwest Seen as 'Unchurched' yet Religious," *Seattle Times*, May 8, 2004, http://community.seattletimes.nwsource.com/archive/?date=20040508&slug=religbook08m.

98. Pew's Religious Landscape Survey in 2015 put the percentage of "Nones" in Seattle at 37%. The 2010 U.S. Religion Census found the Seattle metro area to be the third least religious city. Also, Seattle ranked 37th of 51 for "association" with a religious group in 2013 with 18.1% associated. This rank rose dramatically to 9th in 2016 with 25% indicating they "participated in a church, synagogue, mosque, or a religious institution." This transformation calls for further study. See National Conference on Citizenship, *Greater Seattle* (2013), 10 and National Conference on Citizenship, *Greater Seattle* (2017).

99. Barna, which identifies "post-Christian" individuals as those who meet 60% of their metrics related to beliefs about God, Jesus and the Bible, and participation in Christian practices, ranked Seattle-Tacoma as the ninth most post-Christian metro area in 2017; see "The Most Post-Christian Cities in America: 2017," Barna Group.

100. Pew Research Center, "Religious Composition of Seattle Metro Area," *Pew Research Center's Religion & Public Life Project*, 2014, www.pewforum.org/religious-landscape-study.

101. Killen and Silk, *Religion and Public Life in the Pacific Northwest*, 143.

102. Shipps, "Religion and Regional Culture in Modern America," 36.

103. Ibid.

104. Mark A. Shibley, "Sacred Nature: Earth-Based Spirituality as Popular Religion in the Pacific Northwest," *Journal for the Study of Religion, Nature & Culture* 5, no. 2 (June 2011): 164–185.

105. James K. Wellman Jr., Professor and Chair of the Comparative Religion Program in the Jackson School of International Studies at the University of Washington, suggests ceasing to call the Pacific Northwest the "None Zone" and instead call it the "Abundant Zone"; James K. Wellman Jr., "A Theology for Cascadia: From None Zone to the Abundant Zone," *Christ & Cascadia*, March 4, 2015, http://christandcascadia.com/a-theology-for-cascadia-from-none-zone-to-the-abundant-zone.

106. Frank Newport, "Provo-Orem, Utah, Is Most Religious U.S. Metro Area," Gallup, last modified March 29, 2013, www.gallup.com/poll/161543/provo-orem-utah-religious-metro-area.aspx.

107. "Strength of Affiliation (Over Time)," Association of Religion Data Archives, 2014, www.thearda.com/quickstats/qs_103_t.asp. Gallup research supports these findings, showing that the percentage who consider religion to be "very important" in their lives was 55% in 1980 and 53% in 2016; see Albert Winseman, "Religion 'Very Important' to Most Americans," Gallup, last modified December 20, 2005, www.gallup.com/poll/20539/Religion-Very-Important-Most-Americans.aspx, and "Religion," Gallup, 2016, www.gallup.com/poll/1690/religion.aspx.

108. Christian Smith and Michael Emerson, *American Evangelicalism: Embattled and Thriving* (Chicago: University of Chicago Press, 1998).

109. Killen and Silk, *Religion and Public Life in the Pacific Northwest*, 10.

110. Shibley, "Sacred Nature," 167.
111. James K. Wellman Jr., *Evangelical vs. Liberal: The Clash of Christian Cultures in the Pacific Northwest* (Oxford: Oxford University Press, 2008).
112. According to the Organizing Religious Work Project, conducted in the years leading up to 2000, Seattle's religious ecology differed somewhat from the national scene, with a few more mainline Protestant (32% vs. 25% nationally) and "Other" Christian churches (7% vs. 2%) and a bit fewer Conservative Protestant (50% vs. 55%), African American (3% vs. 7%), and Catholic and Orthodox (4% vs. 6%) congregations. In terms of size, the study found that "Seattle has slightly more small congregations and slightly fewer large ones (over 300 in attendance) than the study sample which intended to parallel the national scene"; see Nancy T. Ammerman, *Doing Good in Seattle: Congregations and Service Organizations Building the Community: A Research Report from the Organizing Religious Work Project* (Hartford, CT: Hartford Institute for Religion Research, February 2001).
113. "Religion 2010: Religions by Tradition, Social Explorer," Infogroup, 2010, www. socialexplorer.com. This tally does not include Mormon, Jehovah's Witness, Christian Science, or several other professedly Christian churches that have non-Trinitarian views and/or have Scriptures in addition to the Bible. However, it does include Seattle's lone Messianic Jewish Synagogue.
114. Pew Research Center, "Adults in the Seattle Metro Area."
115. Mark Driscoll, *A Call to Resurgence: Will Christianity Have a Funeral or a Future?* (Carol Stream, IL: Tyndale House, 2013). Mark Driscoll's Ballard-based Mars Hill Church ballooned several years after its founding in the late 1990s to 13,000 weekly attenders gathering at eleven sites in five Western states, but imploded while this book was being written. Nonetheless, the church planting network that Driscoll founded in 1998, Acts 29, now claims more than 400 member and candidate churches in North America. On August 8, 2014, the board of Acts 29 called for Mark to step down from leadership, and as of January 1, 2015 Mars Hill Church was dissolved and its eleven congregations became independent.
116. See Victoria Johnson, "What Is Organizational Imprinting? Cultural Entrepreneurship in the Founding of the Paris Opera," *American Journal of Sociology* 113, no. 1 (July 1, 2007): 97–127.
117. Christopher B. James, "Some Fell on Good Soil: Church Planting in Religious Ecologies," *Witness: Journal of the Academy for Evangelism in Theological Education* 27 (2013): 114.

CHAPTER 2: SURVEYING THE FIELD

1. For a sense of proportion, consider that a 2010 dataset reported that Seattle was home to roughly 327 churches. Comparing this to my own data on the founding dates of new churches, I estimate that in 2010 roughly 15% of the churches in Seattle had been founded in the previous nine years. This is comparable to a

1999–2000 study of Seattle churches, suggesting that at least during this period, the percentage of new churches in the field has held relatively stable. Infogroup, "Religion 2010: Religions by Tradition, Social Explorer," *Social Explorer*, 2010, www. socialexplorer.com; Nancy T. Ammerman, *Doing Good in Seattle: Congregations and Service Organizations Building the Community: A Research Report from the Organizing Religious Work Project* (Hartford, CT: Hartford Institute for Religion Research, February 2001).

2. These unverified churches are overwhelmingly ethnic minority congregations.

3. Two of the multisite campuses are also "mergers" with longer-standing churches, but in both cases the resources of the existing congregation were simply folded into the multisite church and the building converted to a campus (Mars Hill, West Seattle; City Church, Belltown). The only identified "rebirth" church, OneLife Community Church, underwent an extensive culture shift that coincided with new pastoral leadership, a new neighborhood location, and a new church name. It seems likely that several other Seattle churches have been similarly "born again" but were not identified.

4. Christopher B. James, "New Seattle Churches Map," 2014, www.google.com/maps/d/u/0/viewer?mid=1Ol_nb4caEMe2wTgdfHuGp0-mslo&hl=en_US.

5. Evangelical church planters have, in recent years, increasingly turned their attentions to cities. Consider, for example, Tim Keller's City to City church planting network and the Southern Baptist Convention's Send Cities church planting campaign.

6. "Seattle's Rainier Valley, One of America's 'Dynamic Neighborhoods,'" *Seattle Times*, June 20, 2010, www.seattletimes.com/opinion/seattles-rainier-valley-one-of-americas-dynamic-neighborhoods.

7. On the connections between gentrification and urban church planting, see Sean Benesh, ed., *Vespas, Cafes, Singlespeed Bikes, and Urban Hipsters: Gentrification, Urban Mission, and Church Planting* (Portland, OR: Urban Loft Publishers, 2014).

8. "Conservative Protestant" is comparable to Pew's "Evangelical Protestants" in their Classification of Protestant Denominations used for the U.S. Religious Landscape Survey 2010. See appendix B in Pew Research Center, *America's Changing Religious Landscape*, May 12, 2015, www.pewforum.org/2015/05/12/appendix-b-classification-of-protestant-denominations/. Black Pentecostal and black nondenominational churches are not included here, but are within the historical black church tradition.

9. Nondenominational identity is much more common among new churches than it is in the full congregational ecology. InfoGroup suggests that only 8% of all Seattle churches are nondenominational, but I found the data to be deeply flawed; my research surfaced 32 *new* nondenominational churches (including multisites) operating in 2010, whereas InfoGroup's data identified only 27 total nondenominational churches, including *both* new and established churches. Infogroup, "Religion 2010: Religions by Tradition," 2010, *Social Explorer*, www. socialexplorer.com.

10. The multisite church model—where a single church organization launches multiple campuses and venues for worship—is one of the most important ecclesiological developments of the millennium. Mars Hill Church, before its dissolution in January 2015, was the most prolific multisite church in the area, having established four campuses within the city limits (plus an additional six in the Greater Seattle area, and another four in other Western states). Other noteworthy multisite churches include the Seattle-based Bethany Community Church and three churches based outside the city limits: Eastlake Community Church, City Church, and Calvary, each of which had two sites meeting in Seattle at the time of the study.

11. Twenty percent or more minority participation was used as the standard for a multicultural church. Multicultural identity was determined via analysis of online images of the congregation and, when possible, pastor survey responses and in-person observation of worship.

12. In 2010, the ethnic composition within Seattle was: White (65%), Asian (15%), Black (9%), and Two or More Races (5%). U.S. Census Bureau, Census 2010, 2010, *Social Explorer*, www.socialexplorer.com/tables/C2010/R10769803.

13. As one Pacific Northwest pastor (@joshmrowley) noted on Twitter, "A denomination's resources are more valuable than its brand name." Josh Rowley, Twitter post, August 1, 2014 (1:05 P.M.), https://twitter.com/joshmrowley/status/ 495314381266489344.

14. Six churches include "fellowship" in their name and five self-identify as a "community dinner."

15. This includes eight "community churches," most of which are multisite campuses.

16. National studies suggests that roughly 10% of U.S. congregations have a female senior pastor; among new Seattle churches, it is 6.7%. Hartford Institute for Religion Research, "A Quick Question: What Percentage of Pastors Are Female?," *Hart.sem*, http://hirr.hartsem.edu/research/quick_question3.html.

17. While data collection concluded in March 2014, it is noteworthy that in January 2015, Eastlake Community Church—which at the time had two campuses in Seattle—changed its position to fully include LGBTQ persons in all areas of church life. See Elizabeth Dias, "How Evangelicals Are Changing Their Minds on Gay Marriage," *Time*, January 15, 2015, http://time.com/3669024/ evangelicals-gay-marriage.

18. The significance of the differences between the whole field of new churches and the survey sample is that the tendencies discussed are likely to be more descriptive of Anglo, Conservative Protestant, and digitally connected churches than of all new Seattle churches. When significant, differences between various subgroups are noted. See appendix A for more on survey methodology and respondents and appendix B for the survey instrument.

19. Becker, *Congregations in Conflict*, 14.

20. The two identity "patterns" indicating denominational affiliation are exceptions. Mainline identity is a single variable. Pentecostal/Charismatic identity is

composed of two variables that have a logical relationship—both traditions have an emphasis on the person and work of the Spirit—though they were not correlated in survey responses.

21. Analysis of group differences was conducted, in part, by comparing means of all religious groupings, as well as their subdivisions by ethnic composition (e.g., mainline ethnic, mainline multicultural, and mainline Euro-American churches). Significant differences between these subdivided groups are reported in the text.

22. Surveys were not received from any of the five ethnic churches in sacramental traditions.

23. While most Christian traditions celebrate sacraments, traditionally sacramental traditions include Catholicism, Orthodoxy, and Anglicanism.

24. The five new sacramental ethnic churches in Seattle are not represented in this data point because they did not complete the survey.

25. The Lord's Prayer is used "rarely" or "never" in half the responding churches, and a time of confession is only slightly more common (42%). For more than half (55%), the liturgical Christian calendar is no more than "a little important" to their church culture.

26. Responses from mainline Protestant churches raise the question whether some other type of preaching is more common, since the more favored of the two options was only included "occasionally."

27. It is possible this option was more appealing than descriptive in some cases, where an outside observer might say it is pastors making decisions and selling their vision to other leaders.

28. Five of the 57 surveys were completed by female pastors leading a local congregation.

29. Together with the centrality of Communion in worship, it becomes apparent how central table practices are to new churches.

30. These findings are congruent with scholarly descriptions of American Evangelicalism. The Evangelical pattern in spirituality that emerged from the surveys resonates with three of the four marks of Evangelicalism in Bebbington's classic but still serviceable quadrilateral—namely, biblicism, crucicentrism, and conversionism. Mark Noll captures these three when he describes American Evangelicalism as a form of "biblical experimentalism"; see Mark A. Noll, *American Evangelical Christianity: An Introduction* (Malden, MA: Blackwell, 2001).

31. As members of the larger Evangelical family, Charismatics and Pentecostals are also "biblical experientialists." Whereas the Word features as the primary instrument of God's work in the broad Evangelical tradition indicated above, in these Spirit-filled churches it is the Spirit's direct empowerment and miraculous work that is foregrounded.

32. The survey left "gospel of Jesus" to be proclaimed undefined, but the phrase undoubtedly has nuances of meaning in different theological and cultural traditions. These variations become clearer in chapter 4 of this volume.

33. All eight mainline Protestant churches rated "offering community" as "extremely important."

34. Fifty-nine percent regard "improving society" of little importance, and 69% make the same assessment of "building a refuge."

35. Sixty-nine percent of Conservative Protestants ranked "proclamation of the gospel" as among the top four most time- and energy-consuming highly rated priorities.

36. Eighty percent of white mainline Protestant churches ranked "offering community" in the top two, while 50% of mainline multicultural churches did. Eighty-eight percent of all mainline churches ranked "offering community" in the top four. Mainline and Evangelical churches seem to disagree as to whether offering community or proclaiming the gospel is the primary mission.

37. All biblical quotations are from the New International Version (NIV) unless otherwise noted.

38. Forty-two percent of new churches reference the Great Commission "very often." Matt. 11:28 came in a distant second, with 28% of new churches citing it "very often."

39. Luke 4 is alluded to at least "often" in slightly more than half of new churches (53%), while Acts 1 is cited as frequently in 59%.

40. This may reflect the notion, especially common among Evangelicals, that persons may come to faith through personal relationships and a prayer of salvation, but that participation in a local church is essential to their growth to maturity.

41. Half of the evangelism-only churches were ethnic churches, though they make up only a small portion of the sample. The ethnic churches in the sample favored an evangelism-only approach above all other options (50% selected it).

42. For a summary of these three ways, see the discussion of Unruh and Sider's work in chapter 3 of this volume.

43. Throughout, "priority" and "emphasis" refer to ratings of importance while "commitment" and "investment" indicate ranking in terms of the time and energy devoted to a priority. I suspect that most respondents took "proclaiming the gospel" to refer to what happens from the pulpit and "sharing the good news" as pointing to what happens conversationally.

44. "Faithful presence" is an important mode of mission in contemporary discourse and is described in chapter 4 of this volume.

45. This pattern has strong resemblance to the Sanctuary mission orientation developed in Roozen, McKinney, and Carroll, *Varieties of Religious Presence*.

46. See chapter 2 of this volume, "By the Numbers."

47. This distinguishing of traditions relied on Pew Research Center's denominational classifications. The denominations identified as Charismatic/Pentecostal include: Calvary Chapel, Assemblies of God, and Foursquare. Evangelical (non-Charismatic, non-Pentecostal) denominational identity and nondenominational identities were also explored, but neither was highly correlated to any spirituality or mission pattern.

48. The mean frequency with which ethnic churches invoke the Great Commission was 4.83, while among multicultural and white churches the mean frequency was 3.67 and 3.5, respectively (5 = very often, 4 = often, 3 = sometimes).

49. Note that this correlation between multicultural composition and size is not an indication that the former *causes* the latter. Instead, it is possible that the complex challenges of being a multicultural church are prohibitively difficult to navigate in smaller churches, and those that fail to reach a critical mass disband, thus causing the proportion of multicultural churches to be disproportionately larger. Alternatively, it may be that size promotes diversity, since in a larger church it becomes more likely that those from various ethnic groups may arrive and find others with whom they feel solidarity.

50. While these broad-consensus tendencies must be reckoned with, it would be a serious mistake to simply convert them into proposals, as if reproducing "what has worked, in general" can be trusted as a formula for either theological faithfulness, or even for church plant viability. These broad currents must be theologically evaluated and understood for how they function within the unique dynamics of various ecclesial paradigms and how they play out in particular churches; this is the work of chapters 4 and 5 of this volume.

CHAPTER 3: MODELING CHURCH

1. Roozen, McKinney, and Carroll, *Varieties of Religious Presence*.

2. On models as an interpretive tool, see Osmer, *Practical Theology*, 114–115; Avery Dulles, *Models of the Church* (New York: Image, 1991), 7–25; and Max Black, *Models and Metaphors: Studies in Language and Philosophy* (Ithaca, NY: Cornell University Press, 1962).

3. Nancy T. Ammerman et al., eds., *Studying Congregations: A New Handbook* (Nashville, TN: Abingdon, 1998).

4. Peter L. Berger discusses methodological agnosticism in appendix II of *The Sacred Canopy*. See also Douglas V. Porpora, "Methodological Atheism, Methodological Agnosticism and Religious Experience," *Journal for the Theory of Social Behaviour* 36, no. 1 (March 1, 2006): 57–75.

5. Dulles, *Models of the Church*, 10.

6. See, for example, Margaret M. Poloma and Ralph W. Hood, *Blood and Fire: Godly Love in a Pentecostal Emerging Church* (New York: New York University Press, 2008).

7. This is especially true of studies published in the late 1990s and early 2000s, when there was much interest in, and funding available for, research demonstrating the social benefits of faith-based nonprofits. Some of the contributions most often highlighted include generation of social capital, music and the arts, development of leaders, and social safety-net and transformation.

8. Roozen, McKinney, and Carroll, *Varieties of Religious Presence*; and Carl S. Dudley and Sally A. Johnson, *Energizing the Congregation: Images That Shape Your*

Church's Ministry (Louisville, KY: Westminster John Knox Press, 1993) exemplify the Protestant tendency. Anabaptist John H. Yoder offers an alternative with a triangular typology of Christian approaches to understanding the locus of the meaning of history in "A People in the World," in *The Royal Priesthood: Essays Ecclesiological and Ecumenical* by John H. Yoder and Michael Cartwright (Scottdale, PA: Herald Press, 1999). The "theocratic" vision locates the meaning of history in society at large and thus hopes for "common Christian takeover of all society for the greater glory of God" (71). The "spiritualist" view locates the meaning of history in the personal "stance of the soul" and its eternal destiny (90). Yoder rejects these and argues that the locus of the meaning of history is actually to be found in the believers church itself: "it is the predominant purpose of God neither to direct all of world history coercively toward a predetermined end, nor to make individuals whole each by herself or himself, but to constitute a new covenant people responding freely to God's call" (91).

9. Dulles, *Models of the Church*, 12.
10. The practical ecclesiological models highlighted in this chapter appear to be four of the best suited to the ecclesiastical, cultural, and historical conditions found in Seattle.
11. Dulles, *Models of the Church*, 4, 15, 17, 18, and 21.
12. Healy, *Church, World and the Christian Life*, 32.
13. Ibid., 36.
14. Ibid., 37.
15. Ibid., 50. Healy defends this claim by noting that blueprint approaches direct our ecclesiological reflection into endless searches and unresolvable debates regarding the ideal formulations and their universal implications. Moreover, he notes, even when consensus seems to emerge—as with the "communion" model—closer inspection reveals that the meaning of the formulation to key interpreters is so varied as to render meaningless the agreement on the formulation "communion" itself (43–46). As Healy suggests, the blueprint approach disregards the essential task of attending to the context in which the church is called to live out its discipleship and witness.
16. Ibid.
17. While reflecting to Healy's general proposal, my practical ecclesiological models are constructed as "two-fold construals," something he critiques.
18. For example, see Stetzer and Lim, *Planting Missional Churches*.
19. Healy, *Church, World and the Christian Life*, 27.
20. One of the valuable contributions of models is that they serve as an important interpretive backdrop for understanding the inimitable particularity of local churches—how they illustrate, and perhaps more important, how they deviate from or innovate upon a model.

21. Demonstrating the ecclesiality of these churches is both beyond the scope of this project and, ultimately, impossible. However, the practice of Trinitarian baptism is the most defensible grounds on which to make this judgment, given its centrality to one of the most significant achievements of Christian ecumenical dialogue; the World Council of Churches, *Baptism, Eucharist and Ministry,* Faith and Order Commission, Faith and Order Paper No. 111, Geneva, January 15, 1982. WCC churches, as well as nonmembers including the Catholic Church, have given this report wider formal response and reception of than any Faith and Order text previously or since. See Max Thurian, ed., *Churches Respond to BEM: Official Responses to the "Baptism, Eucharist and Ministry" Text,* vols. I–VI (Geneva: World Council of Churches, 1986).

22. Ecclesiological validity is assumed in each case. Because churches like these exist, and because they gather in Jesus's name and call upon the Triune God as Father, Son, and Spirit, it is presumed that God calls them "my people." As such, I believe that each of these models of church holds promise and is in danger of potential pitfalls and can be served by the ecclesiological and missiological scrutiny of chapter 5 of this volume.

23. Paul S. Minear, *Images of the Church in the New Testament* (Louisville, KY: Westminster John Knox Press, 2004).

24. N. T. Wright, *Paul: In Fresh Perspective* (Minneapolis: Fortress Press, 2009), 109.

25. There is a link between this passive logic of witness and Penny Becker's Community and House of Worship models in *Congregations in Conflict.* This vision of the church is what propelled Paul to "produce and maintain cells of Jews and Gentiles loyal to Jesus as Messiah and Lord, living the power of the Spirit, under the nose of Caesar and in some of the key cities of the empire" which existed to the Jewish (and Christian consciousness) as the central manifestation of darkness on God's earth (Wright, *Paul.* 112, 124, 128–129). It should also be noted that other New Testament authors develop the People of God model in uniquely nuanced ways.

26. See Rom. 12:4–8, 1 Cor. 12:12–30, Eph. 1:22–23 and 4:4–16, and Col. 1:18 and 2:18–19.

27. As Susann Liubinskas has pointed out, Paul's Body of Christ image is in some tension with notions of the whole church as a "sent" body, as missional ecclesiology suggests. Instead, the Body of Christ sends individuals gifted by the spirit for evangelism, apostleship and the like. Susann Liubinskas, "The Body of Christ in Mission: Paul's Ecclesiology and the Role of the Church in Mission," *Missiology: An International Review* 41, no. 4 (October 1, 2013): 402–415.

28. In this model, the mission of the church is primarily seen in its mutual support and ministry.

29. Kevin Giles, *What on Earth Is the Church?: An Exploration in New Testament Theology* (Downers Grove, IL: IVP Books, 2000), 81.

30. Darrell L. Bock, *A Theology of Luke and Acts: God's Promised Program, Realized for All Nations*, ed. Andreas J. Kostenberger (Grand Rapids, MI: Zondervan, 2012), 374.

31. Graham H. Twelftree, *People of the Spirit: Exploring Luke's View of the Church* (Grand Rapids, MI: Baker Academic, 2009), 206.

32. See Luke 19:10.

33. Twelftree, *People of the Spirit*, 205–207.

34. D. Moody Smith, *The Theology of the Gospel of John* (Cambridge: Cambridge University Press, 1995), 136.

35. Raymond E. Brown, *The Community of the Beloved Disciple* (New York: Paulist Press, 1979), 141.

36. Smith, *The Theology of the Gospel of John*, 155.

37. See Robert H. Gundry, *Jesus the Word According to John the Sectarian: A Paleofundamentalist Manifesto for Contemporary Evangelicalism, Especially Its Elites, in North America* (Grand Rapids, MI: Eerdmans, 2002).

38. Raymond Brown develops this theme extensively, identifying six Johannine outgroups in the Gospel, three of which are identified as in some way Christian; Brown, *The Community of the Beloved Disciple*, 62–87.

39. The following paragraphs draw heavily from S. Steve Kang and Christopher B. James, "Christ and Culture," in *Encyclopedia of Christian Education*, ed. George T. Kurian and Mark A. Lamport (Lanham, MD: Rowman & Littlefield, May 7, 2015).

40. H. Richard Niebuhr, *Christ and Culture* (San Francisco, CA: Harper & Row, 1975), 39.

41. Ibid., 177.

42. Ibid., 217.

43. Ibid., 232.

44. Ibid., 256.

45. Dulles, *Models of the Church*, 26. Here, Dulles quotes Robert Bellarmine as affirming that the church is a society "as visible and palpable as the community of the Roman people, or the Kingdom of France, or the Republic of Venice," from *De controversiis*, tom. 2, lib 3, cap. 2 (Naples: Giuliano, 1857), vol. 2, 75.

46. Ibid., 68.

47. Miroslav Volf's Free Church ecclesiology does not fit particularly well into the Herald model—it says virtually nothing about the mission of the church or evangelism—but it offers a robust case for the ecclesiality of the local church as a polycentric community modeled after the Trinitarian fellowship. He anchors his argument in Jesus's well-known and oft-invoked promise from Matt. 18:20 (ESV), "Where two or three are gathered in my name, I am there among them." See Miroslav Volf, *After Our Likeness: The Church As the Image of the Trinity* (Grand Rapids, MI: Eerdmans, 1998).

48. Dulles, *Models of the Church*, 71.

49. Ibid., 77.
50. Ibid., 89.
51. Ibid., 198. Though he does admit the inadequacy of this model for capturing the fullness of the church, it is still somewhat puzzling that Dulles chose to advance a systematic proposal, given his insistence in the original text that justice could be done to the church as a complex reality only by working simultaneously with different models (2). Perhaps, as this book attempts to do in a more robust way, Dulles recognized possibilities for doctrinal construction emerging from his descriptive and evaluative work.
52. Ibid., 250.
53. Ibid., 213. The most prolific and influential exponent of the church as contrast society is Stanley Hauerwas who, drawing heavily on the thought of John Howard Yoder, has argued forcefully for an ecclesiology that divides world from church on the basis of recognition of Jesus as Lord and a witness that inheres in the life and practice of the community of the church itself, that is, in its ethics. See, for example, Stanley Hauerwas, *The Hauerwas Reader* (Durham: Duke University Press, 2001), 371–391.
54. Critiques and responses to Niebuhr's scheme include D. A. Carson, *Christ and Culture Revisited* (Grand Rapids, MI: Eerdmans, 2012); Craig A. Carter, *Rethinking Christ and Culture: A Post-Christendom Perspective* (Grand Rapids, MI: Brazos Press, 2007); Glen H. Stassen, Diane M. Yeager, and John H. Yoder, *Authentic Transformation: A New Vision of Christ and Culture* (Nashville, TN: Abingdon Press, 1996); Graham Ward, *Christ and Culture* (Malden, MA: Blackwell, 2008); Charles Scriven, *The Transformation of Culture: Christian Social Ethics After H. Richard Niebuhr* (Scottdale, PA: Herald Press, 1988).
55. Kevin Christiano, William Swatos, and Peter Kivisto, *Sociology of Religion: Contemporary Developments*, 2nd ed. (Lanham, MD: Rowman & Littlefield, 2008), 87.
56. For a useful, searchable database of congregational studies research, see Congregational Studies Team, *Studying Congregations*, updated August 2016, http://studyingcongregations.org.
57. In an important way, Roozen, McKinney, and Carroll's *Varieties of Religious Presence* was a sociological rendition of Niebuhr's *Christ and Culture* on the congregational level.
58. Ibid., 33.
59. Ibid., 34.
60. Ibid., 87.
61. There are interesting parallels between this work and Dulles's. Both focus on images, but while Dulles describes models of "the Church," Dudley and Johnson offer models for "a church"—that is, they locate the identity work on the congregational level.
62. "The Pillar church has a sense of civic responsibility that embraces the community. The Pilgrim church cares for the cultural group as extended family.

The Survivor church reacts to crises in an overwhelming world. The Prophet church is proactive to translate crises into causes. The Servant church reaches out to support individuals who need help"; Dudley and Johnson, *Energizing the Congregation*, 6–7. Conspicuously, and inexplicably, absent from the Dudley/Johnson scheme is a counterpart to the "evangelist" mission orientation in Roozen, McKinney, and Carroll, *Varieties of Religious Presence*.

63. Heidi R. Unruh and Ronald J. Sider, *Saving Souls, Serving Society: Understanding the Faith Factor in Church-Based Social Ministry* (Oxford: Oxford University Press, 2005), 6.

64. Ibid., 144.

65. Even with these polar types, Unruh and Sider contribute valuable nuance by highlighting the fact that "some dominant social action churches frame their activism as implicit evangelism" and some dominant evangelism churches understand this spiritual work as the "highest form of social compassion" since it is, in their view, the most effective strategy for addressing social ills. Ibid.

66. Ammerman identifies the core tasks expected of congregations in American culture as worship, weekly religious education for children, and some minimal growth opportunities for adults. Nancy T. Ammerman, *Pillars of Faith: American Congregations and Their Partners* (Berkeley: University of California Press, 2005), 49–50.

67. Becker, *Congregations in Conflict*, 7.

68. Ibid., 16.

69. Ibid., 90.

70. Ibid., 81.

71. Ibid., 80.

72. Ibid., 140. Interestingly, none of Becker's models has a distinctive emphasis on evangelism as an approach to religious witness. Whether this is because such an approach was scattered among churches of various models or because none of the churches in the study had a strong evangelistic culture is unknown.

CHAPTER 4: MODELS OF PRACTICAL ECCLESIOLOGY AMONG
NEW SEATTLE CHURCHES

1. These ecclesial options, it is presumed, are, both (1) works in progress that can benefit from critical and theological assessment, and (2) sources of practical and theological wisdom for the contemporary church. Theological assessment is the work of chapter 5 of this volume. Chapters 6 and 7 draw out the practical and theological wisdom and offer practical proposals for their renewal.

2. This is not to say that leaders or participants in these models would necessarily indicate a priority of one dimension over another, but that the model itself may be understood to place logical priority on certain dimensions over others.

3. Congregational studies in American Evangelicalism are numerous, but several noteworthy titles include: Smith and Emerson, *American Evangelicalism*; Shayne Lee and Phillip Sinitiere, *Holy Mavericks: Evangelical Innovators and the Spiritual Marketplace* (New York: New York University Press, 2009); Noll, *American Evangelical Christianity*; Molly Worthen, *Apostles of Reason: The Crisis of Authority in American Evangelicalism* (New York: Oxford University Press, 2013); Tanya M. Luhrmann, *When God Talks Back: Understanding the American Evangelical Relationship with God* (New York: Knopf, 2012).

4. Newbigin insisted that mission was not merely a sign of a healthy church— something the church should do, but part of its essence, part of what the church is. "When the church has ceased to be a mission, then she ceases to have any right to the titles by which she is adorned in the New Testament . . . [she] has certainly lost the *esse*, and not merely the *bene esse* of a Church"; Lesslie Newbigin, *The Household of God: Lectures on the Nature of the Church* (New York: Friendship Press, 1954), 163.

5. Matt. 18:20. Miroslav Volf makes a compelling and theologically robust defense of Free Church ecclesiology, launching from this text; Volf, *After Our Likeness*.

6. Ken Caruthers develops and defends the Church Planters as Church model in his dissertation, "The Missionary Team as Church: Applied Ecclesiology in the Life and Relationships between Cross-Cultural Church Planters," Southeastern Baptist Theological Seminary, 2014, http://gradworks.umi.com/35/81/3581125.html.

7. Linda Berquist's language of a "Spiritual Alpha City" is descriptive; Linda Berquist, "Imagine What God Could Do With a 'Spiritual Alpha City,'" *V3 Church Planting Movement* (blog), May 2015, http://thev3movement.org/2015/05/imagine-what-god-could-do-with-a-spiritual-alpha-city.

8. The Church at Brook Hills was pastored, at the time, by David Platt, who on August 27, 2014, was appointed the head of the Southern Baptist's International Mission Board.

9. Relocation to "pioneer" the area via the "parachute" model of church planting (where a church planter—and spouse, if married—drop into a community and start from scratch) are more common among GCT churches than among other models.

10. It is noteworthy that the metrics used by the groups to produce these statistics, such as One Challenge USA, only include Evangelical churches in their tallies.

11. Smith and Emerson, *American Evangelicalism*. See also Alan Noble, "The Evangelical Persecution Complex," *The Atlantic*, August 4, 2014, www.theatlantic.com/national/archive/2014/08/the-evangelical-persecution-complex/375506.

12. As noted in chapter 1, Conservative Protestants were found more likely to be utilizing Facebook, Twitter, and a church website than other religious traditions. Use is also pronounced among multisite and nondenominational churches, which are disproportionately Conservative Protestant.

13. Just as GCT churches see cities as strategic locations for advancing the gospel, they regard church planting in gentrifying neighborhoods as a cost-effective way

to get a foothold in up-and-coming communities filled with the young, urban hipsters they often hope to reach.

14. The mission priorities highlighted among GCT churches in the New Seattle Churches Survey were evangelism, discipleship, and proclamation. Proclamation of the gospel is closely linked in GCT churches to preaching and will be considered under Spirituality.

15. *Radical* is a book and ministry of David Platt that "exists to serve the church in accomplishing the mission of Christ . . . [and longs] to see the church making disciples who make disciples who make disciples throughout the world—from our neighbors across the street to the unreached people groups across the globe—all for the glory of God. See *Radical: Taking Back Your Faith from the American Dream* (Colorado Springs, CO: Multnomah Books, 2010).

16. Emphasis on "relational evangelism" is a staple of Evangelical life and the topic of countless books. The strategy is also discussed as "personal," "friendship," and "conversational" evangelism.

17. Language in block quotes throughout has been minimally edited (smoothed) for comprehension and readability.

18. The particular meaning of "the Gospel" among GCT churches is discussed on page 94 and following.

19. "Attending worship" was the second most highly rated activity in terms of importance for the "way of life" at The Hallows Church, a GCT exemplar.

20. Brian Steensland and Phillip Goff, eds., *The New Evangelical Social Engagement* (New York: Oxford University Press, 2013).

21. In the last decade, combating sex trafficking has become one of the most popular social-justice issues for Evangelicals to engage, often in partnership with the International Justice Mission. There may be some correlation to Evangelical views on human sexuality that have become major points of friction with the wider culture; Evangelicals are committed to naming sexual sin and so confronting human trafficking is a socially accepted form of religious activism that draws constructively upon their indignation regarding sexual sin.

22. The language of "multiplication" is popular among church planting and disciple-making Evangelicals.

23. During the two years of research both Mosaic and The Hallows Church launched new churches. Downtown Cornerstone Church's vision is to see an expression of the gospel planted in every major neighborhood in Seattle.

24. At The Hallows Church, short- and mid-term international missionaries were featured right before the offering was taken on multiple occasions and Pastor Arthur stressed the link: "this is what your money goes to." Mars Hill Church came under scrutiny for reportedly raising millions of dollars for the Mars Hill Global fund by featuring "highly visible" mission projects but using funds on non-mission efforts. See Warren Throckmorton, "Mars Hill Global Fund: Help the Helpless or Use the Helpless?" *Warren Throckmorton* (blog), October 1, 2014, www.patheos.com/blogs/warrenthrockmorton/2014/10/01/mars-hill-global-fund-help-the-helpless-or-use-the-helpless.

25. These were phrases used by Pastor Arthur at The Hallows Church. Mosaic Church has partners in North Africa in a context of Christian persecution.

26. Tim Challies, "The Gospel-Centered Everything," *Challies.com*, March 7, 2013, www.challies.com/articles/the-gospel-centered-everything.

27. At The Hallows Church, their frequently cited formula for "the Gospel" was: "He lived the life we could not live and died the death we should have died." These are Dualists in the Niebuhrian sense of emphasizing a dichotomy between a righteous God and sinful humanity.

28. The top three contexts in which The Hallows Church participants who completed the congregational survey indicated feeling closest to God were, in order of average importance: "when I learn something new about God," "when I'm out in creation," and "when I'm in a worship service that engages the senses."

29. Nancy T. Ammerman, *Sacred Stories, Spiritual Tribes: Finding Religion in Everyday Life* (Oxford: Oxford University Press, 2013), 292–304.

30. C. S. Lewis, *The Weight of Glory* (New York: HarperOne, 2001), 21.

31. When I visited Mars Hill's University Campus, the song set included classic hymns rearranged and led by an in-house rock band called "Citizens." Songs included "Amazing Grace," "There is a Fountain Filled with Blood," "Jesus Paid it All," "How Deep the Father's Love for Us," and an original song called "The Sweetness of Freedom."

32. This lyric comes from a very popular version of "Jesus Paid it All" by Kristian Stanfill, heard in several GCT churches; Kristian Stanfill, "Jesus Paid It All," *Passion: Everything Glorious*, CD (Six Step Records, 2006).

33. Jesus is also seen as a heroic figure of holiness and confident opposition to culture.

34. Pastor David Parker, interview with author, Seattle, November 6, 2013. The listed actions of God emerged from my analysis of the ways GCT members described their personal experiences of God and God's contemporary actions.

35. Members of The Hallows Church said God had "brought people into our life" and "paved the way to build a relationship with [the local elementary school]" and was "widening the net of our influence."

36. The congregational survey at The Hallows Church found the following to be the most important markers of Christian maturity: 1. relational closeness with God; 2. being obedient to God's will; 3. walking in the power of the Spirit; 4. having Christ-like character; and 5. living missionally in relationships with friends and neighbors. By contrast, "living missionally" was the lowest rated marker of maturity for Wits' End, a church in the NC model.

37. The key networks and affiliations for GCT churches in Seattle are Seattle Church Planting (a wing of the North American Mission Board of the Southern Baptist Convention that is also a resource and place of connection for nondenominational GCT churches), Acts 29, Crosspointe, The Gospel Coalition, Every Nation, and Antioch International Movement of Churches.

38. For example, Mars Hill Church, Church of Brook Hills, Redeemer Presbyterian Church in New York City, and Spanish River Church.

39. See Anchor Church website, www.anchorseattle.org/about/jesus.
40. James Bielo argues that a re-urbanization of Evangelicalism is under way, driven by "a biting cultural critique of suburban megachurches, and a desire for the 'reconciliation' of urban life to 'the kingdom of God.'" See James S. Bielo, "City of Man, City of God: The Re-Urbanization of American Evangelicals," *City & Society* 23, no. s1 (September 2011): 2–23. *Christianity Today* also reflects this trend, especially in their "This is Our City" series.
41. Notwithstanding the fact that the majority of GCT churches meet in church buildings and more than a few gather in community centers.
42. These are only a few of the reasons the trend has gathered steam in the last decade. See Ruth Moon, "Popcorn in the Pews," *Christianity Today*, January 14, 2009, www.christianitytoday.com/ct/2009/january/18.16.html. Regal Entertainment Group even has a dedicated team of Theatre Church Consultants; "Theatre Church," Regal Cinemas, www.regmovies.com/theatres/theatre-church.
43. This practical ecclesiological model is developed qualitatively and theologically from the survey paradigm comprising patterns in Spirit-filled spirituality, Temple-building mission, and Pentecostal/Charismatic and Ethnic Family identity.
44. For some useful congregational studies of Pentecostal, Charismatic, ethnic, and immigrant churches, see Michael W. Foley and Dean R. Hoge, *Religion and the New Immigrants: How Faith Communities Form Our Newest Citizens* (New York: Oxford University Press, 2007); Margaret M. Poloma and John C. Green, *The Assemblies of God: Godly Love and the Revitalization of American Pentecostalism* (New York: New York University Press, 2010); Richard Cimino, Nadia A. Mian, and Weishan Huang, eds., *Ecologies of Faith in New York City: The Evolution of Religious Institutions* (Bloomington, IN: Indiana University Press, 2013); and Arlene M. Sánchez-Walsh, *Latino Pentecostal Identity: Evangelical Faith, Self, and Society* (New York: Columbia University Press, 2003).
45. Pastor Billy Huffman, preaching at City Church's University Campus, July 7, 2013.
46. The New Seattle Churches Survey revealed a negative correlation between strength of neighborhood identification and identification with a cultural or ethnic population.
47. Church growth experts agree that personal invitations to church are far and away the most common reason people begin attending a church. Congregational surveys from three different new churches confirmed that this is true across models in the Seattle context as well.
48. For example, Pastor Serena Wastman told her young congregation, "I'm going to push and contend for you to have all that God has." Pastor Billy Huffman closed the service saying "Hey, let me bless you before we go: Father, thank you for my friends, Lord, I speak a blessing upon their coming and their going."
49. Receiving prayer was rare in my interactions with church leaders of other models.

50. On "niche congregations," see Ammerman, *Congregation and Community*, 130–160.
51. Ryan Bolger and Eddie Gibbs, Evangelical scholars at Fuller Theological Seminary, authored the best, early study of emerging churches and presented them sympathetically, defining them as "communities that practice the way of Jesus within postmodern cultures" that identify with the life of Jesus, transform the secular realm, and live highly communal lives. Eddie Gibbs and Ryan K. Bolger, *Emerging Churches: Creating Christian Community in Postmodern Cultures* (Grand Rapids, MI: Baker Academic, 2005), 44–45. More recently, insider Tony Jones, in his dissertation, expressed preference for the definition found in the *Encyclopedia of Religion in America*: "The emerging church movement is a loosely aligned conversation among Christians who seek to re-imagine the priorities, values and theology expressed by the local church as it seeks to live out its faith in postmodern society. It is an attempt to replot Christian faith on a new cultural and intellectual terrain." Cited in Tony Jones, *The Church Is Flat: The Relational Ecclesiology of the Emerging Church Movement* (Minneapolis, MN: JoPa Group, 2011), 5.
52. Many Evangelical churches that may have once identified as "emerging" now identify more readily with labels such as "missional" or "incarnational." For key Evangelical critiques of the emerging church movement, see D. A. Carson, *Becoming Conversant with the Emerging Church: Understanding a Movement and Its Implications* (Grand Rapids, MI: Zondervan, 2005). Also, Kevin DeYoung, Ted Kluck, and David F. Wells, *Why We're Not Emergent: By Two Guys Who Should Be* (Chicago: Moody, 2008).
53. Noteworthy research on emerging churches includes Gerardo Marti and Gladys Ganiel, *The Deconstructed Church: Understanding Emerging Christianity* (New York: Oxford University Press, 2014); Jones, *The Church Is Flat*; Gibbs and Bolger, *Emerging Churches*; Xochitl Alviso, "A Feminist Analysis of the Emerging Church: Toward Radical Participation in the Organic, Relational, and Inclusive Body of Christ," dissertation, Boston University School of Theology, 2015; and James S. Bielo, *Emerging Evangelicals: Faith, Modernity, and the Desire for Authenticity* (New York: New York University Press, 2011).
54. Becker writes that the "chief form of witness" among Community churches "is in living their values, institutionalizing them in local congregational life . . . like democracies, with more emphasis on formal and open decision making routines that include all members"; Becker, *Congregations in Conflict*, 14. These inclusive processes are in distinction to episcopal and pastor- or staff-driven decision making. During my time among Wits' End I was struck by how openly they talked about money—including as the "main event" during one Sunday gathering. This open process was clearly a part of their distinctive form of community, but also a significant part of their embodied witness.
55. New Community churches typically have somewhat fewer children than churches in the other models.

56. NC churches may not regularly articulate their vision as an eschatological one in such terms, but such it is nonetheless.

57. Participants in the emerging church movement have deconstructed Evangelical theology and practice. As Marti and Ganiel note, faith for emerging Christians is conversation rather than dogma; Marti and Ganiel, *The Deconstructed Church*, 78–108.

58. See, for example, this celebration of Church of the Apostles on the Episcopal Church website, "COTA, Church of the Apostles Seattle," Episcopal Church, last modified March 28, 2013, www.episcopalchurch.org/library/video/ cota-church-apostles-seattle.

59. Gibbs and Bolger, *Emerging Churches*, 217–234; Marti and Ganiel, *The Deconstructed Church*, 122–128.

60. Emerging church insider and scholar Tony Jones asserts that the emerging church movement embodies a "relational ecclesiology"; Jones, *The Church Is Flat*.

61. From Rainer Maria Rilke, *Letters to a Young Poet*, trans. M. D. Herter Norton (New York: W. W. Norton, 1993), 33–35.

62. Authenticity in relationships with one another and with God was a key theme among Wits' End Church, a focus church exemplifying the NC model. It was seen in their desire to "bring to voice" their true selves and to name their painful experiences and difficult emotions. In fact, they welcomed (even celebrated) swearing as an important marker of authenticity. They expressed a desire to also listen and "hold one another" well across difference, in almost a therapeutic manner. Often psychological language was used to describe this.

    One of the stories I heard exemplifies their pursuit of authenticity in relationship: A family in the church was moving and did not get sufficient help from the congregation. Because Pastor Nellis had showed up to help, this impacted his time to prep the sermon for the next day. The following day, he brought this situation before the community for discussion during the sermon time. It was an awkward, hard, emotional discussion about who they are as a church and who they wanted to be—and yet it was celebrated as an example of their unique culture. This authenticity in relationship with one another was echoed in the ways they talked about their relationships with God as including anger, confusion, and grief.

63. *Ressourcement* is a French neologism that could be translated as "renewal through return to sources." Policraticus, "Culture and Theology: The Ressourcement Movement (Part 1)," *Vox Nova*, March 30, 2008, http://vox-nova.com/2008/03/ 30/culture-and-theology-the-ressourcement-movement-part-1.

64. Quote from "New Episcopal Church Video Features Church of the Apostles, Seattle." The task of curating the seasons is assigned to what Church of the Apostles calls their Liturgy Guild. For discussion of worship practices among emerging churches, see Mary Gray-Reeves and Michael Perham, *The*

Hospitality of God: Emerging Worship for a Missional Church (New York: Seabury Books, 2011); and Dan Kimball, David Crowder, and Sally Morgenthaler, *Emerging Worship: Creating Worship Gatherings for New Generations* (Grand Rapids, MI: Zondervan, 2004).

65. During worship, the leader at Valley & Mountain announced: "We are a community here at Valley & Mountain and nothing that you see, nothing that we do is done by one person alone." For more on the collaborative production of worship, see Gibbs and Bolger, *Emerging Churches*, chap. 8; and Marti and Ganiel, *The Deconstructed Church*, 122–128.

66. As Marti and Ganiel have observed, emerging churches strike an apparently contradictory balance in which the autonomy of the individual is a core value, while discourse and other practices emphasize community; Marti and Ganiel, *The Deconstructed Church*, 36.

67. On the Taizé community, see Jason B. Santos, "After Taizé: A Practical Theology of Sustained Spiritual Formation for the Pilgrims of Taizé," dissertation, Princeton Theological Seminary, 2014, http://gradworks.umi.com/36/43/3643491.html; Jason B. Santos, *A Community Called Taizé: A Story of Prayer, Worship and Reconciliation* (Downers Grove, IL: IVP Books, 2008).

68. Jones, *The Church Is Flat*, 100–105.

69. For emerging church practices of engaging Scripture, see Marti and Ganiel, *The Deconstructed Church*, 113–117; Jones, *The Church Is Flat*, 105–108; and Doug Pagitt, *Preaching Re-Imagined: The Role of the Sermon in Communities of Faith* (Grand Rapids, MI: Zondervan/Youth Specialties, 2005).

70. Becca Shirley, "Fighting for Orientation: Thoughts on Psalm 15," *Wits' End Church*, January 30, 2014, www.witsendchurch.org/1/post/2014/01/fighting-for-orientation-thoughts-on-psalm-15.html.

71. Church of the Apostle's website was explicit: "[W]e have an earthy spirituality that affirms the goodness of life and the created world and believes that the extraordinary is to be found in the ordinary."

72. This is yet another instance of NC churches embracing their cultural milieu. A study of Google searches found Seattle to be the fourth-ranked city in the nation for the search term "yoga," an increase of 53% between 2009 and 2013; Othmane Rahmouni, "7 Facts You Didn't Know about Yoga in Seattle," *Seattle Yoga News*, June 9, 2014, http://seattleyoganews.com/yoga-seattle-statistics.

73. All Pilgrims has a long-term relationship with an Islamic mosque. A founding couple at Valley & Mountain came from a Unitarian-Universalist church and, as ongoing pillars of the church, made multiple favorable references to other religions in the span of a single gathering.

74. Respondents to the Wits' End congregational survey rated "adding beauty to the world" as among the top three descriptors of what their church is doing from a list of twenty. It rated above "giving opportunities to worship God" and "proclaiming the gospel of Jesus."

75. Three original abstract icons written by a member are emblematic of the community and are featured on the website of the bE.kON collective, which describes itself as an "alternative faith community" that seeks to be an icon of God on Beacon Hill; see "bE.kON collective," www.bekoncollective.com.

76. Also of note is the multiple meanings several elements hold: the fern as both a local symbol of the Northwest and a traditional Christian symbol of humility; the waves as indicative of Ps. 107, Wits' End logo, exodus, and baptism.

77. The Opiate Mass makes "progressive sacred music for cathedral"; Opiate Mass website, www.theopiatemass.org.

78. Valley & Mountain Fellowship is in partnership with Community Arts Create. Church of the Apostles is partnered with Abbey Arts.

79. Participatory forms of community leadership are a key characteristic discussed in literature on emerging churches. Tony Jones's title asserts the emerging church movement's nonhierarchical character: *The Church Is Flat*. See also Gibbs and Bolger, *Emerging Churches*, 191–215; and Marti and Ganiel, *The Deconstructed Church*, 117–122.

80. There is *almost* a statistically significant relationship between mainline identity and emphasis on innovation (.058, two-tailed significance), but there is a significant relation between Innovation and churches that serve as strong examples of Sacramental-liturgical spirituality (.023, two-tailed).

81. Leaders at Church of the Apostles, All Pilgrims, and Wits' End all described their congregations as mostly composed of wounded and disillusioned post-Evangelicals. The congregational survey at Wits' End confirmed this, as *wounded* was one of the most common words used in open-ended descriptions of the people that are part of the church. The intern leading worship at Valley & Mountain when I visited described his journey from political and religious conservatism had included a stint working for Karl Rove.

    The congregational survey at Wits' End revealed that although 100% of respondents described themselves as "committed Christians" before coming to Wits' End, 79% had not been attending a church regularly. The most common reason indicated was "I had become disillusioned." If Wits' End is representative of NC churches, then it would seem their primary appeal is to the "Dones" described in Josh Packard and Ashleigh Hope, *Church Refugees: Sociologists Reveal Why People Are DONE With Church But Not Their Faith* (Loveland, CO: Group Publishing, 2015).

82. Marti and Ganiel, *The Deconstructed Church*, 34.

83. Indeed, Mark Driscoll, who once identified with the emerging church movement, has been a key foil for progressive emerging churches not only in Seattle but nationally as well.

84. Wollschleger and Porter found that churches existing in the shadow of giants can thrive by developing an identity in distinction; see Jason Wollschleger and Jeremy R. Porter, "A 'WalMartization' of Religion? The Ecological Impact of

Megachurches on the Local and Extra-Local Religious Economy," *Review of Religious Research* 53 (July 29, 2011): 279–299. Given the substantial percentage of participants in NC churches who are disillusioned and de-churched former Evangelicals, it would seem that—counterintuitively—a likely contributor to the vitality and sustainability of NC churches is the towering presence of their Evangelical megachurch foils.

85. The turmoil began to boil over when former members staged protests at the Bellevue campus, declaring "We are not anonymous" in response to a letter released by Mars Hill leadership indicating that they could not reconcile with those who had grievances because they did not know who they were. Mars Hill campuses were cut loose to become, if they wish and are able, autonomous churches.

86. They will need a new villain or, preferably, a better developed (more positively constructed) identity.

87. Episcopal Church, "COTA, Church of the Apostles Seattle."

88. Respondents to the congregational survey at Wits' End rated "offering a community in which to belong and be loved" most highly as descriptive of their church, above nineteen other options.

89. As a further example, a tenant in the home that served as the gathering place for the bE.kON collective did not participate in the religious gathering on Wednesday evenings, but he was described to me as "part of our community."

90. GCT churches—along with Evangelicals more broadly—have in recent years begun speaking of (and in some cases working for) "justice," but in the churches I observed, justice was rarely a matter for prayer.

91. All Pilgrims rejects its designation by outsiders as a "gay church" despite the fact that a strong majority of its members are part of the LGBTQ community. They do not want to be identified by others as "other," but to be identified on their own terms, as a Christian church. That said, being "open and affirming" is central to the identity of All Pilgrims. But "open and affirming" is not limited to inclusion of a diversity of sexual orientation because, as Pastor Turk said, "we first and foremost as human beings serve and love a God we strive to represent and re-present that gospel love to all." Rev. Greg Turk, interview with author, Seattle, August 2, 2013.

92. Christine Clarridge, "Occupy Port Protesters Violent, Officers Say," *Seattle Times*, December 15, 2011, www.seattletimes.com/seattle-news/occupy-port-protesters-violent-officers-say.

93. Mark Chaves, *Congregations in America* (Cambridge, MA: Harvard University Press, 2004), 166–201.

94. In both cases, relatively little concern is placed on effecting real social change through service, since making the world a better place is not the chief priority of either model (as it is of Dulles's Servant model).

95. A flurry of books advocating for variations of the Neighborhood Incarnation model have recently been published, including Paul Sparks, Tim Soerens, and

Dwight J. Friesen, *The New Parish: How Neighborhood Churches Are Transforming Mission, Discipleship and Community* (Downers Grove, IL: IVP Books, 2014); Dan White Jr., *Subterranean: Why the Future of the Church Is Rootedness* (Eugene, OR: Cascade Books, 2015); C. Christopher Smith and John Pattison, *Slow Church: Cultivating Community in the Patient Way of Jesus* (Downers Grove, IL: IVP Books, 2014); Michael Frost, *Incarnate: The Body of Christ in an Age of Disengagement* (Downers Grove, IL: IVP Books, 2014); and Lance Ford and Brad Brisco, *Next Door as It Is in Heaven: Living Out God's Kingdom in Your Neighborhood* (Colorado Springs, CO: NavPress, 2016).

96. Studies of emerging churches typically adopt a broad definition, methodological approach, or sample that includes Neighborhood Incarnation churches within their scope. In other words, samples of emerging churches have typically been developed deductively as those that self-identify as such, attend certain gatherings, or participate in certain networks. While NI churches share certain important similarities with emerging churches, there is a meaningful distinction. The thoroughness of this research in a delimited religious ecology has developed its categorization inductively and suggests the importance of recognizing the fundamental importance of parish identity for a hitherto unresearched cohort of new churches. Distinguishing Neighborhood Incarnation churches from emerging churches offers useful specificity and clarity.

97. Robert Wuthnow distinguishes between two types of neighborhood churches— the small "neighborhood churches" that have been in place for years and have likely seen decline as the environment has changed, and small, intentional churches that are "likely to be a newer congregation, often a mission church that has been started in a new neighborhood and is hoping to become larger with time, or a group that wants to remain small for a variety of reasons." Neighborhood Incarnation churches, of course, resemble the later. See Robert Wuthnow, *Producing the Sacred: An Essay on Public Religion* (Urbana, IL: University of Illinois Press, 1994), 50.

98. On third places, see Ray Oldenburg, *The Great Good Place: Cafes, Coffee Shops, Bookstores, Bars, Hair Salons, and Other Hangouts at the Heart of a Community*, 3rd ed. (New York: Marlowe & Company, 1999).

99. Ed Stetzer describes this model under the heading of missional/incarnational churches that "let their incarnation of Christ drive the mission in their community and beyond; and the church emerges out of that journey"; Stetzer, *Planting Missional Churches* (Nashville, TN: Broadman & Holman Academic, 2006), 161. The focus in this approach is on building relationships and serving rather than recruiting members and launching. The covenant communities resulting from these other-oriented relationships, then, have the potential to incarnate the gospel in a uniquely local and specific way.

100. This paraphrase of John 1:1 from Eugene Peterson's *The Message* is a favorite among NI churches.

101. Parish Collective website, http://parishcollective.org. "Leadership in the New Parish Certificate," Seattle School of Theology & Psychology website, http://theseattleschool.edu/programs/leadership-in-the-new-parish.

102. NI churches might be understood as reflections of what the local church can learn from the new monastic movement, which seeks to emulate the wisdom of Benedictine practices of stability, community, and work in "abandoned" places. For more see Christopher B. James, "What Churches Can Learn from New Monasticism," *Conversations Journal Blog*, July 2013, http://conversations-journal.com/2013/07/what-churches-can-learn-from-new-monasticism-pt-1.

103. These points are emphasized in both Frost, *Incarnate*; and Sparks, Soerens, and Friesen, *The New Parish*. For more on human scale, see Eric O. Jacobsen, *Sidewalks in the Kingdom: New Urbanism and the Christian Faith* (Grand Rapids, MI: Brazos Press, 2003).

104. Sinha et al. describe these as "resident congregations" composed of 50% or more of people who live within ten blocks of the church building. In their study of Philadelphia congregations, resident churches had an average of about 75% living nearby, were older, much more likely to have a pastor who lived nearby, disproportionately Catholic, Orthodox, Lutheran, and Methodist, and more likely located in a stable neighborhood; Jill W. Sinha et al., "Proximity Matters: Exploring Relationships Among Neighborhoods, Congregations, and the Residential Patterns of Members," *Journal for the Scientific Study of Religion* 46, no. 2 (June 1, 2007): 245–260.

105. Pastor Ben Katt estimated that 80% of the Awake church community lives within a few blocks off of Aurora. I suspect this is an overestimate based on my interactions with attendees, but it illustrates the strength of the church's neighborhood identity nonetheless.

106. It might be said that NI churches have an even deeper commitment to a mission of creating community than that typical of the New Community model, simply given their stress on proximate living; they actively encourage relocation and residency within the neighborhood.

107. Craig Van Gelder has famously quipped that the Sunday worship hour has replaced church in America; cited in Lois Barrett, *Treasure in Clay Jars: Patterns in Missional Faithfulness* (Grand Rapids, MI: Eerdmans, 2004), 110.

108. Volf, *After Our Likeness*.

109. Sparks, Soerens, and Friesen, *The New Parish*, 147.

110. Many NI churches give serious thought to how their form of life represents an authentic expression of thier theological tradition. Moreover, most NI churches do satisfy expectations for religious groups in the congregational template, including providing opportunities for worship, fellowship, religious education for children, and outreach. What is novel is how often NI churches *originate* from fellowship or outreach initiatives and mature to include worship, rather than the reverse. On the congregational template, see Ammerman, *Pillars of Faith*, 67.

111. R. Stephen Warner, "Religion and New (Post-1965) Immigrants: Some Principles Drawn from Field Research," *American Studies* 41 (Summer/Fall 2000): 277.

112. The beauty beheld by NI churches in their neighborhoods is not always apparent to the naked eye. While some are located in vibrant hubs of urban life, even those surrounded by blight and brokenness describe their places as full of hope and beauty. David, a man I met at Awake who appeared to be under-housed or homeless, regaled me with a tale of his own eye-opening epiphany to the beauty of the weeds in a local alley.

113. This is one of three components of Union's mission. The other two are an event space and a church community that impacts the neighborhood through worship, prayer, and service.

114. National Conference on Citizenship, *Greater Seattle* (2013), 10.

115. See Oldenburg, *The Great Good Place*.

116. In 2016, a new church, aptly called Bar Church, began working toward launching a bar called "The Cathedral" as a third place. See www.barchurch.com.

117. Lisa Carlson, presentation at Inhabit Conference 2014, Seattle, August 15, 2014.

118. Stories of affirmation from the local community were shared by multiple NI leaders, always validating the unique forms of rooted ministry taking place. This may be especially meaningful to NI churches given the innovative and pioneering nature of their ecclesial life.

119. This approach may be connected to the distinctive emphasis among NI churches upon Christian maturity being evident in Christ-like character.

120. "Faithful presence" is an important mode of mission/ecclesiology in contemporary discourse. James Davidson Hunter prescribes it as an alternative to counterproductive and unfaithful political maneuvering; James D. Hunter, *To Change the World: The Irony, Tragedy, and Possibility of Christianity in the Late Modern World* (New York: Oxford University Press, 2010). The Seattle-based co-author of *The New Parish*, Tim Soerens defines faithful presence as "Entering into your present circumstance responsive to both your limitations and responsibilities for relating to God, to others, and to the created world"; Tim Soerens, comment on David Fitch's blog, August 19, 2015 (at 2:20 P.M.), http://www.missioalliance.org/to-change-the-world-by-james-davison-hunter-five-years-later. David Fitch, B. R. Lindner Chair of Evangelical Theology at Northern Seminary and author of *Faithful Presence: Seven Disciplines that Shape the Church for Mission* (Downers Grove, IL: IVP Books, 2016), defines it in this way:

> Faithful presence names wherever a people gather to become present to Christ. In becoming present to Christ we in turn are enabled to be present to His presence in the world. We are able to participate in His work. It is in and through this faithful presence that His Kingdom breaks in to our lives. It is out of this faithful presence that we invite the world into God's Kingdom in Christ. This is the nature of all true witness: faithful presence.

Fitch posted this definition in a comment on his blog post; see David Fitch, "To Change the World by James Davison Hunter: Five Years Later," *Missio Alliance*, August 19, 2015, www.missioalliance.org/to-change-the-world-by-james-davison-hunter-five-years-later/.

121. The four spirituality patterns in the field are Evangelical, Spirit-filled, Progressive, and Sacramental-liturgical. See chapter 2 of this volume for a discussion of their constituent variables.

122. Community Dinners stresses personal prayers of blessing and healing for the guests at their meals as a primary ministry. Valley & Mountain prayed for "peace and justice in our neighborhoods, in the Rainier Valley, in the Puget Sound region and in all the communities of the earth." Union's mission statement envisions prayer as one of the primary ways they impact their neighborhood.

123. Rev. Randy Phillips, Emmanuel Annual Report June 2012, p. 2, www.emmanuelphinneyridge.org/wp-content/media/EmmanuelAnnualReport2012-2.pdf.

124. The primary patterns that seem to be mixed and matched in various ways are across the field: commitment to the Great Commission, Sacramental-liturgical spirituality, Progressive values, and Neighborhood identity; virtually all new Seattle churches embody one or more of these key patterns.

125. These likely include a Sacramental ethnic-immigrant type and a semi-progressive Evangelical megachurch multisite model, and are discussed briefly in chapter 7 of this volume.

126. Indeed, the average NI church was started mid-2009, which is two years after the average HS was founded (mid-2007) and roughly one year after the average GCT and NC was launched (mid-2008).

127. Bryan Stone makes an argument for the inadequacy of effectiveness as a measure of faithful witness, in Bryan P. Stone, *Evangelism After Christendom: The Theology and Practice of Christian Witness* (Grand Rapids, MI: Brazos Press, 2007), 125.

CHAPTER 5: MISSIONAL THEOLOGICAL ASSESSMENT

1. Healy, *Church, World and the Christian Life*, 50.

2. As Dulles notes, each paradigm "brings with it a particular sent of preferred problems." Dulles, *Models of the Church*, 23.

3. Dana L. Robert, *Christian Mission: How Christianity Became a World Religion* (Malden, MA: Wiley-Blackwell, 2009), 68.

4. According to Van Gelder and Zscheile, the word "missional" first appeared in *The Heroes of African Discovery and Adventure, from the Death of Livingstone to the Year 1882*, written in 1883 by C. E. Borne. See Craig Van Gelder and Dwight J. Zscheile, *The Missional Church in Perspective: Mapping Trends and Shaping the Conversation* (Grand Rapids, MI: Baker Academic, 2011), 42. This book offers an insightful synthesis of the literature that followed the publication of Darrell

L. Guder, ed., *Missional Church: A Vision for the Sending of the Church in North America* (Grand Rapids, MI: Eerdmans, 1998).

5. Minear, *Images of the Church in the New Testament*.

6. Dulles, *Models of Church*, 4. The church which is One is also the church which is Catholic, or universal. In other words, the One church is the diversely embodied church dispersed across the many cultures of the world.

7. Archbishop's Council on Mission and Public Affairs, *Mission-Shaped Church: Church Planting and Fresh Expressions in a Changing Context* (New York: Seabury Books, 2010). For an introduction to the rationale for a "mixed economy" of church, see "What Is the Mixed Economy?" *Fresh Expressions*, www.freshexpressions.org.uk/guide/about/mixedeconomy.

8. According to Robert Schreiter, "reflection on the marks of the church has generally occurred in situations of conflict and controversy. . . . [These struggles] have been of an intrachurch nature. They have been between competing groups within the One church, each claiming to be the true manifestation of the church of Jesus Christ." Robert J. Schreiter, *The New Catholicity: Theology Between the Global and the Local* (Maryknoll, NY: Orbis Books, 2005), 119.

9. This follows the Latin churches' economic construction of the Trinity. More recent scholarship, especially from Luther Seminary, has stressed the need to balance this vision with the Eastern focus on the social Trinity. See Van Gelder and Zscheile, *The Missional Church in Perspective*, 27.

10. Barth articulated this line of thought as early as 1932, speaking of *missio* as "the expression of the divine sending forth of self, the sending of the Son and Holy Spirit to the world" at the Breadenburg Mission Conference. Van Gelder and Zscheile, *The Missional Church in Perspective*, 26–27. Barth's influence on missionary thinking peaked in his 1952 Willingen Conference of the International Missionary Council. See Bosch, *Transforming Mission*, 390.

11. Bosch, *Transforming Mission*, 390.

12. Ibid.

13. Lesslie Newbigin, *The Open Secret: An Introduction to the Theology of Mission* (Grand Rapids, MI: Eerdmans, 1995), 55.

14. Lesslie Newbigin, *The Gospel in a Pluralist Society* (Grand Rapids, MI: Eerdmans, 1989), 119.

15. Jürgen Moltmann, *The Church in the Power of the Spirit: A Contribution to Messianic Ecclesiology* (Minneapolis: Fortress Press, 1993), 64.

16. The same could be said of all Christian practices and life, as well as more fundamentally of human life. As Paul, citing a pagan poet, affirmed, "In him we live and move and have our being" (Acts 17:28; NRSV).

17. Lesslie Newbigin, *Trinitarian Doctrine for Today's Mission* (Eugene, OR: Wipf & Stock, 2006), 83.

18. This union of heaven and earth is the climax of John's vision on Patmos:

> I saw the Holy City, the new Jerusalem, coming down out of heaven from
> God, prepared as a bride beautifully dressed for her husband. And I heard
> a loud voice from the throne saying, "Look! God's dwelling place is now
> among the people, and he will dwell with them. They will be his people,
> and God himself will be with them and be their God." (Rev. 21:2–4, TNIV)

19. Jesus never spoke of building or extending the kingdom, certainly not as some-
    thing people would have the agency to do with respect to God's Reign. See George
    R. Hunsberger, "Is There Biblical Warrant for Evangelism?," in *The Study of
    Evangelism: Exploring a Missional Practice of the Church*, ed. Paul W. Chilcote and
    Laceye C. Warner (Grand Rapids, MI: Eerdmans, 2008), 66–67.
20. Reflections on the implications of the Reign of God for missional ecclesiology are
    plentiful. For example, see George R. Hunsberger, "Missional Vocation: Called
    and Sent to Represent the Reign of God," in *Missional Church: A Vision for the
    Sending of the Church in North America*, ed. Darrell L. Guder (Grand Rapids,
    MI: Eerdmans, 1998), 77–109; Darrell L. Guder, "Pointing Toward the Reign of
    God," in *Treasure in Clay Jars: Patterns in Missional Faithfulness*, ed. Lois Y. Barrett
    (Grand Rapids, MI: Eerdmans, 2004), 126–138; Alan J. Roxburgh and M. Scott
    Boren, *Introducing the Missional Church: What It Is, Why It Matters, How to
    Become One* (Grand Rapids, MI: Baker Books, 2009), 101–114; Van Gelder and
    Zscheile, *The Missional Church in Perspective*, 55–57.
21. Guder, *Missional Church*, 4.
22. Within the mission literature of the early twentieth century it was common to
    describe non-Christian religions as "preparation" for Christianity and the gospel
    as the "fulfillment" of what is good and true within other religions. For an out-
    standing example, see John N. Farquhar, *The Crown of Hinduism* (London: Oxford
    University Press, 1913).
23. As Jacob, awaking from a vision-filled night in Bethel, said, "Surely the LORD is
    in this place, and I was not aware of it" (Gen. 28:16).
24. Newbigin, *Trinitarian Doctrine for Today's Mission*, 36. EIRO, a missional faith-
    based neighborhood-focused initiative in Tucker, Georgia, predicated a recent
    consultation among local leaders on this premise: "As a prerequisite to this
    conversation, we must assume that God is already at work in the communities
    where we live, work, and worship." See Shawn Duncan and Holly Duncan, "An
    Experiment: Riding the Casino Bus," *The Missional Network*, 2015, http://the-
    missionalnetwork.com/who/your-story/an-experiment-riding-the-casino-bus.
25. As Stuart Murray has noted, "church planting that fails to engage with the mis-
    sion agenda of Jesus can easily become church-centered rather than kingdom-
    oriented." Stuart Murray, *Church Planting: Laying Foundations* (Scottdale,
    PA: Herald Press, 2001), 43.
26. Father Richard Rohr has called Jesus the "Archetypal Blueprint for what God has
    been doing all the time and everywhere," noting that the Christmas miracle was

simply the pinnacle of the incarnational practice God began in creation. "Christ Is Plan A," Richard Rohr's Daily Meditation, last modified May 31, 2015, http://myemail.constantcontact.com/Richard-Rohr-s-Meditation--Christ-Is-Plan-A.ht ml?soid=1103098668616&aid=0JLPLPZSMYw.

27. Darrell L. Guder, *The Incarnation and the Church's Witness*, (Eugene, OR: Wipf & Stock, 2005), xii.

28. Van Gelder and Zscheile, *The Missional Church in Perspective*, 114.

29. Phil. 2:5–11. Wilbert Shenk stresses the importance of Jesus's death for Christian witness by asserting that "Mission is patterned after the example of Jesus the Messiah; that is, mission is cruciform." Wilbert Shenk, "New Wineskins for New Wine: Toward a Post-Christendom Ecclesiology," *International Bulletin of Missionary Research* 29, no. 2 (April 2005): 78.

30. Guder, *The Incarnation and the Church's Witness*, xiii.

31. Murray, *Church Planting*, 42.

32. Thus, Newbigin writes, "anything in the nature of manipulation, any exploiting of weakness, any use of coercion, anything other than 'the manifestation of the truth in the sight of God' (2 Corinthians 4:2) has no place in true evangelism." Lesslie Newbigin, "Evangelism in the City," *Expository Times* 98 (September 1987): 355–358. Bryan Stone agrees, "Christian evangelism . . . is pacifist in every way . . . [rejecting] every violent means of converting others to that peace, whether that violence is cultural, military, political, spiritual, or intellectual." Stone, *Evangelism after Christendom*, 11.

33. "Jesus . . . does not seek to take control himself of world history. He rejects every temptation to become himself a ruler and director of events. . . . Nor does he seek to launch a movement which will have power to control world events. When his disciples seek to take such power into their own hands he rebukes them." Newbigin, *Trinitarian Doctrine for Today's Mission*, 39. For biblical examples, see Matt. 20:26, John 18:11, and Luke 9:54.

34. I am indebted to philosopher and spiritual writer Dallas Willard for this insight. As he notes on his observations on the way of Jesus the logician, "Jesus does not try to make everything so explicit that the conclusion is forced down the throat of his hearer. Rather, he presents matters in such a way that those who wish to know can find their way to, can come to, the appropriate conclusion as something they have discovered. . . . [This is decidedly not] the experience of being outdone or beaten down." Dallas Willard, *The Great Omission: Reclaiming Jesus' Essential Teachings on Discipleship* (New York: HarperOne, 2006), 183.

35. Murray, *Church Planting*, 43.

36. Lesslie Newbigin, *Mission in Christ's Way: Bible Studies* (Geneva: WCC Publications, 1987), 11.

37. Newbigin, *The Gospel in a Pluralist Society*, 152.

38. Christopher B. James, "Mission-Shaped Church 2: Book Review," *Jesus Dust*, October 2012, www.jesusdust.com/2012/10/mission-shaped-church-2-book-review.html.

39. Michael Moynagh and Philip Harrold, *Church for Every Context: An Introduction to Theology and Practice* (London: SCM Press, 2012), 105.

40. Newbigin, *The Household of God*, 163.

41. Ibid., 162.

42. Lesslie Newbigin, *Unfinished Agenda: An Autobiography* (London: SPCK, 1985), 138.

43. Johannes Blauw, *The Missionary Nature of the Church: A Survey of the Biblical Theology of Mission* (Cambridge: Lutterworth Press, 2003), 120. Blauw's biblically and theologically developed missionary ecclesiology led him to the "conviction that the Church has been manifested more clearly in the much-defamed groups of 'friends of mission' than in the 'official Church,' which at best accepted a benevolently neutral attitude toward mission" (113).

44. Newbigin, *The Open Secret: An Introduction to the Theology of Mission*, 110.

45. Newbigin, *The Household of God*, 114.

46. Ibid.

47. Theologians influenced by Anabaptist thought are among the most insistent and insightful on this topic. Stanley Hauerwas and, most seminally, John H. Yoder, also develop this core idea of missional ecclesiology. For are recent contribution to missional theology and practice from the Anabaptist tradition, see Stanley W. Green and James R. Krabill, eds., *Fully Engaged: Missional Church in an Anabaptist Voice* (Harrisonburg, VA: Herald Press, 2015).

48. Lohfink advanced an understanding of churches as "contrast societies," in Gerhard Lohfink, *Jesus and Community: The Social Dimension of Christian Faith* (Philadelphia: Fortress Press, 1984), chap. 7. This language picked up by others, most notably, by Will Willimon and Stanley Hauerwas in *Resident Aliens: Life in the Christian Colony* (Nashville, TN: Abingdon Press, 1989). Similar thinking on the missional church as contrast community can be found in Barrett, *Treasure in Clay Jars*, 74–83; and Roxburgh and Boren, *Introducing the Missional Church*, chap. 7.

49. See George R. Hunsberger and Linford Stutzman, "The Public Witness of Worship," in *Treasure in Clay Jars: Patterns in Missional Faithfulness*, ed. Lois Y. Barrett (Grand Rapids, MI: Eerdmans, 2004), 100–116.

50. See Barrett, *Treasure in Clay Jars*, 84–99.

51. Newbigin, "Evangelism in the City," 357.

52. Bosch names the local church as "the primary agent of mission" (*Transforming Mission*, 380). Multiple missional authors have stressed the primacy of the particular congregation in missional perspective. See Guder, *Missional Church*, chap. 8.

    Others have highlighted the importance of a neighborhood orientation among missional churches. See, for example, Alan J. Roxburgh, *Missional: Joining God in the Neighborhood* (Grand Rapids, MI: Baker Books, 2011); and Darrell L. Guder, "Converting the Church: The Local Congregation," in *The Continuing Conversion of the Church*, 7th ed. (Grand Rapids, MI: Eerdmans, 2000), 145–180.

53. Guder, *Missional Church*, 233.
54. Newbigin, *The Gospel in a Pluralist Society*, 232.
55. Ibid., 227. More recently, biblical scholar Michael Gorman has described the church as "a living exegesis of the gospel of God," in Michael J. Gorman, *Becoming the Gospel: Paul, Participation, and Mission: The Gospel and Our Culture* (Grand Rapids, MI: Eerdmans, 2015), 43.
56. From his experience as a missionary in India, Newbigin observes that the "common factor" at work in instances where "people were being drawn to Christ, converted and baptized" was the presence of a believing, worshipping, celebrating congregation of people deeply involved in the ordinary life of their neighbourhood." Newbigin, *Mission in Christ's Way*, 20.
57. As Bosch put it, "for many centuries 'local churches' did not exist, neither in Europe nor on the 'mission fields.'" Bosch, *Transforming Mission*, 379.
58. The congregational nature of missional ecclesiology is not tied explicitly to congregational polity. It is, however, the key reason that this study has focused upon individual local churches in their spiritual, missional, and identity dimensions.
59. Bosch, *Transforming Mission*, 380. Vatican Document *Lumen Gentium* (26) declares that the "Church of Christ is really present in all legitimately organized local groups of the faithful" and that in these local communities "Christ is present through whose power and influence the One, Holy, Catholic and Apostolic Church is constituted." Darrell Guder describes a "growing consensus in worldwide Christianity that the local congregation is the basic unit of Christian witness" (*Continuing Conversion*, 145). Of course, the Anabaptist tradition had come to this conclusion regarding the ecclesiological priority of the local congregation centuries earlier.
60. Bosch, *Transforming Mission*, 378. This ecclesiological shift to the particular coincided with the recognition among the European sending churches that the "younger churches" ought to be regarded as equals (379).
61. Other exceptions include *Church Planting* by Stuart Murray, and *Mission-Shaped Church* by the Archbishop's Council on Mission and Public Affairs. See also Mary Sue D. Dreier, ed., *Created and Led by the Spirit: Planting Missional Congregations* (Grand Rapids, MI: Eerdmans, 2013) and Michael Frost and Christiana Rice, *To Alter Your World: Partnering with God to Rebirth Our Communities* (Downers Grove, IL: IVP Books, 2017).
62. Citations in the following paragraphs for Branson's first priority can be found in Mark L. Branson, "Perspectives from the Missional Conversation," in *Starting Missional Churches: Life with God in the Neighborhood*, ed. Mark L. Branson and Nicholas Warnes (Downers Grove, IL: IVP Books, 2014), 37–38.
63. Branson, "Perspectives from the Missional Conversation," 37. Here Branson is borrowing a phrase popularized by Alan Roxburgh.
64. Indeed, Jesus, the human participant in the *missio Dei* par excellence regularly withdrew to discern, and throughout his ministry declared of the primacy of

God's agency: "the Spirit of the Lord is upon me for he has anointed me to preach good news to the poor." (Luke 4:18–19); "the Son can do nothing by himself; he can do only what he sees his Father doing, because whatever the Father does the Son also does" (John 5:19).

65. George Hunsberger suggests that the call of the missional church is to discern its missional vocation by asking where, when, who, and why they are. Hunsberger, "Missional Vocation."

66. In fact, attention to, discernment of, and participation in God's life and activity among us are foundational to the practice of Christian life and Christian community in general.

67. Branson, "Perspectives from the Missional Conversation," 37.

68. Ibid.

69. Ibid., 38.

70. Ibid.

71. Ibid.

72. Branson attributes this insight to Alan Roxburgh. Ibid., 39.

73. Ibid.

74. Newbigin, *The Gospel in a Pluralist Society*, 82–83.

75. Branson, "Perspectives from the Missional Conversation," 39.

76. The Archbishop's Council on Mission and Public Affairs offers a partial defense of the homogeneous unit principle in *Mission-Shaped Church*, inviting church planters to "accept initial cultural similarity while seeking gradual cultural diversity, expressed in interdependence between groups unlike one another" (109). Michael Moynagh and Philip Harrold do the same in *Church for Every Context*, chap. 9.

77. Branson, "Perspectives from the Missional Conversation," 40.

78. Lesslie Newbigin, *A South India Diary* (SCM Press, 1951), 49–50; and Newbigin, *The Household of God*, 149–150.

79. Lesslie Newbigin, "Pastoral Ministry in a Pluralist Society," in *Witnessing Church: Essays in Honour of the Rt. Rev. Masilamani Azaraiah, Bishop in Madras, Published and Released on the Occasion of His Manivizha Celebrations*, ed. Chris Theodore (Madras, India: Christian Literature Society of India, 1994), 152.

80. Branson, "Perspectives from the Missional Conversation," 40.

81. See Acts, chapters 10–15.

82. Dana Robert argues that the whole of "mission history can be explained as a series of boundary-crossings, driven by a universalist logic." Robert, *Christian Mission*, x–xi.

83. Branson, "Perspectives from the Missional Conversation," 41. Other missional authors have appealed for similar visions of leadership, including Alan Roxburgh in chap. 8 of *Missional Church*; Jeff Van Kooten and Lois Barrett, in Barrett, ed., *Treasure in Clay Jars*, Pattern 8, 139–148; and more recently, J. R. Woodward in *Creating a Missional Culture* (Downers Grove, IL: IVP Books, 2012).

84. Branson, "Perspectives from the Missional Conversation," 41.
85. See Eph. 4:12.
86. Branson, "Perspectives from the Missional Conversation," 42–45.
87. Van Gelder and Zscheile, *The Missional Church in Perspective*, 156. This quotation is cited by Branson, "Perspectives from the Missional Conversation," 41.
88. Branson, "Perspectives from the Missional Conversation," 41.
89. For discussion of what GCT churches understand as "the Gospel," see chapter 4.
90. As Van Gelder and Zscheile point out, missional theology has helped Evangelicals of the sort found among new Seattle churches "to begin to bridge the classic dichotomy that has plagued much of the Evangelical world: the separation of evangelism and social involvement." Van Gelder and Zscheile, *The Missional Church in Perspective*, 75.
91. Luke 19:10.
92. Persons at The Hallows testified to God having "brought people into our life" and "paved the way to build a relationship with [the local elementary school]" and "widening the net of our influence." Various participants, interviews by author, Seattle, 2014.
93. Peter Berger's insights regarding the role of "sustaining conversations" in maintaining faith are relevant here. See Berger, *The Sacred Canopy*, 21–22. This insight is reflected in Nancy Ammerman's finding that "sacred consciousness" is strongest among those who practice their spirituality religiously—that is, who practice it regularly and communally in spiritual contexts that facilitate conversation about their everyday lives. Ammerman, *Sacred Stories, Spiritual Tribes*, 292–304. When churches provide spaces for regular conversation about the practice of evangelism and attending to God's missionary call and transformative work, their members become sensitized to these dynamics in daily life and it shows through in their narratives. These conversations generate and sustain a religious vision of the world, a "sacred consciousness." A similar dynamic is evident in Tanya Luhrmann's excellent study, *When God Talks Back*. If and how we regularly talk about God with reference to our daily lives largely determines if and how we will be able to notice God as a part of our daily lives.
94. Van Gelder and Zscheile, *The Missional Church in Perspective*, 75.
95. The following paragraphs are substantially excerpted from a paper written by the author for a directed study with Dr. Bryan Stone, Boston University School of Theology, Christopher B. James, "Theologies of Church Planting: Comparing Malphurs and Murray," *Jesus Dust*, October 2012, www.jesusdust.com/2012/10/theologies-of-church-planting-comparing.html.
96. Roland Allen, *Missionary Methods: St. Paul's or Ours?* (Grand Rapids, MI: Eerdmans, 1962), 93.
97. For example, Paul instructs slaves to be submissive "so that God's name and our teaching may not be slandered," (1 Tim. 6:1).

98. David J. Bosch, "The Structure of Mission: An Exposition of Matthew 28:16–20," in *The Study of Evangelism: Exploring a Missional Practice of the Church*, ed. Paul W. Chilcote and Laceye C. Warner (Grand Rapids, MI: Eerdmans, 2008), 76–78; Hunsberger, "Is There Biblical Warrant for Evangelism?" 63–64.

99. Alan Roxburgh challenges the dominance of the Great Commission text in missionary imagination on a more contextual basis:

> What starts to emerge is that the paradigmatic nature of Matthew 28 in the social, economic, and geopolitical framing of the last century and a half may no longer have the capacity to frame a Christian imagination in this new space. The language house of empire, power, and control with which Matthew 28 has been invested is an imaginary that can no longer provide us with the resources to understand what Christian life and witness might be in this new place. (Roxburgh, *Missional*, 88)

100. According to Newbigin, there is significant "danger in a kind of thinking which founds the whole missionary task solely upon the doctrine of the person and work of Christ and of the continuing work of the Church which is his body." Newbigin suggests that what is called for is greater attention to the doctrine of the triune nature of God. Newbigin, *Trinitarian Doctrine for Today's Mission*, 82.

101. Van Gelder and Zscheile, *The Missional Church in Perspective*, 75.

102. John 3:8.

103. Van Gelder and Zscheile, *The Missional Church in Perspective*, 75.

104. Humility and mission are the key attributes praised by GCT churches in their exemplars of spiritual maturity. See chapter 4 of this volume, "Spirituality Among Great Commission Team Churches."

105. Van Gelder and Zscheile, *The Missional Church in Perspective*, 75. Sociologist Peter Berger insightfully describes how religious legitimation works: "Religion legitimates social institutions by bestowing on them an ultimately valid ontological status, that is, by locating them within a sacred and cosmic frame of reference . . . Human power, government, and punishment thus become sacramental." Berger, *The Sacred Canopy*, 33–39.

106. This is in contrast to a missional understanding in which the work of ministry is cooperative participation in the *missio Dei* and suitability to the instructions of Jesus with regard to leadership found in Luke 22:24–30.

107. Blaise Pascal is typically credited for first articulating this idea, thanks to this passage:

> What else does this craving, and this helplessness, proclaim but that there was once in man a true happiness, of which all that now remains is the empty print and trace? This he tries in vain to fill with everything around him, seeking in things that are not there the help he cannot find in those that are, though none can help, since this infinite abyss can be filled only with

an infinite and unchangeable object; in other words by God himself. (Blaise Pascal, *Pensees*, trans. A. J. Krailsheimer [London: Penguin Classics, 1995], 45)

108. This was most clearly observed among Community Dinners, a HS/NI church whose missionaries unwittingly approached their table guests as those in need of what the church had to offer—food and spiritual blessing. In one account, the missionary approached a guest with an intention of engaging in "spiritual warfare" to free the individual from addiction to alcohol and was stopped short by a powerful, corporeal experience of Jesus asserting, "Back off! I've got him."

109. As Emmanuel Levinas asserted, encountering the face of the other rejects totalizing efforts: "The face of the Other constantly destroys and overflows the plastic image." That is, the other overturns the ideas we have of the other that are modeled after ourselves." Emmanuel Levinas, *Totality and Infinity: An Essay on Exteriority* (Pittsburgh, PA: Duquesne University Press, 1969), 51.

110. Zscheile and Van Gelder note that in much of the missional literature, focus on the incarnation functions primarily as a way to talk about contextualization. Van Gelder and Zscheile, *Missional Church in Perspective*, 114.

111. Ibid.

112. Stone, *Evangelism After Christendom*, 18.

113. Alan J. Roxburgh, *Moving Back into the Neighborhood: The Workbook* (West Vancouver, BC: Roxburgh Missional Network, 2010), 48.

114. Craig Van Gelder, *The Essence of the Church: A Community Cr Disestablishment eated by the Spirit* (Grand Rapids, MI: Baker Books, 2000), 87. See Luke 18:17–30, Matt.6:33, and Matt. 25:34.

115. Branson, "Perspectives from the Missional Conversation," 37.

116. Van Gelder and Zscheile, *The Missional Church in Perspective*, 84.

117. Ibid., 75.

118. Chapter 6 of this volume offers practical proposals for practitioners and theologians working with churches that embody the Great Commission Team practical ecclesiology.

119. HS churches reflect particular resonance with "Dependence on the Holy Spirit," a pattern among missional congregations explored in Barrett, *Treasure in Clay Jars*, 117–125.

120. This may be more characteristic of the HS churches studied—which were disproportionately Anglo and overlapping with the NI model—than of the churches in the model as a whole.

121. See John 8:28, Heb. 7:25, and Rom. 8:26.

122. Ps. 103:3. As in Mark 2:1–12, forgiveness and healing are often paired in the ministry of Jesus.

123. See chapter 4 of this volume, "Mission Among Household of the Spirit Churches."

124. Accounts of Jesus's healings and exorcisms are abundant in the Gospels. For examples of Jesus's prophetic words of encouragement, see the Beatitudes (Matt. 5:3–12 and Luke 6:20–26), as well as Mark 14:8 and Matt. 19:14.

125. Newbigin, *The Gospel in a Pluralist Society*, 197.
126. Branson, "Perspectives from the Missional Conversation," 37.
127. Sacramental traditions, at their best, while worship centered, awaken worshipers to the presence of God in the ordinary stuff of life.
128. Andy Lord makes a similar critique in his proposal for a Pentecostal missiology, noting that "This mission of God, *missio Dei*, is worked out through the church in the wider world and also directly in the world outside the church." Andy Lord, *Network Church: A Pentecostal Ecclesiology Shaped by Mission* (Leiden: Brill, 2012), 30.
129. My in-depth research among Community Dinners led me to several testimonies that challenged the prevailing notion that the church folks were those who brought the divine presence into the room. I came to refer to these as accounts in which Jesus showed up "on the other side of the table," that is, as the other.
130. In extreme cases, Spirit-filled forms of Christianity produce self-proclaimed apostles and prophets.
131. This is unlike the practice of hospitality, which intrinsically inclines toward experiences of mutuality.
132. See 1 Cor. 12:7.
133. Branson, "Perspectives from the Missional Conversation," 42–46.
134. Newbigin, *The Gospel in a Pluralist Society*, chap. 18.
135. Among the small, opportunistic sample of churches that Branson and Warnes worked with for *Starting Missional Churches*, "worship that is participatory for neighbors" was found to be a common attribute. Branson and Warnes, *Starting Missional Churches*, 192.
136. NC churches speak of and reflect on the Trinity with more intentionality and regularity than the other models. The focus of these reflections, however, tends toward Eastern constructions of the social Trinity, rather than the Western, economic formulations that have most directly informed missional theology. This syncs well with their embrace of divine mystery. The Trinity, NC churches suggest, is not so much to be understood as to be pondered.
137. Pastor Hillesland's words before Communion included, "Take Christ within your bodies, become the body of Christ." Rev. Ivar Hillesland, spoken during worship, Seattle, July 28, 2014.
138. The foil against which their contrast stands out most clearly for NC churches is not, however, the world, but what they perceive to be conservative Evangelicalism's dogmatic and judgmental practice.
139. This echoes the humility that Darrell Guder noted as an aspect of "Pattern 7: Pointing Toward the Reign of God," in Barrett, *Treasure in Clay Jars*, as well as the overall thrust of Guder, *The Continuing Conversion of the Church*.
140. The burdensome duty and spiritual anxiety among GCT and HS churches are rooted theologically in their inflated sense of the church's role in the *missio Dei*.
141. This is a key reason for their reticence toward "evangelism."

142. Nikki MacMillian, Pastor of The Light @ Bare Bulb Coffee, a PC(USA) new worshiping community in Georgia, makes this point: "The boundary that we are crossing with much intentionality is the boundary between the sacred and the secular." Quoted in Branson and Warnes, *Starting Missional Churches*, 119.

143. Marti and Ganiel describe the emerging church movement (ECM) as reflecting disdain for two major conversation partners: "the seeker megachurch" and the "solemn mainline" experience. Marti and Ganiel, *The Deconstructed Church*, 110. For other sources of ECM, see Doug Gay, *Remixing the Church: Towards an Emerging Ecclesiology* (London: SCM Press, 2011).

144. Marti and Ganiel, *The Deconstructed Church*, 25–26. Marti and Ganiel also describe Emerging Christians as "proactive" inasmuch as they "*proactively* appropriate practices from a range of Christian traditions (Gay's "DIY" ecumenism) to nourish their individual spirituality and to enhance their life together as communities." The reference to "Gay's DIY ecumenism" points to Doug Gay's *Remixing the Church*.

145. This practical wisdom is evident in the strengths of GCT churches already discussed.

146. By "evangelism" I mean active Christian witness seeking participate with God's redeeming work of conversion and the formation of a new humanity. While the life of the church itself witnesses to this new humanity and offers an implicit invitation, I reserve the term "evangelism" for activities explicitly oriented toward invitation and initiation into the Reign of God. For a fuller description, see Christopher B. James, "Defining the 'E'-Word: Evangelism as a Christian Practice," *Jesus Dust*, October 2013, www.jesusdust.com/2013/10/defining-e-word-evangelism-as-christian.html.

147. Exceptions are seen among the NC churches that engage in regular advocacy. However, it is conspicuous that the issues on which NC church advocate are almost universally congruent with progressive culture. Even when NC mission becomes proactive, then, it is questionable whether it originates in the Reign of God or whether their mission simply reflects a sacralized version of the agenda (mission) of social progressives. This observation is matched by studies that have found that Evangelical Christians donate more of their time and resources than their mainline counterparts. See Julia Duin, "Giving in Different Denominations," *Philanthropy*, 2001, www.philanthropyroundtable.org/topic/excellence_in_philanthropy/giving_in_different_denominations; "New Study Shows Trends in Tithing and Donating," *Barna.org*, last modified April 14, 2008, www.barna.org/barna-update/congregations/41-new-study-shows-trends-in-tithing-and-donating#.VgieSKJDklM.

148. This reflects the tension between Western emphasis on the "economic Trinity" and Eastern emphasis on the "social Trinity."

149. "The character of Christian evangelism is not only invitation but also summons." Stone, *Evangelism After Christendom*, 12.

150. The points of cultural critique I found among NC churches included critique of individualism and the ways that technology facilitates isolation.

151. H. R. Niebuhr also asserts that liberals mistakenly believe that cultural accommodation is more effective at gaining disciples than countercultural approaches, end up distorting the New Testament figure of Jesus, and have given their fundamental loyalty to contemporary culture; Niebuhr, *Christ and Culture*, chap. 3.

152. Lesslie Newbigin, "A British and European Perspective," in *Entering the Kingdom: A Fresh Look at Conversion*, ed. Monica Hill (Middlesex: British Church Growth Association and MARC Europe, 1986), 60.

153. Lesslie Newbigin, *Foolishness to the Greeks: The Gospel and Western Culture* (Grand Rapids, MI: Eerdmans, 1986), 22.

154. Interestingly, Marti and Ganiel found emerging churches in their study to be more diverse than the other congregations in their area. I did not have a similar finding in a comparison between NC churches and the other models the Seattle context, although NC churches are, I suspect, somewhat more diverse than the other churches in their mainline denominations. Marti and Ganiel, *The Deconstructed Church*.

155. See Roxburgh and Boren, *Introducing the Missional Church*, 33–34. Also, Van Gelder and Zscheile, *The Missional Church in Perspective*, 8–9.

156. D. A. Carson develops a similar line of critique in his analysis of emerging church authors. Carson, *Becoming Conversant with the Emerging Church*, chap. 6.

157. Luke Bretherton, *Hospitality as Holiness: Christian Witness Amid Moral Diversity* (London: Ashgate Publishing, 2006), 147.

158. Jesus's defense of the woman caught in adultery in John 8 is perhaps the most stunning picture of this. He does not condemn, and yet he calls the woman to "go and sin no more."

159. The Christian response to those with whom we disagree is not tolerance. It is hospitality. Bretherton, *Hospitality as Holiness*, 147–151.

160. In fact, this is a liability of all forms of Christian gatherings, community, and practice simply because Americans are formed as consumers. HS and NC churches, however, are the most at risk of losing missional identity as a result because within these models the worship gathering is the clear, singular focal point of the church's life.

161. Among the small, opportunistic sample of churches that Branson and Warnes worked with for *Starting Missional Churches*, they found "focus on a geographic place" to be a common attribute (192).

162. Newbigin, "Evangelism in the City," 357.

163. This is evident among some NC members who affirm God's presence in the ordinary and everyday primarily as a rationale against Evangelical practices like devoted time to personal Bible reading and prayer, rather than as the basis for alternative disciplines for attending to God.

164. It is easy to assert that if God is everywhere, there is no reason one should have to go anywhere to look for God. Not only does this often undercut church attendance, but it can be mistaken to suggest that place is irrelevant—God is everywhere, so nowhere is special, nor calls for special intentionality. Its logic is often extended to undermine the importance of other spiritual practices—prayer, Scripture, solitude, etc.—that tune persons to the presence and voice of God.

165. A form of shorthand prayer common among NI churches adapts the Lord's Prayer, praying, "Thy Kingdom come, thy will be done in [neighborhood name] as it is in heaven." Such a prayer not only confesses the imperfection of the context but also positions the church to anticipate (and participate in) various fulfillments of this prayer. The prayer itself invites a critical missional question: What would it look like if the kingdom came to our neighborhood—and how might we join God in that beautiful future breaking in? GCT churches reflect their own larger frame of reference in their city-size prayers: "Thy Kingdom come, thy will be done, in Seattle as it is in heaven."

166. "In order to receive God's saving revelation we have to open the door to the neighbor whom he sends as his appointed messenger, and—moreover—to receive that messenger not as a temporary teacher or guide who we can dispense with when we ourselves have learned what is needed, but as one who will permanently share our home." Newbigin, *The Gospel in a Pluralist Society*, 83.

167. According to Cheri DiNovo, "evangelism is a movement and that movement is from the queerest of those in our area of ministry to ourselves as church. . . . [E]vangelism is a movement outside/in. . . . [T]he church is the object and not the subject of this movement called evangelism." Cheri DiNovo, *Qu(e)erying Evangelism: Growing a Community from the Outside in* (Cleveland, OH: Pilgrim Press, 2005), 19.

168. This matches Branson's priority of plural leadership that shapes an environment.

169. Neighborhood Incarnation practitioner Karen Reed notes that being available and attentive is "not a passive stance. It's a very active stance where there's this living with the sense of ambiguity, but with a sense of openness and attentiveness and without insisting on this game plan. That you are kind of cooperating with God's game plan." Karen Reed, "Living Slowly in the City," *Journal of Missional Practice*, Summer 2015, http://journalofmissionalpractice.com/living-slowly-in-the-city.

170. According to Alan Roxburgh, "the problem with the "network" idea is the same problem faced and not addressed by too many local churches—homogeneity. . . . The boundary-breaking Spirit is interested not in re-created homogeneous Euro-tribal church but in calling forth local communities that manifest the new creation in a globalized world. Today most neighborhoods are increasingly ethnically mixed and represent the new religiously plural society North America has become." Roxburgh, *Missional*, 168.

171. See Volf, *After Our Likeness*. Operative congregational theology links the gathering with its traditional context on Sunday morning in a religiously defined space.

172. While few NI churches are intentionally exploring the implications of this ecclesiology for ecumenical relations, their nontraditional shape has led to the involvement of local Christians who are active in other congregations.

173. Paul explicitly took issue with factions within the church divided by their loyalty to various teachers.

174. Lesslie Newbigin, *The Reunion of the Church: A Defence of the South India Scheme* (Eugene, OR: Wipf & Stock, 2011).

175. This is possible of all models, but most pronounced among NC and NI churches because they are the most novel forms of Christian community and, thus, must work the hardest to legitimate their unfamiliar mode of existence. Ed Stetzer describes this as a particular danger of the "missional-incarnational" model: "some Missional Incarnational people are reactionary against the established church. Either through railing against or denigration, they vocally attempt to distant themselves from the established church." Ed Stetzer, "Finding the Right Church Planting Model Part 4: The Missional Incarnational Approach," *The Exchange*, August 17, 2015, www.christianitytoday.com/edstetzer/2015/august/finding-right-church-planting-model-part-4-missional-incarn.html.

176. This popular idea is attributed to Patrick Geddes.

177. For example, Valley & Mountain's involvement with immigrant neighbors informs their activism on immigration reform. The prevalence of drug addiction in the neighborhood in which Awake is located informs the programs they develop in the Aurora Commons. Community Dinners encounters many homeless and under-housed individuals and is pursuing a plan to build and provide low-income housing.

178. The authors (Sparks, Soerens, and Friesen) of *The New Parish* describe this as the need for churches to not only be *rooted* in their local context but also *linked* to outside communities and persons.

179. For research on "the Dones," those who have ceased participating in church but who retain their faith, see Packard and Hope, *Church Refugees*.

180. Rodney Stark, *What Americans Really Believe* (Waco, TX: Baylor University Press, 2008), 10–11.

181. While this means that NI churches are unlikely to attract and include many church-seeking returners, their model of recruitment does not depend on advertising (the normal strategy for attracting people "in the market" for something) but on relationships. However, by forging relationships with their neighbors it is possible that they may involve significant numbers of disinterested individuals who would otherwise be unlikely to ever seek out a congregation to belong to.

182. Newbigin, "Evangelism in the City," 357.

183. Robert D. Putnam and Lewis Feldstein, *Better Together: Restoring the American Community* (New York: Simon & Schuster, 2004), 2.

184. These kinds of relationships with neighbors and fellow community members can go a long way toward reducing crime and promoting the local economy.

185. Andrew Sullivan, "I Used to Be a Human Being," *New York Magazine*, September 18, 2016, http://nymag.com/selectall/2016/09/andrew-sullivan-technology-almost-killed-me.html.

186. This form of naiveté—which posits, simply, that the culture is becoming progressive so the church must become progressive to survive—is prolific and demonstrably false. Progressive churches and denominations, as a group, have lost members and closed churches both earlier and more rapidly than their conservative counterparts. Compare, for example, trends between the Episcopal Church USA, one of the most progressive denominations, and the Southern Baptist Convention, one of the nation's most conservative denominations.

187. Consider the "success" of Mars Hill Church. For sociological analysis of the success of countercultural and "strict" churches, see Dean R. Hoge, Benton Johnson, and Donald A. Luidens, *Vanishing Boundaries: The Religion of Mainline Protestant Baby Boomers* (Louisville, KY: Westminster John Knox Press, 1994); Judith Shulevitz, "The Power of the Mustard Seed: Why Strict Churches Are Strong," *Slate*, May 12, 2005, www.slate.com/articles/life/faithbased/2005/05/the_power_of_the_mustard_seed.html; Laurence R. Iannaccone, "Why Strict Churches Are Strong," *American Journal of Sociology* 99, no. 5 (March 1, 1994): 1180–1211.

188. This superseding of the liberal/conservative polarization is a distinct form boundary-crossing, one of Branson's missional priorities.

189. It is true that the localism of NI churches is more closely associated with liberal than with conservative discourse.

190. On the increase of political polarization in recent years, see Pew Research Center, "Political Polarization in the American Public: How Increasing Ideological Uniformity and Partisan Antipathy Affect Politics, Compromise and Everyday Life," June 12, 2014, www.people-press.org/2014/06/12/political-polarization-in-the-american-public. Tobin Grant's map of American denominations illustrates the state of ecclesiastical polarization; Tobin Grant, "Politics of American Churches & Religions in One Graph," Corner of Church and State, *Religionnews.com*, August 27, 2014, http://tobingrant.religionnews.com/2014/08/27/politics-american-churches-religions-one-graph.

191. Henri J. M. Nouwen, *Reaching Out: The Three Movements of the Spiritual Life* (New York: Image, 1986), 51.

192. See Christine Pohl, *Making Room: Recovering Hospitality as a Christian Tradition* (Grand Rapids, MI: Eerdmans, 1999).

193. Ed Stetzer's reflections on the "missional-incarnational" model of church planting (which substantially overlaps with the NI model) affirm this conclusion. He notes that "Missional Incarnational church plants are more conducive in

urban, post-Christian environments" and concludes that "Over time, I believe this "alternative" model (to the Launch Large option) may very well become (and is becoming) more and more prominent." Stetzer, "Finding the Right Church Planting Model Part 4." Leonard Sweet, E. Stanley Jones Professor of Evangelism at Drew Theological School, makes a similar affirmation in his endorsement of a recently published book that elaborates the Neighborhood Incarnation model. He writes, "[A]ll paths to the future of the church must pass through this book"; see Sparks, Soerens, and Friesen, *The New Parish*, front cover.

194. "All kinds of churches for all kinds of people" is a popular phrase found in the writings of Pastor Rick Warren and many others. See, for example, Rick Warren, "It Takes All Kinds of Churches," *Daily Hope with Rick Warren*, last modified May 21, 2014, http://rickwarren.org/devotional/english/it-takes-all-kinds-of-churches.

CHAPTER 6: RENEWING PRACTICE IN THE MODELS

1. John H. Yoder, *Theology of Mission: A Believers Church Perspective* (Downers Grove, IL: IVP Books, 2013), 177.
2. Guder, *The Continuing Conversion of the Church*, 149.
3. Ibid., 144.
4. Ibid., 150.
5. William T. Cavanaugh, *Migrations of the Holy: God, State, and the Political Meaning of the Church* (Grand Rapids, MI: Eerdmans, 2011), 168.
6. Social Psychologist David Myers suggests a more balanced relation between ideas and practices: "If social psychology has taught us anything during the last twenty-five years, it is that we are likely not only to think ourselves into a new way of acting but also to act ourselves into a new way of thinking." David Myers, *Exploring Social Psychology*, 2nd ed. (Boston: McGraw-Hill, 1999), 137.
7. See Matt. 18:20. Volf takes this text as central for addressing the question of ecclesiality; Volf, *After Our Likeness*.
8. For an understanding of cultural logics within congregations see Becker, *Congregations in Conflict*, 3–12.
9. Alan J. Roxburgh, "Conference about leadership with Alan Roxburgh part one," March 2015, https://vimeo.com/122086976. Also, Roxburgh, *Moving Back into the Neighborhood*, 50.
10. In John 4, Jesus initiates the conversation (ignoring social barriers), enters the interaction in a position of seeking assistance (asking for water), spoke in a manner which sparked curiosity, and gently guided the conversation into depth, authenticity, and self-disclosure. Jesus as skilled conversationalist is also on display in the whole of Luke's account of Jesus's journey to Jerusalem (Luke 9:51–19:44). As Eugene Peterson observes, "When Jesus wasn't preaching and when he wasn't teaching, he talked with the men and women with whom he

lived in terms of what was going on at the moment—people, events, questions, whatever—using the circumstances of their lives as his text. . . . What Mark does for preaching and Matthew does for teaching, Luke does for the informal give-and-take language that takes place in the comings and goings of our ordinary lives." Eugene Peterson, *Tell It Slant: A Conversation on the Language of Jesus in His Stories and Prayers* (Grand Rapids, MI: Eerdmans, 2012), 14.

11. Roxburgh suggests several questions for use in contexts where "people can feel you're intruding or threatening them just by asking questions," such as: "When did you first move to the neighborhood? What brought you here? What are your best memories of this neighborhood? What do you like best about the area? Tell me about your family. What would you love to see happen in this community?" Roxburgh, *Moving Back into the Neighborhood*, 50–51.

12. On the built environment, see Jacobsen, *Sidewalks in the Kingdom*; and Leonard Hjalmarson, *No Home Like Place* (Portland, OR: Urban Loft Publishers, 2014).

13. Catholic spiritual writer Emilie Griffin observes, "Essentially there are two ways in which our God-consciousness is heightened. The first is prayer (in the broadest sense of an interaction with God) and the second is reflection." Emilie Griffin, *Doors Into Prayer: An Invitation* (Brewster, MA: Paraclete Press, 2005), 51.

14. Prayer-walking is a recognized Evangelical practice of intercessory prayer. See, for example, Dan R. Crawford, *Prayer Walking: A Journey of Faith* (Chattanooga, TN: AMG Publishers, 2002); Steve Hawthorne and Graham Kendrick, *Prayer-Walking: Praying On-Site with Insight* (Lake Mary, FL: Charisma Media, 1993); and Adele A. Calhoun, *Spiritual Disciplines Handbook: Practices That Transform Us* (Downers Grove, IL: IVP Books, 2005), 254–255.

15. Ammerman notes several examples of lived religion in similar practices of "wondering at the beauty of the outdoors." See Ammerman, *Sacred Stories, Spiritual Tribes*, 83–85.

16. This practice is also recommended in Sparks, Soerens, and Friesen, *The New Parish*, 33 and 148.

17. See Christopher B. James, "Missional Acuity: 20th Century Insights Toward a Redemptive Way of Seeing," *Witness: Journal of the Academy for Evangelism in Theological Education* 26 (2012): 29–43.

18. Twelve or fewer people is recommended as conducive to conversation of the appropriate depth and participation.

19. Roxburgh describes and outlines "Dwelling in the Word" on page 72 of *Moving Back into the Neighborhood Workbook*. He commends Luke 10:1–12 as a focal text.

20. In the words of Jean Vanier, "Each community needs to be in contact with others. They stimulate and encourage, give support, call forth and affirm each other . . . A community that isolates itself will wither and die; a community in communion with others will receive and give life. This is the Church, flowering

over all of humanity and irrigating it." Jean Vanier, *Community and Growth*, 2nd rev. ed. (New York: Paulist Press, 1989), 102–103.

21. For example, "Our hope is to form a stronger network of Christians and good neighbors and to develop a core community that embodies the gospel for this neighborhood."

22. These latter two questions loosely parallel those proposed by Craig Van Gelder: What is God doing? What does God want to do? Craig Van Gelder, *The Ministry of the Missional Church: A Community Led by the Spirit* (Grand Rapids, MI: Baker Books, 2007), 159–161.

23. Churches of every type should consider how they might learn from this strength.

24. Many Seattle GCT churches partner with Seattle's Union Gospel Mission. The two missional communities I observed wrapped gifts to be given to those in need by a Christian agency.

25. Pastor Arthur at The Hallows Church was enthusiastic about this framing when I shared with him the approach of Lux Communities.

26. For a discussion of the function of hospitality in missional practice, see Alan J. Roxburgh, *Missional Map-Making: Skills for Leading in Times of Transition* (San Francisco, CA: Jossey-Bass, 2009), 154–158.

27. The spiritual potency of hospitality is most dramatically illustrated in the Emmaus account of Luke 24, in which Jesus—a stranger on the road—is invited by fellow travelers to stay the evening and share supper, and at table becomes host and, in the breaking of bread and offering of blessing, is revealed.

28. James, "Missional Acuity." This passage draws particularly upon the insights of Thomas Merton, Annie Dillard, and Dorothy Day.

29. This is taking a page from the HS approach of witness through words of encouragement.

30. Notably, Community Dinners and Church of the Undignified were not only examples of HS churches but also reflected key elements of the NI model.

31. This is not to say that the churches that have transitioned in this direction have ceased to be suitable examples of the HS model, but that they have ceased to be ideal examples of it.

32. Because churches in the NC model are characterized by thoughtful reflection on the social formation enacted and effected in worship, they could provide useful partners and resources for HS churches seeking to explore alternative worship practices.

33. Research has found that hand-holding releases oxytocin (a.k.a. the "love hormone"), increasing feelings of trust, generosity and compassion, and decreasing feelings of fear and anxiety. Huffpost Partner Studio and Dignity Health, "The Science Behind the Profound Power of Holding Hands," *Huffington Post*, May 31, 2016, sec. Healthy Living, www.huffingtonpost.com/entry/power-of-holding-hands_us_57435a8be4b00e09e89fc162.

34. When I visited The City Church's University Campus, I was struck by how often applause was included in worship, a total of nineteen separate instances, not including clapping along with the songs. This included clapping after songs, clapping for the guest preacher (four times), clapping for the other pastors (four times), clapping for themselves as "the greatest campus in all The City," clapping for their first time guests, clapping for those who prayed the sinner's prayer, and clapping for the man in the back of the room that those interested in baptism were directed to speak to. This last instance of applause seemed telling, since after applause spontaneously broke out, the pastor said: "Yeah, you can give a hand for T . . . [applause] . . . because T won't do anything unless you applause—that what I heard. He needs the applause of man. I'm just joking . . . probably one of the greatest servants in our church." This particular church, whose lead pastor Judah Smith has spoken publicly and repeatedly of his relationship with Justin Bieber, reflects American celebrity culture in various ways.

35. These select lyrics sung by HS churches I visited exemplify the tendency: "You hold the universe, You hold everyone on earth" conjures a global vista. "Come flood this place and fill the atmosphere," "Hallelujah, grace like rain falls down on me rain down on me," and "into marvelous light I'm running" set worship in a context of immersive spiritual presence. "I hear the voice of many angels sing, 'Worthy is the Lamb'" draws worshipers into a heavenly scene.

36. A couple examples, however, do come to mind: "This little light of mine, I'm gonna let it shine. Shine it all over the neighborhood"; "In my life, Lord, be glorified, be glorified. In my school, Lord, be glorified."

37. A poignant example of incorporation of local elements is found in a song called "Fierce Hope," written by February Birds, a husband and wife band who are also church planters in the Neighborhood Incarnation model located in Bellingham, Washington.

38. The literature on silence in worship comes predominantly from communication scholars and liturgical theologians. Much of it centers on silence as a distinctive practice of Quakerism. Lippard argues that the Quaker practice of silence was a basis for their radical social contributions, including calling for the abolition of slavery. Paula V. Lippard, "The Rhetoric of Silence: The Society of Friends' Unprogrammed Meeting for Worship," *Communication Quarterly* 36, no. 2 (March 1, 1988): 145–156. Also of interest is Adam Jaworski, *The Power of Silence: Social and Pragmatic Perspectives* (Newbury Park, CA: SAGE Publications, 1992).

39. For example, pastoral prayers are often overlaid with musical accompaniment and sprinkled with responses from the congregation.

40. Philip Pruit, "The Gift of Silence: A Renewed Call to Contemporary Pentecostals to the Discipline of Silence," D.Min. dissertation, University of the South, 2013, p. 42.

41. Boddy published these words under the title "The Value of Stillness," in *Pentecostal Evangel*, November 13, 1920, p. 4, cited in Edmund J. Rybarczyk, *Beyond Salvation: Eastern Orthodoxy and Classical Pentecostalism on Becoming Like Christ* (Eugene, OR: Wipf & Stock, 2006), 276.

42. This is unlike the practice of hospitality, which intrinsically inclines toward experiences of mutuality.

43. These suggestions follow loosely Roxburgh's missional transformation process. See Roxburgh and Boren, *Introducing the Missional Church*.

44. Wits' End Church identified their collective culinary expertise as a potential asset as they discerned more intentional missional practice.

45. This suggests the promise of mainline and progressive churches adopting the Neighborhood Incarnation model.

46. Indeed, nearly half of NC churches are also representative of the NI model. The four exemplars in view here are Church of the Apostles, Valley & Mountain, Church of Steadfast Love, and Awake. For Church of the Apostles, located in Seattle's arts district, this has manifested in providing space for a nonprofit arts and community center in their church building as a way to serve the entire community.

47. While including persons of African American, Latino, or Asian descent in the community would certainly be an advantage (especially to their representation of the new humanity in all its diversity), it is more central to this proposal that the persons have been formed in non-American cultural environments. Thus, relationships with first- or second-generation immigrants or members of strong cultural subgroups would be preferred to third-generation immigrants or ethnic minority nonimmigrants.

48. If challenging, the difficulty of forming and sustaining these cross-cultural relationships itself may provoke beneficial introspection among NC churches.

49. One form of partnership worth exploring is sharing facilities. See Brett C. Hoover, *The Shared Parish: Latinos, Anglos, and the Future of U.S. Catholicism* (New York: New York University Press, 2014).

50. The practice of testimony, already common among NC churches, exercises the importance of practices that are both authentically personal, as well as daring, convictional, and proactive. As such, testimony fits with the form of religious individualization characteristic of the emerging church movement. See Marti and Ganiel, *The Deconstructed Church*, 180.

51. Liberation theologians refer to this posture and relationship as "accompaniment." Liberation theology could provide a valuable resource for missional renewal among NC churches, urging them into mutually transformative relationships.

52. Newbigin, *Foolishness to the Greeks*, 22.

53. Guder, *Continuing Conversion*, 144.

CHAPTER 7: PRACTICAL WISDOM FROM
THE FRONTIER OF FAITH

1. Pete Ward, "Blueprint Ecclesiology and the Lived," *Ecclesial Practices* 2, no. 1 (2015): 88.

2. Ibid.

3. Ibid., 83.

4. Don S. Browning, *A Fundamental Practical Theology: Descriptive and Strategic Proposals* (Minneapolis, MN: Fortress Press, 1996).

5. Dorothy C. Bass et al., *Christian Practical Wisdom: What It Is, Why It Matters* (Grand Rapids, MI: Eerdmans, 2016), 4.

6. As a reminder, currents are based largely on the survey data that significantly underrepresents ethnic churches, which may call into question the broadness of this consensus.

7. For a full description of the general consensus among new Seattle churches, see chapter 2 of this volume, "Summarizing the Currents."

8. The increasing prevalence of multisite churches nationwide is a further indication of broader turn to the local.

9. Eric O. Jacobsen, "The Return of the Neighborhood Church," *Better Cities & Towns*, May 2005, p. 6.

10. As the critique of the Neighborhood Incarnation model in chapter 5 indicates, this turn to the immediate local does have some real and potential dangers. While neighborhoods are important to urban environments, they are not the only important geographical unit. Larger regions of the city, as well as the entire metropolitan area including its suburbs, are important levels of analysis for civic and nonprofit leaders to engage as they seek to address urban challenges and enrich urban life. These levels of analysis can begin to account for the uneven distribution of resources and consider solutions that take the broader context into view. Churches with a strong neighborhood focus are in danger of missing the forest for the trees. Indeed, some of the proposals that follow are intended to prevent this.

11. See, for an influential example, Hauerwas and Willimon, *Resident Aliens*.

12. Jer. 7:4–8 (ESV).

13. 1 Pet. 2:12, 17; 3:15–16.

14. Matt. 22:40.

15. Luke 10:25–37.

16. For the metaphor of church as household, see Eph. 2:19 and 1 Tim. 3:15. For church as city, see Matt. 5:14. For church as nation, see 1 Pet. 2:9.

17. Households, cities, and nations have material, geographic dimensions, as well as social dimensions of meaning.

18. This echoes the close association in the Hebrew Scriptures between the People of God and the Promised Land. According to John's vision of the new Jerusalem: "The nations will walk by its light, and the kings of the earth will bring their splendor into it. . . . The glory and honor of the nations will be brought into it (Rev. 21:24, 26).

19. Dunkelman describes the thinning of relationships in the "middle rings" between family and the masses in Marc J. Dunkelman, *The Vanishing Neighbor: The Transformation of American Community* (New York: W. W. Norton, 2014).

20. These are some of the many critiques of contemporary life by the New Urbanism movement.
21. Joseph R. Myers, *The Search to Belong: Rethinking Intimacy, Community, and Small Groups* (Grand Rapids, MI: Zondervan, 2003).
22. Cynthia Woolever and Deborah Bruce, *A Field Guide to U.S. Congregations: Who's Going Where and Why*, 2nd ed. (Louisville, KY: Westminster John Knox Press, 2010), 115.
23. One recent sociological study confirming of the importance of neighborhoods is Robert Sampson, *Great American City: Chicago and the Enduring Neighborhood Effect* (Chicago: University of Chicago Press, 2012).
24. *Lumen Gentium* similarly declares that the "Church of Christ is truly present in all legitimate local congregations of the faithful." Vatican Council, Edward H. Peters, and Gregory Baum, *De Ecclesia; the Constitution on the Church of Vatican Council II Proclaimed by Pope Paul VI, November 21, 1964* (Glen Rock, N.J.: Paulist Press, 1965), *Lumen Gentium* (26). Leonardo Boff builds his case for the ecclesiality of base communities by emphasizing this understanding, stressing that the "particular church is the universal church, manifested— concretized, historicized. . . . The particular church is the church wholly, but not the whole church." Leonardo Boff, *Ecclesiogenesis: The Base Communities Reinvent the Church* (Maryknoll, NY: Orbis Books, 1986), 17–18.
25. Similar models are sometimes designated in the literature as the "missional-incarnational" "place-based," or "new parish" approach.
26. This emphasis on the importance of a church clarifying its focus has been a repeated one from congregational sociologists for more than a decade, but systematic theologians have not, as yet, engaged deeply with the doctrinal implications of these findings and proposals. See, for example, Ammerman, *Congregation and Community*; Cynthia Woolever and Deborah Bruce, *Places of Promise: Finding Strength in Your Congregation's Location* (Louisville, KY: Westminster John Knox Press, 2008).
27. Bivocational and plural forms of leadership are especially critical in churches of this size and nature. Developing alternative funding streams from the offering plate—such as a for-benefit business, or grant-supported nonprofit—is also important. See Hugh Halter, *Bivo: A Modern-Day Guide for Bi-Vocational Saints* (Littleton, CO: Missio Publishing, 2013).
28. Twenty-three percent of new Seattle churches identified with "sacramental" theology while only 4% are in classically sacramental traditions. Traditionally sacramental theological traditions include Catholicism, Orthodoxy, and Anglicanism. This question invited respondents to select which labels described their theology and included: Evangelical, Progressive, Anabaptist, Sacramental, Pentecostal, Charismatic, Baptist, Conservative, Reformed, and Other.
29. This is in contrast to the "Sunday" character of Christian life more broadly.
30. This was observed among several NI/HS churches, as well as among several NC and NI/NC churches.

31. Drescher, *Choosing Our Religion*, 44.

32. According to Guder, Karl Barth was very cautious about describing the church's witness as "ongoing incarnation." Guder, *The Incarnation and the Church's Witness*, 15. Church as ongoing incarnation is traditionally a Roman Catholic ecclesiological paradigm, but it has garnered considerable attention in Protestant ecclesiologies in recent decades, especially missiologically oriented ecclesiologies. See, for example, Michael Horton, *The Christian Faith: A Systematic Theology for Pilgrims on the Way* (Grand Rapids, MI: Zondervan, 2011), 801–802.

33. This understanding of the incarnation can be found, among other places, in the writings of St. John of Damascus:

    > In former times God, who is without form or body, could never be depicted. But now when God is seen in the flesh conversing with men (*Baruch* 3:38), I make an image of the God whom I see. I do not worship matter; I worship the Creator of matter who became matter for my sake, who willed to take his abode in matter; who worked out my salvation through matter. Never will I cease honoring the matter which wrought my salvation! I honor it, but not as God. (John of Damascus, *First Apology of John of Damascus*, trans. David Anderson and Míceál Vaughan, 1980, no. 16, http://faculty.washington.edu/miceal/Courses/CompLit280/John_of_Damascus.html.)

34. In the words of Wendell Berry, "There are no unsacred places; there are only sacred places and desecrated places." Wendell Berry, "How to Be a Poet," in *Given* (Berkeley: Counterpoint, 2006), 18.

35. On "engaged parenting," see Richard Berrett and Kathleen Ramos, *Engaged Parenting* (Boston: Pearson Custom, 2006); and Nelunika G. Rajapakse, *Compassionate, Engaged Parenting as "A Help to Life": To Nurture the Human Body-Mind-Spirit* (Charleston, SC: CreateSpace, 2012).

36. Ecclesiological reflections on church as mother are often grounded in Cyprian's writings, most notably "On the Unity of the Catholic Church," in which he draws close connections between this ecclesiological metaphor and soteriological concerns: "You cannot have God for your Father unless you have the Church for your mother" (Cyprian of Carthage, *On the Unity of the Catholic Church*, ed. and trans. Stanley L. Greenslade, *Early Latin Theology*, Library of Christian Classics [Philadelphia, PA: Westminster John Knox, 1956], 126–129).

37. For example, images and items from everyday life in the community can be included in worship as prompts for both intercessory prayer and thanksgiving.

38. "Modeling God's intentions for humanity" was the sixth most highly rated priority from a list of seventeen. See the New Seattle Churches Survey in appendix B, question 5.

39. J. H. Yoder drew special attention to five such practices at the heart of the early church: binding and loosing (forgiveness), Eucharist, baptism, multiplicity of gifts, and open meeting. John H. Yoder, *Body Politics: Five Practices of the Christian Community Before the Watching World* (Scottdale, PA: Herald Press, 2001).

40. Saint Benedict described his monastery as a "school for conversion." New monasticism has similarly emphasized conversion as a basic Christian practice of witness and formation. See Rubta House, *School(s) for Conversion: 12 Marks of a New Monasticism* (Eugene, OR: Wipf & Stock, 2005).

41. Arthur L. Greil and David R. Rudy, "Social Cocoons: Encapsulation and Identity Transformation Organizations," *Sociological Inquiry* 54, no. 3 (July 1, 1984): 260–278; Christopher B. James, "Making Christians: Conversion as Skill Acquisition," *Jesus Dust*, April 2012, www.jesusdust.com/2012/04/making-christians-conversion-as-skill.html.

42. Religious groups, including "cults," use various forms of encapsulation as do virtually all organizations and enterprises that seek to facilitate personal transformation. Everything from elementary schools, weight-loss programs, and recreational sports transform people by giving them new ways to see the world (ideological encapsulation), providing new relationships (social encapsulation), and gathering people in certain physical spaces (physical encapsulation). These processes, of course, can be abused. Physical encapsulation is especially dangerous because it is so potent. In no case should churches seeking to follow the peaceable way of Jesus use coercion of any kind—physical, emotional, or ideological—to force or manipulate persons into remaining within the transformative environment. Any groups that do so—religious or otherwise—are suspect and inconsistent with God's pattern of relationship with humanity.

43. William J. Abraham, *The Logic of Evangelism* (Grand Rapids, MI: Eerdmans, 1989).

44. For a recent, strong contribution to this literature, see James K. A. Smith, *Imagining the Kingdom: How Worship Works* (Grand Rapids, MI: Baker Academic, 2013). I would be curious to see sociological analysis of the claims that liturgical scholars such as Smith make regarding the formative impact of weekly worship.

45. Robert E. Webber, *Ancient-Future Faith: Rethinking Evangelicalism for a Postmodern World* (Grand Rapids, MI: Baker Books, 1999) kicked off a series of similarly titled books. On the reclamation of the catechumenate see especially, Robert E. Webber, *Ancient-Future Evangelism: Making Your Church a Faith-Forming Community* (Grand Rapids, MI: Baker Books, 2003); Tory K. Baucum, *Evangelical Hospitality: Catechetical Evangelism in the Early Church and Its Recovery for Today* (Lanham, MD: Scarecrow Press, 2008); and Abraham, *Logic of Evangelism*.

46. See Christopher B. James, "Catechumenate: Conversion in the Early Church," *Jesus Dust*, February 2011, http://www.jesusdust.com/2011/02/what-is-normal-christian-conversion.html. Also, William Harmless S.J., *Augustine and the Catechumenate* (Collegeville, MN: Pueblo Books, 1995), 41–58.

47. The doctrine of the social Trinity has been most robustly developed in the Eastern tradition, drawing largely from the Cappadocian Fathers of the fourth century. For a rich discussion of this opportunity for enriching missional theology, see Van Gelder and Zscheile, *The Missional Church in Perspective*, 102–109.

48. Dwight Zscheile, ed., *Cultivating Sent Communities: Missional Spiritual Formation* (Grand Rapids, MI: Eerdmans, 2012), 13.

49. For a sample of Moltmann's reflections on the implication of perichoresis for ecclesial life, see Jürgen Moltmann, "Perichoresis: An Old Magic Word for a New Trinitarian Theology," in *Trinity, Community and Power: Mapping Trajectories in Wesleyan Theology*, ed. M. Douglas Meeks (Nashville, TN: Kingswood Books, 2000), 111-125; and Jurgen Moltmann, *The Trinity and the Kingdom* (Minneapolis, MN: Fortress Press, 1993).

50. Van Gelder and Zscheile, *The Missional Church in Perspective*, 104.

51. For resources on this kind of congregational exegesis, see Congregational Studies Team website, http://studyingcongregations.org.

52. Sixty percent of new Seattle churches did not begin with a launch service, despite the fact that church planting literature and networks overwhelmingly advocate for this approach. It would seem to be unnecessary, unwise, or both in contexts like Seattle.

53. Sixty-three percent of survey respondents indicated that "offering a community in which to belong and beloved" was "extremely important" priority. Another 26% said it was "very important."

54. Given the frequency of this open-ended response, future iterations of the survey should include "word of mouth" as an option. The fact that nearly a fourth of respondents named a relational or word-of-mouth approach makes it seem likely that at least twice that number would have selected this option if it were provided.

55. The significance of this portrait comes into sharper relief in contrast to churches that principally offer appealing events to attend (worship) and who, accordingly, utilize marketing strategies.

56. On missional hospitality as creating spaces see Christopher B. James, "Ecclesiology and Missional Hospitality," in *1001 New Worshiping Communities,* forthcoming.

57. This is especially evident in the scarcity of denominational names among new Seattle churches. Denominational branding makes sense in a Christendom context where new Presbyterians in town will look for a Presbyterian church, but in contexts where denominations are regarded as manifestations of suspect religious institutions, denominational branding can be a liability.

58. Even when this is the case, the elements of hospitable practice—friendship, meals, unstructured conversation, entering homes—have a way of undermining these unequal dynamics.

59. Keith Anderson, *The Digital Cathedral: Networked Ministry in a Wireless World* (New York: Morehouse Publishing, 2015), 208.

60. See Stephen B. Bevans and Cathy Ross, "Introduction: Mission as Prophetic Dialogue," in *Mission on the Road to Emmaus: Constants, Context and Prophetic Dialogue*, ed. Cathy Ross and Stephen B. Bevans (Maryknoll, NY: Orbis Books, 2015), xi–xix.

61. For a sustained critique of church marketing, see Philip D. Kenneson and James L. Street, *Selling Out the Church: The Dangers of Church Marketing* (Eugene, OR: Wipf & Stock, 2003). Also, Stone, *Evangelism After Christendom*, 131–170.

62. For example, jobs working as baristas, bartenders, hairstylists, fitness coaches, college admissions and student life staff, waiting tables, parole officers or social workers.

63. For the effects of megachurches on nearby congregations, see Wollschleger and Porter, "A 'WalMartization' of Religion?"

64. The New Seattle Churches Survey instrument can be found in appendix B.

65. Seven churches in the sample are likely indications of a sacramental-ethnic model, including three Eritrean Orthodox churches, an Ethiopian Orthodox church, a Coptic church, a Spanish-speaking Episcopal church, and a German-speaking Methodist Church. Prime examples of the semi-progressive Evangelical megachurch model would include Eastlake Community Church and Bethany Community Church, which have seemingly formulated distinct combinations of GCT and NC elements that are appealing to large numbers. The size of these churches hints that there may be room in the field for growth among churches who are simultaneously culture affirming and Evangelical with regard to their spirituality and evangelistic mission.

66. Nancy L. Eiesland, *A Particular Place: Urban Restructuring and Religious Ecology in a Southern Exurb* (New Brunswick, NJ: Rutgers University Press, 2000), 11.

67. Ibid., 14.

68. Ibid., 210.

69. For a sample of studies in religious ecology, see Katie Day and Edd Conboy, *Faith on the Avenue: Religion on a City Street* (New York: Oxford University Press, 2014); Eiesland, *A Particular Place*; Roozen, McKinney, and Carroll, *Varieties of Religious Presence*; Omar M. McRoberts, *Streets of Glory: Church and Community in a Black Urban Neighborhood* (Chicago: University of Chicago Press, 2005); Nancy T. Kinney and Todd B. Combs, "Changes in Religious Ecology and Socioeconomic Correlates for Neighborhoods in a Metropolitan Region," *Journal of Urban Affairs*, May 1, 2015, pp 1–20; Cimino, Mian, and Huang, eds., *Ecologies of Faith in New York City*; William Form and Joshua Dubrow, "Ecology of Denominational Fundamentalism in a Metropolis," *City & Community* 7, no. 2 (June 1, 2008): 141–162.

70. For scholars engaging this challenge, see The Network for Ecclesiology and Ethnography website, www.ecclesiologyandethnography.com.

71. "Family Systems Theory," *GenoPro.com*, www.genopro.com/genogram/family-systems-theory.

72. Edwin H. Friedman, *Generation to Generation: Family Process in Church and Synagogue* (New York: Guilford Press, 2011).

73. As Van Gelder and Zscheile write, "We are not on our own in constructing forms of church life and mission that will speak to people." Van Gelder and Zscheile, *The Missional Church in Perspective*, 120.

74. "Bowenian Family Therapy," *PsychPage.com*, www.psychpage.com/learning/library/counseling/bowen.html.

75. Although ethnically identified churches also reflect an identity in distinction from the larger culture, there are good reasons for these minority communities to develop strong differentiated identities which are more about who they are than about who they are not.

76. "Bowenian Family Therapy," *PsychPage.com*.

77. See Gen. 6–8.

78. Envisioning the church as Ark has a long history in Christianity, largely rooted in the writings of Cyprian of Carthage, who linked this ecclesiological image with the assertion that outside the church there is no salvation. A long list of influential theologians and church leaders have similarly developed and utilized the image of the church as ark of salvation, including Pope Pius IX, Jerome, Venerable Bede, Thomas Aquinas, and Robert Bellarmine. For a selection of quotations, see "The Fathers of the Church on Extra Ecclesiam Nulla Salus," *Catholicism.org*, April 25, 2005, http://catholicism.org/eens-fathers.html.

79. Gen. 8:6–8 (ESV).

80. To state this in terms more familiar to missional theological discourse, the *missio Dei* is not only holistic it is also pluriform. Its intention to form a new humanity takes shape in more than a single initiative; it is manifest in more than a single model of church.

81. New Churches Twitter post, August 7, 2015 (7:41 P.M.), http://twitter.com/NewChurches/status/629844730780774400.

82. For example, Nate Cohn, "Big Drop in Share of Americans Calling Themselves Christian," *New York Times*, May 12, 2015, www.nytimes.com/2015/05/12/upshot/big-drop-in-share-of-americans-calling-themselves-christian.html; Laurie Goodstein, "Percentage of Protestant Americans Is in Steep Decline, Study Finds," *New York Times*, October 9, 2012, www.nytimes.com/2012/10/10/us/study-finds-that-percentage-of-protestant-americans-is-declining.html; C. J. Werleman and AlterNet, "Atheists Have Their Number: How the Christian Right Is Hastening Religion's Decline," *Salon.com*, March 25, 2014, www.salon.com/2014/03/25/calling_the_christian_right_soon_you_will_be_outnumbered_partner; Daniel Burke, "Millennials Leaving Church in Droves, Study Finds," *CNN*, last modified May 14, 2015, www.cnn.com/2015/05/12/living/pew-religion-study/index.html; and Cathy Grossman, "Christians Drop, 'Nones' Soar in New Religion Portrait," *USA Today*, last modified May 12, 2015, www.usatoday.com/story/news/nation/2015/05/12/christians-drop-nones-soar-in-new-religion-portrait/27159533.

83. Serious scholars of religion, unlike the media, have generally offered more measured interpretations of recent trends.

84. For example, Wes Granberg-Michaelson, "Think Christianity Is Dying? No, Christianity Is Shifting Dramatically," *Washington Post*, May 20, 2015, www.

washingtonpost.com/news/acts-of-faith/wp/2015/05/20/think-christianity-is-dying-no-christianity-is-shifting-dramatically/?utm_term=.30d340c6cb22; Ed Stetzer, "No, American Christianity Is Not Dead," *CNN*, last modified May 16, 2015, www.cnn.com/2015/05/16/living/christianity-american-dead/index.html; and Vincent Funaro, "Christianity Is Not Dying; Reports Pointing to Decline of Church Are Skewing Data, Says Baylor University Scholars," *Christian Post*, May 13, 2015, www.christianpost.com/news/christianity-is-not-dying-reports-pointing-to-decline-of-church-are-skewing-data-says-baylor-university-scholars-139069.

85. See Robert D. Putnam and David E. Campbell, *American Grace: How Religion Divides and Unites Us* (New York: Simon & Schuster, 2012); Pew Research Center, "'Nones' on the Rise"; and Hunter, *To Change the World*.

86. Ed Stetzer noted these trends and projected their continuation on his blog, "MissionTrends: 4 Trends for Churches to Consider," *The Exchange*, June 2, 2014, www.christianitytoday.com/edstetzer/2014/may/look-back-and-look-ahead-for-church-in-america-4-trends-chr.html.

87. Healy, *Church, World and the Christian Life*, 50.

88. Alan J. Roxburgh, *Joining God, Remaking Church, Changing the World: The New Shape of the Church in Our Time* (New York: Morehouse Publishing, 2015), 7.

89. "And no one pours new wine into old wineskins. Otherwise, the new wine will burst the skins; the wine will run out and the wineskins will be ruined. No, new wine must be poured into new wineskins." Luke 5:37–38. See also Matt. 9:17 and Mark 2:22.

APPENDIX A

1. World Council of Churches, *Baptism, Eucharist and Ministry*. See also Thurian, *Churches Respond to BEM*.

2. According to Pew Research, 76% of U.S. adults, including 86% of millennials and 79% of gen-Xers, list 9/11 among the top ten events with the "greatest impact on the country" to occur in their lifetime. Claudia Deane, Maeve Duggan, and Rich Morin, "Americans Name the 10 Most Significant Historic Events of Their Lifetimes," December 15, 2016, www.people-press.org/2016/12/15/americans-name-the-10-most-significant-historic-events-of-their-lifetimes. *Newsweek* coined the term "Generation 9-11" in a November 12, 2001, cover story. Barbara Kantrowitz, "Generation 9-11: Terror, War, and Recession Hit Home on Campus," *Newsweek*, November 12, 2001. "Generation 9-11" typically refers to those who were between the ages of 10 and 21 on 9/11/2001 In the middle of this study, on 9/11/2014, Generation 9-11 was aged between 23 and 34.

3. Though, unlike New England, the Pacific Northwest still had a greater percentage of Catholics than "Nones." Barry Kosmin et al., *American Nones,*

4. Urban Institute, "NCCS Web Tools," National Center for Charitable Statistics, www.nccsdataweb.urban.org.

5. Christopher B. James, "Ecclesial Pioneers in the Pacific Northwest," *Christ &*
   Cascadia, October 9, 2013, http://christandcascadia.com/ecclesial-pioneers-
   in-the-pacific-northwest-james.
6. Roozen, McKinney, and Carroll, *Varieties of Religious Presence*; and Becker,
   Congregations in Conflict. The findings of these studies, as well as a few others, are
   summarized in chapter 3 of this volume.
7. Survey questions were drawn and adapted especially from Roozen, McKinney,
   and Carroll, *Varieties of Religious Presence*; Becker, *Congregations in Conflict*; Unruh
   and Sider, *Saving Souls*; and Murray, *Church Planting*.
8. Hope Yen, "Census: White Majority in U.S. Gone by 2043," *NBC News*, last
   modified June 13, 2013, http://usnews.nbcnews.com/_news/2013/06/13/
   18934 11-census-white-majority-in-us-gone-by-2043.
9. These percentages are based on Census 2010 data. Forty-five percent represents
   138 million of the U.S. population of 309 million. This percentage has been climb-
   ing, however, from 43% in 2000. Using U.S. Census definitions, "urban areas"
   include both "urbanized areas" ("densely developed territory that contains 50,000
   or more people") and "urban clusters" (which "consists of densely developed territory that has at least 2,500 people but fewer than 50,000 people"). Seventy-one
   percent of the U.S. population lived in "urbanized areas" according to the 2010
   U.S. Census. U.S. Census Bureau, "2010 Census Urban and Rural Classification
   and Urban Area Criteria," www.census.gov/geo/reference/ua/urban-rural-2010.
   html.

Selected Bibliography

Abraham, William J. *The Logic of Evangelism*. Grand Rapids, MI: Eerdmans, 1989.

Allen, Roland. *Missionary Methods: St. Paul's or Ours?* Grand Rapids, MI: Eerdmans, 1962.

Ammerman, Nancy T. *Congregation and Community*. New Brunswick, NJ: Rutgers University Press, 1996.

Ammerman, Nancy T. *Doing Good in American Communities: Congregations and Service Organizations Working Together*. Organizing Religious Work Project, 2001. Hartford, CT: Institute for Religion Research, February 2001. http://hirr.hartsem. edu/orw/orw_cong-report.html.

Ammerman, Nancy T. *Pillars of Faith: American Congregations and Their Partners*. Berkeley: University of California Press, 2005.

Ammerman, Nancy T. *Sacred Stories, Spiritual Tribes: Finding Religion in Everyday Life*. Oxford: Oxford University Press, 2013.

Ammerman, Nancy T. "Spiritual But Not Religious? Beyond Binary Choices in the Study of Religion." *Journal for the Scientific Study of Religion* 52, no. 2 (June 1, 2013): 258–278.

Ammerman, Nancy T., Jackson Carroll, Carl Dudley, and William McKinney, eds. *Studying Congregations: A New Handbook*. Nashville, TN: Abingdon, 1998.

Anderson, Keith. *The Digital Cathedral: Networked Ministry in a Wireless World*. New York: Morehouse Publishing, 2015.

Archbishop's Council on Mission and Public Affairs. *Mission-Shaped Church: Church Planting and Fresh Expressions in a Changing Context*. New York: Seabury Books, 2010.

Barrett, Lois Y., ed. *Treasure in Clay Jars: Patterns in Missional Faithfulness*. Grand Rapids, MI: Eerdmans, 2004.

Bass, Dorothy C., Kathleen A. Cahalan, Bonnie J. Miller-McLemore, Christian B. Scharen, and James R. Nieman. *Christian Practical Wisdom: What It Is, Why It Matters*. Grand Rapids, MI: Eerdmans, 2016.

Baucum, Tory K. *Evangelical Hospitality: Catechetical Evangelism in the Early Church and Its Recovery for Today*. Lanham, MD: Scarecrow Press, 2008.

Becker, Penny E. *Congregations in Conflict: Cultural Models of Local Religious Life*. Cambridge: Cambridge University Press, 1999.

Berger, Peter L. "The Religiously Unaffiliated in America." *The American Interest*. Last modified March 21, 2012. www.the-american-interest.com/2012/03/21/the-religiously-unaffiliated-in-america.

Berger, Peter L. *The Sacred Canopy: Elements of a Sociological Theory of Religion*. New York: Anchor, 1990 [reprint].

Berquist, Linda. "Imagine What God Could Do With a 'Spiritual Alpha City.'" *V3 Church Planting Movement* (blog), May 2015. http://thev3movement.org/2015/05/imagine-what-god-could-do-with-a-spiritual-alpha-city.

Berrett, Richard and Kathleen Ramos. *Engaged Parenting*. Boston: Pearson Custom, 2006.

Bevans, Stephen B., and Cathy Ross. "Introduction: Mission as Prophetic Dialogue." In *Mission on the Road to Emmaus: Constants, Context and Prophetic Dialogue*, edited by Cathy Ross and Stephen B. Bevans, xi–xix. Maryknoll, NY: Orbis Books, 2015.

Bielo, James S. "City of Man, City of God: The Re-Urbanization of American Evangelicals." *City & Society* 23, no. s1 (September 2011): 2–23.

Bielo, James S. *Emerging Evangelicals: Faith, Modernity, and the Desire for Authenticity*. New York: New York University Press, 2011.

Blauw, Johannes. *The Missionary Nature of the Church: A Survey of the Biblical Theology of Mission*. Cambridge: Lutterworth Press, 2003.

Bock, Darrell L. *A Theology of Luke and Acts: God's Promised Program, Realized for All Nations*. Edited by Andreas J. Kostenberger. Grand Rapids, MI: Zondervan, 2012.

Boff, Leonardo. *Ecclesiogenesis: The Base Communities Reinvent the Church*. Maryknoll, NY: Orbis Books, 1986.

Bosch, David J. "The Structure of Mission: An Exposition of Matthew 28:16–20." In *The Study of Evangelism: Exploring a Missional Practice of the Church*, edited by Paul W. Chilcote and Laceye C. Warner, 73–92. Grand Rapids, MI: Eerdmans, 2008.

Bosch, David J. *Transforming Mission: Paradigm Shifts in Theology of Mission*. Maryknoll, NY: Orbis Books, 1991.

Branson, Mark L., and Nicholas Warnes. *Starting Missional Churches: Life with God in the Neighborhood*. Downers Grove, IL: IVP Books, 2014.

Bretherton, Luke. *Hospitality as Holiness: Christian Witness Amid Moral Diversity*. London: Ashgate Publishing, 2006.

Brown, Raymond E. *The Community of the Beloved Disciple*. New York: Paulist Press, 1979.

Browning, Don S. *A Fundamental Practical Theology: Descriptive and Strategic Proposals*. Minneapolis: Fortress Press, 1996.

Carson, D. A. *Becoming Conversant with the Emerging Church: Understanding a Movement and Its Implications*. Grand Rapids, MI: Zondervan, 2005.

Caruthers, Ken. "The Missionary Team as Church: Applied Ecclesiology in the Life and Relationships between Cross-Cultural Church Planters." Southeastern Baptist Theological Seminary, 2014. http://gradworks.umi.com/35/81/3581125.html.

Cavanaugh, William T. *Migrations of the Holy: God, State, and the Political Meaning of the Church*. Grand Rapids, MI: Eerdmans, 2011.

Cavanaugh, William T. *Torture and Eucharist: Theology, Politics, and the Body of Christ*. Challenges in Contemporary Theology. Berlin: Blackwell Publishers, 1998.

Chaves, Mark. *Congregations in America*. Cambridge, MA: Harvard University Press, 2004.

Chilcote, Paul W., and Laceye C. Warner, eds. *The Study of Evangelism: Exploring a Missional Practice of the Church*. Grand Rapids, MI: Eerdmans, 2008.

Christiano, Kevin, William Swatos, and Peter Kivisto. *Sociology of Religion: Contemporary Developments*, 2nd ed. Lanham, MD: Rowman & Littlefield, 2008.

Cimino, Richard, Nadia A. Mian, and Weishan Huang, eds. *Ecologies of Faith in New York City: The Evolution of Religious Institutions*. Bloomington, IN: Indiana University Press, 2012.

Day, Katie, and Edd Conboy. *Faith on the Avenue: Religion on a City Street*. New York: Oxford University Press, 2014.

Deane, Claudia, Maeve Duggan, and Rich Morin. "Americans Name the 10 Most Significant Historic Events of Their Lifetimes." Pew Research Center, December 15, 2016. www.people-press.org/2016/12/15/americans-name-the-10-most-significant-historic-events-of-their-lifetimes.

DeYoung, Kevin, Ted Kluck, and David F. Wells. *Why We're Not Emergent: By Two Guys Who Should Be*. Chicago: Moody Publishers, 2008.

Dias, Elizabeth. "How Evangelicals Are Changing Their Minds on Gay Marriage." *Time*, January 15, 2015. http://time.com/3669024/evangelicals-gay-marriage.

Dougherty, Kevin D., Byron R. Johnson, and Edward C. Polson. "Recovering the Lost: Remeasuring U.S. Religious Affiliation." *Journal for the Scientific Study of Religion* 46, no. 4 (December 1, 2007): 483–499.

Dreier, Mary Sue D., ed. *Created and Led by the Spirit: Planting Missional Congregations*. Grand Rapids, MI: Eerdmans, 2013.

Drescher, Elizabeth. *Choosing Our Religion: The Spiritual Lives of America's Nones*. New York: Oxford University Press, 2016.

Dudley, Carl S., and Sally A. Johnson. *Energizing the Congregation: Images That Shape Your Church's Ministry*. Louisville, KY: Westminster John Knox Press, 1993.

Dulles, Avery. *Models of the Church*. New York: Image, 1991.

Dunkelman, Marc. *The Vanishing Neighbor: The Transformation of American Community*. New York: W. W. Norton & Company, 2014.

Eiesland, Nancy L. *A Particular Place: Urban Restructuring and Religious Ecology in a Southern Exurb*. New Brunswick, NJ: Rutgers University Press, 2000.

Fitch, David E. *Faithful Presence: Seven Disciplines That Shape the Church for Mission.* Downers Grove, IL: IVP Books, 2016.

Florida, Richard. *The Rise of the Creative Class*, rev. ed. New York: Basic Books, 2014.

Foley, Michael W., and Dean R. Hoge. *Religion and the New Immigrants: How Faith Communities Form Our Newest Citizens.* New York: Oxford University Press, 2007.

Ford, Lance, and Brad Brisco. *Next Door as It Is in Heaven: Living Out God's Kingdom in Your Neighborhood.* Colorado Springs, CO: NavPress, 2016.

Form, William, and Joshua Dubrow. "Ecology of Denominational Fundamentalism in a Metropolis." *City & Community* 7, no. 2 (June 1, 2008): 141–162.

Friedman, Edwin H. *Generation to Generation: Family Process in Church and Synagogue.* New York: Guilford Press, 2011.

Frost, Michael. *Incarnate: The Body of Christ in an Age of Disengagement.* Downers Grove, IL: IVP Books, 2014.

Frost, Michael and Christiana Rice. *Alter Your World: Partnering with God to Rebirth Our Communities.* Downers Grove, IL: IVP Books, 2017.

Funaro, Vincent. "Christianity Is Not Dying; Reports Pointing to Decline of Church Are Skewing Data, Says Baylor University Scholars." *The Christian Post*, May 13, 2015. www.christianpost.com/news/christianity-is-not-dying-reports-pointing-to-decline-of-church-are-skewing-data-says-baylor-university-scholars-139069.

Gay, Doug. *Remixing the Church: Towards an Emerging Ecclesiology.* London: SCM Press, 2011.

Gibbs, Eddie, and Ryan K. Bolger. *Emerging Churches: Creating Christian Community in Postmodern Cultures.* Grand Rapids, MI: Baker Academic, 2005.

Giles, Kevin. *What on Earth Is the Church?: An Exploration in New Testament Theology.* Downers Grove, IL: IVP Books, 2000.

Gorman, Michael J. *Becoming the Gospel: Paul, Participation, and Mission.* The Gospel and Our Culture. Grand Rapids, MI: Eerdmans, 2015.

Graham, Elaine, Heather Walton, and Frances Ward. *Theological Reflection: Methods.* London: SCM Press, 2005.

Granberg-Michaelson, Wes. "Think Christianity Is Dying? No, Christianity Is Shifting Dramatically." *Washington Post*, May 20, 2015. www.washington-post.com/news/acts-of-faith/wp/2015/05/20/think-christianity-is-dying-no-christianity-is-shifting-dramatically.

Gray-Reeves, Mary, and Michael Perham. *The Hospitality of God: Emerging Worship for a Missional Church.* New York: Seabury Books, 2011.

Green, Stanley W., and James R. Krabill, eds. *Fully Engaged: Missional Church in an Anabaptist Voice.* Harrisonburg, VA: Herald Press, 2015.

Greil, Arthur L., and David R. Rudy. "Social Cocoons: Encapsulation and Identity Transformation Organizations." *Sociological Inquiry* 54, no. 3 (July 1, 1984): 260–278.

Grossman, Cathy. "Christians Drop, 'Nones' Soar in New Religion Portrait." *USA Today*, May 12, 2015. www.usatoday.com/story/news/nation/2015/05/12/christians-drop-nones-soar-in-new-religion-portrait/27159533.

Guder, Darrell L. *The Continuing Conversion of the Church*, 7th ed. Grand Rapids, MI: Eerdmans, 2000.

Guder, Darrell L. *The Incarnation and the Church's Witness*. Eugene, OR: Wipf & Stock, 2005 [reprint].

Guder, Darrell L., ed. *Missional Church: A Vision for the Sending of the Church in North America*. Grand Rapids, MI: Eerdmans, 1998.

Gundry, Robert H. *Jesus the Word According to John the Sectarian: A Paleofundamentalist Manifesto for Contemporary Evangelicalism, Especially Its Elites, in North America*. Grand Rapids, MI: Eerdmans, 2002.

Halter, Hugh. *Bivo: A Modern-Day Guide for Bi-Vocational Saints*. Littleton, CO: Missio Publishing, 2013.

Harmless S. J., William. *Augustine and the Catechumenate*. Collegeville, MN: Pueblo Books, 1995.

Hauerwas, Stanley, and William H. Willimon. *Resident Aliens: A Provocative Christian Assessment of Culture and Ministry for People Who Know That Something Is Wrong*. Nashville, TN: Abingdon Press, 1989.

Healy, Nicholas M. *Church, World and the Christian Life: Practical-Prophetic Ecclesiology*. Cambridge: Cambridge University Press, 2000.

Hjalmarson, Leonard. *No Home Like Place*. Portland, OR: Urban Loft Publishers, 2014.

Hoge, Dean R., Benton Johnson, and Donald A. Luidens. *Vanishing Boundaries: The Religion of Mainline Protestant Baby Boomers*. Louisville, KY: Westminster John Knox Press, 1994.

Hoover, Brett C. *The Shared Parish: Latinos, Anglos, and the Future of U.S. Catholicism*. New York: New York University Press, 2014.

Hunsberger, George R. "Is There Biblical Warrant for Evangelism?" In *The Study of Evangelism: Exploring a Missional Practice of the Church*, edited by Paul W. Chilcote and Laceye C. Warner, 66–67. Grand Rapids, MI: Eerdmans, 2008.

Hunter, James D. *To Change the World: The Irony, Tragedy, and Possibility of Christianity in the Late Modern World*. New York: Oxford University Press, 2010.

Iannaccone, Laurence R. "Why Strict Churches Are Strong." *American Journal of Sociology* 99, no. 5 (March 1, 1994): 1180–1211.

Jacobsen, Eric O. *Sidewalks in the Kingdom: New Urbanism and the Christian Faith*. Grand Rapids, MI: Brazos Press, 2003.

Jacobsen, Eric O. "The Return of the Neighborhood Church." *Better Cities & Towns*, May 2005, p. 6.

James, Christopher B. "Catechumenate: Conversion in the Early Church." *Jesus Dust*, February 2011. www.jesusdust.com/2011/02/what-is-normal-christian-conversion.html.

James, Christopher B. "Defining the 'E'-Word: Evangelism as a Christian Practice." *Jesus Dust*, October 2013. www.jesusdust.com/2013/10/defining-e-word-evangelism-as-christian.html.

James, Christopher B. "Ecclesial Pioneers in the Pacific Northwest." *Christ &* *Cascadia*, October 9, 2013. http://christandcascadia.com/ecclesial-pioneers-in-the-pacific-northwest-james.

James, Christopher B. "Making Christians: Conversion as Skill Acquisition." *Jesus Dust*, April 2012. www.jesusdust.com/2012/04/making-christians-conversion-as-skill.html.

James, Christopher B. "Missional Acuity: 20th Century Insights Toward a Redemptive Way of Seeing." *Witness: Journal of the Academy for Evangelism in Theological Education* 26 (2012): 29–43.

James, Christopher B. "Mission-Shaped Church 2: Book Review." *Jesus Dust*, October 2012. www.jesusdust.com/2012/10/mission-shaped-church-2-book-review.html.

James, Christopher B. "Some Fell on Good Soil: Church Planting in Religious Ecologies," *Witness: Journal of the Academy for Evangelism in Theological Education* 27 (2013): 105–132.

James, Christopher B. "Theologies of Church Planting: Comparing Malphurs and Murray." *Jesus Dust*, October 2012. www.jesusdust.com/2012/10/theologies-of-church-planting-comparing.html.

James, Christopher B. "What Churches Can Learn from New Monasticism." *Conversations Journal*, July 2013. http://conversationsjournal.com/2013/07/what-churches-can-learn-from-new-monasticism-pt-1.

Jaworski, Adam. *The Power of Silence: Social and Pragmatic Perspectives*. Newbury Park, CA: SAGE Publications, 1992.

John of Damascus. *First Apology of John of Damascus*. Translated by David Anderson and Míceál Vaughan, 1980. http://faculty.washington.edu/miceal/Courses/CompLit280/John_of_Damascus.html.

Johnson, Victoria. "What Is Organizational Imprinting? Cultural Entrepreneurship in the Founding of the Paris Opera." *American Journal of Sociology* 113, no. 1 (July 1, 2007): 97–127.

Jones, Robert P., Daniel Cox, Betsy Cooper, and Rachel Lienesch. *Exodus: Why Americans Are Leaving Religion—and Why They're Unlikely to Come Back*. Public Religion Research Institute. 2016. www.prri.org/research/prri-rns-poll-nones-atheist-leaving-religion.

Jones, Tony. *The Church Is Flat: The Relational Ecclesiology of the Emerging Church Movement*. Minneapolis, MN: JoPa Group, 2011.

Jurjevich, Jason, and Greg Schrock. "Is Portland Really the Place Where Young People Go to Retire? Migration Patterns of Portland's Young and College-Educated, 1980-2010." Nohad A. Toulan School of Urban Studies and Planning, Population Research Center, September 2012. http://pdxscholar.library.pdx.edu/cgi/viewcontent.cgi?article=1004&context=prc_pub.

Kantrowitz, Barbara. "Generation 9-11: Terror, War, and Recession Hit Home On Campus." *Newsweek*, November 12, 2001.

Katz, Bruce. "The Challenge of Seattle's Emerging Society." Brookings Institution. Last modified May 28, 2010. www.brookings.edu/research/opinions/2010/05/28-seattle-katz.

Kaufman, Tone Stangeland. "Normativity as Pitfall or Ally?" *Ecclesial Practices* 2, no. 1 (May 8, 2015): 91–107.

Kenneson, Philip D., and James L. Street. *Selling Out the Church: The Dangers of Church Marketing*. Eugene, OR: Wipf & Stock, 2003.

Killen, Patricia O'Connell. "The Religious Geography of the Pacific Northwest." *Word & World* 24, no. 3 (Summer 2004): 269–278.

Killen, Patricia O'Connell, and Mark Silk, eds. *Religion and Public Life in the Pacific Northwest: The None Zone*. Walnut Creek, CA: Altamira Press, 2004.

Kimball, Dan. *They Like Jesus but Not the Church: Insights from Emerging Generations*. Grand Rapids, MI: Zondervan, 2007.

Kimball, Dan, David Crowder, and Sally Morgenthaler. *Emerging Worship: Creating Worship Gatherings for New Generations*. Grand Rapids, MI: Zondervan, 2004.

Kinney, Nancy T., and Todd B. Combs. "Changes in Religious Ecology and Socioeconomic Correlates for Neighborhoods in a Metropolitan Region." *Journal of Urban Affairs* (May 1, 2015): 1–20.

Kosmin, Barry, Ariela Keysar, Ryan Cragun, and Juhem Navarro-Rivera. *American Nones: The Profile of the No Religion Population*. Hartford, CT: Institute for the Study of Secularism in Society & Culture, 2008. https://commons.trincoll.edu/aris/publications/2008-2/american-nones-the-profile-of-the-no-religion-population.

Lee, Shayne, and Phillip Sinitiere. *Holy Mavericks: Evangelical Innovators and the Spiritual Marketplace*. New York: New York University Press, 2009.

Levinas, Emmanuel. *Totality and Infinity: An Essay on Exteriority*. Pittsburgh, PA: Duquesne University Press, 1969.

Lim, Chaeyoon, Carol Ann MacGregor, and Robert D. Putnam. "Secular and Liminal: Discovering Heterogeneity Among Religious Nones." *Journal for the Scientific Study of Religion* 49, no. 4 (December 1, 2010): 596–618.

Lindsay, D. Michael. *Faith in the Halls of Power: How Evangelicals Joined the American Elite*. Oxford: Oxford University Press, USA, 2008.

Lipka, Michael. "A Closer Look at America's Rapidly Growing Religious 'nones.'" Pew Research Center, May 13, 2015. www.pewresearch.org/fact-tank/2015/05/13/a-closer-look-at-americas-rapidly-growing-religious-nones.

Lippard, Paula V. "The Rhetoric of Silence: The Society of Friends' Unprogrammed Meeting for Worship." *Communication Quarterly* 36, no. 2 (March 1, 1988): 145–156.

Liubinskas, Susann. "The Body of Christ in Mission: Paul's Ecclesiology and the Role of the Church in Mission." *Missiology: An International Review* 41, no. 4 (October 1, 2013): 402–415.

Lohfink, Gerhard. *Jesus and Community: The Social Dimension of Christian Faith*. Philadelphia, PA: Fortress Press, 1984.

Lord, Andy. *Network Church: A Pentecostal Ecclesiology Shaped by Mission.* Leiden, Netherlands: Brill, 2012.

Luhrmann, Tanya M. *When God Talks Back: Understanding the American Evangelical Relationship with God.* New York: Knopf, 2012.

Marti, Gerardo, and Gladys Ganiel. *The Deconstructed Church: Understanding Emerging Christianity.* New York: Oxford University Press, 2014.

McRoberts, Omar M. *Streets of Glory: Church and Community in a Black Urban Neighborhood.* Chicago: University Of Chicago Press, 2005.

Mercadante, Linda A. *Belief without Borders: Inside the Minds of the Spiritual but Not Religious.* New York: Oxford University Press, 2014.

Minear, Paul S. *Images of the Church in the New Testament.* Louisville, KY: Westminster John Knox Press, 2004.

Moltmann, Jürgen. "Perichoresis: An Old Magic Word for a New Trinitarian Theology." In *Trinity, Community and Power: Mapping Trajectories in Wesleyan Theology,* edited by M. Douglas Meeks. Nashville, TN: Kingswood Books, 2000.

Moltmann, Jürgen. *The Church in the Power of the Spirit: A Contribution to Messianic Ecclesiology.* Minneapolis, MN: Fortress Press, 1993.

Moltmann, Jürgen. *The Trinity and the Kingdom.* Minneapolis, MN: Fortress Press, 1993 [reprint].

Moon, Ruth. "Popcorn in the Pews." *Christianity Today.* Last modified January 14, 2009. www.christianitytoday.com/ct/2009/january/18.16.html.

Moynagh, Michael, and Philip Harrold. *Church for Every Context: An Introduction to Theology and Practice.* London: SCM Press, 2012.

Murray, Stuart. *Church Planting: Laying Foundations.* Scottdale, PA: Herald Press, 2001.

Myers, David. *Exploring Social Psychology.* 2nd ed. Boston: McGraw-Hill, 1999.

Myers, Joseph R. *The Search to Belong: Rethinking Intimacy, Community, and Small Groups.* Grand Rapids, MI: Zondervan, 2003.

National Conference on Citizenship. *Greater Seattle: King, Pierce and Snohomish Counties Civic Health Index.* Seattle, WA: Seattle CityClub, 2013.

Network for Ecclesiology and Ethnography. Website. www.ecclesiologyandethnography.com.

Newbigin, Lesslie. "A British and European Perspective." In *Entering the Kingdom: A Fresh Look at Conversion,* edited by Monica Hill, 57–68. Middlesex: British Church Growth Association and MARC Europe, 1986.

Newbigin, Lesslie. *A South India Diary.* London: SCM Press, 1960.

Newbigin, Lesslie. "Evangelism in the City." *Expository Times* 98 (September 1987): 355–358.

Newbigin, Lesslie. *Foolishness to the Greeks: The Gospel and Western Culture.* Grand Rapids, MI: Eerdmans, 1986.

Newbigin, Lesslie. *Mission in Christ's Way: Bible Studies.* Geneva: WCC Publications, 1987.

Newbigin, Lesslie. "Pastoral Ministry in a Pluralist Society." In *Witnessing Church: Essays in Honour of The Rt. Rev. Masilamani Azaraiah, Bishop in Madras. Published and Released on the Occasion of His Manivizha Celebrations*, edited by Chris Theodore, 147–153. Madras, India: Christian Literature Society of India, 1994.

Newbigin, Lesslie. *The Gospel in a Pluralist Society*. Grand Rapids, MI: Eerdmans, 1989.

Newbigin, Lesslie. *The Household of God: Lectures on the Nature of the Church*. New York: Friendship Press, 1954.

Newbigin, Lesslie. *The Open Secret: An Introduction to the Theology of Mission*, rev. ed. Grand Rapids, MI: Eerdmans, 1995.

Newbigin, Lesslie. *The Reunion of the Church: A Defence of the South India Scheme*. Eugene, OR: Wipf & Stock, 2011.

Newbigin, Lesslie. *Trinitarian Doctrine for Today's Mission*. Eugene, OR: Wipf & Stock, 2006.

Newbigin, Lesslie. *Unfinished Agenda: An Autobiography*. London: SPCK, 1985.

Niebuhr, H. Richard. *Christ and Culture*. San Francisco, CA: Harper & Row, 1975 [reprint].

Noble, Alan. "The Evangelical Persecution Complex." *The Atlantic*, August 4, 2014. www.theatlantic.com/national/archive/2014/08/the-evangelical-persecution-complex/375506.

Noll, Mark A. *American Evangelical Christianity: An Introduction*. Malden, MA: Blackwell, 2001.

Nouwen, Henri J. M. *Reaching Out: The Three Movements of the Spiritual Life*. New York: Image, 1986 [reprint].

Oldenburg, Ray. *The Great Good Place: Cafes, Coffee Shops, Bookstores, Bars, Hair Salons, and Other Hangouts at the Heart of a Community*. 3rd ed. New York: Marlowe & Company, 1999.

Osmer, Richard R. *Practical Theology: An Introduction*. Grand Rapids, MI: Eerdmans, 2008.

Packard, Josh, and Ashleigh Hope. *Church Refugees: Sociologists Reveal Why People Are DONE with Church but Not Their Faith*. Loveland, CO: Group Publishing, 2015.

Pagitt, Doug. *Preaching Re-Imagined: The Role of the Sermon in Communities of Faith*. Grand Rapids, MI: Zondervan/Youth Specialties, 2005.

Parish Collective. Parish Collective Website. http://parishcollective.org.

Paas, Stephan. *Church Planting in the Secular West: Learning from the European Experience*. Gospel and Our Culture Series. Grand Rapids: MI: Eerdmans, 2016.

Peterson, Eugene. *Tell It Slant: A Conversation on the Language of Jesus in His Stories and Prayers*. Grand Rapids, MI: Eerdmans, 2012.

Pew Research Center. *America's Changing Religious Landscape*, May 12, 2015. www.pew-forum.org/2015/05/12/appendix-b-classification-of-protestant-denominations.

Pew Research Center. "Changing Attitudes on Gay Marriage." Pew Research Center, Religion & Public Life Project, July 29, 2015. www.pewforum.org/2015/07/29/graphics-slideshow-changing-attitudes-on-gay-marriage.

Pew Research Center. "Majority Now Supports Legalizing Marijuana." Pew Research Center for the People and the Press. Last modified April 4, 2013. www.people-press.org/2013/04/04/majority-now-supports-legalizing-marijuana.

Pew Research Center. "Mobile Technology Fact Sheet." Pew Research Center: Internet, Science & Tech, last modified January 12, 2017. www.pewinternet.org/fact-sheets/mobile-technology-fact-sheet.

Pew Research Center. "'Nones' on the Rise." Pew Research Center, Religion & Public Life Project, October 9, 2012. www.pewforum.org/2012/10/09/nones-on-the-rise.

Pew Research Center. "Political Polarization in the American Public: How Increasing Ideological Uniformity and Partisan Antipathy Affect Politics, Compromise and Everyday Life." Pew Research Center, June 12, 2014. www.people-press.org/2014/06/12/political-polarization-in-the-american-public.

Pew Research Center. "Record Shares of Americans Now Own Smartphones, Have Home Broadband." Pew Research Center: Internet, Science & Tech, January 12, 2017. www.pewresearch.org/fact-tank/2017/01/12/evolution-of-technology.

Pew Research Center. "Religious Composition of Seattle Metro Area." *Pew Research Center's Religion & Public Life Project*, 2014. Accessed January 26, 2017. http://www.pewforum.org/religious-landscape-study.

Pew Research Center. "Social Media Fact Sheet." *Pew Research Center: Internet, Science & Tech*, last modified January 12, 2017. Accessed January 26, 2017. http://www.pewinternet.org/fact-sheet/social-media.

Pew Research Center. "The Future of World Religions: Population Growth Projections, 2010-2050." Pew Research Center, April 2, 2015. www.pewforum.org/2015/04/02/religious-projections-2010-2050.

Piacenza, Joanna. "How Religiously Unaffiliated Is Your City?" Public Religion Research Institute. Last modified March 16, 2015. http://publicreligion.org/2015/03/how-religiously-unaffiliated-is-your-city/#.VoLSG_GpLXn.

Piacenza, Joanna. "The Three Religious Traditions That Dominate the U.S." Public Religion Research Institute, March 4, 2015. http://publicreligion.org/2015/03/top-three-religions-in-each-state.

Platt, David. *Radical: Taking Back Your Faith from the American Dream*. Colorado Springs, CO: Multnomah Books, 2010.

Pohl, Christine. *Making Room: Recovering Hospitality as a Christian Tradition*. Grand Rapids, MI: Eerdmans, 1999.

Poloma, Margaret M., and John C. Green. *The Assemblies of God: Godly Love and the Revitalization of American Pentecostalism*. New York: New York University Press, 2010.

Poloma, Margaret M., and Ralph W. Hood. *Blood and Fire: Godly Love in a Pentecostal Emerging Church*. New York: New York University Press, 2008.

Porpora, Douglas V. "Methodological Atheism, Methodological Agnosticism and Religious Experience." *Journal for the Theory of Social Behaviour* 36, no. 1 (March 1, 2006): 57–75.

Pruit, Philip. "The Gift of Silence: A Renewed Call to Contemporary Pentecostals to the Discipline of Silence." D. Min. dissertation, University of the South, 2013.

Przybylski, Andrew K., and Netta Weinstein. "Can You Connect with Me Now? How the Presence of Mobile Communication Technology Influences Face-to-Face Conversation Quality." *Journal of Social and Personal Relationships* (July 19, 2012): 1–10.

Public Religion Research Institute. *Shifting Landscape: A Decade of Change in American Attitudes about Same-Sex Marriage and LGBT Issues.* February 26, 2014. http://publicreligion.org/research/2014/02/2014-lgbt-survey.

Putnam, Robert D., and David E. Campbell. *American Grace: How Religion Divides and Unites Us.* New York: Simon & Schuster, 2012.

Putnam, Robert D., and Lewis Feldstein. *Better Together: Restoring the American Community.* New York: Simon & Schuster, 2004.

Rajapakse, Nelunika G. *Compassionate, Engaged Parenting as "A Help to Life": To Nurture the Human Body-Mind-Spirit.* Charleston, NC: CreateSpace, 2012.

Randall, Ian. *What a Friend We Have in Jesus: The Evangelical Tradition.* Traditions of Christian Spirituality. Maryknoll, NY: Orbis Books, 2005.

Reed, Karen. "Living Slowly in the City." *Journal of Missional Practice,* Summer 2015. http://journalofmissionalpractice.com/living-slowly-in-the-city.

Robert, Dana L. *Christian Mission: How Christianity Became a World Religion.* Malden, MA: Wiley-Blackwell, 2009.

Roberts Jr., Bob. *The Multiplying Church: The New Math for Starting New Churches.* Grand Rapids, MI: Zondervan, 2009.

Rodrigue, Jean-Paul. "The Burgess Urban Land Use Model." *The Geography of Transport Systems.* https://people.hofstra.edu/geotrans/eng/ch6en/conc6en/burgess.html.

Roozen, David A., William McKinney, and Jackson W. Carroll. *Varieties of Religious Presence: Mission in Public Life.* Cleveland, OH: Pilgrim Press, 1984.

Ross, Sally B. "The Sociological Significance of the Taizé Community as a Religious Phenomenon of Our Time." Fordham University, 1987. http://fordham.bepress.com/dissertations/AAI8727847.

Roxburgh, Alan J. *Joining God, Remaking Church, Changing the World: The New Shape of the Church in Our Time.* New York: Morehouse Publishing, 2015.

Roxburgh, Alan J. *Missional: Joining God in the Neighborhood.* Grand Rapids, MI: Baker Books, 2011.

Roxburgh, Alan J. *Missional Map-Making: Skills for Leading in Times of Transition.* San Francisco, CA: Jossey-Bass, 2009.

Roxburgh, Alan J. *Moving Back into the Neighborhood: The Workbook.* West Vancouver, BC: Roxburgh Missional Network, 2010.

Roxburgh, Alan J., and M. Scott Boren. *Introducing the Missional Church: What It Is, Why It Matters, How to Become One*. Grand Rapids, MI: Baker Books, 2009.

Rubta House. *School(s) for Conversion: 12 Marks of a New Monasticism*. Eugene, OR: Wipf & Stock, 2005.

Saad, Lydia. "U.S. Confidence in Organized Religion at Low Point." Gallup. Last modified July 12, 2012. www.gallup.com/poll/155690/Confidence-Organized-Religion-Low-Point.aspx.

Sampson, Robert. *Great American City: Chicago and the Enduring Neighborhood Effect*. Chicago: University of Chicago Press, 2012.

Sánchez-Walsh, Arlene M. *Latino Pentecostal Identity: Evangelical Faith, Self, and Society*. New York: Columbia University Press, 2003.

Santos, Jason B. *A Community Called Taizé: A Story of Prayer, Worship and Reconciliation*. Downers Grove, IL: IVP Books, 2008.

Santos, Jason B. "After Taizé: A Practical Theology of Sustained Spiritual Formation for the Pilgrims of Taizé." Princeton Theological Seminary, 2014. http://gradworks.umi.com/36/43/3643491.html.

Scharen, Christian B., ed. *Explorations in Ecclesiology and Ethnography*. Grand Rapids, MI: Eerdmans, 2012.

Scharen, Christian B. *Fieldwork in Theology: Exploring the Social Context of God's Work in the World*. Grand Rapids, MI: Baker Academic, 2015.

Schreiter, Robert J. *The New Catholicity: Theology Between the Global and the Local*. Maryknoll, NY: Orbis Books, 2005.

Shenk, Wilbert. "New Wineskins for New Wine: Toward a Post-Christendom Ecclesiology." *International Bulletin of Missionary Research* 29, no. 2 (April 2005): 78.

Shibley, Mark A. "Sacred Nature: Earth-Based Spirituality as Popular Religion in the Pacific Northwest." *Journal for the Study of Religion, Nature & Culture* 5, no. 2 (June 2011): 164–185.

Shipps, Jan. "Religion and Regional Culture in Modern America." In *Can Charitable Choice Work?: Covering Religion's Impact on Urban Affairs and Social Services*, edited by Andrew Walsh, 36. Hartford, CT: Leonard E. Greenberg Center for the Study of Religion in Public Life, Trinity College, 2001.

Shulevitz, Judith. "The Power of the Mustard Seed: Why Strict Churches Are Strong." *Slate*, May 12, 2005. www.slate.com/articles/life/faithbased/2005/05/the_power_of_the_mustard_seed.html.

Sinha, Jill W., Amy Hillier, Ram A. Cnaan, and Charlene C. McGrew. "Proximity Matters: Exploring Relationships Among Neighborhoods, Congregations, and the Residential Patterns of Members." *Journal for the Scientific Study of Religion* 46, no. 2 (June 1, 2007): 245–260.

Smith, Christian. *Christian America?: What Evangelicals Really Want*. Berkeley: University of California Press, 2002.

Smith, Christian, and Michael Emerson. *American Evangelicalism: Embattled and Thriving*. Chicago: University of Chicago Press, 1998.

Smith, Christopher, and John Pattison. *Slow Church: Cultivating Community in the Patient Way of Jesus*. Downers Grove, IL: IVP Books, 2014.

Smith, D. Moody. *The Theology of the Gospel of John*. Cambridge: Cambridge University Press, 1995.

Smith, James K. A. *Imagining the Kingdom: How Worship Works*. Grand Rapids, MI: Baker Academic, 2013.

Sparks, Paul, Tim Soerens, and Dwight J. Friesen. *The New Parish: How Neighborhood Churches Are Transforming Mission, Discipleship and Community*. Downers Grove, IL: IVP Books, 2014.

Stark, Rodney. *What Americans Really Believe*. Waco, TX: Baylor University Press, 2008.

Steensland, Brian, and Phillip Goff, eds. *The New Evangelical Social Engagement*. New York: Oxford University Press, 2013.

Stetzer, Ed. "Finding the Right Church Planting Model Part 4: The Missional Incarnational Approach." *The Exchange*, August 17, 2015. www.christianityto-day.com/edstetzer/2015/august/finding-right-church-planting-model-part-4-missional-incarn.html.

Stetzer, Ed. "MissionTrends: 4 Trends for Churches to Consider." *The Exchange*, June 2, 2014. www.christianitytoday.com/edstetzer/2014/may/look-back-and-look-ahead-for-church-in-america-4-trends-chr.html.

Stetzer, Ed. "No, American Christianity Is Not Dead." *CNN*. Last modified May 16, 2015. www.cnn.com/2015/05/16/living/christianity-american-dead/index.html.

Stetzer, Ed. *Planting Missional Churches: Planting a Church That's Biblically Sound and Reaching People in Culture*. Nashville, TN: Broadman & Holman Academic, 2006.

Stetzer, Ed and Daniel Lim. *Planting Missional Churches: Your Guide to Starting Churches that Multiply*. 2nd ed. Nashville, TN: Broadman & Holman Academic, 2016.

Stetzer, Ed, and Dave Travis. *The State of Church Planting in the United States: Research Overview and Qualitative Study of Primary Church Planting Entities*. Leadership Network, 2007. www.christianitytoday.com/assets/10228.pdf

Stetzer, Ed, Micah Fries, and Daniel Im, *The State of Church Planting in the U.S.* Lifeway Research and NewChurches, 2015. www.newchurches.com.

Stone, Bryan P. *Evangelism After Christendom: The Theology and Practice of Christian Witness*. Grand Rapids, MI: Brazos Press, 2007.

Sullivan, Andrew. "I Used to Be a Human Being." *New York Magazine*, September 18, 2016. http://nymag.com/selectall/2016/09/andrew-sullivan-technology-almost-killed-me.html.

Thurian, Max, ed. *Churches Respond to BEM: Official Responses to the "Baptism, Eucharist and Ministry" Text*. Vols. I–VI. Geneva: World Council of Churches, 1986.

Torres, Blanca. "Seattle's Urban Villages Strategy Is Working—but More Planning Is Needed in the next 20 Years." *Seattle Times*, January 29, 2015. http://blogs.seattle-times.com/opinionnw/2015/01/29/seattles-urban-villages- strategy-is-working-but-more-planning-is-needed-in-the-next-20-years.

Twelftree, Graham H. *People of the Spirit: Exploring Luke's View of the Church*. Grand Rapids, MI: Baker Academic, 2009.

Unruh, Heidi R., and Ronald J. Sider. *Saving Souls, Serving Society: Understanding the Faith Factor in Church-Based Social Ministry*. Oxford: Oxford University Press, 2005.

U.S. Census Bureau. "Seattle QuickFacts." QuickFacts. https://www.census.gov/quickfacts/table/PST045215/5363000,00.

Van Gelder, Craig. *The Essence of the Church: A Community Created by the Spirit*. Grand Rapids, MI: Baker Books, 2000.

Van Gelder, Craig. *The Ministry of the Missional Church: A Community Led by the Spirit*. Grand Rapids, MI: Baker Books, 2007.

Van Gelder, Craig, and Dwight J. Zscheile. *The Missional Church in Perspective: Mapping Trends and Shaping the Conversation*. Grand Rapids, MI: Baker Academic, 2011.

Vanier, Jean. *Community and Growth*. 2nd ed. New York: Paulist Press, 1989.

Volf, Miroslav. *After Our Likeness: The Church As the Image of the Trinity*. Grand Rapids, MI: Eerdmans, 1998.

Ward, Pete. "Blueprint Ecclesiology and the Lived." *Ecclesial Practices* 2, no. 1 (2015): 74–90.

Ward, Pete. *Liquid Ecclesiology: The Gospel and the Church*. Leiden, Netherlands: Brill, 2017.

Ward, Pete, ed. *Perspectives on Ecclesiology and Ethnography*. Grand Rapids, MI: Eerdmans, 2012.

Warner, R. Stephen. "Religion and New (Post-1965) Immigrants: Some Principles Drawn from Field Research." *American Studies* 41 (Summer/Fall 2000): 267–86.

Webber, Robert E. *Ancient-Future Evangelism: Making Your Church a Faith-Forming Community*. Grand Rapids, MI: Baker Books, 2003.

Wellman, James K., Jr. *Evangelical vs. Liberal: The Clash of Christian Cultures in the Pacific Northwest*. Oxford: Oxford University Press, 2008.

Wellman, James K., Jr. "A Theology for Cascadia: From None Zone to the Abundant Zone." *Christ & Cascadia*, March 4, 2015. http://christandcascadia.com/a-theology-for-cascadia-from-none-zone-to-the-abundant-zone.

Werleman, C. J., and AlterNet. "Atheists Have Their Number: How the Christian Right Is Hastening Religion's Decline," March 25, 2014. www.salon.com/2014/03/25/calling_the_christian_right_soon_you_will_be_outnumbered_partner.

White Jr., Dan. *Subterranean: Why the Future of the Church Is Rootedness*. Eugene, OR: Cascade Books, 2015.

Wigg-Stevenson, Natalie. "Reflexive Theology: A Preliminary Proposal." *Practical Matters Journal*, no. 6 (March 1, 2013). http://practicalmattersjournal.org/2013/03/01/reflexive-theology.

Willard, Dallas. *The Great Omission: Reclaiming Jesus' Essential Teachings on Discipleship*. New York: HarperOne, 2006.

Winseman, Albert. "Religion 'Very Important' to Most Americans." Gallup. Last modified December 20, 2005. www.gallup.com/poll/20539/Religion-Very-Important-Most-Americans.aspx.

Wollschleger, Jason, and Jeremy R. Porter. "A 'WalMartization' of Religion? The Ecological Impact of Megachurches on the Local and Extra-Local Religious Economy." *Review of Religious Research* 53 (July 29, 2011): 279–299.

Woodward, J. R. *Creating a Missional Culture: Equipping the Church for the Sake of the World.* Downers Grove, IL: IVP Books, 2012.

Woolever, Cynthia, and Deborah Bruce. *A Field Guide to U.S. Congregations: Who's Going Where and Why.* 2nd ed. Louisville, KY: Westminster John Knox Press, 2010.

Woolever, Cynthia, and Deborah Bruce *Places of Promise: Finding Strength in Your Congregation's Location.* Louisville, KY: Westminster John Knox Press, 2008.

World Council of Churches. *Baptism, Eucharist and Ministry* (Faith and Order Paper No. 111, the "Lima Text"). Faith and Order Commission. Geneva, January 15, 1982. www.oikoumene.org/en/resources/documents/commissions/faith-and-order/i-unity-the-church-and-its-mission/baptism-eucharist-and-ministry-faith-and-order-paper-no-111-the-lima-text.

Worthen, Molly. *Apostles of Reason: The Crisis of Authority in American Evangelicalism.* New York: Oxford University Press, 2013.

Wright, N. T. *Paul: In Fresh Perspective.* Minneapolis, MN: Fortress Press, 2009.

Wuthnow, Robert. *Producing the Sacred: An Essay on Public Religion.* Urbana, IL: University of Illinois Press, 1994.

Yen, Hope. "Census: White Majority in U.S. Gone by 2043." *NBC News.* Last modified June 13, 2013. http://usnews.nbcnews.com/_news/2013/06/13/18934111-census-white-majority-in-us-gone-by-2043.

Yoder, John H. "A People in the World." In *The Royal Priesthood: Essays Ecclesiological and Ecumenical,* edited by Michael Cartwright, 65–101. Rev. ed. Scottdale, PA: Herald Press, 1999.

Yoder, John H. *Body Politics: Five Practices of the Christian Community Before the Watching World.* Scottdale, PA: Herald Press, 2001.

Yoder, John H. *Theology of Mission: A Believers Church Perspective.* Downers Grove, IL: IVP Books, 2013.

Yoder, John H., and Michael Cartwright. *The Royal Priesthood: Essays Ecclesiological and Ecumenical.* Rev. ed. Scottdale, PA: Herald Press, 1999.

Zscheile, Dwight, ed. *Cultivating Sent Communities: Missional Spiritual Formation.* Grand Rapids, MI: Eerdmans, 2012.

Index

communion
  and the early church, 316n39
  frequency of, 42–43, 216, 218
  in GCT churches, 98,
  and liturgical spirituality, 46
  and meals, 108, 119, 216 (*see also*
    meals, sharing)
  in NC churches, 115–116, 119, 166, 216
  open, 116–117, 124–125
community
  beloved, 72
  in church names, 36
  inclusive, 48, 50
  intentional, 57, 61
  longing for, 122–123
  mission pattern, 54
  organizing, 47–49, 55
  outreach events, 52, 80
  in which to belong and be loved,
    47–48, 50, 61, 289n87
  as witness and formation, 113,
    123, 285n53
  See also conversion community;
    missional communities; New
    Community model
Community Dinners (church), 247
  and the actions of Jesus, 302n108,
    303n129
  and low-income housing, 307n177
  as model exemplar, 106, 111, 129–132
  prayer, 106, 293n121
  signboard for, 7–8
  sketch of, 130
Community model (Becker), 82, 113
Community of Disciples, church as, 76
congregation, church as, 56–57, 129–130,
    176. *See also* extracongregational
    identity
congregational studies
  contributions of this book to, 5–6
  and mission, 315n26
  and new churches, 244, 260n9

on religious ecology, 9, 234, 245
  and sociological interpretations of
    church, 64–65
  and surveys, 246
  training in, 224
  See also church-sect theory;
    congregational template;
    congregational typologies
congregational template, 39, 81,
    291n109
congregational typologies, 78–84
Congregations in Conflict. See Becker,
    Penny E.
Conservative Protestants, 271n8
  and identity, 56–57, 59
  vs. mainline Protestants, 40, 61
  and mission, 48, 50–52, 274n35
  and not using sanctuaries, 37
  percentage of, 32–35, 270n12
  and research sample, 246, 272–273n18
  and spirituality, 40–44
  and web presence, 36, 281n12
contrast society, church as
  and church as foretaste, 146–147
  and conversion community, 221–222
  and new Seattle churches, 153,
    158–159, 165
  and technology, 179
  and various authors, 279n53, 297n48
  See also countercultural posture
conversation, 149, 188–189, 191
  and evangelism, 101
  and Jesus, 309–310n10
  and leadership, 224
  with local pastors, 191–192
  and NC/emerging churches, 113, 118,
    169, 221, 296n56
  and sacred consciousness,
    225, 300n93
conversion, 170–171
  of the church, 185, 201, 206
  and encapsulation, 222, 317n42